P9-EEA-898

THE FATHERS OF THE CHURCH

A NEW TRANSLATION

SAINT BASIL

LETTERS

VOLUME 2 (186-368)

Translated by

SISTER AGNES CLARE WAY, C.D.P.
Our Lady of the Lake College

with notes by

† ROY J. DEFERRARI

THE CATHOLIC UNIVERSITY OF AMERICA PRESS
Washington, D. C. 20017

NIHIL OBSTAT:

JOHN M. A. FEARNS, S.T.D.
Censor Librorum

IMPRIMATUR:

✠ FRANCIS CARDINAL SPELLMAN
Archbishop of New York

June 23, 1955

Second (Revised) Printing 1969

Library of Congress Card No. 65-18318

SBN. No. 8132-0028-8

CONTENTS

*Letters** | *Page*

186 (*213*).	To Antipater, the Governor	3
187 (214).	Antipater to Basil	4
188 (*1*).	To Amphilochius, concerning the Canons (1-16)	4
189 (*80*).	To Eustathius, the Court Physician	25
190 (*406*).	To Amphilochius, Bishop of Iconium	34
191 (*398*).	To Amphilochius	37
192 (*329*).	To the Master Sophronius	38
193 (*369*).	To Meletius, the Court Physician	39
194 (*368*).	To Zoilus	40
195 (*312*).	To Euphronius, Bishop of Colonia in Armenia	41
196 (*359*).	To Aburgius	41
197 (*55*).	To Ambrose, Bishop of Milan	42
198 (*263*).	To Eusebius, Bishop of Samosata	45
199 (*2*).	To Amphilochius, concerning the Canons (17-50)	47

* Italicized numbers indicate the older order of the Letters, as distinguished from the Benedictine order which has been followed.

Letters			*Page*
200	*(397)* .	To Amphilochius	62
201	*(402)* .	To Amphilochius	64
202	*(396)* .	To Amphilochius	64
203	*(77)* .	To the Bishops of the Seacoast	65
204	*(75)* .	To the Neo-Caesareans	70
205	*(322)* .	To Bishop Elpidius	79
206	*(348)* .	A Letter of Condolence to Bishop Elpidius	80
207	*(63)* .	To the Clergy of Neo-Caesarea	81
208	*(281)* .	To Eulancius	86
209	*(227)* .	Without Address, in Self-defense	86
210	*(64)* .	To the Most Eloquent Citizens of Neo-Caesarea	87
211	*(170)* .	To Olympius	95
212	*(370)* .	To Hilarius	95
213	*(242)* .	Without an Address, for a Pious Man . .	98
214	*(349)* .	To Count Terentius	99
215	*(250)* .	To Dorotheus, Presbyter	103
216	*(272)* .	To Meletius, Bishop of Antioch	104
217	*(3)* .	To Amphilochius, on the Canons (51-84)	105
218	*(403)* .	To Amphilochius	117
219	*(280)* .	To the Clergy of Samósata	119
220	*(299)* .	To the People of Beroea	121
221	*(298)* .	To the People of Beroea	122
222	*(297)* .	To the Chalcidians	123
223	*(79)* .	Against Eustathius of Sebaste	125
224	*(345)* .	To Genethlius, the Presbyter	135
225	*(385)* .	To Demosthenes, in the Name of the Public	139
226	*(73)* .	To His Monks	141

Letters *Page*

227 (*292*). A Letter of Condolence to the Clergy in Colonia 147
228 (*290*). To the Magistrates of Colonia 150
229 (*193*). To the Clergy of Nicopolis 151
230 (*194*). To the Magistrates of Nicopolis 152
231 (*395*). To Amphilochius 153
232 (*404*). To Amphilochius 155
233 (*399*). To Amphilochius 156
234 (*400*). To Amphilochius 159
235 (*401*). To Amphilochius 161
236 (*391*). To Amphilochius 165
237 (*264*). To Eusebius, Bishop of Samosata . . . 172
238 (*191*). To the Presbyters of Nicopolis 175
239 (*10*). To Eusebius 176
240 (*192*). To the Presbyters of Nicopolis 178
241 (*360*). To Eusebius 181
242 (*182*). To the Westerners 182
243 (*70*). To the Bishops of Italy and of Gaul, concerning the Condition and Confusion of the Churches 184
244 (*82*). To Patrophilus, Bishop of the Church at Aegae 190
245 (*309*). To Bishop Theophilus 200
246 (*66*). To the Nicopolitans 201
247 (*190*). To the Nicopolitans 202
248 (*405*). To Amphilochius 202
249 (*238*). Without an Address, for a Pious Man . 204
250 (*85*). To Patrophilus 204
251 (*72*). To the People of Evaesae 206

Letters		*Page*
252 (*291*).	To the Bishops of the Diocese of Pontus	210
253 (*199*).	To the Presbyters of Antioch	211
254 (*311*).	To Pelagius, Bishop of Laodicea . . .	211
255 (*314*).	To Vitus, Bishop of Charrae	212
256 (*200*).	To Our Most Beloved and Pious Brethren, Fellow Presbyters, Acacius, Aetius, Paulus, and Silvanus, and Deacons, Silvinus and Lucius, and the Rest of Our Brethren, the Monks	213
257 (*303*).	To the Monks Oppressed by the Arians .	215
258 (*325*).	To Bishop Epiphanius	217
259 (*184*).	To the Monks, Palladius and Innocent .	221
260 (*17*).	To Bishop Optimus	222
261 (*65*).	To the Citizens of Sozopolis	232
262 (*344*).	To the Monk Urbicius	236
263 (*74*).	To the Westerners	237
264 (*326*).	To Barses, Bishop of Edessa, during his Exile	243
265 (*293*).	To Eulogius, Alexander, and Harpocration, Bishops of Egypt in Exile	244
266 (*321*).	To Peter, Bishop of Alexandria	250
267 (*327*).	To Barses, Bishop of Edessa, in Exile . .	254
268 (*9*).	To Eusebius in Exile	255
269 (*186*).	A Letter of Condolence to the Wife of the Commander Arintheus	257
270 (*244*).	Without an Address, concerning an Abduction	259

Letters *Page*

271 (*11*). A Letter of Recommendation to Eusebius, His Companion, in Behalf of the Presbyter Cyriacus 260
272 (*330*). To the Master Sophronius 262
273 (*216*). Without an Address, in Behalf of Hera . 264
274 (*416*). To the Master Himerius 265
275 (*217*). Without an Address, concerning Hera . 265
276 (*365*). To the Elder Harmatius 266
277 (*42*). To the Scholar Maximus 267
278 (*425*). To Valerian 269
279 (*274*). To the Prefect Modestus 269
280 (*275*). To Modestus 270
281 (*278*). To Modestus 271
282 (*336*). To a Bishop 271
283 (*284*). To a Widow 272
284 (*304*). To an Assessor, in Behalf of Monks . . 273
285 (*229*). Without an Address, for the Protection of the Church 274
286 (*417*). To a Prison Official 274
287 (*245*). Without an Address, against Retaliators . 275
288 (*246*). Without an Address, against Retaliators . 276
289 (*249*). Without an Address, concerning an Afflicted Woman 277
290 (*323*). To Nectarius 279
291 (*340*). To the Suffragan Bishop Timotheus . . 281
292 (*386*). To Palladius 283
293 (*166*). To Julian 284
294 (*210*). To Festus and Magnus 285

Letters		Page

295 (*295*). To Monks 286
296 (*285*). To a Widow 287
297 (*286*). To a Widow 288
298 (*233*). Without an Address, in Behalf of a Pious Man 289
299 (*352*). To an Assessor 290
300 (*201*). A Letter of Condolence to the Father of a Scholar Who Had Died 291
301 (*346*). A Letter of Condolence to Maximus . . 293
302 (*347*). A Letter of Condolence to the Wife of Briso 295
303 (*423*). To the Prefect of the Emperor's Private Estate 297
304 (*357*). To Aburgius 298
305 (*232*). Without an Address, for Some Virtuous Man 298
306 (*424*). To the Commander at Sebaste 299
307 (*247*). Without an Address 300
308 (*233*). Without an Address, for Patronage . . 301
309 (*230*). Without an Address, for a Needy Person . 302
310 (*237*). Without an Address, in Behalf of Relatives 302
311 (*421*). To an Official 303
312 (*426*). To an Assessor 303
313 (*353*). To an Assessor 304
314 (*231*). Without an Address, in Behalf of a Servant 305
315 (*218*). Without an Address, in Behalf of a Relative 306
316 (*219*). Without an Address, in Behalf of an Oppressed Man 306

Letters		Page
317 *(222)*.	Without an Address, in Behalf of a Needy Person	307
318.	Without an Address, in Behalf of a Countryman	307
319.	Without an Address, in Behalf of a Stranger	308
320 *(221)*.	Without an Address, in Friendly Greeting	308
321 *(212)*.	To Thecla	309
322 *(223)*.	Without an Address, on Celebrating Easter with a Friend	310
323 *(335)*.	To Philagrius Arcenus	311
324 *(375)*.	To Pasinicus, a Doctor	312
325 *(381)*.	To Magninianus	313
326 *(224)*.	Without an Address, for the Sake of Admonition	314
327 *(225)*.	Without an Address, for Encouragement	314
328 *(367)*.	To Hyperechius	315
329 *(282)*.	To Phalerius	315
330 *(176)*.	Without an Address	315
331 *(240)*.	Without an Address	316
332 *(177)*.	Without an Address	316
333 *(178)*.	To a Scribe	316
334 *(180)*.	To a Calligrapher	317
335 *(142)*.	To Libanius	318
336 *(143)*.	Libanius to Basil	319
337 *(144)*.	To Libanius	321
338 *(145)*.	Libanius to Basil	321
339 *(146)*.	To Libanius	323
340 *(147)*.	Libanius to Basil	324

Letters		*Page*
341 (*148*).	Libanius to Basil	325
342 (*149*).	To Libanius	326
343 (*150*).	Libanius to Basil	326
344 (*151*).	To Libanius	327
345 (*152*).	Libanius to Basil	327
346 (*153*).	Libanius to Basil	329
347 (*154*).	Libanius to Basil	329
348 (*155*).	To Libanius	330
349 (*156*).	Libanius to Basil	330
350 (*157*).	To Libanius	331
351 (*158*).	To Libanius	332
352 (*159*).	Libanius to Basil	332
353 (*160*).	To Libanius	333
354 (*161*).	Libanius to Basil	333
355 (*162*).	Libanius to Basil	334
356 (*163*).	To Libanius	334
357.	Libanius to Basil	334
358.	Libanius to Basil	335
359.	To Libanius	335
360 (*205*).	From His Letter to Julian the Apostate	336
361.	To Apollinaris	337
362.	Apollinaris to Basil	339
363.	To Apollinaris	341
364.	Apollinaris to Basil	342
365.	To the Great Emperor Theodosius	343
366.	To Urbicius, a Monk, concerning Continence	345
367.	Gregory to Basil	347
368.	To Gregory	347

INTRODUCTION

VOLUME TWO OF THE LETTERS of St. Basil (Nos. 186-368) includes letters written during his episcopate from the year 374 until his death in 379, letters of uncertain date or authorship, and clearly spurious letters. In the beginning of the year 374, Amphilochius, a disciple of St. Basil, had been consecrated Bishop of Iconium, and, full of apostolic fervor for the reform of his church, consulted St. Basil on many points of discipline and doctrine. St. Basil undertook to furnish the information requested and wrote the so-called three Canonical Letters (188, 199, and 217). These letters—all written within the year 374—were later divided into 84 canons, of which 68 were to be incorporated in the collection of the canons of the Church. The majority of the canons are of a disciplinary character and by defining specifically the penalty to be imposed for the various sins make a great contribution to present-day knowledge of the penitential system of the early Eastern Church.

In assigning the penalty for voluntary murder, for example, St. Basil specifies in Canon 56: 'He who has committed voluntary murder and afterwards has repented shall not partake of the Blessed Sacrament for twenty years. And the twenty years shall be divided thus in his case. For four years he ought to weep as a penitent of the first degree, standing outside the door of the house of prayer and asking the faithful who enter to pray for him, confessing his transgression. And after the four years he will be received among the hearers, and for five years will go out with them. Then, for seven years he will go out, praying with those in the rank of prostrates. For four years he will only stand with the faithful, but will not receive Holy Communion. However, after these have been completed he will partake of the sacraments.' He here gives us the four degrees of penitents: the weepers, the hearers, the prostrates, and the standers.

St. Gregory Thaumaturgus before him had defined in Canon 11 of his Canonical Letter just what is meant by each of the degrees of penance: ' "Weeping" is outside the door of the house of prayer. The sinner standing there must beg the faithful entering to pray for him. "Hearing" is inside the door in the portico. The sinner should stand there as long as the catechumens do and then go out. For, it is said, although he may hear the Scriptures and the instruction, let him be cast out and not deemed worthy of prayer. But the "prostration" is standing inside the door of the church, so as to go out with the catechumens. "Standing" is to remain with the faithful and not to go out with the catechumens. And finally, participation in the Sacrament of the Eucharist is permitted.' St. Gregory, however, mentioned no definite penalty for any particular sin, whereas St. Basil prescribed exactly for each sin.

In addition to the Canonical Letters there are thirteen other letters addressed to Amphilochius, many of which, notably Nos. 233-236, are answers to questions of various kinds on doctrine or explanations of Scriptural passages. These are not as a rule disciplinary nor have they been arranged or treated as canons. They are interesting, however, as showing us the depth of the study which St. Basil has devoted to Scripture and the common sense which he uses in answering his questioner, as in Letter 236: 'Concerning emerging in baptism, I do not know whatever came upon you to ask, if you have actually admitted that the immersion fulfills the figure of the three days. For, it is impossible to be dipped under water three times without emerging just as many times.'

It was during these years, too, that accusations of heresy were brought against St. Basil. In Letter 204 he defends himself to the Neo-Caesareans and in Letter 207 to the clergy of Neo-Caesarea, who, he writes, were united to a man in their hatred of him, and whose principal charge against him was the manner of singing psalms which differed from their own custom. In recounting the manner in which his monks sang the Psalms, St. Basil seems to describe the chanting of the Divine Office as carried out in any monastery of the present day. St. Basil then adds: 'If, then, you shun us on this account you will shun the Egyptians, and the people of both Libyas, the Thebans, Palestinians, Arabians, Phoenicians, Syrians, and those dwelling beside the Euphrates, and, in one word, all those among whom night watches and prayers and psalmody in common have been held in esteem.' To their charge that these things were not done by Gregory Thaumaturgus he asks what witness they had to prove this, and then goes on to show that their own conduct at the time is not at all in conformity with that of St. Gregory during his life.

In Letters 129, 223, 224, and 226, St. Basil denies charges that a letter containing heretical statements had been written by him, and claims that his name was appended to writings of others to make it appear that he was teaching such doctrines. In connection with these charges Letters 361, 362, 363, and 364 may be considered. Two of these, Letters 361 and 363, are attributed to St. Basil, and the other two to Apollinaris. Letter 361 purports to be a petition of St. Basil for an explanation of the meaning of '*ousía*,' and Letter 363, a letter of thanks for the great kindness of Apollinaris in giving so clear an exposition of the subject. Of the answers attributed to Apollinaris, Letter 362 is an explanation of his own on the meaning of '*ousía*' and Letter 364 is a call upon St. Basil to help him in defending the faith, since question has again arisen concerning the meaning of '*homoóusion*' and '*ousía*.' The consensus of opinion at present is that these letters were not written by St. Basil, but were clever forgeries by some of his enemies.

Another group of letters in this volume whose authenticity has been much called into question is that which comprises the so-called Basil-Libanian correspondence (335-359). It is now generally acknowledged that many of these are genuine. They are interesting as being excellent examples of St. Basil's remarkable ability in sophistic writing of a lighter vein.

St. Basil's deep learning and fearless championship of the truths of religion, his profound humility and abhorrence of sin, which made him so forceful a leader of the Church in times of the greatest stress and difficulty due to the rise and spread of heresy, are very apparent in these letters which have come down to us. And the attempts of heretical contemporaries to secure approbation for their doctrines by affixing his name to writings of their own proclaim the high opinion, which in his day all held of him, no less than does the inclusion by the Church of his regulations among its canons.

I wish to acknowledge here my indebtedness to Reverend Mother Mary Angelique Ayres, C.D.P., who read the manuscript of both volumes of the Letters and offered many valuable suggestions.

LETTERS

186-368

Translated by

SISTER AGNES CLARE WAY, C.D.P., PH.D.

Our Lady of the Lake College

with notes by

† ROY J. DEFERRARI, PH.D.

The Catholic University of America

186. To Antipater, the Governor[1]

How admirable is philosophy, since, in addition to its other merits, it denies to its disciples extravagant cures. On the contrary, it uses the same thing as a relish and as a benefit to health. For, you have revived your failing appetite, as I have learned, with cabbage pickled in vinegar, which formerly I could not endure, not only because of the proverb,[2] but also because it was a reminder of its usual companion, poverty.

But now, I think, I shall change my opinion and laugh at the proverb, seeing that cabbage, which has restored our governor to health, is so good a foster-mother. And for the future I will consider that there is nothing that can be compared with it, neither the lotos[3] of Homer, nor even that ambrosia,[4] whatever it was, on which the Olympians fed.

1 Cf. Letters 137 and 187. The date of this letter is 374.

2 The Scholiast on Juvenal 7.154 (*occidit miseros crambe repetita magistros,* 'cabbage twice taken kills the wretched teachers') quotes the proverb, *dìs krámbē thánatos,* 'cabbage twice is death.'

3 Cf. *Odyssey* 9.91ff.

4 Cf. *Odyssey* 5.93.

187. Antipater to Basil[1]

'Cabbage twice is death' the slanderous proverb says. But I, though I have often sought death, shall die but once; and, at any rate, I shall die, even though I had not sought to do so. If, then, at any rate, death comes, do not hesitate to eat a toothsome dish, slandered in vain by the proverb.

1 In answer to the preceding letter and of the same date.

188. To Amphilochius,[1] *concerning the Canons*[2]

First Canonical Letter

'Wisdom,' it is said, 'will be imputed to a fool if he asks questions.'[3] But the question of a wise man, so it seems, makes even the fool wise. And this, by the grace of God, happens to us as often as we receive the letters of your painstaking soul. For, through the question itself we become more observant and more sensible than we were, being taught many things of which we had no immediate appreciation.

1 Amphilochius, while still a young priest, was appointed to the see of Iconium in 374. Cf. also, Letter 150 n. 1. In 387, he was present at the Council of Constantinople as chief pastor of the Lycaonian Church, at the head of twelve other bishops. Two years later he was instrumental in having Emperor Theodosius issue his edict against the Eunomians, Arians, Macedonians, and Apollinarians. He himself presided over a synod held at Sida, in Pamphilia, in which the Messalians were condemned. His death seems to have occurred some time between the years 394 and 403. This letter was written in 374, shortly after his consecration.

2 Letters 188, 199, and 217, in which St. Basil answers certain questions of St. Amphilochius, Bishop of Iconium, chiefly on matters of Church discipline, are called the Canonical Letters, because the answers have been arranged, though not by St. Basil, in the form of canons.

3 Cf. Prov. 17.28 (Septuagint).

Moreover, our solicitude to give an answer becomes for us a teacher. So, since we had never before taken thought of your questions, now we have been driven to examine carefully and to recall whatever we have heard from our elders, and to draw conclusions related to what we have learned from them.

(1) Now, the question[4] concerning the Cathari[5] has been mentioned before[6] and you have kept rightly in mind that it is necessary to follow the practice adopted in each district, since those who made the decision at the time held different opinions[7] concerning their baptism. But, the baptism of the

4 Regarding baptism.

5 A name used for both the Novatians and the Manichaeans. It here refers to the Novatians, a schismatic sect founded by the Roman priest, Novatian, about the middle of the third century. Novatian had himself consecrated bishop by three Italian bishops, and set himself up as an antipope in opposition to St. Cornelius, who had been lawfully elected in 251. Though perfectly orthodox in faith at the outset, Novatian soon gave expression to heretical views on the efficacy of the sacrament of penance. He held that idolatry is unpardonable, and denied to the Church the right to restore to communion anyone who was guilty of it. By his followers this doctrine was extended to all the more grievous sins, such as murder, adultery, and fornication. Second marriages also were condemned and confirmation was rejected. This austerity attracted many followers. Although Constantine the Great ordered their churches and cemeteries to be closed, and persecution and legislation were brought to bear against them, they were still in existence in Alexandria as late as 600.

6 In Canon 8 of the Council of Nice (325) and Canon 7 of the Council of Laodicea (343).

7 All baptism administered outside the Church was declared invalid by three synods of Carthage, held in 220, 255, and 256 respectively, and by two in Asia Minor, one at Iconium and another at Synnada, both held at some time between 230 and 236. St. Basil is probably contrasting the decisions of these councils with those of Nice and Laodicea mentioned above, in which the baptism of the Novatians was recognized as valid.

Pepuzeni[8] does not seem to me to have any sanction;[9] I have wondered how it has escaped the notice of Dionysius,[10] who is well versed in the canons. For, earlier authorities decided to accept that baptism which did not deviate in any manner from that of the faith.[11] Therefore, they used the

8 The Montanists, so called from Pepuza in Phrygia, where they had their headquarters. Montanus, toward the end of the second century, shortly after his conversion to Christianity, pretended to have received revelations from God, and began to prophesy in Phrygia. He spoke in the person of God Himself: 'I am the Father, the Word, and the Paraclete.' 'I, the Lord, the Father, am come.' Two prophetesses, Priscilla and Maximilla, associated themselves with Montanus and founded a schismatic sect. Their doctrine seems to have been orthodox at first, a few disciplinary innovations being their peculiar features. They forbade second marriages, and held chastity and martyrdom in high regard. The grotesque manner in which they delivered their prophesies seems to have been the main accusation against them in the beginning. Later, however, the prophets of the new sect declared that their teaching was higher than that of the Apostles, and even of Christ, and that, as God was unable to accomplish the salvation of the world by His Son, He had sent the Holy Spirit upon Montanus, Priscilla, and Maximilla.

9 The Montanists had been ordered by Canon 8 of Laodicea to be rebaptized upon coming into the Church. Canon 7 of Constantinople and Canon 95 of the Council of Trullo confirmed this decision.

10 Dionysius the Great, Bishop of Alexandria, born toward the end of the second century. A disciple of Origen, whom he greatly admired, he had been ordained a priest for some years when he succeeded Heraclas as Bishop of Alexandria in 247-248, an office which he seems to have retained until his death in 265. An outbreak occurred in Alexandria, the forerunner of the Decian persecution, shortly after he had assumed his episcopacy. Dionysius fled, was captured, and escaped through the intervention of a friend, but he was banished by Valerian in 257. From his places of exile he continued to rule his flock. He took an active part in the famous controversy on rebaptism, and, although he himself carefully obeyed Stephen in refraining from the practice of baptizing heretics, in his correspondence with that Pope and his successor, Sixtus, he advocated moderation in dealing with those Africans and Asiatics who argued in favor of rebaptism of all converts from heresy. His zeal against the false teachings of Sabellius laid him open to the charge of tritheism. St. Basil accused him of having sowed the seeds of the Anomoean heresy, but St. Athanasius vindicated his perfect orthodoxy.

11 That baptism which is administered by those orthodox in faith.

terms heretics, schismatics, and illegal congregations—heretics, those completely broken off and alienated from the faith itself; schismatics, those at variance with each other because of certain ecclesiastical charges and claims capable of being satisfied; and illegal congregations, those assemblies held by insubordinate presbyters or bishops and by the uninstructed laity. For example, if some one, proved to be in fault, was suspended from the ministry and did not submit to the canons but claimed for himself episcopal dignity and the right of ministry, and certain others leaving the Catholic Church went along with him, such a group would be an illegal congregation.[12] But, the being at variance with those belonging to the Church about penance[13] would be schism. And heresies are, for instance, the heresy of the Manichaeans,[14]

12 Thus, an illegal congregation was composed of the orthodox in faith who held the same views as the Catholic Church in regard to the admission of the lapsed to repentance, but had refused to accept the canonical punishment for some misdeed of which they had been guilty, as, for example, Meletius and his followers.

13 I.e., admitting the lapsed to canonical penance, as, for example, the Novatians.

14 The Manichaeans were a Gnostic sect founded by Mani, a Persian, in A. D. 242. Their religion was a mixture of several Eastern cults with a superficial sprinkling of Christian ideas. They believed in two eternal principles, one good and the other evil, as the source of all things. The Good Principle was called 'Father of Majesty'; the Evil Principle, the 'King of Darkness.' Though Adam and Eve were from a female and a male devil, their offspring was not wholly evil but contained germs of light. To free these imprisoned elements was the work of the Saviour, Jesus, the personification of Cosmic Light. By self-denial man was to keep his body free from stain. Those of the sect who practiced self-denial in an extraordinary degree, by abstaining from marriage, animal food, and wine, were called the Perfect or Elect; the weaker ones not capable of sustaining these burdens were named the Hearers. The sect spread rapidly through the East and West, and was especially strong in Babylonia, Mesopotamia, and Turkestan in the East; and in Africa, Spain, France, Italy, and the Balkans in the West. About the time St. Basil wrote his letter it was at the height of its power in the Eastern Roman Empire. It continued until some time after the year 1000, before it died out completely.

the Valentinians,[15] and the Marcionites,[16] and these Pepuzeni themselves, for this is plainly a difference concerning the very belief in God. Accordingly, the Fathers of old[17] thought it best to reject absolutely the baptism of the heretics, but to accept that of the schismatics as of those who still belong to the Church, and also to join again to the Church those in the illegal congregations after they have been healed by a suitable repentance and conversion. Consequently, even those in ecclesiastical orders, who have departed with the

15 A Gnostic sect founded by Valentinus about the middle of the second century. There were two branches of this school: the Oriental, in Egypt, Syria, and Asia Minor; and the Italian, in Italy, Rome, and Southern Gaul. Their system was dualistic pantheism, and all beings arose by emanation from the Primal Being, Bythos. The first to emanate were a series of thirty beings called 'aeons,' paired off sexually into fifteen couples. The sin of Sophia, one of the lowest aeons, brought about the existence of the lower world, in which man is the highest being, participating in both the psychic and material nature. To free the spiritual being from its servitude to the material is the work of Christ and the Holy Spirit. Christ did not have a real body and did not suffer.

16 An heretical sect founded in 144 at Rome by Marcion, an excommunicated bishop, probably a suffragan of his father, Bishop of Sinope, in Pontus. They rejected the Old Testament and refused to identify the Jewish Messias, foretold by the Prophets, with Christ. The former had not as yet come and, although the latter was the Son of God, He was not the son of the God of the Jews. They denied the resurrection of the body, rejected marriage, and baptized only those who were not living in matrimony. After the death of their founder, the Marcionites fell into mere Gnosticism, with this difference, that they thought it sinful to deny their religion in times of persecution.

17 It is not known to whom St. Basil is referring as having made the distinction between the baptism conferred by heretics and that conferred by schismatics. Since he correctly states later on that Cyprian and Firmilian rejected all baptism administered outside the Church by heretics and schismatics alike, it is not they. Possibly, by a false inference, he attributes this opinion to the Fathers at Nice and Laodicea. At both of these councils the baptism of the Novatians, who were schismatics, was recognized as valid, while that administered by the Paulianists and the Montanists, both of whom were heretics, was rejected as invalid. St. Basil, misunderstanding the reason that led the councils to reject the validity of the baptism of these heretics, may have wrongly concluded that it was rejected simply because they were heretics.

insubordinate ones, when they have repented, are frequently received back into the same rank. Now, the Pepuzeni are clearly heretics, for they have spoken blasphemously against the Holy Spirit, unlawfully and shamefully applying to Montanus and Priscilla the name of the Paraclete. Therefore, they are condemned, either as deifying men, or as insulting the Holy Spirit by a comparison with men, and so are liable to eternal condemnation, because blasphemy against the Holy Spirit is unpardonable.[18] What reason is there, then, to accept the baptism of those who baptize in the Father and the Son and Montanus or Priscilla?[19] For, those were not baptized at all who were baptized according to a form[20] not handed down to us. So, if this did escape the notice of the great Dionysius, nevertheless we must not continue to imitate the error.[21] For, the absurdity is evident of itself and is clear to all who claim any, even a small amount, of the power of reason.

The Cathari themselves also belong to the schismatics. But, it seemed best to the men of former times, Cyprian[22]

18 Cf. Matt. 12.31,32.

19 Whether St. Basil really belived that the Montanists had changed the form of baptism by actually supplying the names, Montanus or Priscilla, for the name of the Holy Spirit in the baptismal formula, or whether he means that, because they identified Montanus and Priscilla with the Holy Spirit, they intended to baptize in the name of Montanus and Priscilla is not clear. Tillemont (*Mémoires* 9.228-230) conjectures that St. Basil really assumed that they had changed the form because of the stories he had heard of their doctrine. Baronius (*Annal. ad an.* 260, n. 16), however, thinks that the Montanists had not changed the baptismal form. Hefele (*History of the Church Councils* 2.302) calls both of these positions probable.

20 The Trinitarian formula of baptism, 'In the name of the Father, and of the Son, and the Holy Spirit.' Cf. Zonaras, *PG* 138.583.

21 Cyprian (Letter 73) had expressed the same idea when refuting the argument from tradition against rebaptism of heretics; '*non tamen quia aliquando erratum est, ideo semper errandum est.*'

22 St. Cyprian, Bishop of Carthage.

and our Firmilian,[23] I mean, and their colleagues, to subject all of these—the Cathari, the Encratites,[24] and the Hydroparastates[25]—to one reckoning, because the separation had been initiated through schism, and those who had separated themselves from the Church no longer had the grace of the Holy Spirit[26] in them, its communication having failed because of the breaking of the continuity. In fact, the first ones who had withdrawn had been ordained by the Fathers and by the imposition of their hands they had the gift of the Spirit, but those who were broken off, becoming laymen, had power neither to baptize nor to ordain, no longer being able to bestow upon others the grace of the Holy Spirit from which they themselves had fallen away. Therefore, they commanded those who had been baptized by them, as by laymen, to come to the Church and to be cleansed by the true baptism of the Church. But since, on

23 Bishop of Iconium in Asia Minor. Therefore, 'our own Firmilian,' and according to Zonaras (*PG* 138.583), 'because he had been Bishop of Caesarea.'

24 Literally, 'the continent,' or 'abstainers,' the name given to a sect of Gnostics who, because they regarded matter as essentially evil in its origin, condemned marriage and the use of wine and animal food. Irenaeus (1.28), the first to mention this sect, refers their origin to Saturninus and Marcion. A denial of the salvation of Adam was introduced among them by Tatian. Hippolytus (*Philos.* 8.13) says that they were orthodox in their belief in God and Christ, but that through pride they were water drinkers, abstained from animal food, and forbade marriage. The Encratites were later called Severians from a certain Severus. Cf. J. P. Arendzen, *Cath. Enc.*, art. 'Encratites.'

25 A sect of the Encratites who used water instead of wine in the Eucharist.

26 This was the false argument of Cyprian and Firmilian. It failed to distinguish between the act and the grace of the sacrament. The minister performs the act but does not confer the grace. Once the act is performed, God confers the grace, independently of the merits or demerits of the minister. Cf. Hefele, *History of the Church Councils* 1.144.

the whole, it seemed best for the direction of the many to some of those in Asia,[27] that their[28] baptism be accepted, let it be received.

Yet, we must understand the fraud of the Encratites, because, in order that they might make themselves incapable of admission to the Church, they have attempted to prevent it for the future by a baptism of their own,[29] whence they have violated even their own practice. I think, therefore, that, since there is nothing stated[30] explicitly and openly concerning them, it is proper for us to refuse our assent to their baptism, and, if some one has received baptism from them, to baptize him when he comes over to the Church. Of course, if this is going to be an obstacle to the order in general, we should make use of the usual practice and follow the Fathers who made the regulations for us. In fact, I am apprehensive lest, while we wish to make them hesitant about baptizing, we may be a hindrance to those who are being saved because of the harshness of our proposal. And, if they uphold our baptism, let this not disturb us. For, we have no responsibility to return the favor to them, but to observe the canons with exactness. Moreover, let it be ordained in every case that those coming over from

27 Probably the Asiatic bishops at the Councils of Nice and Laodicea, since both of these councils admitted the Novatians to the Church without rebaptizing them.

28 The Novatians.

29 The Benedictine editors believe that they must have introduced additional ceremonies into the baptismal rite, but did not change the essential form. If they had done so, St. Basil would not have permitted their baptism to be accepted under any condition, a thing that he did for the general good under certain circumstances.

30 The baptism of the Encratites was not questioned either before St. Basil's time or after it. Neither Canon 7 of Constantinople (381) nor Canon 95 of the Council in Trullo, each of which gives a list of those sects whose baptism is to be considered valid or invalid, mentions the Encratites.

their baptism be anointed[31] openly before the faithful and so finally approach the mysteries.[32] On the other hand, I know that we received the brothers, Izois and Saturninus, who were of that sect,[33] into the rank of bishops. So we are no longer able to separate from the Church those who have joined their sect, having set forth a certain canon of communion, as it were, with them through the reception of the bishops.

(2) She who has deliberately destroyed a fetus has to pay the penalty of murder. And there is no exact inquiry among us as to whether the fetus was formed or unformed.[34] For, here it is not only the child to be born that is vindicated, but also the woman herself who made an attempt against

31 I.e., must receive the sacrament of confirmation. Pope Stephen in the controversy against Cyprian and Firmilian had declared that, when one baptized in an heretical sect wished to enter the Church, hands should be placed upon him as a sign of penance. Cf. *Epist. Cypriani ad Pompeium, PL* 3.1128. Cyprian indicates in his Letter 73 that Stephen here refers not only to the sacrament of penance but also to the sacrament of confirmation. Cf. Hefele, I.111-113. Canon 7 of Constantinople and Canon 95 of the Council in Trullo assert that those coming into the Church from sects whose baptism was admitted as valid were anointed with the holy chrism on the forehead, eyes, nostrils, mouth, and ears; while at the same time the formula, 'the seal of the Gift of the Holy Spirit,' was pronounced.

32 The Mass.

33 The Encratites.

34 By a 'formed' fetus is meant one in which the rational soul has already been infused; by an 'unformed' fetus is understood one in which the rational soul has not yet been infused. The distinction between the formed and the unformed fetus is recognized in Exodus 21.22,23, Septuagint and Old Latin versions: *Si autem litigabunt duo viri et percusserint mulierem in utero habentem, et exierit infans eius nondum formatus; detrimentum patietur, quantum induxerit vir mulieris et dabit cum postulatione. Si autem formatum fuerit, dabit animam pro animo.* The Vulgate version, however, and consequently the English, is quite different.

her own life,[35] because usually the women die in such attempts. Furthermore, added to this is the destruction of the embryo, another murder, at least according to the intention of those who dare these things. Nevertheless, we should not prolong their penance until death,[36] but should accept a term of ten years,[37] and we should determine the treatment not by time, but by the manner of repentance.[38]

(3) A deacon who has committed fornication after having been admitted to the diaconate shall be dismissed from the ministry, but, having been reduced to the rank of the laity, he shall not be debarred from communion. For there is an ancient canon[39] that those who have fallen from rank

35 Balsamon (*PL* 138.687) remarks that some, basing their argument on the distinction mentioned in the preceding note, had contended that a woman who had effected the abortion of an unformed fetus should not be subjected to the penalty for murder. According to St. Basil, however, even though the fetus was as yet unformed, the woman must undergo the punishment for murder, because, since the medicines which bring about abortion frequently cause the death of the woman herself, she who takes these medicines is guilty of an attempt on her own life.

36 Canon 63 of the Synod of Elvira had decreed that an adulteress guilty of the crime of abortion should be deprived of Communion even at death. Cf. Hefele 1.164.

37 This is the penance prescribed for this crime by Canon 20 of Ancyra. Cf. Hefele 1.220. Since in Canon 56 St. Basil imposes a twenty-years' penance on the wilful murderer, and in Canons 11 and 57 a ten-years' penance on the involuntary murderer, some concluded that he considered the woman an involuntary murderer. Balsamon, however, believes that the woman was a voluntary murderer, but was not subjected to the full penance of twenty years because grave fear of being detected in shame and punished had led her to the act.

38 St. Basil insists that God's mercy in forgiving sins depends upon the quality of the penance and the sincerity and contrition with which it is performed; not upon the time spent in performing penance.

39 The Benedictine editors think that St. Basil here refers to the twenty-fifth of the Apostolic Canons, which decreed that a bishop, a priest, or a deacon, who had been apprehended in fornication, or perjury, or theft, must be deposed, but must not be deprived of Communion. Drey, however, thinks that this canon was inserted in the Apostolic Canons from the present canon of St. Basil. Cf. *Neue Untersuchungen über die Constitutionem u. Canones der Apostel.* (Tubin. 1832) 403ff., quoted by Hefele 1.453.

should be subjected to this sort of punishment alone, the ancients having followed, as I think, this law: 'You will not punish twice for the same sin.'[40] Another reason is that those who hold the status of laymen, if they fall from the rank of the faithful, are again taken up to the position from which they have fallen, but the deacon once and for all has the lasting penalty of deposition. Therefore, the diaconate not being restored to him, they imposed this penalty alone. This is, then, the explanation according to the regulations. But, on the whole, the withdrawal from the sin is a truer remedy.[41] Consequently, he who, having rejected grace for the pleasures of the flesh, has by mortification of the body and its complete subjection through self-control withdrawn from these pleasures which overcame him, will provide us with solid proof of his cure. We must, then, know both views, that of exact observance and that of custom, and we must follow the rule handed over to us in the case of those things which do not admit of perfect observance.

(4) Concerning thrice-married persons[42] and polygamists[43] they have laid down the same canon as in the case of twice-married persons,[44] but in due proportion; one year,[45] indeed, for those twice-married; however, some say two years; while they excommunicate those thrice-married for three,

40 Cf. Nahum 1.9 (Septuagint).

41 St. Basil calls attention to the contrition and the resolution of amendment that are necessary for the forgiveness of sins, without which the performance of public penance would be worthless.

42 Not those who have three wives at the same time, but those who have married a third time after the death of their former wives by a first and second marriage.

43 Not those who have many wives at the same time, but those who have contracted many marriages successively.

44 Those who have married after the death of their first spouse. Second marriages were looked on with disfavor, especially in the East, where they were regarded as a sign of weakness and a species of incontinence. Although such marriages were permitted, a penance was imposed on those contracting them.

and often for four, years. Moreover, they call such a state no longer marriage, but polygamy, or, rather, a moderate fornication. Therefore the Lord said to the Samaritan woman who had had five husbands in turn: 'He whom thou now hast is not thy husband,'[46] on the ground that those going beyond the limit of two marriages are not worthy of being called by the title of husband or wife. Now, we have accepted a separation of five years as our usual practice in the case of persons thrice-married, not from the canons, but in conformity with those who have gone before us.[47] Yet, there is no need to separate them altogether from the Church,[48] but, in two or three years, to consider them worthy of being 'hearers,' and after this to permit them to stand with the rest at prayer but to exclude them from Holy Communion, and so, only after they have shown some fruit of repentance, to restore them to their place of communion.

(5) Those of the heretics who repent at the hour of death must be received,[49] yet we certainly must not receive them indiscreetly, but after having examined[50] whether they show a true repentance and whether they have fruits to testify to their zeal for salvation.

---

45 It is not known to what authorities St. Basil here refers. Canon 3 of Neo-Caesarea declared that the punishment for those married more than twice was well known, but did not state what the punishment was (Hefele 1.224), and Canon 1 of Laodicea decreed that those who had lawfully and regularly entered upon a second marriage should, after a short period, be pardoned and received into communion. Cf. Hefele 2.299.

46 John 4.18.

47 I.e., from local tradition.

48 Not to place them outside the doors of the church, among the mourners, the lowest grade of penitents.

49 This is in accordance with Canon 13 of Nice, which prescribes that every man, whatever his offense may have been, must, if he requests it, be given Holy Viaticum on his deathbed. Cf. Hefele 1.419.

50 In Canon 13 of Nice, also, the bishop was instructed before giving Communion to the dying penitent to make 'the necessary inquiry.' Cf. Hefele 1.419.

(6) The fornications of canonical persons[51] must not be considered marriage, but their union must by all means be broken. This is both advantageous for the security of the Church, and it will not give the heretics a hold against us on the ground that men are attracted to us because of the license for sinning.

(7) They who defile themselves with men and with beasts—also, murderers, poisoners, adulterers, and idolaters[52] —have been considered deserving of the same punishment.[53] Therefore, whatever regulation you have in the case of the rest, observe also in the case of these. But, those who have spent thirty years[54] in penance for impurity[55] which they committed in ignorance we should not hesitate to receive. Ignorance, as also the voluntary confession, and the long duration of their penance make them worthy of pardon.

---

51 Balsamon and Zonaras understand 'canonical persons' as meaning all those enumerated in the canons, i.e., clerics, monks, nuns, and those girls who, while living at home, have professed virginity (*PG* 138.603-607). Aristenus, however, applied the term only to professed virgins (*PG* 138.606-607). The Benedictine editors agree with the latter because of St. Basil's use of the term in Letters 52 and 173, where it certainly refers to the virgins.

52 Not those who have actually offered sacrifice to idols, but also those who sought the aid of Satan in performing tricks and prodigies. Cf. Balsamon and Zonaras, *PG* 138.607-609.

53 Not that their punishment lasts for an equal period of time, but that all undergo the four grades of punishment. Cf. Balsamon and Zonaras, *PG* 138.607-609.

54 Although the number is supported by all the mss., the Benedictine editors think it clearly an error, since even after a wilful sin of this kind, according to the canons of St. Basil, the person would have been received to communion after twenty years at the most. However, St. Basil is not here prescribing a period of penance for the sin, but merely says that in this given case the person who has already spent thirty years in penance should be admitted. It may be that the case had dragged on unnoticed for more than the prescribed time without an appeal from the penitent.

55 Balsamon and Zonaras think the 'impurity' was incest, which the man committed with a relative, not knowing his relationship to the person. Cf. *PG* 138.607-611.

They have been given over to Satan[56] for almost the whole lifetime of a man in order that they may be taught not to behave in an unseemly manner. Consequently, order them to be received now without delay, especially if they have tears with which to supplicate your Mercifulness, and if they show a life worthy of compassion.

(8) He who in a temper used an axe against his wife is a murderer.[57] And you have have suggested rightly and in a manner worthy of your wisdom that I speak about these matters more fully, because there are many distinctions between voluntary and involuntary acts.[58] Now, to hit a man when throwing a stone at a dog or a tree[59] is entirely involuntary and far from the intention of him who began the act. In fact, the intention was to ward off the beast or to shake down the fruit, and the passer-by fell under the blow

56 I.e., shut out from communion with the faithful. Cf. Balsamon and Zonaras, *PG* 138.607; also 1 Cor. 5.5, where St. Paul orders the Corinthians to deliver the incestuous adulterer 'to Satan for the destruction of the flesh, that the spirit may be saved.'

57 In the Synod of Elvira (Canon 5), murder of a servant committed in anger was punished by a seven years' penance if the blow was delivered with the intent to kill, and by a five years' penance if the blow were not so delivered. Cf. Hefele 1.140. St. Basil punishes voluntary murder with a twenty years' penance (Canon 56), and involuntary murder with ten years' penance (Canon 57). The Benedictine editors think that only those cases of involuntary murder which St. Basil says approach the voluntary were visited with ten years' punishment. Cf. *PG* 138.472; Hefele 1.140.

58 In explaining voluntary and involuntary acts St. Basil seems to be applying the principles laid down by Aristotle in his *Nicomachaean Ethics*. In 3.1 the philosopher teaches that only voluntary acts are imputable to man for praise or blame, and, moreover, that anger or desire does not take away voluntariness from the act. This doctrine is applied to the man who in anger used an axe against his wife, for the act prompted by anger is none the less voluntary and therefore the man is blamed as a murderer. In 5.8 Aristotle proposes the general principle that what is done through ignorance is involuntary. We shall see as we proceed how St. Basil applies his principles to the present case.

59 Here we see the ignorance of the person; hence, the act is involuntary.

accidentally. Therefore, such a deed was involuntary. It is also involuntary if some one wishing to correct another should strike him with a strap or a pliant rod, and the one struck should die. For, it is considered that the intention there is the desire to benefit the one erring, not to destroy him.[60] Among the involuntary occasions there is also this one: when warding off a person in a fight, to aim blows unsparingly at the vital parts with a club or with the hand, so as to injure him but not to destroy him.[61] But, this is already approaching the voluntary.[62] For, he who has used such an instrument for self-defense, or has not applied the blows with caution, is evidently unsparing of the man because he has been overcome by passion. Likewise, if he has used a heavy piece of wood or a stone too large for a man to endure, he is counted among the involuntary murderers, since he wanted one thing, but did another. In his anger he aimed such a blow that he killed the man whom he struck; nevertheless, his intention was, perhaps, to beat him up, but not to take his life entirely. However, he who has used a sword or some such weapon has no excuse, and especially he who hurled the axe. For, it is evident that he did not strike holding it with his hand so that the force of the blow was in his power, but he hurled it, so that the blow necessarily was fatal because of the weight of the iron, its edge, and the momentum gained in traveling over a long distance.

Again, entirely voluntary and admitting no doubt is such an act as that of robbers and hostile invaders. For, the former destroy for the sake of money, fleeing the charge; and they who come in wars to slaughter openly choose

60 Here the death of the one beaten is not intended by the chastiser, who meant merely to correct and not to kill him.

61 Here, too, the death follows contrary to the intention of the one who, in defending himself, killed his assailant. Hence, the murder is involuntary.

62 Cf. note 58.

neither to terrify nor to chasten, but to destroy their opponents. Moreover, even if some one would mix a strange drug for some other cause and he would take away a life, we would consider such an act voluntary murder. Women frequently do this, trying by certain spells and charms to lead on some men to love them, and they also give them drugs which produce a darkness in the understanding. Such women, if they cause death, although in desiring one thing they have done another, nevertheless, because of the strange and forbidden practice, are considered among the voluntary murderers. Moreover, those, too, who give drugs causing abortion are murderers themselves, as well as those receiving the poison which kills the fetus.[63] These, then, are the explanations for such a matter.

(9) The declaration of the Lord concerning the prohibition to depart from marriage except for the reason of fornication,[64] consistent with the sense, applies equally to men or to women. But, such is not the practice; on the contrary, we find great strictness regarding women, since the Apostle said: 'He who cleaves to a harlot, becomes one body with her,'[65] and Jeremias said: 'If a wife shall marry another man, she shall not return to her husband but shall be polluted and defiled,'[66] and again, 'He that keepeth an adulteress is foolish and wicked.'[67] But, custom orders adulterous men and those

63 Cf. notes on Canon 2. St. Basil here subjects to the punishment for murder not only those who take, but also those who administer, drugs causing abortion. This view is traced to Canon 21 of Ancyra, if we accept Routh's (*Reliquiae Sacrae*) rendition of the phrase *kai toútōi suntíthentai,* and translate: 'The same punishment will be inflicted on those who assist them,' i.e., in causing miscarriages. Cf. Hefele 1.220.

64 St. Basil is here referring to the Scriptural prohibition of divorce, contained in Matt. 5.31,32; Matt. 19.9; Mark 10.11,12; Luke 16.18; 1 Cor. 7.10,11; Rom. 7.2.

65 Cf. 1 Cor. 6.16.

66 Cf. Jer. 3.1.

67 Cf. Prov. 18.22.

who are fornicators to be kept by their wives.[68] Consequently, I do not know whether the woman living with a dismissed husband can be styled an adulteress.[69] For, the charge here affects her who dismissed her husband[70]—according to the cause for which she withdrew from marriage. If it was when beaten she did not endure the blows, she should have been patient rather than have been separated from her husband, or, if she could not endure a loss of money, neither is that a reasonable excuse. And, if it was because he lived in fornication, we do not observe this practice in the Church; on the contrary, the wife is not commanded to depart even from the unbelieving husband,[71] but, because of the uncertainty of the consequences, to remain. 'For how dost thou know, O wife, whether thou wilt save thy husband?'[72] Therefore, she who left is an adulteress if she went to another man. But, he who was abandoned is to be pardoned,[73] and she who dwells with such a one is not condemned.[74] However, if the man separating from his wife went to another woman, then he himself is an adulterer, because he has made her commit adultery, and the woman living with him is an

68 The Benedictine editors point out that this custom, which St. Basil admits is at variance with the doctrine of Christ, was probably introduced under the influence of Roman Law, which recognized the husband's right to divorce an adulterous wife, but did not, on the other hand, permit a wife to divorce an adulterous husband.

69 I.e., not whether she is free from sin, but whether she should undergo the canonical punishment for adultery.

70 St. Basil would place the penalty for adultery rather on the wife who illegally dismissed her husband.

71 Cf. 1 Cor. 7.13,14.

72 1 Cor. 7.16.

73 St. Basil clearly does not mean here that the man who, being illegally dismissed by his wife, cohabits with another woman is blameless. Pardon is granted only to the guilty. He simply states that the custom does not authorize the imposing of the canonical penance for fornication on such a man. Cf. Hefele's comment on Canon 10 of Arles, I.189.

74 To public penance for adultery.

adulteress, because she has turned another's husband to herself.

(10) Let not those be compelled to perjure themselves[75] who have sworn that they will not receive ordination, if they have refused under oath. For, even though there seems to be some canon[76] which condones such men, we know by experience that men who forswear themselves do not fare well. Yet, it is necessary to consider also the form of the oath, the words, the spirit in which the oath was taken, and the slightest additions to the words, since, if there is no solution from any side, we must, by all means, dismiss them. However, the matter pertaining to Severus,[77] or rather, the presbyter ordained by him, seems to have some such solution, if you agree with me. Order that district subject to Mesteia, to which the man was assigned, to pay tribute to Vasoda. Thus, that one[78] will not commit perjury, since he is not

75 By inducing them to take orders.

76 This canon is unknown to us. The Benedictine editors think it is the same one that St. Athanasius followed when he gave advice to Dracontius, who upon being raised to the episcopacy had fled in accordance with an oath he had previously taken. St. Athanasius counseled him to disregard his oath and return to his church.

77 This canon is obscure and quite involved. The Benedictine editors have offered the following possible solution. Longinus, a priest in the field subject to Mestia, had been deposed for some delinquency, but had been permitted to retain the honor of the priesthood. Bishop Severus, therefore, had sent another priest named Cyriacus to administer in the place of Longinus. Severus, when he had previously ordained Cyriacus, had forced him to take an oath that he would remain at Mindana. Hence, if Cyriacus remained in the field subject to Mestia, he would be guilty of violating his oath. If, on the other hand, he returned to Mindana, the field subject to Mestia would be without a priest and the responsibility would redound upon Longinus, whose delinquency had caused him to be deposed from active ministry. Hence, St. Basil orders the field that was subject to Mestia to be subjected to Vasoda, the place to which Mindana was subject. In this way the field could retain its priest, Cyriacus, who could remain there without violating his oath, since that place was now subject to the same chorepiscopus as Mindana, where he had sworn to remain.

78 Cyriacus.

withdrawing from the district, and Longinus,[79] having Cyriacus with him, will not desert the church nor will he damn his own soul by idleness.[80] And, we think that we are not doing anything contrary to the canons by showing indulgence to Cyriacus, who, although he had sworn to remain at Mindana, accepted the transfer. For, his return will safeguard his oath. And the fact that he has yielded to the arrangement will not be considered as perjury for him, because it was not added to his oath that he would not withdraw even for a brief space from Mindana, but would remain for the future. But to Severus, who alleges forgetfulness, we shall grant pardon, saying that He who knows hidden things will not suffer His Church to be dishonored by such a man, who has acted uncanonically from the beginning, binding by oath, contrary to the Gospels, and teaching men to perjure themselves by their transfer, and, now, lying by pretending forgetfulness. Yet, since we are not the judge of hearts, but judge from what we hear, let us leave vengeance to the Lord, and ourselves receive him without discrimination, granting pardon for the human frailty of forgetfulness.

(11) He who committed an involuntary homicide[81] has sufficiently paid the penalty in the eleven years.[82] We shall

---

79 Balsamon and Zonaras think that Longinus was a wealthy layman who had threatened to lay waste the church if Cyriacus were withdrawn from the field subject to Mestia, not that he was a priest, as the Benedictine editors believe. Cf. *PG* 138.627.

80 The phrase *dià tês argías* is the principal argument for the Benedictines' interpretation in the preceding note. They show that *argía* is the punishment of deposition in the thirteenth of the Apostolic Canons, and that St. Basil used it in this sense in the letter to Paregorius. He also employs the verb *argéo* in the same sense in Canon 69.

81 According to the Benedictine editors, not all involuntary homicide was punished with ten years' penance, but only that which approached the voluntary. Cf. Canon 8 and notes.

82 Cf. Canon 8 and notes; also, Canon 57.

undoubtedly observe carefully the laws of Moses[83] in the case of those who have been beaten, but we do not consider that he who was indeed laid low by the blows which he received, but again walked with a cane, was murdered. Even if he did not rise again after the blows, although the one who did the beating is a murderer, still, since he did not intend to kill him, he is an involuntary one because of his motive.

(12) The canon[84] absolutely excludes from the ministry those who are twice married.

(13) Our Fathers did not reckon killings in war as murders, but granted pardon, it seems to me, to those fighting in defense of virtue and piety. Perhaps, however, it is well to advise them that, since their hands are not clean, they should abstain from communion alone[85] for a period of three years.

(14) If the tax collector consents to spend his unjust gain on the poor and thenceforward to be free from the vice of avarice, he is acceptable for the priesthood.[86]

(15)[87] I am surprised at your demanding grammatical preciseness in the Scriptures and thinking that the diction is forced in the interpretation which gives the Scriptural mean-

---

83 Cf. Exod. 21.18,19.

84 Cf. 1 Tim. 3.2-13; Tit. 1.5-9; and Canon 17 of the Apostolic Canons; 'If anyone after baptism has been joined in a second matrimony, or have a concubine, he cannot be a bishop, or a priest, or a deacon, or any of those who serve in the sacred ministry.' Cf. Hefele 1.464.

85 Balsamon and Zonaras say that the counsel contained in this canon was never put into effect. However, it was quoted by the bishops against Emperor Phocas when he wished to have all those killed in war honored as martyrs. Cf. *PG* 138.635.

86 Clerics were forbidden to practice usury by the forty-fourth of the Apostolic Canons, Canon 12 of Arles (314), and Canon 17 of Nice (325). Cf. Hefele 1.434.

87 This canon is an answer to some exegetical difficulty involving Ps. 8.9: 'The birds of the air and the fishes of the sea, that pass through the paths of the sea.'

ing but does not exactly transfer the significance of the Hebrew words. However, since we must not idly pass over a question proposed by a man devoted to inquiry, the winged creatures of the heavens and the fishes of the sea were allotted the same origin in the creation. For, both classes were drawn forth from the waters.[88] And the reason is that each has the same peculiar nature. Some swim through the water and others swim in the air. For this cause, then, mention was made of them in common. Now, the form of expression, as referring to the fishes, is used inappropriately, yet, as referring to all creatures that live in the waters, very properly indeed. The winged creatures of the sky have been made subject to man, and so have the fishes of the sea; and not only these, but also all creatures which travel the paths of the seas. For, not everything which lives in the water is a fish, such as sea monsters, whales, hammer-headed sharks, dolphins, seals, and also sea horses, sea dogs, sawfish, swordfish, and sea cows; and, if you wish, there are also sea nettles, scallops, and all the hard-shelled creatures, none of which is a fish yet all are creatures that travel the paths of the seas. Thus, there are three classes: the winged creatures of the sky, the fishes of the sea, and all creatures that, living in the water and differing from fishes, travel the paths of the sea.

(16) Now, Naaman was not great before the Lord, but before his own lord; that is, he was one of those who had great influence with the king of the Syrians. So pay strict attention to the Scriptures and you will find therein the solution of your problem.[89]

---

88 Cf. Gen. 1.20-22.

89 Cf. 4 Kings 5, which deals with Naaman, general of the army of the king of Syria, and how he was cleansed of leprosy by Eliseus.

189. To Eustathius, the Court Physician[1]

Truly, humanity is the concern of all of you who follow the profession of medicine. And it seems to me that he who would prefer your profession to all other life pursuits would make a proper choice, not straying from the right, if really the most precious of all things, life, is painful and undesirable unless it can be possessed with health. And your profession is the supply vein of health. But, in your case, especially, the science is ambidextrous, and you set for yourself higher standards of humanity, not limiting the benefit of your profession to bodily, but also contriving the correction of spiritual ills. I say this, not only because of common reports, but also because I have been taught by my own experience on many occasions, especially now, in the midst of the indescribable wickedness of the enemies. This, as it flowed through our life like a destructive flood, you skillfully dispelled, dissipating that grievous fiery pain of our heart by the pouring on of consoling words. For I, when I looked upon the continuous and varied assaults of our enemies against us, thought that I ought to be silent and to receive in silence these accusations and not to contradict those armed with deceit, that base weapon, which frequently thrusts its point even through truth. But, you acted rightly, urging me not to betray the truth but to expose the false accusers,

---

1 Letter 151 was written to this same Eustathius. The authorship of this letter has been much contested since it is found among both the works of St. Basil and those of St. Gregory of Nyssa. On the margin of one ms. (Regius 2896) these words are found: 'It should be known that some say that this letter belongs to him of Nyssa: and it seems probable judging from the character of its style.' Although most earlier scholars assigned it to St. Basil, at the present time St. Gregory is generally acknowledged to be its author. The date given for its composition is 374 or the beginning of 375.

lest many be harmed incidentally if the lie gained its point against the truth.

Now, they who adopted that undisguised hatred against us seemed to me to be inventing something very similar to Aesop's fable. For, he made the wolf bring certain charges against the lamb, ashamed, as he pretended, to seem to be destroying without just excuse one who had never caused distress, and, when the lamb easily put an end to every charge deceitfully brought forward, the wolf did not slacken in any degree his attack, but, being defeated in justice, was victorious with his teeth. In the same way, they who are zealous in their hatred against us as something good, blushing, perhaps, at seeming to hate without cause, fabricate accusations and charges against us and persist in none of their imputations for the whole time, but they now give this cause for their ill will toward us, and a little later that one, and again some other. Their malice has no foundation, but whenever they have been shaken from one charge, they cling to another, and from that one they again seize upon another, and, even if all their charges have been dissolved, they do not desist from hating. They claim that we worship three gods, dinning this into the ears of the people, and not ceasing to build up this slander in a most specious manner. Truth, however, is fighting on our side, since we show, both in public to all men, and in private to those who visit us, that we anathematize everyone who says that there are three gods and we judge such a one to be no Christian. But, whenever they hear this, they have Sabellius at hand against us, and his diseased doctrine is noisily proclaimed along with our words. Against this we again put forward truth, our customary weapon, pointing out that we shudder at such a heresy as much as at Judaism.

What then? After such attempts have they been wearied

and reduced to silence? Not so. They accuse us of innovation, thus framing the charge against us because we confess three Persons. They claim that we say one Goodness, one Power, and one Divinity. And this they say not without truth, for we do say it. But, they allege in their charge that their custom does not have this, and that Scripture does not agree. What, therefore, shall we reply to this? We do not think that it is right to make the custom that prevails among them the law and norm of right doctrine. For, if custom is the strong point for a proof of correctness, it assuredly is also possible for us to propose in its stead the custom prevailing among us. And, if they reject this, clearly we need not follow them. Therefore, let the God-inspired Scripture be judge for us, and to those whose teachings are found to be in harmony with the divine words will belong by all means the verdict of truth. What, then, is the charge? Really, two points have been set forth at the same time in the accusation against us: one, the dividing of the Persons; and the other, our not yet using in the plural any of the names proper to God, but, as was said before, expressing in the singular as one the Goodness and the Power and the Godhead, and ali such names. Now, those teaching the distinction of substances in the divine nature would not be averse to the division of the Persons. For, it is unreasonable for those who say that there are three substances not to say that there are three Persons, also. Consequently, the only thing in the charge is this—we proclaim in the singular the names given to the divine nature.

But, we have a ready and clear argument against this. For, he who condemns those proclaiming one Godhead necessarily agrees with him who says that there are many, or with him who says that there is none. For, it is not possible to conceive of something else beyond this statement. And on the other hand, the divinely inspired doctrine does not permit us to say that there are many, since, wherever it makes mention of it, it refers to the Godhead in the singular; for example, 'For in him dwells all the fullness of the Godhead.'[2] And elsewhere, 'For since the creation of the world his invisible attributes are clearly seen—his everlasting power also and divinity—being understood through the things that are made.'[3] If, then, it is characteristic only of those who have suffered the error of polytheism to spin out the number of godheads to a plurality, and to deny the Godhead absolutely would be a mark of atheists, what argument is there which brings us into discredit in our confession of the one Godhead? But, they reveal more openly the aim of their speech—they admit, in the case of the Father, that He is God, and that in like manner they honor the Son with the name of the Godhead, but that the Spirit, who is numbered with the Father and the Son, they no longer include in the idea of the Godhead, but, while admitting the power of the Godhead as extending from the Father as far as the Son, they exclude the nature of the Spirit from the divine glory. Therefore, we must put up a brief defense, as well as we may be able, against this idea.

What, then, is our argument? The Lord, in handing over the saving faith to those who are being instructed in His doctrine, joins the Holy Spirit with the Father and the Son. And that which has been once associated, we say, remains united always. For, He was not ranked with Them in one instance and excluded in others. But, in the life-giving power through which our nature is transformed from the perishable life to immortality, the power of the Spirit is possessed in common with the Father and the Son, and in many other

2 Cf. Col. 2.9.
3 Rom. 1.20.

respects, as in the concept of goodness, and also of holiness and eternity, of wisdom, righteousness, authority, ability, and, plainly everywhere, He is inseparable in all the terms which are understood in the higher sense. Accordingly, we consider that it is right to believe that that which is joined with the Father and the Son in such sublime and divine concepts is separated in none other. For, we do not know any difference in regard to the greater or the inferior terms for the divine nature so as to think that it is lawful to concede to the Spirit the joint ownership of terms of the inferior attributes and to judge Him unworthy of the more exalted ones. In fact, all the concepts and terms proper to God are equal to each other in honor, since they show no variation at all in regard to the designation of the subject.[4] For, the name of goodness does not lead the thought to one subject, and that of wisdom and of power and of righteousness to another, but, whatever terms you may say, the thing signified is the same in all. And, if you say 'God,' you have indicated the same One whom you meant by the rest of the terms. But, if all the terms used in connection with the divine nature have equal force with each other in the indication of the subject, guiding our thought to the same object, some with one emphasis, others with another, what reason is there, when the Spirit is granted partnership with the Father and the Son in the other terms, to exclude Him from the Godhead alone? It is absolutely necessary either to give the partnership in this also or not to grant it in the other terms. For, if He is deserving in the former, He surely is not undeserving in the latter. But, if He is of too little importance, according to their reasoning, to be capable of the partnership of the term 'Godhead' with the Father

4 I.e.; since all the Persons are equal, all the terms applied to Them are of equal honor.

and the Son, He is not worthy of sharing any other of the terms proper to God. For, if the terms are considered and compared with each other according to the significance observed in each, none will be found to be inferior to the title of 'God.' And a proof of this is that many inferior things also are called by this name. Moreover, the divine Scripture does not refrain from using this equivocal term, not even in inconsistent matters, as when it calls images by the name of 'God.' 'For,' it says, 'let the gods who did not make the heaven and the earth be destroyed and be cast under the earth.'[5] It also says, 'All the gods of the Gentiles are devils.'[6] And the witch[7] with her magic arts summoning up the souls sought by Saul said that she saw gods. Furthermore, even Balaam,[8] a certain diviner and soothsayer, who bore his oracles in his hand, as the Scripture says, and who successfully procured for himself instruction from the demons through his divining trickery, is related by the Scripture to have taken counsel with God. And, it is possible, collecting many such passages from the divine Scriptures, to allege that this name has no precedence above the other appellations proper to God, since, as it has been said, we even find it used equivocally in incongruous matters. But the name of holiness, and of eternity, and of righteousness, and of goodness, we are taught by the Scriptures, is nowhere communicated to things that are unfit. Therefore, if they do not deny that the Holy Spirit shares with the Son and the Father in the names piously used exclusively in the case of the divine nature alone, what reason is there to try to make out that He has no partnership in this one alone which

5 Cf. Jer. 10.11.
6 Cf. Ps. 95.5.
7 Cf. 1 Kings 28.13.
8 Cf. Num. 22.20.

both evil spirits and idols have been shown to share through a certain equivocal use?

But, they say that this term is indicative of nature, and that the nature of the Spirit is not shared with Father and Son, and for this reason He does not share the partnership implied in this name. Let them show, then, by what means they have come to know the difference of the nature. For, if it were possible for the divine nature itself to be discerned by itself, and for that which is peculiar to it and that which is foreign to it to be discovered from what is seen, we certainly would not have needed words or other proofs for the perception of the object of our search. But, since it is too sublime for the understanding of those who are searching and we draw conclusions from certain signs concerning matters which are beyond our knowledge, it is very necessary for us to be guided in our investigation of the divine nature by its operations. Accordingly, if we see that the operations of the Father and the Son and the Holy Spirit differ from each other, we will infer from the dissimilarity of the operations that the natures which are producing them are different. It is not possible that things which are distinct in nature should correspond with each other in the form of their operations: fire does not cool, nor does ice heat; but, because of the dissimilarity of their natures even the operations produced by them differ from each other. But, if we consider the operation of the Father and of the Son and of the Holy Spirit to be one, differing or varying in no way at all, it is necessary because of the identity of the operation for the oneness of the nature to be inferred.

Equally the Father and the Son and the Holy Spirit sanctify and vivify and enlighten and console and do all such things. And let no one especially assign the sanctifying power to the action of the Spirit, after he has heard the

Saviour[9] in the Gospel saying to His Father concerning the disciples, 'Father, sanctify them in thy name.' In like manner, all other things are equally accomplished for those who are deserving of them by the Father and the Son and the Holy Spirit; every grace and virtue, guidance, life, consolation, transition to immortality, transference to freedom, and whatever other good there is which comes down to us. But, the dispensation above us in both the intellectual and sensible creation, if there is any need to conjecture by means of what is known to us concerning that which is beyond us, not even this is established without the operation and power of the Holy Spirit, since each thing receives a share of His assistance according to its own desert and need. Now, if the arrangement and administration concerning those things which are above our nature are not manifest to our perception, nevertheless, by analogy one would more reasonably conclude through things familiar to us that the power of the Spirit is active in those things also, rather than that it is alienated from the dispensation in what is above us. In fact, he who makes that statement utters a bare and naked blasphemy, and without reasoning establishes a logical absurdity. But, he who infers that matters beyond us are administered by the power of the Spirit with the Father and the Son affirms confidently concerning these things, supported by clear testimony accruing from his own life. Therefore, the identity of the operation in the case of the Father and of the Son and of the Holy Spirit clearly proves the precise similarity of the nature. So that, if the name of 'Godhead' points out the nature, the common sharing of the substance proves that this name is validly applicable to the Holy Spirit, also.

Yet, I do not know how those who are fabricating every-

9 Cf. John 17.11,17.

thing apply the name of 'Godhead' in proof of the nature, as if they have not heard from the Scripture that the nature is not something acquired by appointment. Moses was appointed god of the Egyptians when He who was giving the revelation[10] spoke to him in this manner: 'I have appointed thee the God of Pharao.' Therefore, the title conveys an indication of some power, either protective or active. But, the divine nature in all the names which may be contrived remains, just as it is, inexplicable, as is our teaching. For, having learned that it is beneficent, judicious, good, and righteous, and all other such things, we have been taught the different forms of its operations, but we cannot at all recognize any better the nature of the one acting, through a consideration of the operations. When one gives a definition of each of these names and of the nature itself to which these terms have reference, he will not give the same definition of both. But, of things which have a different definition, the nature also is different. Therefore, the substance, of which an enlightening definition has not yet been found, is one thing, but the meaning of the names referring to it, derived from some operation or value, is another.

From the partnership of the names, therefore, we arrive at the fact that there is no distinction in the operations, but we arrive at no clear proof of variation in nature, since, as it was said, identity of the operations indicates community of nature. Therefore, if 'Godhead' is the name of an operation, as we say there is one operation of the Father and Son and Holy Spirit, so we say that there is one Godhead; or if, according to the opinions of the many, the name of 'Godhead' is indicative of nature, because we find no diversity in the nature, we do not unreasonably declare the Blessed Trinity to be of one Godhead.

10 Exod. 7.1.

190. To Amphilochius, Bishop of Iconium[1]

You have attended to the affairs of the Isaurian[2] church in a manner worthy of your tact and zeal, of which I am always an admirer. That it would be more advantageous for everyone if the responsibility were divided among a greater number of bishops I believe is self-evident to any chance observer. And, in fact, your Intelligence is not unaware of this, but you have both clearly perceived and have made known to us how the matter stands. Since, however, it is not easy to find worthy men, shall we not, perchance, while we wish to have the credit due to numbers and to cause the Church of God to be administered more accurately by a larger number, unwittingly let the doctrine fall into contempt through the untrustworthiness of those called, and induce in the people a habit of indifference? For, you yourself also know that, for the most part, it is usual for the characters of the governed to be the same as that of their leaders. Therefore, perhaps it would be better, at least if this also is not too hard, to put forward one certain man of approved character as leader of the city, and rely on him to administer the details on his own responsibility. We say this only if there is some servant of God, 'a worker that cannot be ashamed,'[3] one looking not to his own interests, but to those of the many[4] in order that they may be saved, who, if he sees that he is unequal to the office, will take on helpers for

1 Concerning Amphilochius cf. Letter 188 n. 1. This letter was written in 374.

2 A titular see in the province of Lycaonia, under the ecclesiastical jurisdiction of Iconium. The Isaurians, although in the heart of the Roman monarchy, had long continued as a nation of wild barbarians, never reduced to obedience by arms or policy, and raids and Arian persecution had disorganized the Isaurian episcopate.

3 Cf. 2 Tim. 2.15.

4 Cf. Phil. 2.4.

the harvest. If, then, we find such a man, I admit that the one is worth many, and that it is an advantage to the churches and without danger to us to handle the care of souls in this way. But, if this is not easy, let us be zealous, first, to give leaders to the little towns and villages which formerly had a bishop's see. And we shall appoint the bishop of the city then, so that he who is proposed may not become a hindrance to us in our future government, whereupon we may become involved in a domestic quarrel, because he wishes to rule larger numbers and does not accept the appointment of the bishops. But, if this is difficult, and the time does not permit it, let your Intelligence busy yourself about this—to cause to be defined the special sphere of action for the bishop of the Isaurians, because he has been ordaining certain neighbors. After this it will be a right reserved for us to give bishops to all the rest at the proper time, after approving by close examination those whom we ourselves judge to be the more capable.

We have questioned George,[5] as your Reverence urged, and he said the same as your Reverence reported, about which matters we must be at peace, throwing the care of the house upon the Lord. I have confidence in the holy God that He will give us wisdom to deliver ourselves from our necessities in another way and to attain to a life free from pain or sorrow. Now, if this does not seem best, be so kind as to send me a suggestion yourself as to what dignity[6] we should endeavor to obtain, so that we may begin to ask each one of our friends in power for this favor, either gratis or for a moderate payment, as the Lord may prosper us.

5 Not identified.

6 This dignity, according to the Benedictine editors, seems to have been some rank or office conferred by a document in the emperor's own hand, a *codicillaria dignitas,* which St. Basil was seeking for a friend.

I have written to our brother Valerius,[7] as you proposed. The affairs of Nyssa are in the same state as they were left by your Reverence, and with the help of your prayers they are making progress for the better. Of these who at that time had broken off from us, some have gone to the court; others remain, awaiting the report from there. But, the Lord is able to bring to naught the hopes of these latter and to make unavailing the return of the former.

In explaining the manna, Philo said, as if taught by some Jewish tradition, that its quality was such that it changed its nature according to the fancy of the one who was eating, and that it was of itself like millet boiled in honey, and it gave the taste now of bread, and now of meat—flesh either of birds or of beasts—and now of vegetables according to each one's liking, and of fish, so that the peculiar flavor of each species was accurately preserved in the taste of the person eating.

The Scripture acknowledges chariots with three riders,[8] because other chariots had two riders, the charioteer and the armed soldier, but those of Pharao had two warriors and one who held the reins of the horses.

Sympius[9] wrote us a letter expressive of courtesy and concord, and we have sent the letter answering him to your Reverence, so that, if you entirely approve of it, you may order it to be sent to him, of course with the addition of your own letter.

May you be in good health, cheerful in the Lord, and praying for me, and may you be preserved to me and to the Church of God by the clemency of the Holy One.

---

7 Probably a bishop.

8 *Anabátas tristátas* in Exod. 15.4 is translated 'captains.' Its meaning here, however, seems to be 'three riders,' which could also be the meaning in Exodus.

9 Bishop of Seleucia in Isauria. He attended the Council of Constantinople in 381, and was buried in the martyry of St. Thecla.

191. To Amphilochius, Bishop of Iconium[1]

On reading the message from your Reverence we felt very grateful to God, because in the words of the letter we found traces of an earlier charity; you, at least, were not affected by the feelings of the many, nor did you cling contentiously to a refusal to begin a friendly correspondence, but, as one who has learned the splendor which the saints gain from humility, you chose by taking the second place to be proved to be ahead of us. This is the law of victory among Christians, and he who does not refuse to be the lesser is crowned. In order, therefore, that we may not be wanting in the noble rivalry, behold, we ourselves also are saluting your Dignity and we declare our opinion, that, since by the grace of God the agreement in faith between us is strong, there is nothing to hinder us from being one body and one spirit as we were called in one hope of our calling.[2] Now, it is the duty of your Charity to give with this goodly beginning also what comes next—to organize the like-minded brethren around you and to indicate the time and place for the meeting, in order that, having in this way by the grace of God received one another, we may administer the churches according to the ancient pattern of love, admitting as our own members the groups of brethren coming from each party, sending forth as to friends and welcoming them in

---

1 It is very evident that this title is wrong, since in the letter St. Basil is attempting to renew friendly relations with the one to whom it is addressed, which certainly was unnecessary in the case of Amphilochius, his close friend. Tillemont (note 70) thinks that it was written to one of the Lycian bishops mentioned in Letter 218 or to Sympius or Symposius mentioned in the preceding letter, Bishop of Seleucia, who took part in the Council of Constantinople in 381. This latter view seems to be the truer one and is confirmed in Letter 204, where St. Basil mentions the Isaurians as in communion with him. This letter was written in 374.

2 Cf. Eph. 4.4.

turn as from among friends. For, this was once the boast of the Church, that the brethren from each church, journeying from one end of the world to the other furnished with small tokens, found all to be fathers and brothers. This, now, together with everything else, the enemy of the churches of Christ has taken away from us, and we are confined in our cities and hold our neighbor in suspicion. And, what else shall I say, except that we have let our charity grow cold,[3] by which alone our Lord said that His disciples were distinguished?[4] If you think best, do you yourselves first become acquainted with one another, in order that we may know with whom we shall be in agreement. So, having chosen by common consent some spot convenient for both and a time suitable for the journeys, we shall hurry to meet each other and the Lord will give us success. May you be in good health and cheerful, praying for me, and may you be preserved for me by the clemency of the Holy One.

192. To the Master Sophronius[1]

If you yourself were the recipient of a double blessing, as in your unsurpassed desire for good works you wrote to us, the one in having received my letter, and the second in having given assistance in our need, how much gratitude must we be thought to have, who have read your letter with its most welcome words and have seen the need for which we begged so speedily satisfied! Therefore, although

3 Cf. Matt. 24.12.
4 Cf. John 13.35.

1 For Sophronius and the other letters addressed to him, cf. Letters 32, 76, 96, 177, 272. This letter was written in 374.

we received with pleasure your dispatch because of its own special nature, we accepted it much more gladly because you were the one who directed its preparation. May the Lord allow us to see you soon so as to express our thanks in words and to enjoy all your virtues close at hand.

193. To Meletius, the Court Physician[1]

It is not granted to us as it is to the cranes to escape the hardships of winter, but, as regards the foreseeing of the future, we, perhaps, are not worse off than the cranes; while in the matter of freedom of choice in life we are almost as far behind the birds as we are in the ability to fly. For, first of all, some of the business affairs of life held me back; next, continuous and violent fevers so wasted my body that there has seemed to be something thinner even than I—myself thinner than myself. Then came attacks of the quartan fever lasting for more than twenty cycles. And now, when I seem to have been delivered from the fevers, I am so weak that I do not at all in this respect fall short of a spider's web. Therefore, every road is impassable to me, and every gust of the wind brings more danger than mighty waves do to sailors. Accordingly, I must hide myself in my bedroom and await the spring, if only we may be able to last until then and not fall beforehand under the disease that has settled in our intestines. But, if the Lord will preserve us by His mighty hand, we shall most gladly make the journey to your country and most gladly embrace you, our dear friend. Only pray that our life may be ordered to the advantage of our soul.

1 Nothing is known of this Meletius. The date of this letter is 375.

194. To Zoilus[1]

What are you doing, admirable Sir, getting ahead of us in the measure of humility? You, although you are so very learned and so skilled in writing, as your letter clearly shows, ask pardon of us as if for some undertaking too daring and even surpassing your dignity. But, put aside this pretence and write to us at every opportunity. If we have any claim to eloquence, most gladly shall we read the letter of an eloquent man, and also, if we are taught from the Scripture how great is the beauty of love, above all things do we treasure the communication with a man who loves us. May it be possible for you to write of the blessings—the bodily health and the prosperity of your whole house—which we are praying for you.

Be assured that our affairs are not at all more endurable than usual. But, it is enough to say this much and to inform you of the weakness of our body. Regarding the intensity of the illness now possessing us, it is not easy either to show by word or to be convinced of it in fact, if, in truth, we have experienced anything more in the matter of illness than that which you yourself have known. But, it is the work of the good God to give us the strength to bear in patience the blows inflicted on our body for our advantage by our beneficent Lord.

1 Nothing more is known of this Zoilus beyond what is found in this letter written in 375.

195. To Euphronius, Bishop of Colonia in Armenia[1]

Because Colonia, which the Lord has handed over to you for guidance, has been settled far from the highway, frequently, even if we write to the other brothers in Lesser Armenia, we hesitate to send a letter to your Reverence, since we do not suppose that there is any carrier going that far. But now, hoping that either you yourself will be present or that the letter will be sent on by the bishops to whom we have written, we are writing also to your Reverence and by the letter are saluting you, both making it evident that we seem still to be upon the earth and, at the same time, urging you to pray for us, in order that the Lord may lessen our afflictions and may remove from us the great burden of pain now lying on our heart like some cloud. And this will come to pass if He will grant a speedy return to the bishops, dearly beloved of God, who are now dispersed, paying the penalty for their devotion to religion.

196. To Aburgius[1]

Rumor, the messenger of good news, does not cease announcing to us that you have been darting about like the stars, appearing sometimes in one part of the barbarian land, again in another, now furnishing provision money for the soldiers, and now in brilliant apparel seen with the emperor.

---

1 This is the same Euphronius who was later made Metropolitan of Nicopolis. Cf. Letters 227, 228, 229, and 230. This letter was written in 375.

---

1 Other letters addressed to Aburgius, an old friend and countryman of St. Basil, are Letters 33, 75, 178, and 304. This present letter, assigned to the year 375, is also found among the Letters of St. Gregory of Nazianzus, numbered 241, with the title *Abougriōi.*

And we pray to God that your undertaking may proceed according to its merits, that you may go forward to greatness, and may be seen in your native land at some time or other while we are upon earth and inhale this air. For, only so far do we have a share in life, in that we breathe.

197. To Ambrose, Bishop of Milan[1]

Always magnificent and abundant are the gifts of our Lord, and neither can their magnitude be measured nor their quantity numbered. But, one of the greatest gifts to those keenly aware of receiving His favors is this present one—that He has granted us, though far separated by the position of our countries, to be united with each other through the declarations in our letters. And He has favored us with a twofold means of becoming acquainted: one, by personal conference, and the other, through intercourse by letter. Seeing, therefore, that we know you through what you have said, and we know you, not by having imprinted on our memories your bodily characteristics, but by having learned in the variety of your utterances the beauty of the inner man, because out of the abundance of the heart each of us speaks,[2] we have glorified our God who has chosen in each generation those who are well pleasing to Him. He formerly raised up from His sheepfold a ruler for His people,[3] and having through the Spirit strengthened Amos[4] He elevated him from the goat pasture to the rank of Prophet; and now, a man from the imperial city, a trusted ruler of a whole

1 This letter, written to St. Ambrose in 375, a year after his accession to the episcopal throne, is the answer to a request for the relics of St. Dionysius of Milan who had died in Cappadocia.

2 Cf. Matt. 12.34.

3 Cf. Ps. 77.70.

4 Cf. Amos 1.1.

nation, lofty in intellect, in the illustriousness of his birth, in the renown of his life, in the power of his words, conspicuous among all throughout the world, He has drawn forth for the care of the flocks of Christ. This man, having thrown away worldly advantages and having counted them as loss in order that he might gain Christ,[5] was permitted to receive the helm of a ship great and famous because of its faith in God, the Church of Christ. Come, therefore, man of God, since you did not receive nor learn from men the Gospel of Christ, but the Lord Himself transferred you from the judges of earth to the chair of the Apostles, fight the good fight, and correct the infirmities of the people, if by chance the malady of Arian madness has seized upon anyone. Renew the ancient footprints of the Fathers, and by the frequency of your salutations be zealous to build upon the foundation of love toward us, which you have laid down. In this way we shall always be able to be near each other in spirit, even if in our earthly dwelling we are very far apart.

Your loving esteem and zeal for the most blessed Bishop Dionysius[6] give evidence of your perfect love for the Lord, your respect for your predecessors, and your earnestness concerning the faith. For, our disposition toward the well-disposed of our fellow servants is referable to the Lord, whom they have served, and he who honors those who have gone through struggles for the faith is clearly possessed of an equal zeal for the faith, so that one act in itself bears testimony of much virtue. Moreover, we are informing your Charity in Christ that the most zealous brothers, those selected

5 Cf. Phil. 3.8.

6 The successor of Protasius to the bishopric of Milan in 346. Mention is made of him in connection with the Council of Milan in 335. Although through the influence of Emperor Constantius he affixed his name to a document partially condemnatory of St. Athanasius, his name is said to have been erased by Eusebius of Vercelli. He died in Cappadocia in 374 where he had been banished by the emperor.

by your Reverence for the ministry of the good work,[7] have, first of all, brought praise upon the whole clergy through the graciousness of their manners; in fact, by their own decorum they have made known the steadfastness of all. In the next place, exercising all zeal and care, they had courage to face a formidable winter, and with all their energy persuaded the faithful guards of the blessed body to yield to them this safeguard of their own lives. And, realize this, that neither the rulers nor the influential men would ever have been able to force those men, if the strength of purpose of these brethren had not shamed them into compliance. Especially was assistance to accomplish the task given through the presence of our most beloved and most pious son, Therasius,[8] the fellow presbyter, who undertook the exertion of the journey of his own choice, checked the violent attack of the faithful there, and, having won his opponents by his persuasive speech in the presence of the presbyters, deacons, and many others who fear the Lord, took up the relics with becoming reverence and assisted the brethren in preserving them. Receive these relics with as much joy as was the grief of the guards who sent them forward. Let no one hesitate,[9] let no one doubt: this is that unconquerable athlete. The Lord knows these bones which struggled to the end with the blessed soul. He will crown these bones with this soul on the just day of His retribution according to what is written, 'for, we must stand before the tribunal of Christ so that each one may receive according to his works in the body.'[10] There was one coffin which had received that honored body; no one else was laid near him; his burial was

7 The action taken regarding Dionysius.
8 Therasius is not otherwise known.
9 The abuse of relics was at this time causing much concern. It is for this reason that St. Basil is so insistent on the authenticity of the relics.
10 Cf. 2 Cor. 5.10.

a notable one; his honor that of a martyr. Christians who had entertained him as a guest buried him with their own hands then, and now took him up. They cried as if bereaved of a father and a leader; but they sent him on, preferring your joy to their own consolation. Those, therefore, who handed him over are pious; those who received him are scrupulously careful. Nowhere is there falsehood, nowhere deceit—we ourselves bear witness; let the truth be free from misrepresentation in your presence.

198. To Eusebius, Bishop of Samosata[1]

After the letter which was brought to us by the officials we received one other, which had been sent to us later. And we ourselves wrote letters—not many, in truth, because of not meeting with any setting out in your direction, but at least, more than four—with which we sent under seal to the most revered brother Leontius,[2] the Peraequator[3] of Nicaea, those brought to us from Samosata after your Reverence's first letter, urging that through him they be carried to the steward of the house of our most revered brother Sophronius that he might have charge of conveying them to you. Now, since the letters are passing through many hands, it is probable that want of leisure or indifference on the part of some one man is the cause of your Reverence's

1 For Eusebius of Samosata cf. previous letters addressed to him: Letters 27, 30, 31, 34, 47, 48, 95, 100, 127, 128, 136, etc. This letter was written in the spring of 375, during the exile of Eusebius. Cf. Loofs, *op. cit.* 22, 46 n. 5.

2 Otherwise unknown as is the case with Sophronius.

3 Officials who made local and extraordinary revisions in the census after Diocletian. They were chosen either from the old magistrates or from the chief municipalities.

not receiving them. Therefore, pardon, we urge you, the dearth of letters.

But, as to the fact that, when we should have sent someone from ourselves, we did not do it, you in your wisdom have rightly inquired and have reproached us. But, realize that the winter here has been so severe that all the roads were closed until the Easter days, and we had no one who possessed the courage to face the difficulties of the journey. For, even if our clergy seem somehow to be numerous, the men are unprepared for journeys, because they never travel nor do they choose outside employment, but the majority engage in sedentary crafts from which they have the means of their daily livelihood. Immediately, then, summoning from the country this brother whom we have now sent to your Reverence, we used him as a carrier of the letter to your Holiness, in order that he might give accurate information of our affairs and by the grace of God clearly and speedily report to us again the conditions there. And we held back, waiting for mild weather, the most beloved brother Eusebius,[4] the reader, who has long been eager to press on to your Reverence. Yet, even now I am in no slight anxiety lest the unaccustomed journey may produce an injurious effect upon him, causing illness to his body, which is inclined to weakness.

It is really unneedful for us to mention in our letter the innovations in the East, since the brothers are able of themselves to give accurate information. But realize, my most honorable friend, that, while I have been writing these things, I have felt so bad that all hopes of living have now failed me. For, it is not possible for the great number of the symptoms attacking me, the weakness, the intensity of the fevers, and the nature of my sufferings, to be recounted; but from all, one fact is drawn, that we have now fulfilled the time of our sojourn in this wretched and painful life.

4 Otherwise unknown.

199. To Amphilochius, concerning the Canons[1]

Some time ago, when I answered the questions proposed to us by your Reverence, I did not send what I had written, being hindered partly by a long and dangerous illness and partly by the lack of messengers. Few of our men are both experienced in journeying and prepared for such kind of services. And so, having learned the causes of our delay, pardon us.

We were in admiration of your love of learning along with your humility, because you who have been entrusted with the position of teaching do not refuse to learn, and to learn from us who possess no great knowledge at all. Nevertheless, since you consent through fear of God to do a task not easily done by another, it is necessary for us also to co-operate, even beyond our power, in your desire and in your noble effort.

(17) You asked us about Bianor, the presbyter, if he is acceptable for the ministry because of his oath. Now, I know that I have already set a certain general condition[2] for the clergy in Antioch concerning all those who took the oath at the same time with him, that they keep away from the public assemblies and carry on in private the works of presbyters. And this same condition grants him freedom for his ministry, because his priestly service is not in Antioch but in Iconium, which, as you yourself wrote to us, he took in exchange for Antioch as his dwelling place. Therefore, that man is acceptable after he has been required by your Reverence to do penance for the ease and the lightness of taking that oath which he swore in the presence of an

1 Cf. Letter 188 n. 1. This letter was written in 375.
2 This letter is not extant.

unbeliever[3] because he was not able to endure the annoyance of that little danger.

(18) Concerning the fallen virgins who had vowed to the Lord a life of chastity, then, having submitted to the passions of the flesh, denied their vows, our Fathers,[4] accommodating themselves simply and gently to the weakness of those who slip, ordained that they be received after a year, classifying them in the same way as those married a second time. But, it seems to me that, since the Church, advancing by the grace of God, is becoming stronger and the order of virgins is now increased, we should turn our attention carefully to the affair as it appears on reflection, and also to the spirit of the Scripture, which can be discovered from the following. Widowhood is inferior to virginity; therefore, the sin of widows also is definitely secondary to that of virgins. Moreover, let us see what Paul has written to Timothy: 'But refuse younger widows, for when they have wantonly turned away from Christ, they wish to marry, and are to be condemned because they have broken their first troth.'[5] If, then, a widow lies under a very grave judgment as having set at naught her faith in Christ, what must we think of the virgin, who is the bride of Christ and a hallowed vessel dedicated to the Lord? It is, in truth, a great sin for a slave, bestowing herself in secret marriage, to fill the house with corruption and through her evil life to treat the master insolently. But, surely, it is much more grievous for the bride to become an adulteress and, having esteemed lightly her union with her bridegroom, to give herself up to un-

3 According to the Benedictine editors the 'unbeliever' was one of the influential Arians of Antioch who during the absence of Meletius had imposed some unorthodox oath on the clergy.

4 Canon 19 of Ancyra decreed that 'all who have taken a vow of virginity, and have broken that vow, must submit to the decrees and prescriptions concerning bigamists.' Cf. Hefele I.218.

5 1 Tim. 5.11,12.

bridled pleasures. Therefore, the widow is condemned as a corrupted slave, but the virgin lies under the sentence of adultery.[6] Now, as we call him who has intercourse with another's wife an adulterer, not receiving him to communion before he has desisted from his sin, it is evident that we should be disposed in the same way in the case of him who holds the virgin. But, now it is necessary for us to agree on this beforehand, that she is called a virgin who has willingly attached herself to the Lord and renounced marriage, preferring a life of holiness. And we accept the professions from the age which possesses fullness of reason. It is not proper to consider the words of a child valid in such cases, but she who is beyond sixteen or seventeen years, being mistress of her own reasoning powers, after having been further examined, and having remained firm and persevered with prayers to be received, should finally be listed among the virgins and should attain to the profession of such; the violation of this profession should be inexorably punished. Parents and brothers and some relatives bring forward many before the proper age, not because the virgins are eager of their own accord for celibacy, but to provide some sort of material advantage for themselves.[7] We must not easily receive these until we have thoroughly examined their personal inclination.

(19) We do not recognize the professions of men, except of those who have enrolled themselves in the order of monks. These seem silently to have taken celibacy upon themselves. But, even in their case, I think that it is proper that

---

6 In Canon 58 St. Basil prescribes a fifteen years' punishment for adultery.

7 Balsamon cites the example of those who because of their poverty find it difficult to provide for their daughters. Zonaras gives the example of relatives who would not then be obliged to supply them with a dowry. Cf. *PG* 138.651.

this course of action should precede: that they be questioned and that a clear profession be received from them,[8] so that, when they change to a carnal and voluptuous life, they may be subjected to the punishment of fornicators.

(20) Those women who professed virginity when they were in heresy, then afterwards preferred marriage, I do not think ought to be condemned.[9] For, 'whatever the Law says, it is speaking to those who are under the Law.'[10] And those who have not yet come under the yoke of Christ do not observe the laws of the Master. So that they are acceptable to the Church, and have the forgiveness of these sins with all others because of their faith in Christ. And, on the whole, the things done during their life as a catechumen are not called into account. But, of course, those without baptism the Church does not receive. Therefore, the rights of birth[11] are a most necessary measure among them.

(21) Whenever a man living with a wife becomes dissatisfied with his marriage, and falls into fornication,[12]

---

8 St. Basil advocates an explicit profession of the vow of chastity instead of a tacit one which he claims that the monks usually make. Women living in the world often took a vow of chastity, as well as nuns living in their monasteries, but St. Basil says that to his knowledge there is no such custom among the men and only a tacit vow of celibacy among monks. He recommends an explicit vow of celibacy for the monks in the future.

9 According to the Greek commentators, St. Basil is here speaking of women who, while heretics, transgressed a vow of virginity by entering the state of marriage. Upon entering the Church they were not called to account for the violation of their vow which had occurred while they were living in heresy, for they were not yet subject to the law of the Church. Moreover, their sin had been forgiven by baptism just as the sins of those in the catechumenical state. Cf. *PG* 138.654-657.

10 Rom. 3.19

11 Probably the rights of spiritual birth of the soul, i.e., of baptism.

12 A married man who cohabited with an unmarried woman was subjected to the punishment for fornicators, that is, seven years, and

we call such a one a fornicator, and we keep him longer under penalty. However, we do not have a canon by which to bring him under a charge of adultery if the sin is committed against an unmarried woman, because, it is said, the adulteress 'shall be polluted and defiled,'[13] and she shall not return to her husband, and 'He that keepeth an adulteress is foolish and wicked.'[14] However, he who has committed fornication is not excluded from cohabitation with his wife. Therefore, the wife will receive her husband when he returns from fornication,[15] but the husband will send away from his home a defiled wife. And the reasoning for this is not easy, but custom has so ruled.

(22) Those who have abducted women, if they have seized for themselves some betrothed to others, must not be received before separating themselves from the women and putting them under the jurisdiction of those to whom they had first been promised, whether the latter wish to take them back or to give up all claim to them.[16] But, if one has carried off

---

not to that for adultery, which was fifteen years. This is in accord with the Mosaic and Roman Law, but not with the Christian law, which declares any carnal intercourse in which either of the parties is married, adultery.

13 Cf. Jer. 3.1; also Canon 9 and note.

14 Prov. 18.22; also Canon 9 and note.

15 Canon 9 and note.

16 The eleventh canon of Ancyra had decreed that 'Damsels who are betrothed, who are afterwards carried off by others, shall be given back to those to whom they are betrothed even when they have been treated with violence.' Hefele 1.211 comments on this canon as follows: 'This canon treats only of betrothed women (by the *sponsalia de futuro*), not of those who are married (by the *sponsalia de presente*). In the case of the latter there would be no doubt as to the duty of restitution. The man who was betrothed was, moreover, at liberty to receive his affianced bride who had been carried off, or not. It was thus that St. Basil had already decided in Canon 22 of his canonical letter to Amphilochius.' There is an error here in placing St. Basil's decree before that of the Synod of Ancyra. The latter was held in 314, while the present letter was written in 375.

a girl who is free, she must be taken away and restored to her relatives, and the matter left to their decision, whether they be parents, or brothers, or any guardians whatsoever of the girl;[17] if they wish to hand her over to him, the marriage must stand,[18] but, if they refuse, force must not be used. Nevertheless, he who possesses a wife through either secret or somewhat violent seduction must accept the penalty for fornication. The punishment prescribed for fornication lasts four years. During the first year they must be banished from prayers, and must weep at the door of the church; in the second year they must be admitted to the state of 'hearer'; in the third, to penance; in the fourth, to 'standing' with the people, abstaining from Holy Communion; finally, they must be permitted the communion of the good Gift.[19]

(23) Concerning men who marry two sisters, or women who are married to two brothers, we have published a short letter,[20] of which we sent a copy to your Reverence. He who has taken his own brother's wife will not be received until he has separated from her.[21]

(24) A widow who has been enrolled among the widows, that is, is supported by the Church, the Apostle judged should

17 Therefore, without the consent of the parents or guardians the girl could not be received. Cf. Canons 38, 40, 42.

18 Cf. Canon 25, where St. Basil advises that those guilty of fornication be separated. If they so wished, however, they might be permitted to enter matrimony.

19 Holy Communion.

20 Cf. Letter 160, in which St. Basil condemns the marriage of a man to the sister of his deceased wife, as being contrary to custom.

21 The second canon of the Synod of Neo-Caesarea decreed: 'If a woman married two brothers, she shall be excommunicated till her death; if she is in danger of death and promises in case of recovery to break off this illegitimate union, she may, as an act of mercy, be admitted to penance. If the woman or husband die in this union, the penance for the survivor will be very strict.' Cf. Hefele 7.225.

be disregarded[22] if she marries. However, no law is imposed on a widower, but the penalty for second marriage is sufficient for such a one. Nevertheless, if the widow sixty years old prefers to live again with a husband, she will not be deemed worthy of the communion of the good Gift until she checks the passion of impurity. If, however, we enrolled her before the age of sixty,[23] the responsibility is ours, not the woman's.

(25) He who retains for his wife the woman seduced by him will submit to the penalty for seduction but will be permitted to keep his wife.[24]

(26) Fornication is not marriage; it is not even the beginning of marriage. Therefore, if it is possible for those joined together through fornication to be separated, that is best. But, if they are in every way satisfied with their union, let them acknowledge the penalty for fornication.[25] But let them be permitted to remain together in order that something worse may not happen.

(27) Concerning the presbyter who through ignorance

---

22 No longer be supported out of Church funds. Cf. Acts 6.1. According to 1 Tim. 5.9, those who were sixty years or over and had been married only once were permitted to perform certain temporal ministrations in the Church. These are probably the ones that St. Basil refers to as those who are enrolled among widows. Here he implies that such widows were forbidden to marry. Not all widows, however, were so forbidden. St. Paul (1 Cor. 7.39) permitted them to marry, 'but if her husband dies she is free. Let her marry whom she pleases, only let it be in the Lord.'

23 Cf. 1 Tim. 5.9.

24 As in the case of fornication, rape did not prevent the man from marrying the girl if she and her parents consented. This marriage, however, did not free him from the necessity of performing the penance for rape. Cf. Canon 22.

25 Cf. Canon 22.

became involved in an unlawful marriage,[26] I have defined what is necessary: he should retain his seat but refrain from the rest of his duties.[27] In the case of such a man pardon is sufficient. But, it is inconsistent for one who should take care of his own wounds to bless another. And how will he who does not have this blessing because of his transgression through ignorance communicate it to another? Accordingly, let him not bless either publicly or privately; let him not distribute the Body of Christ to others, nor perform any other religious service, but being content with his seat of honor, let him beg the Lord with tears that the transgression committed through ignorance be forgiven him.

(28) This, assuredly, appeared to me to be ridiculous—to vow to abstain from pork. Therefore, deign to teach them to refrain from foolish prayers and promises; nevertheless, allow the use to be a matter of indifference.[28] No creature of God which is received with thanksgiving is to be rejected.[29] Therefore, the vow is ridiculous; the abstinence is not necessary.

(29) It is entirely proper to correct the action of rulers swearing to wrong their subjects.[30] The remedy is twofold:

---

26 The Greek commentators give various examples of a possible unlawful marriage in which a priest might be unknowingly implicated. Balsamon offers three: marriage with a girl of whom he or his father was the tutor, with a nun, or with a blood relation. Zonaras mentions only the last two, while Aristenus names as forbidden partners in matrimony, a widow, an idiot, an actress, or one consecrated to God. Cf. *PG* 138.677-682.

27 He could retain his seat of honor among the priests, but could perform no priestly offices in pubilc or in private.

28 A vow should be made only in regard to a better possible good; hence, a vow made in regard to things in themselves indifferent has no binding force.

29 Cf. 1 Tim. 4.4.

30 A vow made to do evil, besides having no binding force, must also be broken.

to teach them, first, not to swear rashly, and, secondly, not to persist in their wicked decisions. Therefore, if someone has been apprehended taking an oath for the injury of another, let him give evidence of repentance for the rashness of the oath, but let him not, of a truth, confirm his wickedness under a pretext of piety.[31] It did not profit Herod to keep his oath, who, in order that he might not forswear, as he pretended, became the murderer of the Prophet.[32] The oath, then, is once and for all forbidden,[33] and it is more reasonable, surely, for the oath made for an evil purpose to be condemned. Therefore, he who has sworn must change his mind and not be eager to treat as valid his unholy act. Now, examine the absurdity more in detail. If someone would swear to dig out the eyes of his brother, would it be something good to bring such an oath to accomplishment? And, if someone would swear to commit a murder? If, in short, someone would swear under oath to transgress any commandment? 'I have sworn and am determined' not to commit the sin, but 'to keep the judgments of thy justice.'[34] As it is proper that the commandment be confirmed with unalterable judgments, so it is consistent that sin be canceled and wiped out in every way.

(30) Concerning seducers we do not have an ancient canon, but we have made our own decision[35]—that they and those co-operating with them be excluded from prayers for

31 I.e., let him not, under the pretence of performing a sacred duty in fulfilling his vow, carry out the evil which he swore to do.
32 Cf. Matt. 14.9,10.
33 Cf. Matt. 5.34.
34 Cf. Ps. 118.106.
35 Canon 11 of Ancyra, quoted in n. 16, did not prescribe any punishment for the abductor.

three years.[36] If violence is not used, the act is not liable to punishment when neither rape nor theft precede it. The widow is responsible for herself, and the power to follow lies with her.[37] Therefore, we must not take heed of her pretences.[38]

(31) She who, after her husband departed and disappeared, lived with another man before she was convinced of her husband's death is an adulteress.[39]

(32) Those clerics who have committed the sin unto death[40] are deposed from their rank but are not debarred

36 The Benedictine editors distinguish between two classes of prayers: 'the prayers of the prostrates' and 'the prayers of the faithful.' They consider this reference to have been made to the 'prayers of the faithful.' Since Aristenus (*PG* 138.691) says that the punishment for abduction is the same as for fornication, the Benedictines, following Canon 22, place the abductor in the first year among the 'mourners,' in the second among the 'hearers,' in the third among the 'prostrates,' and finally in the fourth admit him to the 'prayers of the faithful' among the 'standers.' This explanation seems plausible.

37 Cf. 1 Cor. 7.39.

38 Balsamon (*PG* 138.687-690) interprets *tôn schēmátōn* in the sense of 'pretences,' and explains the case in question as follows: If a widow who wishes to be married but is ashamed to enter a second marriage should pretend that she has been abducted, whereas she willingly went off with the man, no heed should be given to her pretences. He did not employ force and so there is no question of abduction. Zonaras (*PG* 138.690-691) interprets *tôn schēmátōn* as 'the apparel,' and understands the case to refer to a widow who has already assumed the customary dress of the widows of the Church, but who has not yet dedicated herself by vow to continence. Hence, she is still free to marry, and no heed is to be given to the apparel.

39 This canon was published together with Canons 36 and 46 as one canon (93) in the Council in Trullo. Cf. *PG* 137.830-831.

40 Cf. 1 John 5.16,17. Different interpretations are given for the 'sin unto death.' Balsamon thinks that it is one of the more grievous mortal sins, which is punished by death, such as murder. According to this interpretation, the present canon is a complement to Canon 4 of the first letter, where it is laid down that a deacon who committed fornication should be deposed but not excommunicated. Fornication, since it was not punishable by death, would not be a sin unto death, in this sense. St. Basil, asked here if a cleric who committed a sin even graver than fornication, one, for example, punishable by death,

from the communion of the laity. 'For you shall not exact punishment twice for the same thing.'[41]

(33) Let the woman who gave birth on the road and neglected the child[42] lie under the charge of murder.[43]

(34) Women who have committed adultery and through piety confessed,[44] or who have been convicted in any way whatsoever, our Fathers did not command to be publicly exposed, in order that we might not furnish an occasion of conviction and death for them,[45] but they ordered them to refrain from communion until the completion of the time of penance.[46]

(35) In the case of the man abandoned by his wife it is necessary to consider the cause of the desertion;[47] if she seem to have departed without reason, he is deserving of

---

like murder, is to be deposed only and not also excommunicated, answers in the affirmative. Cf. *PG* 138.694-695. Zonaras understands the 'sin unto death' to be a sin consummated in deed, as opposed to a sin not unto death or one that exists in the mind only and has not been executed in act. Cf. *PG* 138.695. Artistenus interprets the 'sin unto death' as a carnal sin. Cf. *PG* 138.695. The Benedictine editors think that St. Basil here refers to the more grievous mortal sins.

41 Cf. Nahum 1.9.

42 When she could have cared for it. If the mother was not physically able to care for it, and the child died of neglect, the mother was pardoned. Cf. Canon 52.

43 According to Balsamon and Zonaras, the woman was to be punished thus even when the infant did not die but was found and taken care of by someone else. Cf. Canon 2.

44 I.e., privately. This canon furnishes evidence for the practice of private confession of sin to the priest. Cf. O. D. Watkins, *A History of Penance* 1.323.

45 Lest her husband, if he saw her performing all the grades of penance, become suspicious of her sin and kill her. Cf. *PG* 138.698-702. Another explanation is lest the civil law punish her with death, the penalty for adultery. Cf. Migne, 'Penitence,' Sec. 2, Chap. 2, Adoncissements a la confession publique—*Theologiae Cursus Completus* 20.377, 378.

46 The time of penance for adultery was fifteen years. Cf. Canon 58.

47 Cf. Canon 9, in which St. Basil mentions some reasons that do not justify a woman in separating from her husband.

pardon,[48] but she of punishment. And permission will be given to him to be in communion with the Church.

(36) Wives of soldiers who married when their husbands disappeared are subject to the same rule as those also who during their husbands' sojourn abroad would not await his return,[49] except that here the matter has some excuse because the supposition of death is greater.

(37) He who has married after the wife of another has been taken from him will be charged with adultery[50] in the case of the first woman, but in the case of the second will be guiltless.[51]

(38) Girls who follow a man contrary to the wish of their father[52] commit fornication, but, if their parents are reconciled, the matter seems to admit of a remedy. They are not restored to communion immediately, however, but will be punished for three years.[53]

(39) She who lives with an adulterer is an adulteress the whole time.[54]

(40) She who has given herself over to a man against

---

48 He is not to be separated from the Church, but he may not cohabit with another woman. Cf. Zonaras, *PG* 138.702. According to Aristenus (*ibid.*) the sense is that, even if he does live with another woman, he is to be pardoned, that is, he is not to be subjected to the punishment for adultery.

49 Cf. Canon 31 and note.

50 I.e., the punishment of fifteen years. Cf. Canon 58.

51 The adulterer who has dismissed the wife of another will not be impeded from entering matrimony with a woman who is free to marry. Cf. Balsamon, Zonaras, Aristenus, *PG* 138.703-706.

52 Canon 22 n. 2; also, Canons 40 and 42.

53 This canon applies, not to girls who have been raped, but to those who have married without the knowledge of their father. The Benedictine editors and Aristenus agree that this period of three years refers to their time as 'prostrates,' but that an additional year was required of them among the 'standers.'

54 She cannot, therefore, be received to penance until she separates from the adulterer. Cf. Zonaras and Aristenus, *PG* 138.710.

the will of her master has committed fornication,[55] but, if after this she has engaged in a freely authorized marriage, she is married. So the former was fornication; the latter, marriage. For, the contracts of those who are subject to another have no force.

(41) She who in her widowhood has authority over herself[56] can without blame live with a husband if there is no one to disrupt the marriage, since the Apostle says: 'But if her husband dies, she is free. Let her marry whom she pleases, only let it be in the Lord.'[57]

(42) Marriage contracted without the consent of those in authority are fornications.[58] If neither the father is alive, nor the master, those living together are without blame. It then takes on the force of marriage, just as if the persons in authority consent to the cohabitation.

(43) Whoever gave the blow that caused death to his neighbor is a murderer,[59] whether he gave the first blow or was retaliating.

(44) The deaconess[60] who committed fornication with

55 Cf. notes on Canon 22; also, Canons 38 and 42.

56 I.e., from the jurisdiction of parents, superiors, or guardians. Cf. Canon 42.

57 1 Cor. 7.39; cf. also, Canons 24 and 30.

58 According to this canon, the consent of parents, masters, or guardians is necessary for the validity of the marriage of those subject to them. Canons 22, 38, 40, and 41 contain applications of this general principle.

59 Either voluntary or involuntary, depending on his intention and the instrument used. Cf. Aristenus, *PG* 138.718. The punishment for the former was a penance of twenty years (cf. Canon 56), for the latter ten years (cf. Canon 57). Cf. also, Canon 8 for the different kinds of voluntary and involuntary murder.

60 There is little definite information on the institution of deaconesses in the early Church. It has been identified by some with the order of widows. There is, however, sufficient evidence to believe that the two orders were distinct. The deaconesses received a sort of formal consecration from the hands of the bishops, performed for women the temporal acts of charity which the deacons performed for men, and assisted at the baptismal ceremony of women. These functions

the Greek is acceptable for penance and she will be admitted to Holy Communion in the seventh year, provided, of course, that she is living in chastity. But the Greek who, after accepting the faith, again enters upon sacrilege returns to his vomit. But, we no longer permit the body of the deaconess, having been consecrated, to be given over to carnal uses.

(45) If anyone who has taken the name of Christian[61] mocks Christ,[62] he has no profit from the title.

(46) She who unwittingly has married a man deserted at the time by his wife, then has been dismissed because his former wife returned to him, committed fornication, but in ignorance. Therefore, she will not be debarred from marriage. But, it is better if she remains unmarried.[63]

(47) Encratites[64] and Saccophori[65] and Apotactitae[66]

---

are assigned to the deaconesses by the *Didascalia Apostolorum*. In the Apostolic Constitutions they are given the duty of maintaining order among the women in church, and of acting as intermediaries between the clergy and the women of the congregation. Although deaconesses were forbidden to give any blessing or to fulfill any function of priest or deacon, abuses existed, especially in Syria and Asia.

61 By receiving baptism and accepting the orthodox faith.

62 By rejecting ecclesiastical traditions and the canonical definitions or by refusing to live according to the precepts of the Christian religion. Cf. Balsamon, *PG* 138.722.

63 This canon, together with Canons 31 and 36, appears as Canon 93 of the Synod in Trullo.

64 Cf. note on Canon 1.

65 These were Manichaean solitaries. They were denounced under pain of capital punishment in a law of Theodosius of the year 382.

66 Apotactitae, or Apostolici, were an ascetic sect in Phrygia, Cilicia, and Pamphilia of the third and fourth centuries, who rejected private property and condemned marriage. They sought authority for their views in the Apocryphal Acts of Andrew and of Thomas. There was probably no real historical connection between this sect and the Marcionists, as St. Basil asserts.

are not[67] subject to the same reckoning as the Novatians,[68] because concerning the latter a canon[69] has been promulgated, even though it is different, but matters pertaining to the former have been passed over in silence. Nevertheless, for one and the same reason we rebaptize such. But, if rebaptism is forbidden among you, just as it also is among the Romans because of some regulation, let our principle have force. Since the heresy among them is, as it were, an offshoot of the Marcionists,[70] who abominate marriage and turn away from wine and say that the creature of God is defiled, we do not receive them into the Church unless they have been baptized into our baptism. Let them not say: 'We are baptized in the Father and the Son and the Holy Spirit,' who, in truth, represent God as the author of evils, equally with Marcion and the other sects. Therefore, if this is satisfactory, more bishops should convene and explain the canon in such a way that he who acts may be free from danger and he who answers may be worthy of trust in his response concerning such things.

(48) She who has been abandoned by her husband ought, in my opinion, to remain.[71] If the Lord said, 'If anyone puts away his wife, save on account of immorality, he causes her to commit adultery,'[72] because she is named an adulteress, he debars her from union with another. For,

---

67 With the Benedictine editors I have inserted 'not' in the text, since it seems necessary for the context.

68 Cf. the note on Canon 1.

69 Canon 8 of Nice and Canon 7 of Laodicea, in which the baptism of Novatians was recognized as valid.

70 Cf. the note on Canon 1.

71 I.e., she ought not to marry again during the lifetime of her first husband. Cf. *PG* 138.730-734.

72 Matt. 5.22.

how can the man be responsible, as the cause of adultery, but the woman be blameless who was called an adulteress by the Lord because of her intercourse with another man?

(49) Let seductions suffered through violence be free from censure. Therefore, the slave, if she was forced by her own master, is guiltless.

(50) There is no law concerning a third marriage.[73] Therefore, a third marriage is not contracted by law. And in fact, we look at such things as pollutions of the Church.[74] But, we do not subject them to public penalties,[75] on the ground that they are preferable to unrestrained fornication.

200. To Amphilochius, Bishop of Iconium[1]

Maladies following one after another attack us, and duties arising from ecclesiastical affairs and from persons who act insolently toward the churches have kept us busy the whole winter, even to the time of this letter. Therefore, it has not been possible for us either to send someone or to visit your Reverence. But, we surmise that your situation is just another such as ours. I do not mean in respect to the illness—

73 I.e., no ecclesiastical law, although third marriages were recognized by civil law. Cf. Balsamon, Zonaras, Aristenus, *PG* 138.735.

74 Cf. Canon 4, in which St. Basil refers to third marriages as a moderated fornication. From Balsamon it appears that, although the Church did not sanction third marriages, once the parties had lived together by mutual consent, she did not order them to separate. St. Basil says in Canon 4 that custom authorized the imposition of a five-year separation for trigamists.

75 I.e., to 'mourning' outside the doors of the church. They were immediately received to the place of 'hearers.' Cf. Aristenus, *PG* 138.735; also, Canon 4.

1 For Amphilochius, cf. note 1 of the preceding letter. This was written in the spring of 375. Cf. Loofs, *op. cit.* 22,46 n. 5.

may that not be; may the Lord, in truth, grant health to your body sufficient for the execution of His commands—but that the anxiety concerning the churches inflicts the same distraction on you, also. And at present I was intending to send someone for this very purpose, so that he might inform us concerning the state of your affairs. But, when our most beloved son Meletius,[2] who is escorting the newly recruited troops, reminded us that it was possible to salute you through him, we gladly welcomed the opportunity of writing and we hastened to the messenger of our letter, a man capable even of taking the place of a letter, not only because of his truth-loving character, but also because of his knowledge of our affairs. Through him we urge your Reverence, first of all, to pray for us in order that the Lord may grant to me release from this wearisome body and to His churches peace, and to you rest and, when you have disposed of the matters in Lycaonia in an apostolic manner as you have begun, also the freedom to visit the place here, whether we are living on in the flesh or have been enjoined to depart to the Lord. We urge this, in order that you may care for our regions as your own, which certainly they are, may steady what is unsound, rouse what is sluggish, and by the grace of the Spirit which is in you may rearrange all things according to what is pleasing to the Lord.

As regards our most honorable sons, Menetius and Melitius,[3] whom you have known for a long time and look upon as your own, keep them as a sacred trust and pray for them. This is sufficient for their complete safety. And be so kind as to extend a greeting from us to those with your Holiness, to all the clergy, and to the laity tended by you,

2 A young recruiting officer and a friend of St. Basil. He is not mentioned elsewhere.

3 Nothing more is known of him than is mentioned here.

and to our brethren and fellow ministers dearly beloved of God. Bear in mind the commemoration of the most blessed martyr Eupsychius,[4] and do not wait for a second reminder; furthermore, do not strive to present yourself upon the appointed day, but anticipate it and gladden us if, perchance, we shall still be upon earth. Meanwhile, then, be strong in the Lord, pray for us, and preserve yourself for us and for the churches of God by the grace of the Holy One.

201. To Amphilochius, Bishop of Iconium[1]

For many reasons I am eager to meet you, both so that I may make use of your counsel concerning the affairs in hand, and, as it is so long since I have seen you, that I may have some palliation for your absence. But, since the same forces hinder both of us—your present illness and our more prolonged ailment which has never left us—let us both, if you are willing, make allowances for each other, so as to free each other in turn from blame.

202. To Amphilochius, Bishop of Iconium[1]

A meeting with your Dignity means much to me in any event, but especially now when the matter which is bringing us together is of such great importance. Yet, the aftereffects

4 For Eupsychius, cf. Letter 100 and note.

1 For Amphilochius, see previous letters addressed to him. This letter was written in the spring of 375. Cf. Loofs, *op. cit.* 47 n.

1 On Amphilochius see previous letters addressed to him. This letter was written in the early summer of 375. Cf. Loofs, *op. cit.* 22, 47 n.

of my illness are such as not to permit me the slightest movement. For, just in attempting to be conveyed by carriage as far as the martyrs,[2] I almost succumbed again to the same disease. I shall need to have your pardon. If it will be possible to postpone the affair until a few days later, by the grace of God I will both be with you and will share your anxieties. If the matter is urgent, then with the help of God attend to the business at hand, but count me with you as though I were present and taking part in the well-performed tasks. May you be in good health and cheerful in the Lord, and continue to pray for me. And may you be preserved by the grace of the Holy One for the Church of God.

203. To the Bishops of the Seacoast[1]

Although I have been very eager for a conference with you, there has always been some obstacle that thwarted my desire. Either the infirmity of my body hindered me (you are not at all ignorant of how serious this has been from my earliest days until my present old age, growing up with me, as it has, and chastising me according to the just judgment of God, who manages all things in His wisdom), or the

2 I.e., to the chapel of certain martyrs. It cannot be ascertained who these martyrs were.

1 A part of the seacoast of the Pontus had been separated from the Church of Caesarea by the efforts of Eustathius. St. Basil was much grieved and by the advice of the bishops of Cappadocia wrote a protest to these bishops remonstrating with them for not coming to him. This letter was written in the late summer of 375. Cf. Loofs, *op. cit.* 21.

cares of the churches, or the conflicts with those who have risen up against the word of truth. Up to the present, therefore, I have endured in great affliction and grief, being conscious that my duty toward you has been left undone. For I have heard from God, who took upon Himself a sojourn in the flesh for this reason, that He might not only shape our lives by the example of His own actions but also through His own words announce to us the gospel of the Kingdom: 'By this will all men know that you are my disciples, if you have love for one another.'[2] I also heard, that, when He was about to complete His life in the flesh, the Lord left His peace, as His parting gift to His disciples, saying: 'Peace I leave with you, my peace I give to you.' Therefore, I cannot convince myself that I can be called a worthy servant of Jesus Christ without mutual love and without, as far as depends on me, being at peace with all men. I have waited a long time to see whether I would receive some visit from your Charity. You certainly are not unaware that we, set out in public before all like the promontories jutting out into the sea, receive the fury of the heretical waves, and that these, while they break around us, do not overflow that which is behind us. And when I say 'we,' I do not refer to human power but to the grace of God, who in the weakness of men shows forth His own power, just as the Prophet speaking in the person of the Lord says: 'Will not you, then, fear me? I have set the sand a bound for the sea.'[4] For, by this weakest and most contemptible of all things, sand, the Mighty One has bound the great and ponderous sea. Therefore, since our condition is somewhat similar, it would follow that some of the true brethren should be sent continuously from your

---

2 Cf. John 13.35.
3 John 14.27.
4 Cf. Jer. 5.22.

Charity to visit us in our afflictions, and that affectionate letters should come more frequently to us, on the one hand to strengthen our zeal, and on the other to correct us if we fail in any respect. Indeed, we do not deny that we are subject to many faults, since we are men and are living in the flesh.

But, since in former times, either because of your being unaware of what was proper you neglected your obligations toward us, or because of your having been by some predisposed to the slanders against us you did not think that we were worthy of a friendly visit, behold, now we ourselves are the first to write, and we profess that we are ready to clear ourselves in your presence of the charges brought against us, if only those who are treating us despitefully will consent to stand face to face with us before your Reverence. If we are convicted, we shall acknowledge our fault, and you yourselves after the conviction will receive pardon before the Lord, since you are withdrawing yourselves from partnership in our sins. Moreover, those convicting us will receive a reward on the ground that they have made public our hidden evil. But, if you condemn us before the hearing, we shall not, in truth, have been harmed in any way beyond being deprived of that possession which is the most precious of all to us, charity with you. And you, since you will not have us, will seem not only to suffer this same loss, but also to be fighting against the Gospel which says: 'Does our law judge a man unless it first give him a hearing, and know what he does?'[5] Further, he who is pouring out slanders against us and not bringing forward the proofs of what is said will be obviously giving himself a bad name by his wicked use of words. How else shall we call the slanderer than by applying to him the name which he has made for himself by his acts? Therefore,

5 John 7.51.

let not him who is reproaching us be a slanderer, but an accuser; or, rather, let him not even receive the name of accuser, but let him be a brother, admonishing in charity and bringing forward his evidence in order to correct. Do not you yourselves listen to slanders, but examine evidence. Let us not be left uncured, with our sins not manifested to us.

Now, do not let this reasoning hold you back, namely, that we who dwell along the seashore are outside of the misfortunes of the majority and not in want of aid from others; therefore, what need is there for us of communion with others? The Lord has separated the islands from the mainland by the sea, but He has bound the islanders and the dwellers on the mainland together by charity. Nothing separates us from each other, brethren, unless we by deliberate choice consent to a separation. We have one Lord, one faith, and the same hope. Even if you consider yourselves the head of the Church as a whole, the head is not able to say to the feet: 'I have no need of you.' Or, if you also rank yourselves in any other position among the ecclesiastical members, you are not able to say to us who are in the same body: 'We have no need of you.' The hands have need of one another, and the feet support each other, and the eyes possess distinctness of perception by their concerted action. Now, we admit our weakness and we seek union with you. We know that, even if you are not bodily present, you will furnish great assistance to us in our most trying times by the aid of your prayers. But, it is not seemly before men nor pleasing to God for you to make use of such words as not even the Gentiles, who do not know God, employed. Yet, we hear that they, even if they live in a country that is self-sufficient in all things, at any rate because of the uncertainty of the future, welcome an alliance with each other, and they seek intercourse with one another on the ground that it holds some advantage. We, however, although we are sprung from those Fathers who ordained by law that tokens of unity should be borne from one end of the world to the other through slight signs, and that all should be fellow citizens and friends to all, do we now cut ourselves off from the world, and are we not even ashamed in our isolation? Do we neither consider it a loss to endure the severance from unity, nor shudder that the dread prophecy of our Lord is applicable to us, when He said: 'Because iniquity will abound, the charity of the many will grow cold'?[6]

Do not, most honorable brethren, do not permit this, but console us for the past with peace-bearing letters and friendly greetings, as if soothing with a gentle touch the wound of our heart which you caused by your former carelessness. And, if you yourselves wish to come to us and to examine for yourselves our maladies so as to see if they are really such as you hear, or, if in the report to you our sins are made more serious by the addition of falsehoods, let this be done. We are ready to welcome your arrival with open hands and to offer ourselves for a strict examination; only let charity guide the proceedings. Or, if you wish to suggest some place in your district to which we shall go and discharge our debt of a visit, which we owe you, and present ourselves, as far as possible, for the examination, so as to heal the past and for the future to leave no place for slanders, then let this be done. On the whole, even though we bear about with us weak flesh, nevertheless, as long as we draw breath, we have the responsibility of leaving nothing undone for the edification of the churches of Christ.

Now, do not misconstrue this request of ours, nor bring us to the necessity of speaking out to others our distress. Realize, brethren, that up to the present time we have been

6 Matt. 24.12.

hiding our grief within ourselves, being ashamed to noise abroad tò those who are in communion with us at a distance your estrangement from us, lest we afflict them and cause delight to those who hate us. I alone have written these things now, but I have sent them with the consent of all the brethren in Cappadocia, who also asked me not to use any chance messenger for the letter, but a man who will be able to fill out through his own sagacity, which he has from the grace of God, those things which we have omitted in the letter through the fear that we may prolong our explanation excessively. We mean the most beloved and pious brother, Peter, our fellow presbyter. Receive him in charity and send him on to us in peace, in order that he may be a messenger of good tidings to us.

204. To the Neo-Caesareans[1]

For a long time we have maintained silence toward each other, most honorable and dearly beloved[2] brethren, like men roused to anger. Yet, who would be so exceedingly wrathful and hard to reconcile with one who has grieved him as to prolong the anger which springs from hatred almost the whole lifetime of a man? But, this it is possible to see

1 Newman (*Church of the Fathers*, p. 98) says by way of introduction to this letter: 'If Basil's Semi-Arian connexions brought suspicion upon himself in the eyes of Catholic believers, much more would they be obnoxious to persons attached, as many Neo-Caesareans were, to the Sabellian party, who were in the opposite extreme to the Semi-Arians, and their special enemies in those times. It is not wonderful, then, that he had to write to the church in question in a strain like the following.' Atarbius, Bishop of Neo-Caesarea, was probably the principal agent in the slandering of St. Basil. This letter was written in the late summer of 375. Cf. Loofs, *op. cit.* 21.

2 *Peripóthētoi*—a title of distinction used by St. Basil in speaking of the clergy.

happening in our case, although there is no just occasion for a separation, as least as far as we ourselves know, but, contrariwise, there have been present from the beginning many strong reasons for a most profound friendship and unity between us. One of these, in truth the greatest and the first, is the command of the Lord, who says explicitly: 'By this will all men know that you are my disciples, if you have love for one another.'[3] And, again, the Apostle clearly presents to us the excellence of charity, on the one hand, when he shows that love is the fulfillment of the law,[4] and on the other, when he prefers the excellence of charity to all other great advantages, in the words: 'And if I should speak with the tongues of men and of angels, but do not have charity, I have become as sounding brass or a tinkling cymbal. And if I have prophecy and know all mysteries and all knowledge, and if I have all faith so as to remove mountains, yet do not have charity, I am nothing. And if I distribute all my goods to feed the poor, and if I deliver my body to be burned, yet do not have charity, it profits me nothing.'[5] This is not said as if each of the qualities enumerated could at any time be possessed apart from charity, but on the ground that the Holy One by His extravagant manner of expression wishes, as He Himself said, to confirm in His precept its superiority over all things.[6]

And a second point is that, if the sharing of the same teachers makes a great contribution to union, you and we not only have the same teachers of the mysteries of God, but also the same spiritual Fathers, who from the beginning laid the foundations of your church. I mean the eminent Gregory[7]

---

3 Cf. John 13.35.
4 Cf. Rom. 13.10.
5 1 Cor. 13.1-3.
6 B. Jackson suggests that St. Basil has in mind Mark 11.23.
7 Gregory Thaumaturgus, Bishop of Neo-Caesarea about 233-270.

and all who after him succeeded to the episcopal throne among you; one after another, like rising stars, they followed along the same footsteps, so as to leave clearly distinguishable signs of a heavenly administration to those who wished them. And truly, if blood relationships are not to be cast aside, but even contribute greatly to an unbroken union and fellowship of life, these birthrights also exist between you and us. Why, therefore, most revered of cities (for through you I am addressing the whole city), is there no courteous letter from you, no kindly word, but your ears are open to those who attempt to slander? In consequence, I ought so much the more to lament, the more I see their endeavors being brought to a successful issue, for the work of slander has a manifest author, who, being already known for his many wrongdoings, is characterized especially by this form of wickedness, so that the sin even becomes his name.[8] Yet, endure my freedom of speech; you have opened wide both ears to those who are slandering us, and are receiving everything without investigation into your mind; there is no one who distinguishes the falsehood from the truth. Who, when struggling alone, was ever free from malicious charges? Who was ever convicted of lying when the person he denounced was not present? What speech is not plausible to the hearers if the reviler maintains of a surety that it is so, and the one reviled is not at hand and does not hear the slanders? Does not the very practice of the world teach you in this regard that he who intends to be a fair and impartial listener must not be wholly led away by the first comer, but await also the defense of the accused in order that the truth may thus be clearly manifested by the comparison of the two arguments? 'Give a just judgment';[9] this precept is one of the most necessary for salvation.

8 *Ho diábolos.*
9 Cf. John 7.24.

And I say these things, not forgetful of the words of the Apostle that, fleeing human judgments, he reserved his entire life for the accounts to be rendered before the court that cannot be deceived, when he said: 'But with me it is a very small matter to be judged by you or by man's tribunal.'[10] Nevertheless, since slanderous lies have taken possession beforehand of your ears and our life has been brought into discredit and our faith in God has been attacked, I am aware that the slanderer is inflicting injury on three persons at one time; he is, in fact, harming him who is reviled, and those with whom he holds speech, and himself. I would have kept silence concerning my own injury, rest assured, not because I disdain your esteem (for how could that be, since I, to avoid suffering the loss of it, am now writing this letter and arguing?), but because I see that of the three who are injured, he who suffers the least loss is myself. For, though I am deprived of you, you have lost the truth, and, though he who is responsible for these things is separating me from you, he is estranging himself from the Lord, because it is not possible to be reconciled with God through forbidden things. Therefore, it is more on your account than my own and also for the sake of delivering you from unendurable harm that I am saying this. For, what greater evil could anyone suffer, once he has lost the most valued of all things, the truth?

What, then, am I saying, brethren? Not that I am some sinless person, nor that my life is not full of thousands of defects; for I know myself and I certainly do not cease to shed tears over my sins in the hope that I may somehow be able to appease my God and escape the threatened chastisement. But, I say, if he who judges our actions is positive that he has an eye that is pure, let him pick the mote out of

10 1 Cor. 4.3.

our eye.[11] We admit that we need much care from those who are sound. But, if he would not say this (and the freer he is from error, so much the more he will not say it, because it is characteristic of the perfect not to exalt themselves, since they will become liable to the charge of the arrogance of the Pharisee who, while justifying himself, condemned the publican), let him seek with me a physician and 'not pass judgment before the time, until the Lord comes, who will bring to light the things hidden in darkness and make manifest the counsels of hearts.'[12] And let him remember also Him who said: 'Do not judge, that you may not be judged';[13] and 'Do not condemn, that you may not be condemned.'[14] And, on the whole, brethren, if our faults are curable, why does he not obey the teacher of the churches who says: 'Reprove, rebuke, entreat'?[15] And, if our lawlessness is incurable, why does he not oppose us face to face, and by making public our transgressions free the churches from the harm done by us? Do not, therefore, tolerate the slander that is covertly spoken against us. This is what one of the maidservants from the mill might do, or even one of the market loungers whose tongue is whetted for all slander might show off extravagantly. But there are bishops; let them be summoned for a hearing. There are clergy in each diocese of God; let the most esteemed be brought together. Let him who wishes speak with freedom, in order that what takes place may be a trial and not abuse. Let my hidden wickedness be brought into view; let him not hate me, then, but rebuke me as a brother. We sinners are perhaps more

---

11 Cf. Matt. 7.4,5.
12 Cf. 1 Cor. 4.5.
13 Matt. 7.1.
14 Cf. Luke 6.37.
15 2 Tim. 4.2.

justly to be pitied by the blessed and sinless men than to be treated harshly.

But, if the error is one of faith, let the document be shown to us; again, let a fair and impartial tribunal be set up. Let the charge be read. Let an examination be made to ascertain whether the charge does not seem to be due to the ignorance of the accuser rather than that the writing is condemned because of its character. Many beautiful things do not seem to be such to those who do not possess an accurate judgment of mind. And even equal weights of material bodies do not seem to be equal when the scale pans are not equally balanced with each other. Moreover, honey actually seems bitter to some whose sense of taste is ruined by suffering. Also, when the eye is not healthy, it does not see many of the things which exist, and it assumes many things which do not exist. And, again, with regard to the force of words, I frequently see the same thing happening when the judge lacks the skill of the writer. For, both the critic and the writer should begin with almost the same equipment. Certainly, he who is not skilled in farming is not able to judge the works belonging to agriculture, and he who has no understanding of music will not distinguish between the dissonance and the harmony of the musical rhythms. Yet, whoever wishes will straightway be a literary critic, even though he is not able to point out his teacher nor the time in which he studied and understands nothing at all, neither little nor much, about letters. And I perceive that in regard to the words of the Holy Spirit, also, not every one should apply himself to an examination of what is said, but only he who has the Spirit of discernment, as the Apostle has taught us, when he said concerning the distribution of gifts: 'To one through the Spirit is given the utterance of wisdom; and to another the utterance of knowledge, according to the same Spirit; to another faith, in the same Spirit; to another the working of miracles; to another prophecy; to another the distinguishing of spirits.'[16] Consequently, if our affairs are spiritual, let him who wishes to judge our affairs show that he possesses the gift of the discernment of spiritual matters. But if, as he himself slanderously says, they are of the wisdom of this world, let him show himself experienced in the wisdom of the world, and then we will entrust to him the votes of judgment. And let no one think that we are planning these things as a means of escape from the examination. For I permit you, most beloved brethren, to make for yourselves an examination of the charges against us. Are you so dull of intellect as to stand in need of all the advocates for the discovery of the truth? But, if the matters seem to you to be incontestable in themselves, persuade those who are trifling to put aside all contentiousness. And, if something seems to be ambiguous, question us through some mediators who are able to serve our interests faithfully, or, if it seems best, demand of us written explanations. But, strive by all means and in every way not to leave these matters without investigation.

What clearer proof of our faith could there be than that we were brought up by our grandmother, a blessed woman, who came from among you? I have reference to the illustrious Macrina, by whom we were taught the words of the most blessed Gregory, which, having been preserved until her time by uninterrupted tradition, she also guarded, and she formed and molded me, still a child, to the doctrines of piety. But, after we received the power of understanding, and reason had been perfected in us through age, having traversed much of the earth and sea, whenever we found any who were

16 1 Cor. 12.8-10.

walking according to the traditional rule of piety, we claimed them as our fathers and made them the guides of our soul on the journey to God. And up to this very hour by the grace of Him who has called us by His holy calling to a knowledge of Him we are aware of having received in our hearts no teaching averse to the sound doctrine, nor of having ever defiled our souls with the hateful blasphemy of the Arians. But, if we have at any time received into communion any who came from that teacher, we have admitted them because they concealed their disease in the depths of their hearts and spoke pious words, or did not resist what we said; and we did not entrust all the judgment regarding them to ourselves, but we followed the decrees pronounced before by our Fathers concerning them. For, I have received writings from the most blessed Father Athanasius, Bishop of Alexandria, that I have at hand and offer to those who ask for them, in which he has plainly declared that, if anyone from the heresy of the Arians should wish to retract, acknowledging the Nicene Creed, we should receive him unhesitatingly. And, as he cited for me all the bishops both of Macedonia and of Achaea as supporters of this view, believing that because of the dependability of the lawmakers I should follow such a man, and at the same time, wishing to receive the reward of peacemaking, I enrolled those who admitted this creed in the party of communicants.

It is more just to judge our affairs, not from one or two of those who do not walk uprightly in the truth, but from the multitude of bishops throughout the world who are united with us by the grace of the Lord. Let the Pisidians, the Lycaonians, the Isaurians, the Phrygians of both provinces, such Armenians as are your neighbors, the Macedonians, the Achaeans, the Illyrians, the Gauls, the Spaniards, all

Italians, the Sicilians, the Africans, the untainted Egyptians, whatever remnant of Syrians is left, that is, whoever send letters to us and again receive them from us, be closely questioned. From these letters, both those brought from them and those sent back in answer from here, it is possible for you to learn that we are all united in spirit, having one thought. Therefore, let it not escape the notice of your Integrity that he who shuns communion with us severs his union with the whole Church. Consider, brethren, with whom you are in communion. When you are not received by us, who, henceforth, will recognize you? Do not make it necessary for us to take any harsh measures concerning the Church that is nearest and dearest to us. There are things which I now hide in my own heart, groaning within myself and bewailing the wickedness of the time, in that the greatest of the churches and those which of old occupied the position of brothers to each other without reason are now separated. Do not, oh! do not cause me to complain of these things to all who are in communion with us. Do not compel me to utter words, which until now with the curb of reason I have hidden within myself. Better is it for us to be out of the way and for the churches to agree with each other than through our childish pettiness to bring such evil upon the people of God. Ask your fathers and they will declare to you that, even if the dioceses seemed to be divided by their location, they were one at least in thought and were guided by one opinion. Continuous was the intermingling of the people with each other; continuous the visits of the clergy; and among the pastors themselves there existed such mutual love that each of them used the other as teacher and guide in matters pertaining to the Lord.

205. To Bishop Elpidius[1]

Again we have sent our beloved fellow presbyter Meletius to carry our greetings to your Charity. Even though we had determined to spare him because of his weakness, which he voluntarily brought on himself in the subjugation of his flesh according to the Gospel of Christ, we decided that it was proper for us to address you through men of this kind, who can easily supply by themselves whatever escapes the letter, and be, as it were, a sort of living letter for both the writer and the recipient. We are also satisfying his longing to see your Perfection, which he has always entertained ever since he has had experience of your good qualities. Consequently, we have now besought him to go to you, and through him we are paying our debt of a visit and urging you to pray for us and for the Church of God in order that the Lord may grant us the grace to lead a quiet and peaceful life, free from the abuse of the enemies of the Gospel.

If it really seems fitting and necessary to your Intelligence for us to join each other and to meet also the rest of the most honorable brothers, the bishops of the seacoast, do you yourself assign for us the place and the time at which this shall be done. Write the brethren in order that, each leaving the task in hand to the care of men whom he shall appoint, we may be able to do something for the edification of the Church of God, rid ourselves of the causes of grief which now exist among us because of suspicions against each other, and confirm the charity without which the Lord Himself has declared to us that the observance of every precept is imperfect.

---

1 Elpidius was evidently the bishop of a maritime town in the East whom Eustathius of Sebaste separated from his communion because he was a friend of St. Basil. Cf. Letter 251; also Letter 206, in which St. Basil consoles him for the loss of a little grandson. This letter was written in 375.

206. A Letter of Condolence to Bishop Elpidius[1]

Now, especially, am I sensible of the weakness of my body, when I see that it is such a hindrance to the betterment of my soul. If matters were succeeding according to my wish, not through letters nor through messengers would I salute you, but I myself would personally pay my debt of love, and in your company would enjoy spiritual profit. Now, however, I am in such a state that I can scarcely support the journeys in my own country, which we must make in our visitations of the parishes of the district. But, may the Lord provide for you strength and readiness, and for me, in addition to the eagerness I now have, ability to procure for us, as I have urged you, this pleasure when we are in the confines of Comana.

I fear, however, for your Modesty, lest, perchance, the grief for your relative should become an obstacle to you. For, I have learned that the death of a little child has afflicted you. His loss to you as a grandfather would reasonably be painful, but to a man who has already advanced to so high a degree of virtue and who understands human nature both from the experience of a lifetime and from his spiritual training, the separation from his nearest kin should not, as a consequence, be altogether too hard to bear. In fact, the Lord does not demand the same from us as from ordinary men. For they live according to custom, but we use as the rule of our life the precept of the Lord and the previous examples of blessed men,[2] whose nobility of mind was made manifest especially in precarious circumstances. In order, therefore, that you yourself may leave an example of manli-

1 On Elpidius, cf. the preceding letter and note. This letter was written in 375.

2 The martyrs.

ness and of a true regard for the hoped-for blessings, show yourself not bowed down by suffering, but raised above your distresses, submitting patiently to the affliction and rejoicing in hope. Let none of these things, then, be an obstacle to our eagerly awaited meeting. For little children age is sufficient in itself to free them from blame, but we are responsible for serving the Lord in the duties assigned to us and for being ready in all things for the administration of the churches, for which our Lord has reserved great rewards for the faithful and prudent stewards.

207. To the Clergy of Neo-Caesarea[1]

Your concurrence in hatred toward us and the fact that all of you, even to the last man, follow the leader[2] of the war against us, tempted me to maintain silence toward all alike and not to be the first with a friendly letter or with any other communication, but in silence to give myself over to my grief. However, we must break this silence in the presence of slanders, not in order that through the contrary assertion we may avenge ourselves, but that we may not acquiesce in the success of a lie, nor leave those who have been deceived to harm. Therefore it appeared necessary both to explain this to all and to write to your Intelligences, although lately, when I wrote to all the clergy in common, I was not considered worthy of an answer from you. Do not, brethren, flatter those who are introducing evil doctrines into your souls, and do not knowingly allow yourselves to disregard

1 Cf. Letter 204 and note 1. This letter was written in the late summer of 375. Cf. Loofs, *op. cit.* 21.

2 Atarbius of Neo-Caesarea.

the fact that the people of God are being undone through impious teachings. Sabellius the Libyan[3] and Marcellus the Galatian[4] alone of all men have dared to teach and to write these things which now the leaders of the people endeavor to promote among you as their own discoveries. They talk endlessly, and are not even capable of bringing these sophisms and fallacies to a plausible shape. These men publicly say unutterable things against us, and in every way they avoid meeting us. And why? Is it not because they view with uneasiness the examination of their wicked teachings? They have, at any rate, behaved so shamelessly toward us that they invent certain dreams against us, attacking our doctrines as harmful. Even if they entertain in their heads all the fantasies of the autumn months, they will be unable to attribute to us any blasphemy, since there are many witnesses to the truth in each church.

Now, if they are asked the reason for this unheralded and truceless war, they mention psalms and a manner of chanting which differs from the practice prevailing among you, and similar things, of which they ought to feel ashamed. Moreover, a charge is brought against us that we maintain men of ascetic life who have renounced the world and all worldly cares, which the Lord compares to thorns, since they do not permit the word to come to fruition. Such men bear around in their body the death of Jesus; lifting their own cross, they follow God. I would think it worth my whole life that my crimes were such, and that I had beside me, under my training, men who have deliberately chosen this ascetic life. I hear that in Egypt at the present time there is virtue of such

3 St. Basil is considered the oldest authority for the statement that Sabellius was an African by birth.

4 I.e., of Ancyra. In attempting to refute the heterodox writings of Asterius he was accused of teaching doctrine combining the errors of Sabellius and Paul of Samosata, although earlier at the Nicene Council he had been on the side of the orthodox.

kind among men, and perhaps there are also some in Palestine living successfully the life based on the Gospel. I also hear that in Mesopotamia there are some perfect and blessed men. We, however, are children, certainly, in comparison with the perfect. And, if there are women also who choose to live according to the Gospel, preferring virginity to marriage, bringing into subjection the proud designs of the flesh, and living in that sorrow which is pronounced blessed, they will be happy in their choice, wherever they may be on earth. But among us this is rare, since the people are still being instructed in the first principles and introduced to the practice of piety. And, if any disorder is cited in the life of the women, I do not undertake to speak in their defense. Yet, I call upon you to witness this, that, what up to this time Satan, the father of lies, did not permit himself to say, these bold hearts and unbridled mouths are always proclaiming without scruple. However, I wish you to know that we profess to have orders of men and women whose conduct of life is heavenly, who have crucified the flesh with its passions and desires, who are not solicitous about food and clothing, but, being free from distractions and constantly waiting on the Lord, continue in their prayers night and day. Their mouths do not speak idly of the works of men, but they chant hymns to our God continuously, working with their hands in order that they may be able to share with those who are in need.

As to the charge regarding psalmody, by which especially our slanderers terrify the more simple, I have this to say, that the customs now prevalent are in accord and harmony with those of all the churches of God. Among us the people come early after nightfall to the house of prayer, and in labor and affliction and continual tears confess to God. Finally, rising up from their prayers, they begin the chanting of psalms. And now, divided into two parts, they chant antiphonally, becoming master of the text of the Scriptural passages, and at the same time directing their attention and the recollectedness of their hearts. Then, again, leaving it to one to intone the melody, the rest chant in response; thus, having spent the night in a variety of psalmody and intervening prayers, when day at length begins to dawn, all in common, as with one voice and one heart, offer up the psalm of confession to the Lord, each one making His own the words of repentance. If, then, you shun us on this account, you will shun the Egyptians, and also those of both Libyas,[5] the Thebans, Palestinians, Arabians, Phoenicians, Syrians, and those dwelling beside the Euphrates—in one word, all those among whom night watches and prayers and psalmody in common have been held in esteem.

But these things did not exist, it is said, in the time of the great Gregory.[6] But neither did the litanies[7] of which you now make use. And I do not say this to denounce you; in fact, I have prayed that all of you might live in tears and in continual penance. For we also do nothing else but offer up supplications for our sins, except that we appease our God, not so much with human words, as you do, but with the sayings of the Spirit. Whom do you have as witnesses that these things did not exist in the time of the wondrous Gregory, you who certainly have not preserved any of his practices until now?[8] Gregory did not cover his head at

5 Upper Libya and Lower Libya, a division made after the time of Diocletian for purposes of administration.

6 Gregory Thaumaturgus.

7 According to the Benedictine editors, 'litanies' here does not mean processions or supplications, but penitential prayers, a meaning supported by the following sentence.

8 The Benedictine editors call attention to an apparent contradiction between this passage and *De Spiritu Sancto* 74, where St. Basil says that the Church in Neo-Caesarea had apparently rigidly preserved the traditions of Gregory. However, this rigid conformity may be confined to matters of importance.

prayer. In fact, how could he, since he was a true disciple of the Apostle, who said: 'Every man praying or prophesying with his head covered, disgraces his head,'[9] and 'A man indeed ought not to cover his head, because he is the image and glory of God.'[10] He avoided oaths, that pure soul, worthy of fellowship with the Holy Spirit, being satisfied with 'yes' and 'no' because of the command of the Lord, who said: 'But I say to you not to swear at all.'[11] He did not dare to call his brother a fool, for he feared the threat of the Lord. Indignation and wrath and bitterness did not proceed from his mouth. Slander he hated, because it did not lead to the kingdom of Heaven. Envy and arrogance were excluded from his guileless soul. He would not stand at the altar before he was reconciled with his brother. Speech that was deceitful and skillfully contrived for the slander of someone he so loathed as one who knows that the lie is born of the Devil and that the Lord 'will destroy all that speak a lie.'[12] If there is none of these things in you, but you are free from all, truly you are disciples of him who was learned in the commands of the Lord. But, if not, look to it lest you are, on the one hand, straining out a gnat[13] in being exacting about the raising of the voice in psalmody, and, on the other, rendering null the greatest of the commandments. The necessity of a defense has led me to these words, in order that you may be taught to cast out the beam from your own eyes, and then to remove the mote from others. We, however, pardon everything, even though nothing is left unscrutinized by God. Only, let the essentials be sound, and silence the innovations concerning the faith.

9 1 Cor. 11.4.
10 1 Cor. 11.7.
11 Matt. 5.34; cf. Matt. 5.22.
12 Cf. Ps. 5.6,7.
13 Cf. Matt. 23.24.

Do not reject the Persons. Do not deny the name of Christ. Do not misinterpret the words of Gregory. Otherwise, so long as we draw breath and are able to speak, it will be impossible for us to be silent in the presence of such harm wrought on souls.

208. To Eulancius[1]

You have been silent for a long time, even though you are most loquacious and make it your practice and art always to speak something and to draw attention to yourself through your words. But, Neo-Caesarea is probably the cause of your silence toward us. Perhaps we should receive as a kindness the fact that we are not remembered by those there, since the mention of us is not kind, according to the report of those who have heard. But, you were formerly of those who were hated on our account, not of those who were content to hate us because of others. Therefore, be the same, and write, wherever you may be, thinking of us without bias, if you have any care for justice. It is just, I presume, for those who have taken the initiative in love to be repaid with equal love.

209. Without Address, in Self-Defense[1]

You were doomed to griefs and struggles in our defense. And this is proof of your vigorous soul. Indeed, God, who directs our affairs, procures for those who are able to endure mighty conflicts greater occasions of winning public esteem.

1 Otherwise unknown. This letter was written in 375.

1 Written in 375.

And you, moreover, have put forward your own life as a test of the genuineness of your virtue in regard to your friends, as the furnace is the test for gold. Therefore, we pray God that other men may become better and that you may remain like yourself and may not cease bringing such charges as you have now brought, reproaching us with a deficit of letters as a great wrong. That is the accusation of a friend; so continue to demand such debts. In this way, in fact, I am not an exceptional debtor of friendship.

210. To the Most Eloquent Citizens of Neo-Caesarea[1]

I had no obligation at all to divulge my opinion[2] to you or to tell the reasons for which I am now in this locality. I am not, in fact, one who wishes to attract attention, nor is the matter deserving of so much publicity. But we are not doing, I believe, what we wish, but that to which the leaders challenge us. Yet, I have always striven more zealously to be altogether ignored than the lovers of glory strive to be conspicuous. However, since the ears of all in your city are deafened, as I hear, and there are some newsmongers, makers of lies, hired for this very purpose, who are explaining my affairs to you, I have thought that I should not disregard the fact that you are being informed by an evil mind and a filthy tongue, but should myself tell you how my affairs stand. Both through my acquaintance with this place from childhood (for I was raised here by my grandmother[3]) and

1 Cf. also Letter 223, in which St. Basil defends himself more specifically against the calumnies of Eustathius of Sebaste which he had endured for more than three years. This letter was written in the late summer of 375. Cf. Loofs, *op. cit.* 20f.

2 On matters of religion.

3 Macrina, whose home was in Annesi.

through my long stay here afterwards, when I was fleeing political disturbances, I realized that this place was suitable for studying philosophy because of the silence of the solitude; and I spent many successive years here. Moreover, because my brothers[4] now dwell here, I gladly came to this solitude, not by this means to cause trouble for others, but to satisfy my own desire.

Why, therefore, is it necessary to have recourse to dreams and to hire dream interpreters, and to make us the subject of talk over the cups in the public banquets? Truly, if the slanders had arisen among any others, I would have submitted you as witnesses of my opinions. Now, I ask each of you to recall those circumstances of former days when the city was summoning us to take charge of its youths, and a deputation of your magistrates waited upon us, how afterwards they all crowded around us in a body. What offers did they not make us? What did they not promise? Nevertheless, they were not able to prevail upon us. How could I, then, who did not heed at the time when I was called, be attempting at present, unbidden, to intrude? How could I, who fled those praising and admiring me, now be likely to seek the favor of those who are slandering me? Do not think so, most noble Sirs. Our cause is not so contemptible. For, no one, if he were wise, would board a ship without a steersman, nor would he turn to a church in which those who are sitting at the helm are themselves causing the waves and the storm. In fact, why has the city been full of confusion, when some were fleeing, although no one was pursuing, and others were stealing away, although no one was following, and all the soothsayers and dream interpreters were spreading fear? What else is the cause of these things?

4 Cf. Letter 216, in which St. Basil mentions that he went to his brother Peter's house near Neo-Caesarea.

Is it not known even to a child that it is due to the leaders of the people? The reason for their hatred it is unbecoming for me to mention, but it is very easy for you to perceive. When bitterness and disagreement have no limit to their harshness, and the explanation of the cause is altogether unsubstantial and ridiculous, there is evidently a disease of the soul which not only affects the good of others, but is properly and primarily an evil to the possessor. Yet, they have another clever trait. Though severely stung and feeling pained, they do not permit themselves through shame to speak openly of their misfortune. Now, this suffering of their soul is known both from their actions against us, and from the rest of their conduct. And, even if it should be unknown, there would be no great harm in the matter. The truest reason, however, for which they think that a meeting with us must be avoided, and which, perchance, has escaped the notice of many of you, I shall explain. Now, listen.

A perversion of faith is being practiced among you, hostile both to the apostolic and evangelical doctrines and to the tradition of the truly great Gregory[5] and his successors up to the blessed Musonius,[6] whose teachings are certainly even now ringing in your ears. The evil of Sabellius, stirred up long ago, but extinguished by the tradition of that great man, these men are now endeavoring to revive; fearful of refutation, they are inventing dreams against us. But you, bid farewell to your wine-heavy heads which the vapor, rising from your drunken bouts and raging like the waves, terrifies with visions, and hear from us, watching and unable to be silent through fear of God, the damage done to yourselves. Sabellianism is Judaism introduced into the preaching of the

5 Thaumaturgus.

6 Musonius, Bishop of Neo-Caesarea, died in 368. Nothing is known of him except what is contained here and in Letter 28.

Gospel in the guise of Christianity. He who says that the Father and Son and Holy Spirit are one thing manifold in character, and explains the Person of the three as one, what else does he do but deny the eternal existence of the Only-begotten One? And he also denies His sojourn among men through the Incarnation, His descent into Limbo, His Resurrection, the Judgment; he denies, too, the activities proper to the Spirit. And now, I hear that among you there have been attempted even more daring things than those of the weak-minded Sabellius. For they say, and they speak as persons who have heard, that the wise men among you maintain and declare that a name of the 'Only-begotten' has not been handed down but a name of the adversary exists,[7] and they rejoice in this and are as proud as over a discovery of their own. For it is written, He says: 'I have come in the name of my Father, and you have not received me; if another come in his own name, him you will receive.'[8] And because it is said: 'Make disciples of all nations, baptizing them in the name of the Father, and of the Son, and of the Holy Spirit,'[9] it is evident, they say, that there is only one name. For it is not said 'in the names,' but 'in the name.'

I blush at writing these words to you, because those guilty of these wrongs are from our blood,[10] and I sigh from the depths of my soul that I am compelled, like men who fight against two persons, to restore the proper strength to the truth by striking with my arguments and throwing down the perversions in doctrine on both sides. On this side Anomoeus attacks us, and on the other, as it seems, Sabellius. I urge you to pay no attention to these sophisms so disgusting and

7 The contrast here is between Christ and the Devil.
8 John 5.43. St. Basil has changed the tense of his verbs.
9 Matt. 28.19.
10 The allusion is probably to Atarbius.

incapable of perverting anyone, but to know that the name of Christ, which is above every name, is actually His being called the Son of God, and that according to the saying of Peter: 'There is no other name under heaven given to men by which we must be saved.'[11] In regard to the words 'I have come in the name of my Father,' it must be understood that He says these things in claiming His Father as His beginning and cause. And, if it is said: 'Going, baptize in the name of the Father and of the Son and of the Holy Spirit,' we must not believe from this that one name has been handed over to us. For, just as he who says 'Paul and Silvanus and Timothy' has mentioned three names, but has joined them to each other by the syllable 'and,' so he who says the name of the Father and of the Son and of the Holy Spirit, while mentioning three, has connected them with the conjunction, showing that a distinct meaning is suggested for each name, inasmuch as names are significant of things. And no one who enjoys even a little intelligence doubts that things have their individual and independent existence. Now, the nature of the Father and of the Son and of the Holy Spirit is the same, and there is one Godhead; but the names are different, presenting to us concepts circumscribed and exact. In fact, it is impossible for the mind, unless it is without confusion as regards the properties of each, to be able to offer the doxology to the Father and to the Son and to the Holy Spirit. If, then, they deny that they so say and teach, our efforts have been crowned with success. Yet, I see that the denial is hard for them, because we have many witnesses of these speeches. However, we do not look to the past; only let the present be sound. But, if they continue in the same sentiments, it will be necessary for us to proclaim your misfortune to the other churches, also, and to cause

11 Acts. 4.12.

letters to be sent to you from more bishops in order to tear down this great mass of secretly and gradually prepared impiety. Either there will be some good effect for our pains, or the present protest will free us absolutely from blame at the Judgment.

Even in their personal writings they have already inserted those expressions which they sent first to the man of God, Bishop Meletius,[12] but, after receiving from him the proper reply, like mothers of monsters ashamed of the deformities of nature, they, too, concealed their shameful offspring and are bringing them up in consistent darkness. They made some attempt by letter against Anthimus,[13] Bishop of Tyana, a man of like mind with us, on the ground that Gregory said in his *Exposition of the Faith*[14] that Father and Son were two in thought, but one in Person.[15] That this is not said dogmatically, but controversially in the argument with Aelian,[16] they were not able to understand, they who were congratulating themselves on the subtlety of their minds. In this dispute there are many copyists' errors, as we shall show you in the writings themselves, God willing. In fact, at the time in trying to persuade the Greek, Gregory did not think that it was necessary to be exact about his words, but that he should in a way make concessions to the custom of him

12 Meletius of Antioch.

13 Anthimus of Tyana appears first on friendly terms with St. Basil. Cf. Letters 58 and 92. But soon after, in the year 372, dissensions due to the division of Cappadocia broke out between the two. In the same year peace was made between them by the intercession of St. Gregory, but it did not last. Cf. Letters 110, 121, and 122. A reconciliation seems to have been again effected as we see from the present letter.

14 The *écthesis tês pisteōs* of St. Gregory Thaumaturgus is given at length in the Life of Gregory Thaumaturgus by St. Gregory of Nyssa and also appears in the Latin Psalter that Charlemagne gave to Adrian I.

15 The Benedictine editors do not believe that St. Gregory used so Sabellian an expression.

16 Evidently a pagan. He is known only from this letter and St. Gregory Thaumaturgus' *Frag. de Trin.* (*PL* 10.1103,1143).

who was being brought in, so that the latter might not offer resistance in matters of importance. Therefore, you might truly find many words there which furnish the greatest support to the heretics, such as 'creature' and 'thing made' and the like. Then, too, many words spoken concerning the union with man are referred to the doctrine of the divinity when heard by those lacking instruction in the writings, and of such a sort is this expression which is being bruited about by them. It must be well understood that, as he who does not confess a community of substance falls into polytheism, so he who does not grant the individuality of the Persons is carried away into Judaism. Our mind, supported, as it were, by some underlying principle, must stamp upon itself clear impressions and thus arrive at an understanding of the object of its desire. If we have not grasped the meaning of Paternity, nor considered Him about whom this attribute is defined, how can we receive the concept of God the Father? In fact, it is not sufficient to enumerate the differences in the Persons, but it is necessary to admit that each Person exists in a true hypostasis. Not even Sabellius rejected the illusion of Persons without hypostasis, saying that the same God, though He is one in essence, is transformed on each occasion according to the needs arising and is spoken of now as Father, now as Son, and now as Holy Spirit. This error, long ago suppressed, is at present being revived by the inventors of this anonymous heresy, who reject the Persons and deny the name of the Son of God. And, if they do not cease speaking iniquity against God,[17] they will have to mourn with the Christ-deniers.

We have written this to you of necessity, in order that you may guard yourselves against harm from the evil doctrines. Really, if we should compare evil teachings to deadly drugs,

17 Cf. Ps. 74.6.

as the dream interpreters among you say, these things are hemlock and bane and any other murderous drug. These things and not our words, as the drunken brains full of fancies from their condition cry out, are destructive of souls. If they were sound of mind, these should know that the prophetic gift shines in souls that are undefiled and cleansed from every stain. In fact, it is neither possible for the reflections of images to be received in a filthy mirror, nor for the soul preoccupied with the cares pertaining to life and blinded by the passions arising from the pride of the flesh to receive the illuminations of the Holy Spirit. Not every vision seen in sleep is forthwith a prophecy, as Zacharias says: 'The Lord has made a vision and wintry rain, because those who speak out have uttered disturbances, and they told false dreams.'[18] But these, according to Isaias 'sleeping and loving dreams,'[19] are ignorant of this, that frequently an illusion is sent to 'unbelievers.'[20] And there is a lying spirit which, arising in the false prophets, deceived Achab.[21] Knowing this, they should not be so lifted up as to ascribe prophecy to themselves, who are shown to lack the exactness even of the seer Balaam. Summoned with great gifts by the king of the Moabites, he did not dare to utter a word contrary to the will of God, nor to curse Israel, which the Lord did not curse.[22] If, then, their visions seen in sleep concur with the precepts of the Lord, let them be satisfied with the Gospels which need no additional aid from dreams for reliability. If the Lord has left His peace to us, and has given us a new commandment that we should love one another, but

18 Zach. 10.1,2 (Septuagint).
19 Cf. Isa. 56.10.
20 Cf. Eph. 2.2.
21 Cf. 3 Kings 22.22.
22 Cf. Num. 22.11,12.

dreams lead to strife and separation and a destruction of love, let them not give an opportunity to the Devil to assail their souls in sleep, and let them not deem their own fancies more authoritative than the doctrines of salvation.

211. To Olympius[1]

After reading the letter from your Honor I became more content than I had been and more cheerful, and, when I conversed with your most beloved sons, I seemed to behold you yourself. Although they found my soul exceedingly afflicted, they so disposed me that I forgot the hemlock which the dream-peddlers and dream-hucksters among you bear around against us for the delight of those who have hired them. I have sent some letters; others we shall give later, if you wish. Only I hope there may be some benefit from them to the recipients.

212. To Hilarius[1]

How do you think I felt or what thought do you think I entertained when I journeyed to Dazimon and a few days after our arrival learned that your Eloquence had departed? It is not only because of the admiration which I had for you from boyhood, even from my very school days, that I have always valued your discourse highly, but also because nothing now is so excellent as a truth-loving soul endowed with a

1 On Olympius cf. Letters 4, 12, 13, and 131. This letter was written in 375.

1 This letter is the only source of our information about Hilarius. It was written in the late summer of 375. Cf. Loofs, *op. cit.* 20f.

sound judgment in practical affairs. And this, we think, has been preserved in you. We see most other men divided, as at the horse races, shouting out together with the factions, some for these and others for those. But, since you are far above fear and flattery and every ignoble feeling, it is likely that you are viewing the truth with unprejudiced eye. I also perceive that you do not treat the affairs of the churches cursorily, since, as a matter of fact, you even sent us a message concerning these matters, as you declared in this recent letter. I would be glad to learn who it was who consented to bring it, so as to know the one who wronged me. I have not yet received a letter from you on this subject.

How great a price, then, do you think I would pay for a chance to talk with you in order to acquaint you with my grievances (for the act of speaking out affords, as you know, some relief for those who are pained), and to answer your questions, not trusting to lifeless letters, but personally telling each point clearly and going through it in detail. Living words, indeed, have a more effective persuasiveness; they do not at all resemble the written words in their susceptibility either to attack or to misrepresentation. Yet nothing is left untried by anyone, since even those whom we trusted most, who, after seeing them with other men, we realized were somewhat greater than the common run of men, even these permitted themselves to send on someone else's writings, whatever they were, as ours, and by them to bring us into discredit with the brethren, so that now there is nothing more abhorrent to the pious than our name. Although I have deliberately striven from the beginning to be unknown, as perhaps no other of those who have considered human weakness has, now, just as if, on the contrary, I preferred to make myself known to all men, I have been talked about everywhere on earth, and I may add, on the sea, also. Those who make the utmost limit of impiety their business and introduce into their churches the godless dogma of Anomoeanism are at war with me. And those who take the middle course,[2] as they think, though starting from those same principles, but not admitting the consequences of their reasoning because of its opposition to the views of the many, are hostile to us and load us with calumnies as much as they are able. Furthermore, they refrain from no intrigue, even though the Lord has made their attempts unavailing. How is it possible for these things not to be distressing? How is it possible for them not to make life painful for me? I have, at any rate, one consolation in my troubles, the weakness of my flesh, because of which I am convinced that I shall not long remain in this wretched life. So much, then, for this.

I exhort you in your bodily sufferings to bear yourself nobly and in a manner worthy of the God who called us. If He sees that we have received with thanksgiving our present condition, He will either release us from our distress, as in the case of Job, or will requite us with the great crowns of patient endurance in our future life.

---

2 The Benedictine editors remark that, although at first sight Eustathius of Sebaste seems to be the one to whom St. Basil is referring here, because in Letter 128 he speaks of him as occupying a contemptible half-and-half position, yet on second thought he evidently means those heretics whom he attacks in *De Spiritu Sancto,* sections 13, 25, 34, 52, 60, 69, 75.

213. Without an Address, for a Pious Man[1]

May the Lord, who has provided for me speedy relief in my afflictions, Himself grant you the help of that consolation which you have bestowed upon us in your present visit by letter, and reward you with a true and great joy of spirit for the consolation given to our Lowliness. It happened that I was in a way distressed in soul, when I observed in a large gathering a kind of beastlike and altogether irrational indifference in the people and an inveterate and stubborn habit of baseness among their leaders. But, when I saw the letter and its treasure of love, I recognized that He who manages our affairs had made a sweet solace to shine upon us who are living in bitterness. Therefore I, in turn, address your Holiness, making my customary appeal, that you will not cease praying for my wretched life, lest at any time, overwhelmed by the imagery of this world, I may forget God who raises up the needy from the earth,[2] or, feeling some elation, may 'incur the condemnation passed on the devil,'[3] or, being remiss in my administration, may be found by the Master asleep; or even lest, handing it over through hurtful deeds, or wounding the conscience of my fellow servants,[4] or again, associating with drunken men, I may suffer what was threatened to the wicked stewards in the righteous judgment of God. I beg you, then, in all your prayers ask of God that we may be sober in all things in order that we may not become a shame and a reproach to the name of Christ in the unveiling of the secrets of our heart on the great day of the manifestation of our Saviour Jesus Christ.

1 This letter was written in 375.
2 Cf. Ps. 112.7.
3 Cf. 1 Tim. 3.6.
4 Cf. 1 Cor. 8.12.

I want you to know, moreover, that I am in expectation of being summoned to court as an insult on the part of the heretics, on a pretext, to be sure, of peace; and that the bishop here,[5] when he heard this, wrote to us to go with speed to Mesopotamia, and, after gathering together the brethren of like opinion there, who control the affairs of the churches, to set out with them to the emperor. But, probably, even my body itself will not be adequate for the journey in winter. Meanwhile, the matter does not seem pressing, unless you yourself advise it. In fact, I shall await the advice of your Reverence so that my opinion may be confirmed. Consequently, I urge you to make known to us quickly through one of our zealous brethren what solution occurs to your Perfection and divinely inspired Intelligence.

214. To Count Terentius[1]

When we heard that your Dignity has been forced into the care of public affairs, we were immediately disturbed (for the truth will be told). We considered how contrary it was to your inclination, after you had been freed once and for all from public duties and were devoting yourself to the care of your soul, to be again compelled to turn back to the former responsibility. Then it occurred to our mind that, perhaps, the Lord, wishing to grant this one consolation for the innumerable griefs which now oppress the churches among us, had directed that your Dignity should again appear in the public affairs, and we were certainly more

5 Maran, *Vita Basilii* 6, believes that this is Bishop Meletius.

1 On Terentius, cf. Letters 99 and 105. This letter was written in the autumn of 375. Cf. Loofs, *op. cit.* 21.

cheerful as we were likely to meet your Honor at least once more before we departed from this life.

But again, another report reached us, that you were delaying at Antioch and that you were managing the affairs at hand with the chief authorities. In addition to this report, tidings reached us that the brethren of the company about Paulinus were having some talk with your Rectitude concerning union with us, and by 'us' I mean those of the party of the man of God, Meletius,[2] the bishop. And I also hear now that they are circulating a letter from the Western[3] bishops transferring to them the episcopate of the church in Antioch, and misrepresenting Meletius, who is the admirable bishop of the true Church of God. And I do not wonder at this. The former[4] are entirely ignorant of our affairs, and the latter, who seem to know, interpret matters to them more contentiously than truthfully. Yet, it is altogether likely that either they are ignorant of the truth or are concealing the reason for which the most blessed bishop, Athanasius, was compelled to write to Paulinus. We urge your Perfection, since you have men who are able to explain clearly and in detail what took place between the bishops in the reign of Jovian,[5] to be fully informed by them. But, since we accuse no one and pray to have charity toward all and especially toward the members of our faith,[6] we congratulate those

2 St. Basil supported Meletius, whose orthodoxy was unquestioned. The Eustathians, however, because of his Arian nomination, bitterly opposed him. For the trouble involving Paulinus and Meletius, cf. Letters 57, 68, 89, 120, 129, and notes.

3 This description favors the first of the two letters written by Pope Damasus to Paulinus on the matter of admitting to communion Vitalius, bishop of the Apollinarian schism at Antioch.

4 The Western bishops.

5 Jovian, emperor from June 27, 363, until Feb. 16, 364, while firm for orthodoxy and, especially, for the re-establishment of St. Athanasius, was anxious for peace and toleration among his subjects.

6 Cf. Gal. 6.10.

who have received the letter from Rome. And, if it contains some honorable and great testimony for them, we pray that this may be true and confirmed by the facts themselves. Not, however, for this reason, at any rate, can we ever persuade ourselves either to ignore Meletius or to forget the church subject to him or to consider as trifling the questions from which the disagreement arose, and to think that it makes little difference in regard to the aim of piety. For my part, not only will I refuse to draw back if someone becomes elated because he received a letter from men, but not even if it came from the very heavens, yet does not agree with the sound reasoning of faith, am I able to consider him as in communion with the saints.

Lay to heart, then, O admirable Sir, that the falsifiers of the truth, who introduced the Arian schism into the sound faith of the Fathers, put forward no other reason for not having accepted the pious teaching of the Fathers than the doctrine of consubstantiality, which they interpret in an evil manner with a view to slandering the whole faith, saying that we assert that the Son is consubstantial in Person. If we give any opportunity to them because of our being carried away by those who through simplicity rather than through wickedness use these expressions or expressions very similar to them, there is nothing to prevent us from giving unanswerable arguments against ourselves and from establishing strongly the heresy of those whose one care in their utterances about the Church is, not to maintain their own teachings, but to slander ours.

What slander could be more serious than this, or more able to cause the many to waver, than if some among us should seem to be saying that there is one Person of the Father and of the Son and of the Holy Spirit, even though we teach very clearly the difference of the Persons, and especially because this same idea was started before by Sabellius? He said that God is one in Person, but is represented in different Persons by the Scriptures according to the specific need underlying each case, and that now it applies to Him the terms belonging to the Father whenever there is an occasion for this Person, and again those proper to the Son whenever He descends to the care of us or to some other activities relating to the Incarnation, and again the mask of the Holy Spirit is put on whenever the situation demands terms expressive of this Person. If, then, some among us are evidently saying that the Father and the Son and the Holy Spirit are one in substance (*hypokeímenon*) while admitting three perfect Persons (*hypóstasis*), how is it possible that they will not seem to be providing clear and irrefutable proof that the things said about us are true?

Now, in regard to the fact that person (*hypóstasis*) and substance (*usía*) are not the same thing, even the brethren from the West, as I think, themselves gave evidence, when, viewing with suspicion the inadequacy of their language, they transferred into the Greek language the word for 'substance' (*usía*), in order that, if there should be any difference of meaning, it would be preserved in the clear and unconfused differentiation of the terms. And, if we must say briefly what we think, we shall say this, that substance (*usía*) has the same relation to person (*hypóstasis*) as the general has to the particular. Each of us shares in 'existence' by the common meaning of 'substance,' and he is So-and-so or So-and-so through his own particular characteristics. Thus, here also the meaning of substance is common, as in 'goodness' or 'divinity' or anything else that may be conceived, but the person is perceived in the peculiar properties of paternity or sonship or sanctifying power. If, then, they say that the Persons are without hypostasis, from that point their doctrine is absurd; but, if they concede that the Persons themselves are in a true hypostasis, as they admit, let them enumerate them, in order that the doctrine of consubstantiality may be preserved in the unity of the Godhead, and the pious acknowledgement of the Father and of the Son and of the Holy Spirit in the perfect and complete Person of each of those names may be proclaimed. Yet, I wish your Dignity to be convinced of this, that you and everyone who, like you, has a care for the truth and who does not disdain those who are struggling for the sake of piety, ought to wait for leaders of the churches to be the guides for this unity and peace, for I consider them to be pillars and a support of the truth and of the Church. I revere them the more, the farther they have been banished, since exile was inflicted on them as a punishment. I urge, then, keep yourself unprejudiced for our sake, in order that we may be able to rest on you, at least, whom God has granted to us as a staff and a prop in all things.

215. To Dorotheus, Presbyter[1]

As soon as I found an occasion, I sent a letter to the admirable man, Count Terentius,[2] for I considered that my writing to him through strangers about the matter under discussion would be viewed with less suspicion, and at the same time I wanted our most beloved brother Acacius[3] to meet with no delay in the affair. Therefore, I gave the letter to the collector of revenues in the office of the prefects,

1 Letter 243 mentions this Dorotheus as carrying a letter for St. Basil. This letter was written in the autumn of 375. Cf. Loofs, *op. cit.* 21.
2 Cf. the previous letter and note 1.
3 This may be the presbyter of Beroea mentioned in Letters 220 and 256.

who was traveling by public conveyance, and I bade him show the communication to you first. As regards the road to Rome, I do not know how it is that no one reported to your Intelligence that in the winter it is entirely impassable, since the intervening country from Constantinople to our district is full of enemies. If it is necessary to travel by sea, it will be an opportune time, provided that my brother Gregory,[4] the bishop most dearly beloved of God, will consent to the voyage and to an embassy on such matters. I do not even see who are going along with him and I know that he is entirely inexperienced in the affairs of the churches. Moreover, while his conference with a sensible man would excite respect and be worth much, yet, what benefit would there be to our common interests from the conversation of such a man as Gregory, whose disposition is averse to servile flattery, with a mighty and eminent man who holds a somewhat high position, and for this reason is not able to hear those who speak the truth to him from the lower position?

216. To Meletius, Bishop of Antioch[1]

Many and varied journeys have drawn us away from the fatherland. In fact, we went as far as Pisidia to settle with the bishops there matters concerning the brethren[2] in Isauria. And from that place our travels next took us to the Pontus, since Eustathius had considerably disturbed Dazimon and

4 St. Gregory of Nyssa.

1 Other letters addressed to Meletius, Bishop of Antioch, are Letters 57, 68, 89, 120, and 129. This letter was written in the autumn of 375. Cf. Loofs, *op. cit.* 21.

2 The Christians. Cf. Tillemont, 'Basil,' *op. cit.* note 71.

induced many there to separate from our church. We also proceeded even to the home of our brother Peter;[3] and this fact, because of our proximity to the region of Neo-Caesarea, furnished an occasion for much trouble to the Neo-Caesareans, and gave them an excuse for much insolence toward us. They began to flee, although no one was pursuing them, and we were believed to be forcing ourselves uninvited upon them out of a desire of obtaining their commendation.

When we had returned, having contracted a severe illness from the rains and discouragements, immediately a letter reached us from the East which declared that certain letters with a semblance of some authority had been brought to the party of Paulinus from the West, and that the leaders of that party were elated and glorying in the correspondence, and so were offering a creed, and on these terms were ready to be joined with our Church. In addition to this, it has also been announced to us that they have brought over to their support Terentius, a most excellent man. I wrote to him quickly in order to restrain his impetuosity and to explain their subtleties.

217. To Amphilochius, on the Canons[1]

Having just returned from a long journey (I had gone as far as the Pontus on business for the Church and for a visit to my relatives), even though I had brought back a shattered body and a comparably distressed spirit, when I took your Reverence's letter into my hands I at once forgot all, for I had received a memento of a voice the sweetest of all to me

3 St. Basil's brother, Peter, had succeeded St. Basil at the head of the monastic establishment on the Iris.

1 Cf. Letter 188 n. 1. This letter was written in 375.

and of a hand the dearest. Since, then, I was made so happy by your letter, you should be able to surmise how much I would value a meeting with you; may the Holy One so manage that it will take place at your convenience and your invitation. In fact, if you should come to the house at Euphemias, it will not be difficult for me to be there at the same time, not only getting away from my troubles here, but also hastening to your sincere Charity. Besides, perhaps the sudden departure of Bishop Gregory, dearly beloved of God, of which the cause is unknown up to the present time, may make the journey to Nazianzus necessary for me. But, I want you to know that the man about whom I was talking with your Perfection and who you yourself were hoping was now ready has contracted a lingering illness and is further suffering an affliction of his eyes due to a former malady and to the disease recently attacking him, rendering him entirely useless for any duty. Moreover, there is no one else with us. Therefore, it is better, even though they have entrusted the affair to us, for someone from among themselves to be put forward. We must believe that these are the words of necessity and that their spirit desires that which they sought from the beginning—that he who is their leader be one of their own. And, if there is any one of the newly baptized, whether it seem best to Macedonius or not, let him be put forward for ordination. And you will form him for his duties, the Lord being your Co-worker in all things and granting you the grace for this also.

(51) The canons are indefinite in their explanation regarding clerics, commanding that one penalty shall be assigned for those who fall, deposition from the ministry,[2]

2 Cf. Letter 188, Canon 3, especially notes 39 and 40; also Letter 199, Canon 32. Canon 51, according to Balsamon's interpretation, is a complement to Canon 32, and determines the sense of the word

whether they happen to be in orders or are still in the unordained stage of the ministry.

(52) As regards the woman who left her new-born child uncared for on the road, if, although she was really able to save it, she disregarded it, either thinking in this way to conceal her sin or scheming in some entirely brutal and inhuman manner, let her be judged as for murder. But, if she was unable to protect it and the child perished through destitution and the want of the necessities of life, the mother is to be pardoned.

(53) Probably the widowed servant did not fall seriously in procuring a second marriage for herself on a pretext of abduction.[3] Therefore there is no need for any charge to be brought on this account. The pretext is not judged, but the intention. It is evident, however, that the penalty for a second marriage awaits her.[4]

(54) I know that I formerly wrote to your Reverence to the best of my ability on the distinctions to be made in

---

'cleric' in that canon. Some had objected that Canon 32 applied only to clerics in those orders which were conferred by the imposition of hands, such as priests, deacons, and subdeacons (according to Balsamon and Zonaras, *PG* 138.738-739), but also cantors and lectors (according to Aristenus, *PG* 138.739). St. Basil here states that immunity from excommunication applies also to clerics in minor orders, or those orders which are conferred without the imposition of hands.

3 Cf. Letter 199, Canons 24 and 41. In the present case, the widow was evidently not enrolled among the widows of the Church, was not yet sixty years of age, and was not subject to the jurisdiction of parents or masters. Therefore, she was free to marry. Cf. also Canon 30, especially notes 37 and 38. Balsamon considers that Canon 53 refers to a widow who wished to remarry, but feared to arouse the opposition of her children or the relatives of her first husband. Hence, she pretended to have been abducted, while as a matter of fact she had gone voluntarily with her future husband with the intention of marrying him. St. Basil's decision is that, since she is free to marry and really intended matrimony when she went to live with him, she is not subject to punishment on that account nor is the deception which she practiced such as to warrant public penance.

4 Cf. Letter 188, Canon 1, notes 44 and 45.

involuntary murders[5] and I am unable to say more about them. However, it is the privilege of your Intelligence to extend or even to lessen the penalties according to the particular circumstances of the case.[6]

(55) Those who march out against robbers, if they are of the laity, are excluded from the communion of the Good Gift, but, if they are clergy, they are deposed from their orders. For it is said: 'Everyone who takes the sword will perish by the sword.'[7]

(56) He who has committed voluntary murder and afterwards has repented shall not partake of the Blessed Sacrament for twenty years.[8] And the twenty years shall be divided thus in his case. For four years he ought to weep as a penitent of the first degree, standing outside the door of the house of prayer and asking the faithful who enter to pray for him, confessing his transgression. And after the four years he will be received among the hearers, and for five years will go out with them. Then for seven years he will go out, praying with those in the rank of prostrates. For four years he will only stand with the faithful, but will not receive Holy Communion. However, after these have been completed he will partake of the sacraments.

(57) He who has unintentionally killed someone shall not partake of the Blessed Sacrament for ten years.[9] And

5 Cf. Letter 188, Canon 8.

6 Cf. Letter 217, Canons 74 and 84.

7 Cf. Matt. 26.52.

8 St. Basil is more lenient in this regard than the Synod of Ancyra, which permitted Communion to be given to wilful murderers only at the end of their lives. Cf. Hefele, *History of the Church,* 1.220-221.

9 The Council of Ancyra shows more leniency than St. Basil here, imposing only a five years' penalty for unintentional murder. Cf. Hefele, *op. cit.* 1.221. The Benedictine editors think that St. Basil's punishment of ten years was not imposed for all cases of involuntary murder, but for those only which he says approached voluntary murder. Cf. Letter 188, Canon 8.

the ten years shall be divided thus in his case. For two years he shall weep as a penitent of the first degree, and for three years he shall continue to be among the hearers, for four in the rank of prostrates, for one year he shall only stand, and in the following be admitted to the sacred rites.

(58) The adulterer[10] shall not partake of the Blessed Sacrament for fifteen years;[11] weeping for four years, being a hearer for five, in the rank of prostrates for four, and standing without Communion for two.

(59) The fornicator[12] shall not partake of the Blessed

10 The Council of Elvira (Canon 69) had sentenced the married man who had committed adultery once to five years' penance. Cf. Hefele, *op. cit.* 1.15. A married man was punished for adultery when he had sinned with a married woman, but for fornication if the woman was unmarried. Cf. Letter 199, Canon 21.

11 The Council of Elvira (Canon 47) had decreed that a married man who had frequently committed this sin was to be given Communion before death if he promised to amend his ways; if, however, he should recover and again fall into the same sin, he was not to be given Communion even *in articulo mortis.* Cf. Hefele, *op. cit.* 1.157. The adulterer was given a seven-years' penance by Canon 20 of Ancyra. Cf. Hefele, *op. cit.* 1.219-220. St. Basil's legislation is more severe than either of these earlier ordinances.

12 The Greek commentators, Balsamon and Zonaras, consider that St. Basil has changed the earlier legislation of the Fathers, who, he said in Canon 22, imposed a four years' penance on the fornicator. Here, he intends to impose a severer penance for the sin. The Benedictine editors, however, would distinguish two kinds of fornication: one, which is committed by two unmarried people, as mentioned by St. Basil in Canon 22, and for which four years' penance is prescribed; the other, which is committed by a married man with an unmarried woman, as mentioned by St. Basil in the present canon, and for which seven-years' penance is prescribed. They confirm this interpretation from Canons 21 and 77. In the former St. Basil states that the married man who has intercourse with an unmarried woman is adjudged a fornicator and not an adulterer by the canons. He says, however, that in this case the penance for fornication is prolonged. In Canon 77 St. Basil says that such a man is really an adulterer according to the sentence of the Lord, but that according to the canons he is subjected to seven years' penance and not to the fifteen years' prescribed for adultery. This seems a consistent and reasonable explanation.

Sacrament for seven years; weeping for two, being a hearer for two, in the rank of prostrates for two, and for one standing only; in the eighth year he will be admitted to Communion.

(60) She who has professed virginity and has been unfaithful to her promise shall complete the length of time allotted for the sin of adultery[13] in a life spent in continence. The same holds also in the case of those who have professed the life of monks and have fallen.

(61) If the thief, after having repented, should accuse himself of his own accord, he will be debarred for one year from partaking of the Blessed Sacrament only; but, if he should be convicted, for two years. The time will be divided for him into a period of prostrating and one of standing; and then let him be considered worthy of Communion.

(62) He who commits shameful deeds with men will be allotted the time prescribed for him who transgresses by adultery.[14]

(63) He who admits his shameful behavior with animals will observe the same time in penance.[15]

(64) The perjurer will not partake of Communion for ten years;[16] for two years weeping, for three being a hearer, for four among the prostrates, and for one year standing only; and then he will be considered worthy of Communion.

(65) He who confesses witchcraft or poisoning will do penance the length of time prescribed for homicide,[17] being treated as one who has accused himself of that sin.[18]

---

13 Cf. Letter 199, Canon 18.
14 I.e., fifteen years.
15 This is less severe than the legislation of Ancyra, which (Canon 16) had prescribed a twenty years' punishment for bestiality.
16 Canon 74 qualifies the legislation of the present canon.
17 I.e., for twenty years.

(66) The grave-robber shall not receive Communion for ten years; weeping for two, being a hearer for three, among the prostrates for four, standing for one year, and then being admitted.

(67) Incest between brother and sister will incur the penalty for the length of time prescribed for the murderer.[19]

(68) The uniting in marriage of persons within the prohibited degrees of kinship, if it should be discovered to have taken place in sin, will receive the penalty prescribed for adulterers.[20]

(69) A lector, if he should have intercourse with his betrothed before marriage, after being suspended for a year, will be allowed to read,[21] remaining without promotion.[22]

---

18 Cf. Canon 56. According to the Council of Elvira (Canon 6) he who caused the death of another by witchcraft or sorcery would not be received to communion even at the end of his life. Cf. Hefele, *op. cit.* 1.140. The Council of Ancyra (Canon 24) had prescribed a five years' penance for those who foretold the future, followed pagan customs, or admitted people to their homes in order to discover magic remedies. Cf. Hefele, *op. cit.* 1.221.

19 I.e., twenty years. Cf. Canon 56. Aristenus notices that St. Basil is here speaking of a full brother and sister. In Canon 75 he prescribes a twelve years' penance for one who has had sexual relations with his half-sister. Cf. *PG* 138.763. The Council of Elvira denied Communion even at death to him who was guilty of incest by marriage with his daughter-in-law. Cf. Hefele, *op. cit.* 1.165.

20 I.e., either seven or fifteen years, according to the degree of consanguinity violated, in the opinion of Aristenus. He distinguishes two classes of adultery. The first, that in which a married man has intercourse with an unmarried woman, is punished with a seven years' penance, and the other, committed with a married woman, which is punished with a fifteen years' penance. Cf. *PG* 138.763-766. Hence, the lighter adultery is identical with the graver fornication, which is also punished with a seven years' penance. Cf. Canon 59 and note 12. This view is supported by the fact that in Canon 78 St. Basil imposes on him who marries two sisters a seven years' penance, the same as he imposes on the unfaithful husband to whom he refers as a fornicator in Canon 21.

21 The Scriptures, the proper office of the lector.

22 He must remain a lector all his life, and may not be ordained to the diaconate or the priesthood.

But, if he has sought illicit love without betrothal, he will be deposed from the ministry. It is the same in the case of a minister.[23]

(70) A deacon who has incurred defilement by his lips[24] and has confessed that he has sinned to this extent will be debarred from public service; but he will be considered worthy of partaking of the Blessed Sacrament with the deacons. The same holds true also for the presbyter. But, if it is discovered that anyone has sinned more than this, in whatever order he may be he shall be deposed.

(71) He who was privately aware of any of the aforementioned sins and did not confess, but was convicted, shall remain under the penalty for the same length of time as the doer of the evils.[25]

(72) He who has given himself over to diviners or any such persons[26] shall be allotted the time prescribed for the murderer.

(73) He who has denied Christ and transgressed against the mystery of salvation ought to weep and to do penance

---

23 I.e., a subdeacon according to Balsamon and Zonaras (*PG* 138.765-770); a cleric in the minor orders which were conferred without the imposition of hands, according to Aristenus (*PG* 138.770). The Benedictine editors prefer the former opinion and point out that '*hypērétēs*' is certainly a subdeacon in Letter 54.

24 A sin which one has expressed the intention of committing but has never committed, according to the Benedictine editors. The Greek commentators (*PG* 138.769-774) interpret this as lascivious kisses, etc., but this seems less probable.

25 According to Balsamon, only he who had been an accomplice in the crime was bound by this canon to confess. Cf. *PG* 138.775. Watkins (*A History of Penance* 1.324-325), understands the regulation as binding on all men who had a knowledge of the sin of any other man, and calls it a 'grossly unfair' provision. Zonaras thinks that all the sins of the clergy had to be reported by him who had knowledge of them. Cf. *PG* 138.775. The most convincing argument against Watkins' interpretation is the fact that, as he admits, there is no historical evidence that any such law was observed. Balsamon's interpretation seems the more reasonable here.

26 Cf. Canon 65 and note 17.

during the whole time of his life.[27] At the moment at which he departs from this life he will be considered worthy of the Holy Eucharist[28] because of trust in the mercy of God.

(74) Yet, if each one of those who have fallen into the sins written above should be earnest in doing penance, he who by the mercy of God has been entrusted with the power to loose and to bind will not be deserving of condemnation[29] if, on seeing the excessive penance of the sinner, he would show mercy to the extent of lessening the time of the penalty. The account in sacred Scripture[30] makes known to us that those who do penance with greater suffering quickly receive the mercy of God.

75) Let him who has been defiled with his own sister on the father's or mother's side not be permitted to be present in the house of prayer until he shall cease from his wicked and unlawful conduct.[31] After having come to an awareness of that dread sin, let him weep during a period of three years, standing at the door of the houses of prayer and begging the people entering for prayer, each one, to offer with sympathy for him earnest petitions to the Lord. And after this let him be admitted for another three-year period to hearing only, and, although hearing the Scriptures and the doctrine, let him be put out and not considered worthy of prayer. Then, if he has sought with tears and prostrated himself before the Lord with contrition of heart and very

27 This sin of apostasy is the only one for which St. Basil demands lifelong penance. Cf. Canon 81 and notes 37, 38, and 39.

28 Canon 13 of Nice had forbidden anyone who had requested Holy Viaticum on his deathbed to be deprived of it. Cf. Hefele, *op. cit.* 1.419-420.

29 This canon sheds a softer light on the severe penitential decrees found in the rest of this letter.

30 St. Basil here refers to the stories of Manassa, Ezechia, and others, according to Zonaras. Cf. *PG* 138.783.

31 Cf. Canon 67 and note 19.

much humility, let prostration be granted to him for another three years. And thus, when he shall show fruits worthy of repentance, let him be admitted in the tenth year to the prayer of the faithful, but without Communion. After standing for two years for prayer with the faithful let him finally be considered worthy of partaking of the Good Gift.

(76) The same rule holds also for those who take their own daughters-in-law.[32]

(77) He who leaves the wife lawfully joined to him and unites himself with another, according to the sentence of the Lord lies under the charge of adultery.[33] And it has been ruled by our Fathers that such should weep for one year, should be hearers for a period of two years, should be prostrates for a period of three years, and in the seventh stand with the faithful. And then they will be considered worthy of Holy Communion if they do penance with tears.

(78) And let the same rule be observed also in the case of those who take two sisters,[34] even if at different times.

(79) They who rage with passion for their stepmothers are subject to the same canon as they who rage after their sisters.

(80) The Fathers left polygamy[35] unmentioned, as something beastlike and altogether foreign to the human race. And it occurs to us that the sin is somewhat greater than fornication. Therefore, it is reasonable that such persons be subjected to the canons, that is to say, having wept for one

32 The Council of Elvira (Canon 36) had decreed that he who married his daughter-in-law was to be adjudged guilty of incest and was to remain without Communion even at the end of his life. Cf. Hefele, *op. cit.* 1.165.

33 Cf. Letter 188, Canon 9, and Letter 199, Canon 21.

34 Cf. Letter 199, Canon 23 and notes.

35 Balsamon and Zonaras interpret polygamy here as meaning four or more successive marriages. Cf. *PG* 138.789-794. The Benedictine editors, however, think that it includes also trigamy. Cf. Letter 188, Canon 4 and notes, also Letter 199, Canon 50 and notes.

year, and having been among the prostrates for three years, that they be then received.[36]

(81) Since many in the incursion of the barbarians violated their faith in God, swearing heathen oaths and eating certain unlawful foods which had been offered to them in the magic temples of the idols, let regulations be made for them according to the canons already put forth by our Fathers.[37] Those who were subjected to harsh constraint through torture and not enduring the sufferings were drawn into a denial are not to be received for three years, and are to be hearers for two years, and after they have been prostrates for three years they are then to be received into communion.[38] But they who betrayed their faith in God without great constraint,[39] and touched the table of the demons, and swore heathen oaths are to be kept out for three years, to be hearers for two, and, after praying in the grade of prostrates for three, and for another three standing with the faithful for prayer, they are then to be admitted to the communion of the Good Gift.

(82) And concerning those who have committed perjury,

36 I.e., to standing without communion according to Balsamon and Zonaras (cf. *PG* 138.789-794), but to Holy Communion according to Aristenus (cf. *PG* 138.794). The former opinion is more conformable to Canon 4, where a five years' penance was prescribed. If the polygamists are placed for one year among the 'standers,' perfect harmony is established between this canon and Canon 4.

37 Of Ancyra, according to the Benedictine editors. In Canons 4, 5, 6, 7, and 8 of that synod, various penalties, less severe than those of St. Basil, were laid down for those who had sacrificed, taken part in pagan festivities, etc. Cf. Hefele, *op. cit.* 1.205-209.

38 Although St. Basil prescribes eight years of penance, the Council of Ancyra (Canon 4) punished those who had sacrificed under compulsion for six years if they had done it willingly, for four years if they had performed the task enjoined upon them sorrowfully (Canon 5). Cf. Hefele, *op. cit.* 1.205.

39 The Council of Ancyra (Canon 6) punished with a six years' penance those who yielded under the mere threat of confiscation of their property or of exile and offered sacrifices. Cf. Hefele, *op. cit.* 1.206.

if they transgressed their oaths because of force and constraint, they are subject to lighter penalties, and therefore are to be received after six years. But, if without constraint they betrayed their faith, only after weeping for two years, being hearers for two years, praying in the grade of prostrates for five years, and for another two years being received without Holy Communion into the fellowship of prayer, and finally, after having shown, of course, a worthy repentance, shall they be restored to the communion of the Body of Christ.[40]

(83) Let those who consult oracles and follow the practices of the Gentiles, or introduce persons into their houses for the discovery of remedies and for purification, fall under the canon of six years. After having wept for one year, been hearer for one year, prostrate for three years, and standing with the faithful for one year, so let them be received.[41]

(84) But we write all these things for the purpose of testing the fruits of repentance. Not entirely by time do we judge these matters, but we give heed to the manner of the repentance. If men are with difficulty restrained from their own ways, and desire to serve the pleasures of the flesh rather than the Lord, and do not accept the manner of life according to the Gospel, there is no common ground between them and

40 There seems to be a discrepancy between this canon, which imposes an eleven years' penance on perjury, and Canon 64, which imposes a ten years' penance on the same sin.

41 As Balsamon explains, this canon does not contradict the legislation laid down in Canon 65 and 72 on the same subject, where a penance of twenty years was imposed. Canon 65 spoke of those who with malicious intent had prepared poisonous drugs for men. Canon 72 spoke of those who, hiring themselves out to a magician or a seer, had co-operated directly with him in the practice of his art, while the present canon speaks only of those whose co-operation is more or less indirect in an attempt to procure remedies for ills by means of magic. Cf. *PG* 138.199-804. The Council of Ancyra (Canon 21) grouped together those who foretold the future, followed pagan customs, and admitted into their houses magicians in order to discover magical remedies, or to perform expiations, and sentenced all to a five years' penance. Cf. Hefele, *op. cit.* 1.221.

us. For, in the midst of a disobedient and contrary people we have been taught to hear: 'Save thy soul.'[42] Let us not, therefore, permit ourselves to be destroyed with such men, but, fearing the stern judgment, and keeping the terrible day of retribution of the Lord before our eyes, let us be unwilling to perish by the sins of others. If the terrifying works of the Lord did not teach us, nor such scourges lead us to a realization that the Lord had abandoned us because of our sinfulness and handed us over into the hands of the barbarians, and that the people were led away captive among the enemies and were given over to dispersion because those bearing the name of Christ dared these things; if they have not known or perceived that the wrath of God has come upon us because of these things, what ground do we have in common with them? Yet, we ought to testify to them night and day both in public and in private. Let us not, however, permit ourselves to be led away likewise by their wickedness, praying especially to win them and to snatch them away from the snare of the Evil One. But, if we are unable to do this, let us strive to save our own souls, at least, from everlasting condemnation.

218. To Amphilochius, Bishop of Iconium[1]

Our brother Aelian[2] by himself brought to a successful conclusion the business about which he had come, without need of any assistance from us. Moreover, he bestowed on

42 Cf. Gen. 19.17.

1 For Amphilochius, see note 1 of the preceding letter. This letter was written in the autumn of 375. Cf. Loofs, *op. cit.* 21.

2 Otherwise unknown.

us a twofold pleasure in bringing a letter from your Reverence and in furnishing us an opportunity of writing a letter to you. Therefore, through him we greet your genuine and inimitable Charity, and we urge you to pray for us, who now, if ever, have need of the assistance of your prayers. My body, shattered from the journey to the Pontus, is unbearably afflicted by illness. Yet, this I have wanted for a long time to make known to your Intelligence (it is not that, hindered by another more important cause, I forgot); I am mentioning it now in order that you may deign to send a zealous man to Lycia to investigate who are the followers of the true faith. Indeed, we must not by any chance neglect them, if that is true which one of the pious men coming from there has related to us—that they, having been entirely alienated from the belief of the Asians,[3] are willing for us to enroll them as fellow communicants. Now, if anyone intends to go, let him seek out in Corydalia,[4] Alexander, the bishop, from the monks; in Limyra,[5] Diatimus; in Myra,[6] Tatian and Polemo[7] and Macarius, the presbyters; in Patara,[8] Bishop Eudemus;[9] in Telmesus,[10] Hilarius, the bishop, and in Phelus, Lollianus, the bishop.

A certain person commended these and several more to us as men who are sound in the faith, and I felt very grateful to God if there are any at all in the region of Asia who are clear of the evil of the heretics. If, then, it is possible, let us in the meanwhile make an investigation without letters; and, if we are convinced, then we shall also send a letter and

3 This has reference to the Roman province of Asia. Cf. Acts 20.4.
4 Now Hadginella, on the road between Lystra and Patara.
5 Now Phineka.
6 Cf. Acts 27.5. The Vulgate here reads 'Lystra' instead of 'Myra.'
7 Afterwards Bishop of Myra.
8 Cf. Acts 21.1.
9 Bishop at Constantinople in 381.
10 Now Macri.

make haste to invite one of them to a conference with us. May all things turn out advantageously for your most beloved church of Iconium. Through you we greet all the honorable clergy and those who are with your Reverence.

219. To the Clergy of Samosata[1]

The Lord determines all things for us by measure and by weight[2] and lays upon us temptations not exceeding our strength, but tests the champions of piety by adversity, not allowing them to be tempted beyond what they are able to bear.[3] He gives for drink tears in measure[4] to those who ought to show whether in their afflictions they preserve gratitude toward God. He has manifested His benignity especially in His dispensation concerning you, for He did not permit such a persecution by the enemy to be inflicted on you as could pervert or shake any from faith in Christ. In fact, having matched you with shallow and easily conquered adversaries, He prepared for you the reward of patient endurance in your victory over them. But the common Enemy of our life, he who opposes the goodness of God by his wiles, when he saw that you, like a mighty wall, regarded the attack from the outside with contempt, contrived, as I hear, that there should arise among you yourselves certain grievances against each other and meanness of spirit. Although these at first are slight and easy to cure, yet, increasing by contention as time advances, they are inclined to turn into something entirely incurable. I have hastened, therefore, to warn you by this letter. If it had been possible, I myself

1 This letter was written in 375.
2 Cf. Wisd. 11.21.
3 Cf. 1 Cor. 10.13.
4 Cf. Ps. 79.6.

would have been present and would have besought you personally. Since, however, circumstances do not permit this, we tender you this letter in lieu of the olive branch of the suppliant, in order that, showing regard for our requests, you may bring to an end all contention with each other and quickly send me the good tidings that you have dismissed the grounds of common complaint.

I wish your Intelligence to realize this, that he is great before God who humbly submits to his neighbor and, having no cause for shame, allows charges against himself, even if they should not be true, for the sake of bestowing upon the Church of God the great blessing of peace. So, let there be among you a noble strife as to who first will be deemed worthy of being called the son of God, procuring this honor for himself through his peacemaking. Moreover, the bishop dearly beloved of God has written to you what is proper, and he will write again what concerns him. But, we, also, because it has been granted to us up to now to be closer to you, are not able to have no care for your affairs. Hence, when our most pious brother Theodorus, the subdeacon, came, saying that the Church was in a state of grief and disorder, being exceedingly crushed and smitten in heart with the most grievous pain, we could not be silent, but we urged you to cast aside every accusation against each other and to obtain peace for yourselves, in order that you may not afford pleasure to your opponents nor betray the glory of the Church which now is proclaimed to the whole world—that you all so live in one body as if ruled by one soul and one heart. We salute all the people of God through your Reverence, both those in positions of honor and in political offices, as well as the entire body of the clergy; and we urge you to remain ever your old selves. In fact, we ask for nothing more, because you yourselves precluded further improvement by your display of good works.

220. To the People of Beroea[1]

The Lord has granted a great consolation to those who are deprived of personal contact with each other, namely, communication by letter, from which it is possible to learn, not the characteristics of the body, but the disposition of the soul itself. Hence, having just now received a letter from your Reverences, we became acquainted with you and at the same time conceived in our heart a love for you, without the need of a long time to form an acquaintance. For we were enkindled with love for the beauty of your souls from the very thoughts contained in your letter. In fact, besides the letter, which was so beautiful, the friendliness of the brothers who were making the negotiations showed us still more clearly the spirit among you. Our most beloved and pious fellow presbyter Acacius,[2] recounting more details than the letter, and bringing your daily struggle and your vigorous opposition for religion's sake under our very eyes, produced such wonder in us and roused so great a desire for the personal enjoyment of your excellent qualities that we have prayed to the Lord that there may be at some time an opportunity for us to become acquainted with your affairs through our own experience. He reported to us, indeed, not only the exactitude of those of you who are entrusted with the ministry of the altar, but also the harmony existing among all the people, the nobility of manners of the rulers of the city and of its chief officials, and the sincerity of their disposition toward God, so that we proclaimed the Church

1 Beroea in Syria. This letter was written in 375.

2 Letter 256 is written to Acacius and others to condole with them on the loss of their monastery, which had been burnt by the heretics. This is doubtless the same Acacius who, together with Paulus, urged Epiphanius to produce a work on heresies, and also the one who was Bishop of Beroea in Syria from 379-436.

blessed which was composed of such men. And we now pray that spiritual tranquility be given to you in a greater degree in order that in the time of rest you may receive the reward of those works manifested in the present time of struggle. It is natural, somehow, that things which are disagreeable when experienced bring pleasure when they are recalled. But, as to your present state, we urge you not to become faint-hearted nor to grow weary because of continual sufferings. For, near are the crowns and near the support of the Lord. Do not throw away that which you have obtained by previous labor; do not render useless the toil proclaimed throughout all the world. Human affairs are short-lived; 'All flesh is grass, and all the glory of man as the flower of the grass. The grass is withered, and the flower is fallen; but the word of our Lord endureth forever.'[3] Clinging to the enduring precept, let us despise the passing fancy. Your example has restored many churches. You have, unawares, secured for yourselves much recompense because you have aroused the more inexperienced to a like zeal. And rich is the Rewarder and able to bestow upon you worthy recompense for your struggles.

221. To the People of Beroea[1]

We knew you heretofore, most beloved friends, because of your widely proclaimed piety and the crown of your confession of Christ. And perhaps, one of you might say: 'And who is he who has carried these reports to such a distant land?' The Lord Himself, who, having set His worshipers

3 Isa. 40.6-8 (Septuagint).

1 This letter was written in 375.

like a lamp upon a lampstand, makes them shine forth through the whole world. Is it not usual for the prize of victory to proclaim the winner among the contestants, and the design of the work the designer? And, if in these and such like things the memory endures unforgettable, as regards those who live piously in Christ, concerning whom the Lord Himself says: 'Whosoever shall glorify me, him will I glorify,'[2] how is it possible that He will not make them illustrious and renowned before all, overspreading with the rays of the sun the splendor of their dazzling brightness? Moreover, you have again inspired in us a greater longing to see you by deeming us worthy of a letter, and such a letter. In addition to your previous struggles for religion, you have in it abounded in a rich and more vigorous strength of spirit in behalf of the true faith. For these things we rejoice with you and we pray that the God of the universe, whose contest it is, who assigns the arena, and through whom are given the crowns, may infuse zeal, may provide strength of soul, and may bring your work to a final approval in His sight.

222. To the Chalcidians[1]

Your Reverences' letter, coming to us in our time of affliction, became a relief such as water frequently is to race horses, when poured into their mouths at high noon in the midst of their course, as they draw in the dust with their violent panting. We have recovered breath after our continuous trials, and at the same time we have been strengthened

2 Cf. 1 Kings 2.30.

1 Syrian Chalcis is now Kinesrin. According to the Benedictine editors (*Vit. Bas.* Chap. 33), this letter was carried by Acacius along with Letter 221. It was written in 375.

by your words, while by the remembrance of your struggles we have received more power to endure without yielding the conflict lying before us. Indeed, the conflagration which has spread over many parts of the East is already stealthily creeping into our country and, having burned everything around, it is endeavoring to fasten also upon the churches in Cappadocia, which the smoke from the neighboring places[2] is meanwhile moving to tears. At present, moreover, it is hastening to seize upon us, too, but may the Lord divert it by the breath of His mouth and may He check the flame of this wicked fire. For, who is so cowardly and unmanly or so unprepared for the labors of the athlete as not to be strengthened for the contest by your acclamation and not to pray to be proclaimed victor with you? You have been the first to strip yourselves in the race of religion and you have beaten off many attacks in the bouts with the heretics; moreover, you have borne the great heat of trials, both you, the leaders of the Church to whom the service of the altar has been entrusted, and every individual of the laity, even the more influential. And this, in fact, is especially admirable in you and deserving of all praise, that you are all one in the Lord, some being leaders toward the good, and others united followers. Therefore, you are superior to the attacks of your adversaries, since in no member do you provide a hold for your antagonists.

For this grace we pray night and day to the King of Ages, to preserve the people in the integrity of the faith, and to preserve the clergy for them as a sound head placed at the top and itself supplying foresight for the members of the body subject to it. For, when the eyes perform their functions, then the labor of the hands is skillful, and the movement of the feet without stumbling, and no part of the body is

2 This apparently refers to the general spread of heresy throughout the East, not to any particular persecution.

deprived of its proper care. Therefore, we urge you, as you are doing and intend to do, to cling to one another, and you to whom has been entrusted the care of souls to hold together each and every one and to cherish them as your beloved children. And the people we urge to preserve toward you the reverence and honor owed to fathers, in order that in the proper maintenance of the Church your strength as well as the foundation of the faith in Christ may be preserved, and that the name of God may be glorified, and that the blessing of charity may abound and be multiplied. And may we hear and rejoice in your advancement in God. Moreover, if we are still bidden to dwell in the flesh in this world, may we at some time see you in the peace of God. But, if we are commanded soon to depart from this life, may we see you in the splendor of the saints, crowned along with those who are held in honor for patient endurance and for every example of good works.

223. Against Eustathius of Sebaste[1]

'A time to keep silence, and a time to speak,' says the maxim in Ecclesiastes.[2] Surely, then, since the time of silence has been long enough, it is now opportune to open our mouth for a disclosure of the truth concerning matters which are misunderstood. The great Job also long endured his misfortunes in silence, in this very manner displaying his courage, remaining firm under the most grievous sufferings,[3]

---

1 On Eustathius of Sebaste and his relation with St. Basil, cf. Letters 79 and 119. This letter, answering Eustathius, who with a view of proving St. Basil himself a heretic had published with alterations a letter written by St. Basil to the heresiarch Apollinaris twenty-five years before, when both were laymen, was written in 375.

2 Eccle. 3.7.

3 Cf. Job 1.1ff.

but, when he had struggled sufficiently in silence, and had persevered in hiding the pain in the depth of his heart, then he opened his mouth and uttered those words known to all. And so for us this third[4] year of silence has been in emulation of the Prophet who made the boast: 'I became as a man that heareth not and that hath no reproofs in his mouth.'[5] Therefore, we buried in the depth of our heart the pain caused us by the calumny. For, truly, calumny humiliates a man, and calumny troubles the poor man.[6] Although the evil of calumny is so great that it brings down both the perfect man (this the Scripture means by the word 'man') from his height, and the poor man (that is, the one who lacks great learning, as it seems to the Prophet[7] who says: 'Perhaps they are poor . . . ,' therefore they will not hear; 'I will go to the great ones,' meaning by 'the poor' those wanting in intelligence, and here, of course, those not yet made orderly in the inner man nor having attained to the perfect measure of their age;[8] these, the proverb says, are troubled and made to waver), nevertheless, I thought that I should bear my grievances in silence, awaiting some rectification through the deeds themselves. I believed that these things had been said against us not from any malice, but from ignorance of the truth.

Since, however, I see that the enmity is increasing with time and that they show no repentance for what they said in the beginning and do not manifest any solicitude as to how they will make amends for the past, but that they renew their efforts and organize themselves to attain the aim which

4 Since 372. St. Basil had suffered much at the hands of Theodotus, Bishop of Nicopolis, because of Eustathius' vacillations of doctrinal belief.

5 Ps. 37.15.

6 Cf. Eccle. 7.8.

7 Cf. Jer. 5.4,5.

8 Cf. Eph. 4.13.

they originally adopted—to afflict our life and to besmirch our reptutation with the brethren—no longer is the soundness of silence evident. Still, the saying of Isaias[9] has come to my mind: 'I have kept silence, I shall not always keep silence and endure, shall I? I have been patient as a woman in labor.' May it be that we both receive the reward for our silence and acquire some power for the refutation, so that, when we have given our proofs, we may dry up this bitter torrent of falsehood poured out against us; also, that we may say: 'Our soul hath passed through a torrent,'[10] and this, too: 'If it had not been that the Lord was with us, when men rose up against us, perhaps they had swallowed us up alive, perhaps the waters had swallowed us up.'[11]

After I had wasted much time in vanity and had spent nearly all my youth in the vain labor in which I was engaged, occupying myself in acquiring a knowledge made foolish by God,[12] when at length, as if aroused from a deep sleep, I looked upon the wondrous light of the truth of the Gospel and saw the futility of the wisdom 'of the rulers of this world who are passing away,'[13] having mourned deeply my piteous life, I prayed that guidance be given me for my introduction to the doctrines of religion. And before all things else, I was careful to amend my ways, which for a long time had been perverted by my companionship with the indifferent.[14] Accordingly, having read the Gospel and having seen clearly there that the greatest means for perfection is the selling of one's possessions,[15] the sharing with needy brethren,

---

9 Cf. Isa. 42.14.
10 Ps. 123.5.
11 Ps. 123.2-4.
12 St. Basil here refers to his years of study, especially in the schools of rhetoric. Cf., also, 1 Cor. 1.20.
13 Cf. 1 Cor. 2.6.
14 Cf. 1 Cor. 15.33.
15 Cf. Matt. 19.21; also, Mark 10.21; Luke 12.33, 18.22.

the complete renouncing of solicitude for this life, and the refusing of the soul to be led astray by any affection for things of earth, I prayed to find some one of the brethren who had chosen this way of life, so as to pass with him over life's brief and troubled waters.

And in truth, I found many in Alexandria and many throughout the rest of Egypt, and others in Palestine and Coele Syria and Mesopotamia, the self-discipline of whose manner of living I admired. I marveled, too, at their endurance in toil; I was amazed at their attention at prayers, their victory over sleep, being overcome by no physical necessity, always preserving lofty and unconquered the resolution of their soul, in hunger and thirst, in cold and nakedness,[16] not paying attention to the body nor consenting to waste any thought on it, but, as if living in flesh not one's own,[17] they showed by their deeds what it is to dwell among those on this earth[18] and what to have their citizenship[19] in heaven. I admired these things and I considered the life of the men blessed because they show by their works that they bear around in their body the dying of Jesus.[20] And I prayed that I, also, as far as was possible, might be a zealous follower of those men.

Therefore, when I saw some men in our country trying to emulate their deeds, I thought that I had found some assistance for my own salvation, and I considered the things seen as an indication of the things unseen.[21] Since that which lies hidden within each of us is not apparent, I thought that

16 Cf. 2 Cor. 11.27.
17 Cf. Thuc. 1.70: *allotriōtátois toîs sōmasin chrēsthai* ('to deal with one's body as if it belonged to another').
18 Cf. Ps. 118.19; also. Heb. 11.13.
19 Cf. Phil. 3.20.
20 Cf. 2 Cor. 4.10.
21 Cf. Aristotle, *Nic. Ethics* 2.2.6.

a lowly garment was sufficient indication of a lowly spirit, and the coarse mantle, the girdle, and the sandals of untanned hide sufficed to give full assurance to me. Moreover, although many were attempting to lead me away from association with these, I did not permit it, seeing that they preferred a life of hardship to one of pleasure; because of their extraordinary manner of life, I was filled with zeal in their regard. For this reason I did not admit the charges concerning their doctrines, although many affirmed that they did not have correct notions about God but, having been instructed by the leader[22] of the present heresy, were secretly sowing his teachings. Since I myself had never heard these things, I believed that those who reported them were slanderers. But then we were called to take charge of the Church. The guards and spies of our life, given to us under a pretext of assistance and affectionate fellowship, I pass over in silence in order that I may not seem either to be bringing myself into discredit by saying what is incredible, or, if I am believed, to be inspiring those who believe me with hatred for mankind. And this would almost have happened to me if the mercies of God had not quickly overtaken me. For I became suspicious of almost everybody, and, being smitten in soul by their treacherous wounds, I believed that there was nothing trustworthy in anyone. Nevertheless, it seemed that for a time we had some semblance of intimacy with them. And even once or twice we had conferences concerning doctrines,[23] and, having expressed the same opinions, we seemed not to be at variance. In this way they found out

---

22 Arius.

23 In 372 St. Basil arranged a meeting with Eustathius at Sebaste to satisfy the suspicions of Theodotus, Bishop of Nicopolis, against himself and Eustathius. The two agreed substantially on matters of faith, but Eustathius refused to sign an agreement and later denied having made it. In a second meeting in 373, although he signed, he broke his promise and began openly to attack St. Basil.

that we made the same statements concerning faith in God which they had always heard from us. For, even if other matters are deserving of our groans, yet of this one thing at least I dare to boast in the Lord, that never have I held false opinions[24] concerning God, nor did I, thinking otherwise than now, learn differently later. But the concept of God which in childhood I received from my blessed mother[25] and from grandmother Macrina, this unfolding more completely, I have held within me, for, on arriving at full reason I did not exchange one teaching for another, but confirmed those principles which they had handed over to me. Just as the growing seed from a small size becomes larger, yet is the same one in itself, not changing in kind, but made perfect through growth, so I consider that in my case the same doctrine has grown through progressive stages, not that the one which I now hold was made in place of that which I held from the beginning. Therefore, let them, mindful of the judgment seat of Christ, examine their own conscience: whether they have ever heard anything else from us contrary to what we are now saying, they who have now spread abroad that we are heretical, and have deafened the ears of all by invective letters which they have written against us. It is for this reason I was obliged to make this defense.

We are accused of blasphemy against God, although we cannot be convicted either from any writing which we ourselves formerly put out or from any unwritten words which we have spoken, always openly, to the churches of God. And no witness has been found who says that he has heard from us any sacrilegious words uttered in private. Whence, then, are we judged, if we neither write anything sacrilegious nor

24 St. Basil was accused by Eustathius in public assemblies of holding unorthodox views on the divinity of the Holy Spirit.
25 Emmelia.

preach anything injurious nor in our conversations in private pervert those whom we meet? O novel fabrication! 'A certain man[26] in Syria,' it says, 'wrote something not at all piously; and you wrote to him twenty years ago and more. Conequently, you are an accomplice of the man, and let the charges against him become also against you.' But, O friend of the truth, you who have been taught that a lie is the child of the Devil, how have you been persuaded that that letter is mine? You have not written, nor have you asked, nor have you been informed by me, who am able to tell you the truth. Even if the letter were mine, whence is it evident that this writing which has now fallen into your hands is contemporaneous with my letter? Who is he who has told you that this is a writing of twenty years ago? And how is it evident that it is the treatise of that man to whom my letter was sent? Moreover, if the man is the author and I wrote him a letter and the time of my letter and the treatise are the same, what is the proof that I accepted it in my mind and hold that opinion in myself?

Ask yourself: How often did you visit us at the monastery on the Iris River when, moreover, our brother Gregory, dearly beloved of God, was with me, pursuing the same goal of life as I was? Did you hear any such thing? Or did you receive any such impression either slight or weighty? How many days were we in the village on the other side of the river at my mother's home, living there as friends with each other and engaging in conversations night and day? Were we found to have anything akin to that in our views? And when we visited the blessed Silvanus[27] together, did not our journey include conversations concerning these matters? And

26 Apollinaris; cf. Letters 130 and 224.
27 Of Tarsus. Cf. Letters 34.

at Eusinoe,[28] when, as you were about to set out for Lampsacus[29] with several bishops, you summoned me, was not our conversation about faith? Were not your shorthand writers at hand all the time while I was dictating objections to the heresy? Were not the most genuine of your disciples with me all the time? When I visited the brotherhoods and passed the night with them in prayer, always speaking and listening without contention to matters pertaining to God, did I not provide exact proofs of my opinions? How, then, did your experience over so great a period of time seem of less value than a suspicion so unsound and weak? And who, in preference to you, should be witness of my state of mind? The statements which we made at Chalcedon pertaining to faith and those frequently advanced in Heraclea, and those earlier in the suburb at Caesarea, were they not all concordant on our part? Were they not all consistent with one another, except, as I have said, for some amplification being observed in the matters discussed due to progress, which is not a change from the worse to the better, but through additional knowledge a bringing to fulfillment of what was left unfinished? And how is it that you do not consider this, that 'the father shall not bear the iniquity of the son, nor shall the son bear the iniquity of the father,'[30] but each shall die in his own sin? Yet, he who is brought into discredit among you is neither a father to me, nor is he a son. He was neither my teacher nor my pupil. But, if it is necessary that the sins of the parents become the accusations against the

28 Perhaps Eusene, on the north coast of Pontus.

29 In 364, the year after St. Basil had been ordained presbyter and had written his work against Eunomius. The Council at Lampsacus (364), at which St. Basil was not present, repudiated the creeds of Ariminum and Constantinople (359 and 360), and reasserted the second Dedication Creed of Antioch of 341.

30 Cf. Ezech. 18.20.

children,[31] much more justly those of Arius must be charged against his disciples. And in the case of him who begot Aetius,[32] the heretic, the charges against the son must pass back upon the head of the father. If it is not just for anyone to be blamed for those things, surely it is much more just that we should not have to give an account for those who have nothing at all to do with us, even if they have actually sinned, and if they have written something that is worthy of condemnation. I must be pardoned if I mistrust what is said against them, since my own experience gives proof of the tendency of accusers to calumniate.

In fact, even if they began the slander against me because, having been deceived, they thought that I shared the opinion of the men who wrote those words of Sabellius which they themselves are circulating, they were not even in that case deserving of pardon, since before they had definite proofs they immediately attacked with blasphemies and wounded us who had done no wrong, not to mention our being bound to them by the closest friendship, and that a proof of their not being led by the Holy Spirit is the fact that among themselves they hold false beliefs. Indeed, it is proper for him who intends to cut himself off from friendship with a brother to meditate much and to endure many sleepless nights, as well as to seek the truth from God with many tears. The rulers of this world, in fact, when they are about to condemn some malefactor to death, draw aside the veils and summon the most experienced for a consideration of the facts lying before them, and spend much time, now looking to the severity of the law, now revering their common

31 Cf. Exod. 20.5.

32 Aetius was the first to carry the doctrines of Arius to their natural conclusion, maintaining in opposition to both the Homoousians and Homoiousians that the Son was unlike (*anómoios*) the Father. Hence, his followers were called Anomoeans.

human nature, lamenting much and deploring the necessity, and they become to all men public servants of the law through necessity and not men urging the condemnation according to their own pleasure. Of how much more zeal and solicitude and consultation with the many should he esteem the affair worthy who is about to break off from a long-confirmed friendship of the brethren? Yet, there is but one letter and that doubtful. For, not even they would say that they recognized it from the identifying handwriting of the signature who certainly did not receive in their hands the original, but a copy. Therefore, the charge comes from one letter, and that an old one. It is twenty years to the present time since anything was written to that man.[33] And in all the intervening time I have no better witnesses of my principles and life than the accusers who are now standing against me.

Yet, the letter is not responsible for the separation, but something else which I am ashamed to say is the pretext for the severance, and I would have kept silence forever if their recent acts had not forced me for the advantage of the many to a disclosure of their whole purpose. The good men thought that communion with us was an impediment to the recovery of their power. And, since they were prejudiced because of a certain outline of faith which we tendered them—not mistrusting their opinions (I admit it), but wishing to allay the suspicions against them which many of our like-minded brethren held—in order that nothing from that confession of faith might seem to prove for them a hindrance to their being received by the men now in power,[34] they renounced communion with us, and as an excuse for the

33 Apollinaris.

34 The Benedictine editors think that the reference here is to Euzoius, who was now in high favor with Valens.

separation this letter was invented. A very clear proof of what has been said is that, after having denounced us and composed the complaints against us as they wished, before writing to us, they sent the letter around everywhere. In fact, seven days before it reached my hands, the letter appeared in the possession of others, and these, having received it in their turn from others, were about to send it on. They had intended thus for one to hand it over to another, in order that they might exchange it quickly throughout the whole country. Moreover, this was told to us at that time by men who reported their actions to us with the greatest certainty, but we decided to keep silence until He who reveals the depths should make public their deeds by the clearest and most indisputable evidence.

224. To Genethlius, the Presbyter[1]

I received your Reverence's letter, and I approved the name which you aptly gave to the document composed by them, calling it a bill of divorce.[2] What defense, in truth, the authors, asserting that they have separated themselves from our love, have prepared for it before the tribunal of Christ which is not to be deceived I cannot imagine. They set forth the charge and inveighed violently against us and described in detail, not what was the truth, but what they wished, making a show of their own great humility and attributing to us inordinate arrogance on the ground that we did not receive those sent by them. Thus, all, or, not to speak rashly, at least most of what they have written are falsehoods, as if prevailing upon man and not God, and

1 Nothing more is known of Genethlius. This Letter was written in 375.
2 Cf. Deut. 24.3.

seeking to please man and not God, to whom nothing is more precious than truth. Then they attached heretical expressions to the letter against us, concealing the author of the impiety in order that the greater number and especially the more simple, since the accusation against us was placed before, might think that the words subjoined were ours because the name of the originator of the evil doctrines was kept secret by those artfully slandering us; it was left for the more guileless to suspect that we were the ones who either invented or wrote these expressions. Inasmuch, therefore, as you know these facts, we urge you not to be troubled yourself and to calm the agitation of those who are vacillating, although we know that our defense is hard to believe because the wicked blasphemies against us are already accepted by trustworthy persons.

Now, concerning the fact that those words which are being circulated as ours are not our words, I think that, although the feeling against us quite darkens their reasoning so that they are not conscious of what is advantageous, nevertheless, if they were asked by you, they would not proceed to such a degree of stubbornness as to dare to utter the falsehood with their own mouth and to say that the words added are mine. But, if they are not mine, why am I condemned for another's words? Well, they will say that I am in communion with Apollinaris[3] and hold within myself such perverted doctrines. Let them be asked for proofs. For, if they know how to search the heart[4] of a man, let them admit it, and do you acknowledge their truthfulness in all

3 Apollinaris the Younger, Bishop of Laodicea, who flourished in the second half of the fourth century. Although he at first adhered to the Nicene Creed, he later developed the christological heresy called Apollinarianism. He seceded in 375 and died about 392.

4 Cf. Rom. 8.27; also, Wisd. 1.6; Jer. 17.10; Apoc. 2.23.

things. But, if they attempt to prove my communion with him from things that are clear and evident to all, let a canonical letter which I sent to him be shown, or one he sent me, or the association of his clergy with us, or any one of them whom we have ever received in communion of prayer. But, if they now bring forward a letter written to him twenty-five years ago, from a layman to a layman, and this not as it was written by me, but changed, God knows by whom, then acknowledge the injustice; for no bishop is accused if, while a layman, he wrote somewhat carelessly about a matter of indifference, and this not even concerning faith, but a simple letter with a friendly greeting. And, possibly, they themselves are known to have written to the Greeks and the Jews without incurring any blame. Until today no one has been brought to trial for this act for which we now are condemned by those who strain out the gnats.[5] But, that we neither wrote those words, nor have approved them, but even anathematize those who hold that evil opinion of the confusion of the Persons, in which the most impious heresy of Sabellius has been renewed, certainly is well known to God who discerns hearts; it is also well known to all the brotherhood which has had experience of our Lowliness. And let those men themselves, who are now our violent accusers, examine their own conscience, and they will know that from childhood we have been far from such doctrines.

If, indeed, some one asks what our belief is, he will learn from the document itself in which their signature appears in their own handwriting, but, because they wish to repudiate it, they cover over their change of position by calumny against us. They do not admit that they have repented of having

5 Cf. Matt. 23.24.

signed the document which I presented to them, but they bring forward accusations of impiety against us, thinking that it is not known that their separation from us is a pretext, while in truth they have withdrawn from the faith which they frequently professed in writing in the presence of many, and finally both accepted and subscribed, when I presented it to them. This it is possible for all to read, and from the letter itself to learn the truth. Their intention, moreover, will be known if anyone, after seeing the signature they gave to us, reads the creed which they presented to Gelasius[6] and perceives how great is the difference between that confession and this. Accordingly, let not those who change so easily to the opposite examine the specks of others, but let them cast out the beam in their own eye.[7]

However, we are defending ourselves and explaining everything more completely in another letter,[8] which will convince those who are seeking more information. But you, at the present time, since you have received this letter of ours, put aside all grief and assure us of your love for us,[9] because of which I strongly cling to union with you. Moreover, it is the greatest grief to us and an inconsolable pain to our heart, should the slanders against us ever prevail over you to such an extent as to cool your brotherly love and estrange us from each other. Farewell.

---

6 Bishop of Caesarea in Palestine from 367 to 395.
7 Cf. Matt. 7.3-5; also, Luke 6.41-43.
8 Letter 223.
9 Cf. 2 Cor. 2.8.

225. To Demosthenes, in the Name of the Public[1]

We always feel very grateful to God and to the rulers who have charge over us when we see that the administration of our country has been entrusted to a man who, first of all, is a Christian and, secondly, is upright in character and a strict guardian of the laws by which we manage human affairs. But, especially, on the occasion of your visit did we acknowledge this gratitude to God and to the emperor, dear to God. Perceiving, however, that some of the enemies of peace were intending to influence your revered court against us, we were waiting to be summoned by your Lordship so that we might explain the truth to you, if only your mighty Wisdom would consent to make your own the examination of ecclesiastical affairs. But the court ignored us, and your Highness, disturbed by the slanders of Philochares, ordered our brother and fellow minister Gregory to be carried to prison. He heeded the command (how could he refuse?), yet, because he was suffering from a pain in the side and at the same time from a chill, his kidney disease having made its usual assault, he was compelled, unmercifully detained as he was by the soldiers, to be removed to some place of quiet for the purpose of securing care for his body and relief from the intolerable pains. For this reason

1 Probably the same Demosthenes, superintendent of the kitchen, who had previously attempted by threats to compel St. Basil to accede to the emperor's wishes. This Demosthenes, Vicar of Pontus, was an enemy of the orthodox faith and a firm supporter of the semi-Arians. At a council of semi-Arians at Ancyra which he convoked he tried to procure the arrest and imprisonment of St. Gregory of Nyssa on a charge of misappropriation of church funds. In 376 Demosthenes summoned another such synod which deposed St. Gregory and gave his see to an Arian. On the death of Theodotus, Demosthenes also tried to force upon the church at Nicopolis a bishop consecrated by Eustathius of Sebaste, but he did not succeed. Cf. Letters 231 and 237. This letter was written as if by common consent of a group of bishops in December of 375. Cf. Loofs, *op. cit.* 9, n.2.

we have all come to beseech your Greatness[2] not to be displeased at the postponement of his trial; no public concern is in a worse condition because of our delay, and none of the interests of the Church suffers harm from it.

But, if the discussion is about money, on the grounds that it has been wasted, the treasurers of the church funds are here, ready to give an account to whoever wants it and to prove the slander of those who have made a bold bid for your careful hearing. It is easy for them from the actual writings of the blessed bishop to make the truth evident to those who search for it. If, however, there is something else pertaining to the canons which needs examination and your Lordship consents to undertake the hearing and judgment of it, there is need of us all, because, if something is lacking in what pertains to the canons, those who did the consecrating are responsible, not he who was forced by every form of constraint to undertake the ministry.

Therefore we beg you to keep the hearing for us in the fatherland and not to drag us to a foreign land, nor to impose upon us the necessity of a meeting with the bishops with whom we have not yet settled matters concerning ecclesiastical questions.[3] At the same time we beg you to spare our old age and weakness. You will know through your investigation itself, God willing, that nothing pertaining to the canons, either small or great, was omitted in the consecration of the bishop. Therefore we pray that under your administration both concord and peace with the brethren may be achieved. Since this has not yet been done, even a meeting is difficult for us, because many of the simpler brethren are frustrated by our disagreement with one another.

---

2 *Mégethos*—a title of address used by St. Basil only in this instance.

3 According to Letter 237, Demosthenes was at this time probably in Galatia, where he had summoned a heretical synod. Cf. *Cod. Theod.* IX, *tit.* 1.10.

226. To His Monks[1]

The holy God can bestow even the gratification of a conference upon us who are always eager to look upon you and to hear about you, because in nothing else do we experience rest[2] of soul except in your progress and perfection through the commands of Christ. But as long as this is not granted to us, we hold it necessary to visit you through our true and God-fearing brethren and to converse with your Charities by letter. Now, for this very reason we have sent our most reverent and true brother and co-worker of the Gospel, our fellow presbyter Meletius, to describe for you the longing desire which we have for you and the solicitude of our soul, how night and day we implore the Lord for your good name that we may have confidence in the day of our Lord Jesus Christ through your salvation, and that you may shine forth in the brightness of the saints, because your work has been approved by the just judgment of God.[3]

At the same time, the difficulty of this present critical situation, in which all churches have been shaken and all souls are sifted,[4] causes us much anxiety. For, some have opened their mouths unsparingly against their fellow servants. Falsehood is fearlessly spoken; the truth is completely veiled. The accused are condemned without trial; the accusers are believed without examination. For this reason, although I heard that many letters are being circulated against me, marking and denouncing us and bringing accusations about affairs for which we have a defense ready at the tribunal of truth, I decided to keep silence, and I did. Now, this is

1 Written in December, 375; cf. Loofs, *op. cit.* 19.
2 Cf. Matt. 11.29.
3 Cf. Rom. 2.5.
4 Cf. Luke 22.31.

already the third year since, smitten by the slanders, I have been bearing the scourges of the accusation, being content that I have the Lord, the Knower of hidden things, as the witness of this false charge. But, since I see that many have already accepted our silence as a confirmation of the slanders and have believed, not that we have been silent through forbearance but through the inability to open our mouth against the truth, I have attempted to write to you, beseeching your Charities in Christ not by any means to receive as true these partisan slanders, because, as it is written: 'The law judges no man, unless it first give him a hearing, and know what he does.'[5]

Yet, for a reasonable judge the matters themselves are sufficient for a proof of the truth. Accordingly, even if we shall be silent, it is possible for you to see clearly what is happening. In fact, they who are bringing an accusation of heterodoxy against us have now openly appeared siding with the party of the heretics; they who condemn us through the writings of others are shown to be contradicting themselves by their own confessions, which they have deposited in writing with us. Consider the practice of those who dare to do such things, that it is always their custom to change over to the powerful party and to trample under foot their weaker friends while they flatter those who get the upper hand. Indeed, they who are writing those much-spoken-of letters against Eudoxius[6] and all his party, and sending them around to all the brotherhoods asserting that they shun communion with them as destructive to souls, and for this reason not having admitted the votes brought forward for their deposi-

5 Cf. John 7.51.

6 This 'worst of all Arians,' as he was called by Baronius, was intruded into the sees of Germanica, of Antioch, and finally of Constantinople, as its eighth bishop (360-370). Many comments about his 'blasphemous oratory' have come down to us from ancient sources.

tion, since the votes had come from heretics, as they then tried to persuade us—these men now, forgetting all these things, have united with them.[7] There is, moreover, no denial left for them, for they openly laid bare their policy by embracing their communion privately in Ancyra since they had not yet been received by them publicly. Ask them, then, if Basileides,[8] who is in communion with Ecdicius,[9] is now orthodox, why, on returning from Dardania, they were overthrowing his altars in the country of Gangra[10] and setting up their own; and why, even up to the present time[11] they have been attacking the churches of Amaseia and Zela[12] and appointing presbyters and deacons from their own men? If they are in communion with them as being orthodox, why do they attack them as though they were heretics? But, if they have supposed them to be heretics, how is it that they do not give up communion with them? Is this not evident even to a child's intelligence, most honorable brethren, that, always looking to their own advantage, they attempt either to slander some or to unite with them?

7 About ten years before the present letter the semi-Arians had summoned Eudoxius to Lampsacus, and in his absence from his see deposed him.

8 Bishop of Gangra; nothing is known of him, except from the references here and in Letter 251.

9 A presbyter whom Demosthenes, Vicar of Pontus, in the synod he convoked at Ancyra, placed in the bishopric of Parnassus in Cappadocia Tertia to succeed Hypsinus whom he had caused to be deposed in 375. Cf. Letter 237.

10 Modern Kiangeri, in Turkey, Asia Minor.

11 Tillemont explains this by saying that Eustathius in 375 was persecuting the Arians in Amasea and Zela in order to win the orthodox party to his side and estrange them from St. Basil. The Benedictine editors, however, believe that this is too strict an interpretation, that Eustathius, at that time friendly with the Arians, would not risk attacking them and putting orthodox bishops in their sees. They hold that, since the expression, *méchri nûn,* is often used to refer to something in the past but more recent than another past act, St. Basil simply means that Eustathius had persecuted the churches in Amasea and Zela later than those of Gangra.

12 Modern Amasieh and Kazarklar, in Turkey, Asia Minor, on the Iris.

Therefore, they stood aloof from us, not being annoyed because we did not write in answer to their charge (for it is this, especially, for which they say that they are provoked), nor because we did not receive the suffragan bishops whom they say they had sent. Yet, those who are trumping this up will give an account to the Lord.[13] One certain Eustathius,[14] indeed, who was sent and who handed over a letter to the company of the vicar, after staying three days in the city, when he was about to depart for his own home, is said to have approached our home late in the evening when I was asleep. On hearing that I was asleep, he went away and did not again come near us on the following day, but, having thus acquitted himself of his obligation toward us, he returned. Now, this is the fault which we have committed, and those long-suffering men have not weighed our previous service, which we gave them in love, against this error, but they have made their wrath against us so much more grievous in view of this sin that they have caused us to be excommunicated from all the churches throughout the world, at least as far as depends on them.

This, however, is not truly the cause of the separation, but, since they thought at that time that they would be highly esteemed by Euzoius[15] if they would estrange themselves from us, they invented for themselves those pretexts in order that they might find some commendation among them[16] through the war against us. These now also attack the Nicene Creed and call us defenders of sameness of substance, because in that creed the only-begotten Son is confessed to be of the same substance as God the Father, not on the

13 Cf. Rom. 14.12.
14 A suffragan bishop, not Eustathius of Sebaste.
15 An intimate friend of Arius from an early age, who was appointed Arian bishop of Antioch after the deposition of Meletius in 361.
16 Euzoius and his party.

grounds that He is from one substance divided into two cognate parts, God forbid, for such a thing that holy and God-loving assembly did not have in mind, but that whatever the Father is in substance, this the Son also should be believed to be. They themselves have thus interpreted for us saying: 'Light from light.' And it is the Nicene Creed, carried by them from the West,[17] which they delivered to the synod in Tyana, and because of it also they were admitted. But they have a certain subtle principle for their change of this kind—namely, that they make use of the words of the Creed as doctors do, according to circumstances, adapting them now in one way, again in another, to the conditions presented. It is not for me to refute the unsoundness of this sophism, but for you to ponder it. The Lord will give you understanding[18] to know what is the right doctrine and what the false and distorted one. In fact, if it is necessary at one time to write one creed and at another another one, and to change with the times, the assertion of him who says, 'One Lord, one faith, one baptism,'[19] is false. But, if those words are true, 'let no one lead you astray with these empty words.'[20] They slander us on the ground that we are making innovations concerning the Holy Spirit. Ask, therefore, what the innovation is. For we confess what we have also received —that the Paraclete is ranked with the Father and the Son, that He is not reckoned with the creature. We have believed in the Father and the Son and the Holy Spirit; we are baptized in the name of the Father and of the Son and of

17 The Eastern semi-Arian deputies received a letter from Pope Liberius upholding the doctrine of the Council of Nicaea, and at a council of Sicilian bishops held in December 366 received another letter confirming that of Pope Liberius. These two letters they brought to the bishops at the Council of Tyana, Cappadocia, in 367. Cf. Hefele, 1.976,979.

18 Cf. 2 Tim. 2.7.

19 Cf. Eph. 4.5.

20 Cf. Eph. 5.6.

the Holy Spirit. Because of this we never separate the Paraclete from the union with the Father and the Son. Indeed, our mind, spiritually enlightened by the Spirit, looks upon the Son, and in Him as in an image sees the Father. Therefore, we neither invent names of ourselves, but we call Him Holy Spirit and Paraclete, nor do we allow ourselves to reject the glory owed to Him. This, in all truth, is our stand. Let him who accuses us in these matters make his accusation; let him who persecutes us persecute; let him who believes these slanders against us be ready for the judgment. 'The Lord is near, let us have no anxiety.'[21]

If someone in Syria[22] is writing, this is nothing to us. 'By thy words thou wilt be justified,' He says, 'and by thy words thou wilt be condemned.'[23] Let my own words judge me; let no one condemn us for the errors of others, nor bring forward letters we wrote twenty years ago as a proof of our being at present in communion with those who have written these things. Before these documents and before any such suspicion even was stirred up against them, we wrote as layman to layman; and we wrote nothing concerning the faith, nor the sort of things which these are now slanderously circulating against us, but mere greetings, returning a friendly salutation. We, in fact, shun as impious and excommunicate equally those who fall into the errors of Sabellius and those who vindicate the teaching of Arius. If anyone says that the Father is the same as the Son and the Holy Spirit, and suggests one thing under many names and one Person addressed by three titles, such a one we place in the party of the Jews. Likewise, if anyone says that the Son is unlike the Father according to substance, or reduces the Holy Spirit to a creature, we excommunicate him and we hold that he

21 Cf. Phil. 4.5,6.
22 I.e., Apollinaris. Cf., also, Letters 130 and 223.
23 Matt. 12.37.

is near the error of the Gentiles. But it is impossible for the mouths of our accusers to be held in check by our writings; really, it is more probable that they will be roused to wrath by our defense and make ready greater and more harsh charges against us. Nevertheless, it is not hard for you to guard your ears. Therefore, do as much as is in you. Keep your hearts sincere toward us and unprejudiced by the slanders, and demand of us an account in regard to the charges brought forward. If you find the truth with us, do not give place to falsehood. But, if you perceive that we are too weak in our defense, then believe our accusers as speaking the truth. In planning to injure us they lie awake; this we shall not ask of you. They, pursuing a mercantile life, make the slander against us their merchandise; but we urge you to remain at home and to behave with decorum, in silence fulfilling the work of Christ,[24] yet to avoid intercourse with them, which becomes by deceitful means the undoing of those who listen, in order that you may keep your love toward us sincere, may preserve intact the faith of the Fathers, and, as friends of the truth, may appear glorious in the presence of the Lord.

227. A Letter of Condolence to the Clergy in Colonia[1]

What, indeed, is so beautiful and pleasing in the sight of God and men as perfect love, which we have been taught by

24 Cf. 1 Thess. 4.11.

1 Because the orthodox Catholics would not submit to Fronto, consecrated through the efforts of the Eustathians to fill the see left vacant by the death of Theodotus, Poemenius of Satala sent the Bishop of Colonia, Euphronius, to fill the vacancy. The Colonians, clergy and laity, were much disturbed at being deprived of their bishop. This occurred in 375 and St. Basil wrote this and Letters 228-230 to allay the trouble.

the wise master is the fulfillment of every law? Therefore, I approve the ardor of your affection for your shepherd. Now, as the loss of a good father is unendurable to a son who loves his father, so also the departure of a shepherd and teacher is unbearable to a church of Christ. Therefore, you offer a proof of your good and noble will in your intense affection for your bishop. While this worthy disposition of yours toward your spiritual father is to be approved when it is within measure and reason, yet, when it oversteps due bounds, it is no longer deserving of the same approbation.

An excellent arrangement in the case of the brother dearly beloved of God, your fellow minister Euphronius, has been made by those who were entrusted with the management of the churches—an arrangement necessary for the occasion and advantageous both for the church to which he was transferred and to you yourselves from whom he has been taken. Do not believe that this is a human ordering, nor that it was called forth by the reasoning of men who think only of mundane affairs, but be persuaded that those who have dependent upon them the care of the churches of God have done this by the customary co-operation of the Holy Spirit, and, impressing this origin on your mind, be zealous to perfect it. Accept, therefore, in silence and with thanksgiving what has happened, being convinced of this, that they who do not accept from the churches of God that which is decreed by the churches oppose the command of God. Do not come to an issue with your mother, the church at Nicopolis. Do not be angry with those who have taken upon themselves the care of your souls. For, in the firm establishment of the affairs of Nicopolis your part also will be saved, but, if some disturbance shall fasten upon it, even if you have countless numbers guarding you, the part will be destroyed along with the head. Now, just as they who live beside rivers, when they see some men afar off throwing up embankments against the streams, know that they are acting beforehand for their safety by turning back the onward flow of the streams, so also those, who now take upon themselves the weight of the care of the churches, in their protection of the others provide security for you; and you will be sheltered from all tumults, since the others will intercept the attacks of war. Consequently, you must consider that he has not cast you off, but has taken on the others. We are not, certainly, so malicious that we compel him who is able to share his gifts with others to confine his favor to you and restrict it to your region alone. In fact, neither he who obstructs the spring and impairs the outflow of water nor he who hinders the further progress of sufficient teaching is free from the passion of jealousy. Therefore, let him have the care of Nicopolis, too, and let solicitude for you be added to his cares there. More labor has accrued to the man, but his care of you is not at all lessened.

This, however, has grieved me exceedingly, and it has seemed to be beyond bounds—your having said: 'if we fail to obtain what we are seeking, we shall go to court, and we shall appoint over our affairs men to whom the overthrowing of the churches is the chief object of their prayer. Never, then, let any, borne along by senseless wrath, prevail upon you to make some public utterance, and thereupon some disaster be brought on and the weight of what is happening be turned upon the heads of those who are furnishing the cause. But receive both our advice, which is offered through our paternal affection for you, and also the appointment of the bishops dearly beloved of God, since it was made according to the will of God. Also wait for us, who, if the Lord will lend us His assistance, shall come and personally propose what it is not possible to recommend to your Reverences through a letter, and we shall attempt by our very deeds to procure for you all possible consolation.

228. To the Magistrates of Colonia

I received your Modesties' letter and I thanked the all-holy God, because, although you are engaged in the care of public affairs, you do not give those of the churches second place, but each one has shown solicitude in the same way as for a personal concern and one involving his own livelihood, and because you wrote to us when you were grieved at the departure of Euphronius, your bishop dearly beloved of God. Nicopolis has not taken him from you, but would say in pleading its case that it has recovered its own, and, cherishing you, will tell you in a voice proper to an affectionate mother that it will hold in common with you the father who will share his favor in turn with each. He will not allow them to suffer anything from the incursions of their opponents nor will he deprive you of his customary care. Considering the difficulty of the time and understanding by prudent thought the necessity of the appointment, pardon the bishops who adopted this way of strengthening the churches of our Lord Jesus Christ; propose to yourselves what is becoming to men who possess a mature intelligence of their own and know how to accept also the suggestions from those who love them. Indeed, it is probable that you fail to understand many of the disturbances because you are situated in the remote part of Armenia, but we who are in the midst of affairs and from all sides daily are struck with the reports of churches being overthrown are in great anxiety lest the common enemy, begrudging the long-enduring peace of your life, should at any time be able to sow his weeds[1] also in the regions about you; and the district of the Armenians should become food of the opponents. But for the present, be at peace, permitting your neighbor to have the common

1 Cf. Matt. 13.25.

use, as it were, of a goodly vessel. A little later, if the Lord grants us the journey, you shall receive a more perfect consolation for the things which have happened, if this shall seem necessary to you.

229. *To the Clergy of Nicopolis*[1]

We are convinced that action taken by one or two pious men is done through the counsel of the Spirit. Since there is no human motive placed before their eyes, and saintly men are moved to action not with an aim of personal advantage, but after having proposed to themselves what is pleasing to God, it is evident that it is the Lord who directs their hearts.[1] And, whenever spiritual men are the initiators of plans, and the people of the Lord follow them in harmony of thought, who will doubt that the plan has been arrived at in communion with our Lord Jesus Christ, who poured out His blood for the churches? Therefore you yourselves have also rightly inferred that our brother and fellow minister dearly beloved of God, Poemenius,[2] was moved by God, he who came to you at an opportune time and devised this method of consolation. Not only his discovery of something beneficial do I praise, but I also admire the nobility of his mind, because he did not drag the affair out by long delays, undermining the eagerness of those who were making demands, giving time to the opponents for defense, and stirring up the plots of those lying in wait, but he immediately brought it to accomplishment by his excellent plan. May

1 Cf. 2 Thess. 3.5.

2 Bishop of Satala, who was responsible for the appointment of Euphronius to the vacancy caused by Theodotus' death, and an intimate friend of St. Basil, who had appointed him to the see of Satala.

the Lord preserve him with all his household in His grace, so that the Church may continue unchanging under successors as equally honored as their predecessors, and may not give place to the Evil One who now, if ever, will be angry at the settled condition of the churches.

We have also given many exhortations to the brothers in Colonia by letter, and you, too, rather than irritate them as if they were overlooked because of their insignificance, ought to approve their disposition, and not to lead them on to contention by your contempt. Those who are contentious somehow naturally become more inconsiderate, and direct many of their personal affairs badly for the sake of grieving their opponents. But no one is so insignificant as not to be able now to provide an opportunity for great evils to those who want the opportunity. And we say this, not from conjecture, but taught by the experience of our own troubles, which may God avert by your prayers. Pray also with us for a good journey, in order that on our arrival we may rejoice with you over your present shepherd,[3] and may mutually be consoled for the death of our common father.[4]

230. To the Magistrates of Nicopolis

The government of the churches depends upon those who are entrusted with their care, but they are strengthened by the laity. And so the duty of the bishops dearly beloved of God has been fulfilled; what is left now depends upon you, if you will deign to cleave dauntlessly to the bishop[1] given to you and strongly to beat off the attacks from the outside.

3 Euphronius.
4 Theodotus.

1 Euphronius.

Nothing so puts to shame both leaders and people who envy your peaceful condition as the agreement in your love for him who has been given to you, and the strength of your resistance. In fact, it inspires them with a despair of every wicked attempt if they see that neither clergy nor people are accepting their artifices. Therefore, whatever opinion you hold about the good man, make it public in the city; hold discussions with the people and with all the inhabitants of the district, strengthening their noble resolutions, so that the genuineness of your love toward God may be proclaimed among all. And would that we may at some time be considered worthy to come to you and to visit your church, the promoter of piety, which we honor as the metropolis of orthodoxy because from earliest times it has been governed by most honorable men, chosen of God, who have held fast 'the faithful word which is in accordance with the teaching.'[2] You have approved as worthy of these him who has now been appointed, and we have agreed. Only may you be preserved by the grace of God who puts an end to the wicked plans of the enemy and engenders strength and vigor in your souls for the defense of what has been rightly determined.

231. To Amphilochius, Bishop of Iconium[1]

I find few opportunities of writing to your Reverence and this grieves me not a little. It is just as if, although it was possible to see you frequently and to enjoy you, I rarely did

2 Cf. Titus 1.9.

1 This letter was written during the last days of 374 or at the beginning of 375. According to Loofs, *op. cit.* 9 and 12 n. 4, this letter should be dated December, 375. On Amphilochius, cf. previous letters.

so. But it is impossible for me to write because of the lack of persons traveling from here to your country; otherwise, there was nothing to hinder my letters from being, as it were, a daily record of my life, notifying your Charity of the happenings of each day. It brings me relief to tell you about the state of our affairs, and I know that you care for nothing so much as what concerns us. At present, however, Elpidius[2] is hastening to his master to lay bare the slanders falsely trumped up against him by certain enemies, and he has asked us for a letter. Through him we are both saluting your Reverence and are recommending the man to you as being worthy of protection from you not only for justice' sake but also for our own. Even though we have no other testimony to give for him but that he valued highly the privilege of being the carrier of our letter, regard him as a friend, remember us, and pray for the Church.

But I want you to know that our brother[3] dearly beloved of God is in exile, being unable to endure the annoyances of shameless men. And Doara[4] is exposed to the storm, since the fat sea monster[5] is throwing everything there into confusion. The enemies are devising plots against us at court, as is the report of those who know, but the hand of the Lord meanwhile is with us.[6] Only pray that we be not abandoned in the end. Our brother continues calm, and Doara has received the old muleteer;[7] it could do nothing more, and the Lord will scatter the plots of our enemies. Our deliverance from all griefs present and awaited is in

2 A servant of Amphilochius. It is doubtful whether he is to be identified with any other of the same name mentioned in the letters.
3 St. Gregory of Nyssa. Cf. Letter 225 n. 1.
4 One of the bishoprics in Cappadocia Secunda under Tyana.
5 Demosthenes, Vicar of Pontus.
6 Cf. Luke 1.66; also, Acts 11.21.
7 Probably Demosthenes again.

seeing you. Therefore, if it shall ever be possible for you while we are on earth, deign to come to see us.

We have been writing the book on the Spirit[8] and it is now finished, as you yourself know. The brethren who are with me prevented me from sending it written on paper, saying that they had orders from your Nobility to write it on parchment. In order, therefore, that we may not seem to do anything contrary to your command, we are holding it back now, but shall send it a little later, if only we obtain some suitable messenger. May you by the kindness of the Holy One be given to me and to the Church of God in good health and spirits and praying to the Lord for us.

232. To Amphilochius, Bishop of Iconium[1]

Every day which brings a letter from your Reverence is a feast day for us, and the greatest of feasts. And, when the tokens[2] of a feast also are added, what else must we call it but a feast of feasts, just as the ancient Law was accustomed to use the expression Sabbath of Sabbaths? Therefore, we give thanks to the Lord, since we have heard that you are strong in body and that you have celebrated the commemoration of the Incarnation with the Church at peace.

Some tumults, however, have disturbed us; truly, we have not spent the time without sadness, for the reason that our brother dearly beloved of God has been exiled. But pray for

---

8 The *De Spiritu Sancto*.

---

1 According to Maran, *Vit. Basil.* 35, this letter is to be placed late in 375, if the Nativity was celebrated on December 25, or early in 376, if it was celebrated after the Epiphany according to Oriental usage up to the end of the fourth century, as seems likely here. Loofs, *op. cit.* 8 n. 3, places it specifically in January, 376.

2 Christmas presents.

him in order that God may allow him at some time to behold his Church cured of the wounds caused by the stings of the heretics. And do have the great kindness to visit us while we are still upon earth. Perform an act that is consistent with yourself, but for us is deserving of the greatest prayers. We can only wonder at the meaning of your blessings, since enigmatically you prayed for a strong old age for us. In fact, you have explained that by your lamps you wake us for nightly labors, and that by your sweetmeats you guarantee us to be strong in all our members. In truth, at my age munching is not for me at any rate, since my teeth have long ago been worn away through time and illness. Therefore, to your questions I have given in this memorandum some answers such as I was able and the time allowed.

233. To Amphilochius, Who Had Questioned Him[1]

I myself know this, having heard it, and I am also acquainted with the constitution of man. What, then, shall we say in answer to these things? That the mind is a thing of beauty; and in it we have that which is made according to the image of the Creator; also a thing of beauty is the operation of the mind; and, since the mind is ever active, it frequently forms images of non-existent things as though they did exist; and it frequently is borne straight to the truth. Since, however, two powers have grown side by side in it, according to our understanding who believe in God, the one wicked, which is of the demons, drawing us along to their own apostasy, the other more divine and good, leading us up to the likeness of God, whenever the mind remains

1 This letter was written in January, 376. Cf. Loofs, *op. cit.* 8 n. 3.

within itself, it descries little things and those which are commensurate with itself, but, when it gives itself over to those who deceive it, it does away with its own judgment and is haunted by strange phantasies. Then it even thinks that wood is not wood, but God, and it judges that gold is not money, but an object of worship. But, if it inclines toward the more divine part and receives the graces of the Spirit, then it is able to discern the more divine things, as far as is commensurate with its nature.

Now, there are, as it were, three conditions of life,[2] and equal in number with these are the operations of our mind. For, either our habits of life are wicked—and, of course, the movements of our mind are wicked, such as adulteries, thefts, idolatries, slanders, contentions, anger, intrigues, pride, and whatever the Apostle Paul counted among 'the works of the flesh'[3]—or there is a certain indifferent operation of the soul which involves nothing either condemnable or laudable as the acquisition of those mechanical arts which we truly call indifferent, since they incline in no way to virtue or to evil by reason of themselves. For, what is the evil of the art of steering and of medicine? These are certainly not virtues in themselves, but according to the will of those using them they incline toward the one or the other of the opposite states. Yet, the mind that is permeated with the divinity of the Spirit is already initiated in the mighty contemplations, and beholds the divine beauties, as far, of course, as grace is granted and its constitution admits.

Therefore, let them dismiss those dialectic questions and, not in a mischievous manner, but with reverence, examine the truth. The judgment of our mind has been given to us

2 Virtuous, wicked, and indifferent.
3 Cf. Gal. 5.19-21.

for the comprehension of the truth. But our God is truth itself. So, the principal duty of our mind is to know our God, but to know Him in such a way as the infinitely great One can be known by the very small. Now, when the eyes are applied to the perception of visible things, not immediately are all visible things brought within their view. In fact, not even the hemisphere of the heavens is observed in one glance, but a visual representation surrounds us, and truly many things in it, not to say all, are not known: the nature of the stars, their magnitude, intervals, movements, concourses, distances, the other temporary conditions, the substance itself of the firmament, the depth from the concave circumference to the convex upper surface. Nevertheless, we would not say that the heavens are invisible because of the things which are not known, but visible because of a limited perception of them. And so it is concerning God. If the mind is misled by the demons, it will practice idolatry or will turn aside to some other form of impiety, but, if it has given itself over to the aid of the Spirit, it will understand the truth and will learn to know God. And it will know, as the Apostle says, imperfectly, but more perfectly in the life after this. 'For when that which is perfect has come, that which is imperfect will be done away with.'[4] Therefore, the judgment of the mind is good and is directed toward a useful end, the knowledge of God, but operating only so far as it is able to go.

---

4 1 Cor. 13.10.

234. To the Same,[1] *in Answer to Another Question*

'Do you worship what you know or what you are ignorant of?' If we shall answer: 'What we know, that we adore,' very quickly will come the retort from them: 'What is the substance of that which is adored?' And if we shall admit that we are ignorant of the substance, again turning on us they say: 'Surely, then, you adore what you do not know.' But we say that 'know' is a word of many meanings. We say that we know the greatness of God, and His power, and wisdom, and goodness, and the providence with which He cares for us, and the justice of His judgment, not His substance itself. And so the question is insidious. He who says that he does not know the substance does not admit that he is ignorant of God, since from the many attributes which we have enumerated the concept of God is formed for us. 'But,' he says, 'God is simple, and everything which you enumerate of Him as knowable belongs to His substance.' This is a sophism which contains innumerable absurdities. Since there are so many attributes enumerated, are all these names of one substance? And are His awesomeness and kindliness equivalent to each other, His justice and His creative power, His foreknowledge and His requiting, His splendor and His providence? Or, if we mention any of these, do we reveal the substance? If they say this, let them not ask if we know the substance of God, but let them inquire of us whether we know that God is awesome, or is just, or is kind. We admit that we know these things. But, if they say that the substance is something else, let them not mislead us on the score of simplicity. In fact, they themselves have admitted that the

1 Another letter written in January, 376 (cf. Loofs, *op. cit.* 8 n. 3) during the contest with the Arians over the substance of God and the divine Persons individually.

substance and each of the attributes enumerated are different things. 'But the operations are varied, and the substance is simple.' We say that from His operations we know our God; we do not undertake to approach His substance itself. His operations come down to us, but His substance remains inaccessible.

'Well, if you are ignorant of the substance,' they say, 'you are ignorant of Him.' But you retort: 'If you say that you know His substance, you do not know Him.' He who has been bitten by a mad dog on beholding the dog in a dish does not see more than those who are well; on the contrary, he, is to be pitied for this reason, that he thinks that he beholds what he does not see. Do not, therefore, admire him for his announcement, but judge him deserving of pity for his madness. Furthermore, be assured that from mockers is the saying: 'If you are ignorant of the substance of God, you adore what you do not know.' I know that He exists, but what His substance is I consider as beyond intelligence. How, then, am I saved? Through faith. Faith is sufficient of itself to know that God exists, not what He is, and that He becomes the rewarder of those who seek Him.[2] The knowledge of His divine substance is the perception of its incomprehensibleness, and that which is to be worshiped is that which we understand—not what its substance is, but that its substance exists.

And let them be questioned in turn thus. 'No one has at any time seen God. The only-begotten Son, who is in the bosom of the Father, he has revealed him.'[3] What has the Only-begotten revealed of the Father: the substance or the power? If the power, we know as much as He revealed to us. If the substance, tell me, where did He say that His was

2 Cf. Heb. 11.6.
3 John 1.18.

an unbegotten substance? When did Abraham adore? Was it not when he believed? And when did he believe? Was it not when he was called? Where, then, is his comprehension attested by the Scriptures? When did the disciples adore Him? Was it not when they saw that creation was subject to Him? From the sea and the waves obeying Him they knew His divinity. Therefore, from the works is the knowledge, and from the knowledge is the adoration. 'Do you believe that I can do this? I believe, Lord; and falling down he worshiped him.'[4] Thus, adoration follows faith, and faith is confirmed by power. But, if you say that he who believes also knows, it is through these things which he believes that he also knows, or also conversely, through these things which he knows that he also believes. We know God through His power. Therefore, we believe in Him who is known, and we adore Him who is believed.

235. To the Same,[1] in Answer to Another Question

Which is first: knowledge or faith? We say that, on the whole, in the case of sciences, faith precedes knowledge, but in our teaching, even if anyone says that knowledge begins before faith, we do not disagree—but, a knowledge commensurate with human comprehension. In the case of sciences we must believe first that alpha is so called, and afterwards, having learned the letters and their pronunciation, gain also an accurate notion of the force of the letter. But in our faith concerning God the thought that God exists goes before, and this we gather from His works. We recognize by obser-

4 Cf. Matt. 9.28 and John 9.38.

1 Written in January, 376; cf. Loofs, *op. cit.* 8 n. 3.

vation His wisdom and power and goodness and all His invisible attributes from the creation of the world.[2] Thus, then, we accept Him as our own Lord. Since, in fact, God is the Creator of all the world, but we are a part of the world, then God is also our Creator. Faith follows this knowledge, and adoration follows such faith.

Now, since the word 'knowledge' has many meanings, those mocking at the simpler souls and likewise making a show of themselves by their paradoxes, like men in the theatres spiriting away the pebbles in the sight of all, do away with everything by their questioning of the matter as a whole. Although the word 'knowledge' pertains to many things, and although something can be known in respect to number, magnitude, power, the manner of existence, the time of generation, and substance, these men, taking in the whole meaning in their question, if they catch us admitting that we know, demand of us the knowledge of the substance, but, if they see that we are cautious in our assertion, they turn and bring against us the censure of impiety. We admit that we know what can be known of God, and again that it is impossible to know anything which is beyond our comprehension. So, then, if you ask me if I know what sand is, and if I answer that I understand, you will evidently be quibbling if immediately you demand the number of the grains of sand, because your first question referred to the appearance of sand; the second, a verbal trap, turned toward its number. This is like the sophism of him who says: 'Do you know Timothy? Then, if you know Timothy, you know also his nature; but you have admitted that you know Timothy, accordingly, give us an account of Timothy's nature.' But I truly know Timothy, and I do not know him; not,

2 Cf. Rom. 1.20.

that is, in the same manner and in the same respect. It is not in respect to what I know that I do not know, but in respect to one thing I know, and in respect to another I am ignorant. I know him through his figure and his other personal qualities, but I am ignorant of his substance. Then, also, by this reasoning, I thus know myself and am ignorant of myself. I know myself, who I am; and I do not know myself, in so far as I am ignorant of my substance.

Now, let them explain to us in what sense Paul said: 'Now we know in part.'[3] Do we know His substance in part, as if we know parts of His substance? That is absurd, for God is indivisible. Do we know His whole substance? How, then, do we explain: 'When that which is perfect has come, that which is imperfect will be done away with'?[4] And why are the idolaters accused? Is it not because, having known God, they did not give Him glory as God? Or why are the senseless Galatians[5] reproached by Paul, who says: 'But now that you have come to know God, or rather to be known by God, how is it that you turn again to the weak and beggarly elements?'[6] And how was God known in Judea? Was it because the nature of His substance was known in Judea? 'The ox,' it is said, 'knoweth his owner.'[7] That is to say, according to you, the ox knows the substance of his master. 'And the ass his master's crib.' Therefore, the ass also knows the substance of the crib. 'But Israel,' it is said, 'has not known me.' According to you, Israel is accused of this, that it has not known the nature of the substance of God. 'Pour out,' it is said, 'thy wrath upon the nations

3 1 Cor. 13.9.
4 1 Cor. 13.10.
5 Gal. 3.1.
6 Gal. 4.9.
7 Isa. 1.3.

that have not known thee';[8] that is, the nations that have not understood Your substance. But knowledge, as we have said, is of many kinds. There is the apprehension of Him who created us, and the consideration of His wonders, and the observance of His commands, and the affection toward Him, but they, rejecting all these things, reduce knowledge to one signification, the contemplation of the substance itself of God. 'You will place them,' it is said, 'before the testimonies, wherefore, I will make myself known to you there.'[9] Is it not 'I will make Myself known,' instead of 'I will reveal My substance'? 'The Lord knows who are his.'[10] Did He know, then, the substance of those who were His, and not know the substance of those who were disobedient? 'Adam knew his wife.'[11] Then did he know her substance? And concerning Rebecca it is said: 'She was a virgin, and was not known to man.'[12] And 'How shall this happen, since I do not know man?'[13] Is it that no one knew the substance of Rebecca? And did Mary mean this: 'I have not known the substance of any man'? Or it is that it is the custom in the Scriptures to use the word 'know' in the case of conjugal embraces? And for God to be known from the mercy seat[14] means that He will become manifest to His servants. And the expression, 'The Lord knows who are his,'[15] means that, because of their good works, He has received them into familiarity with Him.

8 Ps. 78.6.
9 Cf. Exod. 25.21,22.
10 2 Tim. 2.19.
11 Cf. Gen. 4.1.
12 Cf. Gen. 24.16.
13 Luke 1.34.
14 Cf. Exod. 37.6; also, 25.18.
15 2 Tim. 2.19.

236. *To the Same Amphilochius*[1]

Many have already inquired into the evangelical saying concerning our Lord Jesus Christ not knowing the day and the hour of the end,[2] and especially have the Anomoeans put it forward for the destruction of the glory of the Only-begotten, as a proof of His unlikeness in substance and of His subordination in dignity, on the ground that He who does not know all things is neither able to have the same nature nor to be understood in one likeness with Him who encompasses the knowledge of all things by His foreknowing and cogitative power regarding the future. Your Intelligence has now proposed this to us as something new. Now, the truths which since childhood we have heard from our fathers and which we have received without question because of our love for the good, these we can declare. Even if they do not put an end to the shamelessness of those hostile to Christ (what argument could appear stronger than their attack?), yet for those who love the Lord and who possess a previous concept from faith stronger than the exposition from reason they do, perhaps, provide sufficient assurance.

Although 'no one' seems to be a universal term, so that not even one person is excluded by this expression, it is not so used in the Scriptures, as we have observed in the passage, 'No one is good but God only.'[3] Not even there does the Son in saying this place Himself outside of the nature of good. But, since the Father is the first good, we believe that 'no one' was said with 'first' understood with it; as also the expression, 'No one knows the Son except the Father.'[4] For,

1 Written in January, 376; cf. Loofs, *op. cit* 8. n. 3.
2 Cf. Mark 13.32.
3 Mark 10.18.
4 Matt. 11.27.

not even there does He charge the Spirit with ignorance, but testifies that the knowledge of His own nature belongs first to the Father. Thus, also, we think that the words 'no one knows'[5] are said because He was attributing to the Father the first knowledge of things present and future, and by every means He was teaching men the First Cause. Otherwise, how is the expression consistent with the remaining testimonies of Scripture or how can it agree with our general convictions, since we believe that the Only-begotten is an image of the invisible God, but an image, not of a bodily figure, but of the very divinity and of the magnificent qualities attributed to the substance of God, an image of power, and image of wisdom, as Christ is called the power of God and the wisdom of God?[6] But, certainly, knowledge is a part of wisdom, which He does not represent as a whole, if He is wanting in any of its parts. But, just how did the Father not show to Him through whom He made the ages 'that day and hour,' the least part of the ages? And how is the Creator of all things wanting in the knowledge of the least part of that which was created by Him? And He who says that toward the end of the world various signs will appear[7] in the heaven and in places upon earth, how is He ignorant of the end itself? When He says: 'The end is not yet,'[8] He makes His declaration, not as one who doubts, but as one who knows. Then, if one considers fairly, the Lord also speaks many things to men as man, such as 'Give me to drink,'[9] which is an utterance of the Lord to satisfy His bodily need. Yet, He who asked was not a soulless body,[10]

5 Matt. 24.36.
6 Cf. 1 Cor. 1.23,24.
7 Cf. Matt. 24.
8 Matt. 24.6.
9 Cf. John 4.7.
10 Cf. Letter 261 n. 2.

but divinity using a soul-endowed body. If anyone now receives in this way the meaning of ignorance in the case of Him who accepted all things in accordance with the Incarnation and advanced before God and man[11] in wisdom and grace, he will not be carried beyond the interpretation of true religion.

It would be appropriate to your Diligence[12] to set forth the evangelical words and to compare with each other the words of Matthew and Mark. These alone seem to have agreed with each other concerning this passage. The reading of Matthew is as follows: 'But of that day and hour no one knows, not even the angels of heaven, but the Father only.'[13] And that of Mark: 'But of that day and hour no one knows, neither the angels in heaven, nor the Son, but the Father.'[14] Now, what is worthy of note in these? That Matthew said nothing about the ignorance of the Son, but he seems to agree with Mark in meaning, because he said: 'but the Father only.' And we think 'only' was said in contradistinction to the angels, and the Son was not included with His own servants in ignorance.[15]

He, indeed, is without deceit who said: 'All things that the Father has are mine.'[16] But one of the things which He has is the knowledge of 'that day and hour.' In the reading of Matthew, omitting mention, therefore, of His Person as a fact admitted, the Lord said that the angels were ignorant, but the Father alone knew; saying by His silence that the knowledge of the Father was also His own, because He had

11 Cf. Luke 2.52.
12 *Philoponias*—used by St. Basil as a title only in this place. It is not used as a title by other writers.
13 Matt. 24.36.
14 Cf. Mark 13.32.
15 I.e., of the hour and the day.
16 John 16.15.

also said elsewhere: 'Even as the Father knows me and I know the Father.'[17] And, if the Father knows the Son wholly and entirely, so that He knows all the wisdom residing in Him, in equal measure, certainly, will He also be known by the Son, with all His inherent wisdom and foreknowledge of the future. Therefore, we think that the passage occurring in Matthew, 'But the Father only,' demands this explanation. But the saying of Mark, since he also plainly seems to separate the Son from the knowledge, we understand in this way: that no one knows, neither the angels of God, but not even the Son would have known, unless the Father had known, that is, the cause of the Son's knowledge is from the Father. And this explanation is not far-fetched if one listens with a fair mind, since 'only' is not added, as in Matthew. Therefore, the meaning in Mark is as follows: Concerning that day or hour no one knows, neither the angels of God, but not even the Son would have known unless the Father had known, for from the Father was knowledge first given to Him. And this is to speak most reverently and becomingly concerning the Son, because from Him with whom He is consubstantial He also received His knowledge and His attribute of being beheld in all wisdom and in glory becoming to His divinity.

Concerning Jechonias, whom the Prophet Jeremias declares had been cast out from the land of Judea when he said: 'Jechonias was dishonored as a vessel of which there is no need; and because he himself was rejected and his seed, neither shall any man rise from his seed to sit on the throne of David, to have power in Judea,'[18] the statement is simple and clear. When Jerusalem was demolished by Nabucho-

17 John 10.15.
18 Cf. Jer. 22.28-30.

donosor,[19] the kingdom was destroyed, and no longer were there hereditary successions to the sovereignty as formerly; at that time, moreover, being out of power, the posterity of David were living in captivity. But, when the followers of Salathiel and Zorobabel[20] returned, they led the people more democratically, transferring the rule henceforth to the priesthood because of the intermingling of the priestly and royal tribes. Therefore, the 'lord[21] is both king and high priest in the matters pertaining to God.'[22] And the kingly race did not fail until the coming of Christ; nevertheless, the seed of Jechonias no longer sat on the throne of David. The 'throne,' of course, means the royal dignity. At any rate, recall the history—that all Judea was tributary to David, the Idumean country as well as that of the Moabites, and whatever parts of Syria were near at hand, and the more distant lands up to Mesopotamia, and on the other side as far as the river of Egypt. If, then, no one of his descendants was seen in such a dignity, why is the word of the Prophet not true—that no longer will one from the seed of Jechonias sit on the throne of David? No one descended from him appears to have succeeded to this dignity. However, the tribe of Juda did not fail until He came for whom it was reserved, who did not Himself sit upon a material throne, for the kingdom of Judea had now been transferred to Herod, the son of Antipater, the Ascalonite, and to his sons, who divided Judea into four provinces when Pilate was governor and Tiberius held the power over the whole Roman province. But His indestructible kingdom he calls the throne of David on which the Lord sat. He Himself is 'the expectation of nations,'[23]

19 The story is told in 2 Par. 36, and also in 4 Kings 23.34-25.
20 Cf. 1 Esd. 3.2.
21 Ruler or leader.
22 Cf. Heb. 5.1,2.
23 Cf. Gen. 49.10.

not of the least part of the world. 'For there will be the root of Jesse,' it is said,[24] 'and he who rises up to rule the Gentiles, in him the Gentiles will hope.' 'For I have placed you for a covenant of the people, for a light of the Gentiles.'[25] 'And I shall establish,' it is said, 'his seed forever, and his throne as the days of the heavens.'[26] So, then, God remained both a priest—even if he did not receive the sceptre of Judea—and king of all the earth, and the blessing of Jacob was confirmed; 'And in his seed shall all the tribes of the earth be blessed,'[27] and all the Gentiles shall bless the Christ.

Now, to the subtle Encratites, in answer to their solemn question why we do not eat all things, let this be said, that we loathe also our excrement. According to their value the vegetables of the field are meats for us, but according to our judgment of what is beneficial; just as among vegetables we distinguish the harmful from the healthful, so also in our meats we separate the harmful from the useful. Even the hemlock is a vegetable, just as the vulture's flesh is meat; nevertheless, one who has any sense would neither eat henbane nor touch dog's flesh, unless extreme necessity forced him; while, certainly, he who ate it did not act unlawfully.

In answer to those who say that human affairs are governed by fate, do not seek explanations from us, but wound them with their own rhetorical darts; the question is too long for my present state of weakness.

Concerning the emerging in baptism, I do not know what ever came upon you to ask, if you have actually admitted that the immersion fulfills the figure of the three days. It is impossible to be dipped under water three times without emerging just as many times.

24 Isa. 11.10. (Septuagint).
25 Cf. Isa. 42.6.
26 Cf. 2 Kings 7.13.
27 Cf. Gen. 22.18.

As to the word '*phágos,*'[28] we put the acute accent on the penult.

'Substance' and 'person' have the same difference as the general has in regard to the particular, just as a living being has in regard to this or that man. For this reason, we acknowledge one substance in the Godhead so as not to explain variously the definition of 'existence'; but we acknowledge a person which is individual, in order that the concept concerning the Father and Son and Holy Spirit may be unconfused and clarified for us. For, if we do not consider the definite qualities of each, such as paternity and sonship and holiness, but confess God from the general idea of existence, it is impossible to give a sound account of our faith. Therefore, it is necessary to add the particular to the general, and thus to profess our faith; the Godhead is common, the paternity is individual; and joining these we must say: 'I believe in God the Father.' Again, in the confession of the Son we must do about the same, that is, join the particular to the general and say: 'I believe in God the Son.' So also in the case of the Holy Spirit; fashioning our utterance in conformity with the pronouncement, we must say: 'I believe also in the divine Holy Spirit,' so that, throughout the whole, both the oneness is preserved in the confession of the one Godhead and the individuality of the Persons is confessed in the separation of the distinctive characteristics understood in each. But they who say that substance and person (*hypóstasis*) are the same are compelled to confess only different Persons (*prósōpa*), and in avoiding the declaration of three Persons (*hypóstaseis*) they are found not to escape the evil of Sabellius, who also, although frequently himself confusing the idea, undertakes to distinguish the Persons (*prósōpa*), saying that the same Person (*hypóstasis*) is changed according to the need occurring each time.

---

28 The Doric form is *phagós.*

Concerning your question as to how the neutral and indifferent matters about us are ordained, whether by some spontaneous chance, or by the just providence of God, we say this: that health and sickness, wealth and poverty, honor and dishonor, inasmuch as they do not make their possessors good, are not of the things which are good according to nature, but, inasmuch as they furnish some happiness in our lives, those first mentioned are preferable to their opposites and have some value in being mentioned. Yet, these are given by God to some for distribution, as to Abraham, and to Job, and to suchlike men. To the wicked they are a challenge to improve their habits, so that he, who after such a pledge of friendship from God perseveres in his iniquity incontrovertibly renders himself liable to condemnation. But the just man neither turns his mind to his wealth when he has it nor seeks it when he does not; he is not devoted to the enjoyment of what has been given him, but to its administration. And no one who has any sense is eager for the business of distributing others' possessions, unless he looks to the praise of the many who admire and envy those who are established in any office of power. Moreover, the just accept sickness as a conflict, awaiting their crowns made great because of their patience. For someone else to be appointed for the administration of these things is not only absurd, but also impious.

237. To Eusebius, Bishop of Samosata[1]

I both intended to send a letter to your Reverence through the Vicar of Thrace and I wrote other letters to send through a certain prefect of the treasury of Philippolis who was crossing from our country into Thrace, and I asked him to

1 Written in the spring of 376; cf. Loofs, *op. cit.* 11.

take them up when he was setting out. But the vicar did not take our letter. While we were traveling around our diocese, he stopped at the city in the evening and left again in the early morning, so that the arrival of the man escaped the notice of the administrators of the church and, in consequence, the letter remained with us. Then the prefect, when, by chance, some unexpected circumstance pressed upon him, set out in haste, without either picking up the letters or seeing us. It was not possible to find anyone else. Therefore, we remained grieved that we could neither write to you nor receive a letter from your Reverence. Yet, I was wishing, if it were possible, to announce to you what was happening to us each day. There are so many things and they are so contrary to expectation that there is need of a daily report, which I would have drawn up, you may be well assured, if I had not had my mind forcibly turned from my intention by the continuous succession of mishaps.

The vicar[2] visited us—the first and greatest of our evils. Whether the man is a heretic at heart I do not know (I think, in fact, that he is inexperienced in all doctrine, and does not even have any interest or care for such things, for in other matters I see him engrossed, soul and body, both night and day; but he is certainly a friend of the heretics. Yet, he loves them no more than he hates us. Indeed, he summoned a synod of impious men in the middle of winter at Galatia,[3] and, excommunicating Hypsinus, put Ecdicius[4] in his place. Further, he ordered my brother, who had been accused by one man, and him insignificant, to be removed. Then, after having been engaged about the camp for a short time, he again came breathing rage and slaughter,[5] and handed over to the senate all the clergy of the church in

2 Demosthenes; cf. Letter 225.
3 At Ancyra.
4 At Parnassus, a few miles higher up the Halys than Tchikin Aghyl.
5 Cf. Acts 9.1.

Caesarea in one sentence. He presided in Sebaste for many days, choosing his friends, calling those in communion with us senators and condemning them to the service of the state, but treating with the greatest honor the adherents of Eustathius.

Again, he ordered a synod of the clergy of Galatia and Pontus to be summoned at Nyssa.[6] They obeyed, and having assembled, sent a certain man[7] to the churches; what his character is I would not like to say, yet it is possible for your Wisdom to surmise of what sort he is likely to be who seconds such policies of men. And at present, while I have been writing these things, this same band has started for Sebaste to be united with Eustathius and with him to overthrow the affairs of the Nicopolitans. For the blessed Theodotus[8] has fallen asleep. Meanwhile, they have nobly and strongly beaten off the first attacks of the vicar, for he tried to persuade them to receive Eustathius and through him to accept the bishop. But, as he saw that they were not yielding willingly, he is now trying with a more violent hand to establish the one[9] who is being given. However, some expectation of a synod is being hinted at, to which they are planning to summon us and either to receive us in communion with them or to enjoy their friendship. Such, then, are the affairs of the churches. As to what state of health I am in, I believe that it is better to be silent than to write, since I will only cause distress by telling the truth, and I cannot endure to tell a lie.

6 The first synod held at Ancyra was of no avail. On St. Gregory's deposition and banishment, cf. his *De vita Macr.* 2.192 and Letters 18, and 22; also St. Gregory Nazianzus, Letter 142.

7 The Benedictine editors consider that this refers to the unknown intruder into the see of Nyssa. St. Basil mentions him contemptuously in Letter 239.

8 Cf. Letter 121.

9 Fronto.

238. To the Presbyters of Nicopolis[1]

I received the letter of your Reverence, and I was not able to learn anything of more recent date from it than what I had already known. The report had come beforehand to all the country around, relating the disgrace of the one among you who fell, who because of a desire of empty glory brought shameful dishonor upon himself, and was found to have fallen from the rewards of his faith through self-love, but who because of the just hatred of those who fear the Lord did not attain that wretched little glory through the longing for which he had been betrayed into impiety. But that man by his present course of action has disclosed very clear evidence of his whole life—that never did he live in the hope of the promises reserved for us by the Lord, but if he engaged in any human undertakings for his own interests, he used all, both words of faith and forms of piety, to deceive those with whom he came in contact.

But, why is a chance event afflicting you? In what respect have you become worse than you were in consequence of this? One of your number has left, but, even if perhaps another one or two went along, they are to be pitied for their fall, yet your body is whole by the grace of God. What was rendered useless has fallen away, and what has remained is not mutilated. And, if it grieves you because you have been cast outside of the walls, nevertheless you shall abide under the protection of the God of heaven; moreover, the guardian angel of the Church has gone out with you. So they lie down in empty houses day by day, preparing for themselves a grave judgment because of the dispersion of

1 Written in the spring of 376; cf. Loofs, *op. cit.* 13ff. On the consecration of Fronto, Semi-Arian bishop, cf. Letter 227; on Theodotus, cf. Letter 121.

2 Cf. Ps. 90.1.

the people. Even if there is some suffering in the situation, I trust in the Lord that this will not turn out fruitless for you. Therefore, the greater the trials you experience, so much the more glorious reward may you expect from the just Judge. Do not be impatient over the present troubles, and do not flag in hope. 'For yet a very little while, and he who is your helper will come, and will not delay.'[3]

239. To Eusebius, Bishop of Samosata[1]

The Lord has given us even now through our fellow presbyter, the most beloved and pious brother, Antiochus, an opportunity to address your Holiness and to urge you to pray as usual for us and through our conversations by letter to find for yourself some consolation for our long separation. Moreover, we beseech you in your prayers to ask this as the first and greatest favor from the Lord—that we be delivered from the wicked and malicious men who have gained the mastery over the people to such an extent that now our condition resembles nothing other than the Jewish captivity.[2] For, the weaker the state into which the churches sink, the more does the lust of men for power increase. And now the name of bishop has devolved upon wretched household slaves, since no one of the servants of God wishes to put himself in opposition except desperate men, such as they are who have now been sent by Anysius, the disciple of Euippius, and Ecdicius the Parnassian, and he who appointed him

3 Cf. Heb. 10.37.

1 Written in the spring of 376; cf. Loofs, *op. cit.* 8-17.

2 Undoubtedly a reference to the capture of Jerusalem in the year 70 and the events which then transpired, as the Benedictine editors suggest.

has put into the churches an evil traveling-companion for himself for the future life. These men have now driven my brother from Nyssa and have introduced in his stead a man, or rather a slave worth a few obols, but, as regards the corruption of the faith, a match for those who appointed him. Further, to the village of Doara a wretched fellow, a household slave of orphans, who ran away from his masters, has been sent in order to flatter an impious little woman who formerly used George according to her own will, and now has got this man as his successor, and the piteous name of the episcopate is insulted. Who could bewail the affairs of the Nicopolitans as they deserve, since the wretched Fronto first assumed, as he pretended, the advocacy of the truth, and, finally, betrayed shamefully both the faith and himself, receiving as a reward of his betrayal a name of dishonor? He received from them the dignity of the episcopate, as he thinks, but, by the grace of God, he has become the common abomination of all Armenia. Nevertheless, there is nothing that they will not dare, nor do they lack co-workers worthy of themselves. The rest of the news of Syria brother Antiochus both knows and will relate better than we could.

You, however, have met with these conditions of the West before, since brother Dorotheus has told you everything. What sort of letters should be given to him when he again departs? Perhaps he will share the journey of the noble Sanctissimus,[3] who has great zeal and is going around the East collecting signatures and letters from each of the men of distinction. Now, as to what I should write through them, or how agree with those who are writing, I am at a loss; if you shall find some soon who are coming to us, be so kind as to inform us. It comes to my mind to speak the words of Diomede:

3 Sanctissimus seems to have made two visits to the East as the envoy of Damasus. Cf. Letters 120, 132, 221, 225, 253, and 254.

'Would that thou never hadst sought, because,' he says, 'haughty is the man.'[4] In truth, arrogant characters, when they are honored, often become more disdainful than they were. Yet, if the Lord will be propitious to us, what other assistance do we need? But, if the anger of God remains, what help is there for us from Western superciliousness? They neither know the truth, nor are they willing to learn, but, being preoccupied with false suspicions, they now do the same as they did formerly in the case of Marcellus,[5] contending with those who are announcing the truth to them and themselves confirming the heresy. In fact, I myself wished to write to their leader apart from the joint document, not at all, however, about ecclesiastical matters—except so much as to hint that they neither know the truth about our affairs, nor do they accept the means through which they might learn—but in general concerning the fact that there is no need to afflict those humbled under trials, nor to judge dignity to be pride, a sin which alone is sufficient to produce enmity against God.

240. To the Presbyters of Nicopolis[1]

You did well in writing to us, especially in writing through such a man. He would suffice even without letters to provide considerable consolation for us in our anxieties and to give an accurate explanation of the situation. In fact, because of the scattered rumors coming across to us, there were many things which we were eager to learn from one who

4 Homer, *Iliad* 9.698-699.
5 Cf. Letter 69.

1 Written in 376.

had a clear understanding of them. All of these the most beloved and most honored brother, our fellow presbyter Theodosius, explained to us consistently and practically. Consequently, we are writing to your Reverences the counsels which we are recommending to ourselves, that these things which are befalling you have happened to many; not only at the present time, but even in the past, there have been innumerable examples of such occurrences; some have been left in written accounts, others we have received through unwritten memory from those who knew them, for both individually and by cities trials for the sake of the name of the Lord have beset those who have hoped in Him. Nevertheless, all have passed by and no darkness has held unending distress. As the hails and the torrents and any other chance evils easily harm and ruin soft objects, but suffer more harm than they cause if they meet with unyielding ones, so also the fierce trials stirred up against the Church have been clearly shown to be weaker than the firm foundation of our faith in Christ. Just as the cloud of hail passed by and the torrent flowed beyond its gully (the one was dissolved in the open air and the other disappeared in the deep, leaving the path through which it flowed dry and without moisture), so also the storms now overtaking us will in a short time cease. If only we would permit ourselves not to see the present, but to gaze steadfastly with hope at things a little more distant!

If, then, the trial is heavy, brethren, let us endure the pains; no one is crowned unless he has been assailed in the contest and covered with dust. And, if these sports of the Devil are light and they who have been sent against us are troublesome because they are his servants, but despicable because God has joined powerlessness to their wickedness, let us guard against the condemnation that we are making great lamentations over slight sufferings. One thing is worthy of grief—the loss of that person who for the sake of transient glory (if, indeed, we must say that behaving unseemly in public is glory) deprived himself of the everlasting honor of the just. You are the children of confessors, you are the children of martyrs who have resisted sin unto blood.[2] Let each use his own relatives as examples for constancy in defense of true religion. No one of us has been torn to pieces by lashes; no one's house has been confiscated; we have not lived in exile; we have no experience of prison. What evil have we suffered? Unless, perhaps, this is distressing—that we have in no way been ill treated nor considered worthy of suffering for Christ.[3] But, if this—the fact that so-and-so occupies the house of prayer, and you worship the Lord of heaven and earth in the open air—grieves you, reflect that the eleven disciples were shut up in the upper room, but those who crucified the Lord fulfilled the Jewish service in the celebrated Temple. Judas, in preferring death by hanging to living with shame, proved himself better, perhaps, than those of the present time who are past blushing before the universal condemnation of men, and who for this reason are not affected with shame for disgraceful acts.

Only, do not be deceived by the falsehoods of these when they profess correctness of faith. Such men, in fact, are traffickers in Christ, and not Christians, since they prefer always to make profit for themselves in this life rather than to live according to the truth. When they thought that they were obtaining this empty power, they associated themselves with the enemies of Christ; when they saw that the people were angry, they made a show again of true religion. I do

2 Cf. Heb. 12.4.
3 Cf. Acts 5.41.

not recognize a bishop, nor would I number among the priests of Christ[4] one put forward for leadership by unhallowed hands to the dissolution of the faith. This is my decision. If you have any part with us, you will, of course, hold the same opinion as we do. But, if you take counsel of yourselves, each is responsible for his own opinion and we are innocent of this blood. I have written these words, not distrusting you, but by a declaration of my opinion confirming the uncertainty of some, so that no one may be taken prematurely into communion, nor any, having received the imposition of hands from them, afterwards, when peace has been made, may use force to have themselves numbered in the body of the clergy. All the clergy, both in the city and in the diocese, together with all the people who fear the Lord, we greet through you.

241. To Eusebius, Bishop of Samosata[1]

It is not to increase your despondency that in our letters we seldom refrain from mentioning our troubles to your Honor, but to give some consolation to ourselves by our lamentations, which, when expressed, somehow are able to dissipate the pain in the depth of our heart. We also wish to spur your Lordship to more fervent prayer for the churches. Assuredly, Moses prayed always for his people, yet, when his struggle against Amalec[2] had begun, he did not let his hands drop down from dawn until evening. The outstretching of the holy man's hands ended only with the cessation of the fighting.

4 Cf. Letter 54.

1 Written in 376.
2 Cf. Exod. 17, especially 11-13.

242. To the Westerners[1]

Since the holy God has promised those who hope in Him a means of escape from every affliction, we, even if we have been cut off in the midst of a sea of evils and are racked by the mighty waves stirred up against us by the spirits of wickedness, nevertheless endure in Christ who strengthens us, and we have not slackened the intensity of our zeal for the churches, nor do we, as in a storm when the waves rise high, expect destruction. We still hold fast to our earnest endeavors as much as is possible, sensible of the fact that he who was swallowed by the whale was considered deserving of safety because he did not despair of his life but cried out to the Lord.[2] So, then, we ourselves, having reached the uttermost limit of evils, do not give up our hope in the Lord, but watch and see His help on all sides. Therefore, we have now looked to you, too, our most honored brethren, who frequently in the time of tribulations we expected would come to us. When we were disappointed in our hope, we also said to ourselves: 'I looked for one that would grieve together with me, but there was none; and for those that would comfort me, and I found none.'[3] Our sufferings are such as to have reached even to the limits of our inhabited world; if, when one member suffers, all the members suffer along with it,[4] surely it was proper for your Mercifulnesses also to be compassionate toward us who have been suffering for a long time. Not the nearness of the places, but the union of spirit, is wont to engender the friendship which we believe is entertained for us by your Charities.

1 This plea to the Westerners was successful in winning sympathy for the East. The Benedictine editors object to the earlier date for this letter determined by Tillemont, and place it no earlier than Easter, 376.

2 Cf. Jonas 2.

3 Ps. 68.21.

4 Cf. 1 Cor. 12.26.

Just why, then, has there been no letter of consolation, no visit of the brethren, nothing else of what is owed to us by the law of love? This is the thirteenth year[5] since the war of the heretics against us originated. In this time there have been more afflictions in the churches than those mentioned since the Gospel of Christ was proclaimed.[6] We are unwilling to describe each of them separately to you, lest at some time the insufficiency of our speech might weaken the clear evidence of the evils. At the same time, we do not think that you stand in need of information, since you have long ago learned the truth of our troubles by report. However, here is a summary of the evil: the laity, who have now left the houses of prayer, assemble in the solitudes. It is a pitiable sight—women, children, old men, and those who are in other ways feeble, enduring hardships in the open fields in the most violent rainstorms, snows, winds, and frosts of winter, as well as in summer under the heat of the sun. And they suffer these things because they are unwilling to be of the base leaven[7] of Arius.

But how could speech represent these facts to you clearly, unless experience itself and personal observation should rouse you to compassion? Therefore, we urge you, now at least, to stretch out your hand to the churches in the East which have already fallen to their knees, and to send some men to remind us of the rewards reserved for the patient endurance of sufferings for Christ. Ordinary speech is not wont to be so efficacious as the unfamiliar voice is to produce consolation, especially when it belongs to men who by the grace of God are everywhere recognized as among the noblest; and rumor

5 The thirteenth year of Valens' reign began March 376. This fact furnished reasons to the Benedictine editors for dating this letter as they have done. Cf. *Vita Basil.* 35.

6 As Jackson says, 'a rhetorical expression not to be taken literally.'

7 Cf. Matt. 16.6.

reports to all men that such you are who have persisted in the faith unwounded, preserving inviolate the deposit of the Apostles. Yet, not such is our position, but we have some men who with a desire for glory and with the pride which above all tramples on the souls of Christians, have boldly used certain innovations in their expressions, and for this reason the churches, having become rotten, like vessels made porous, received the heretical corruption that was streaming in. But you, O beloved and much desired brethren, be the physicians of our wounded members and the trainers of our sound ones, healing that which is ill and stimulating to piety that which is sound.

243. To the Bishops of Italy and of Gaul; concerning the Condition and Confusion of the Churches[1]

To our truly most beloved of God and most dear brethren and fellow ministers of like mind, the bishops of Gaul and Italy, Basil, Bishop of Caesarea in Cappadocia.

Our Lord Jesus Christ, who deigned to call the whole Church of God His body, and who declared each one of us members of one another, also granted all of us the privilege of friendship for all through the harmonious union of the members. Therefore, even if we are very distant from each other in our dwellings, nevertheless, by reason at least of our union we are near to each other. Since, then, the head is not able to say to the feet, 'I have no need of you,'[2] certainly, you will not dare to reject us, but you will feel as much compassion for our afflictions, to which we have been handed

1 Cf. Letter 242 n. 1. This letter was written in the early summer of 376; cf. Loofs, *op. cit.* 41.

2 1 Cor. 12.21.

over because of our sins, as we feel joy at your glory in the peace which the Lord has granted you. We have already at another time called upon your Charities for help and compassion toward us, but, assuredly, because our retribution had not been paid in full, you were not allowed to rise up to our assistance. We request especially that through your Reverences the confusion in our affairs may be evident to the emperor[3] himself of your country; if this is difficult, we ask that some may come from among you to visit and console those who are afflicted, in order that they may see with their own eyes the calamities of the East. It is impossible to realize them by hearsay, because no word can be found which can clearly describe to you our condition.

A persecution has seized upon us, most honorable brethren, the most grievous of persecutions. The shepherds are persecuted in order that the flocks may be scattered. And the hardest part is that neither do those who are wronged receive their sufferings in the full assurance of martyrdom, nor do the people cherish the athletes in the rank of martyrs, because the name of Christian embraces the persecutors. There is one charge now for which severe punishment is allotted—the exact observance of the traditions of the Fathers. For this the pious are banished from their native lands and are led into the solitary places. Gray hair is not held in reverence by the judges of iniquity, nor the practice of piety, nor a life spent according to the Gospel from youth till old age. No malefactor, indeed, has been condemned without clear evidence, but bishops have been convicted on slander alone, and, although no proof has been brought forward for the charges, they are handed over for punishment. Some did not even know their accusers nor see the courts, nor were they falsely accused to begin with, but, carried off by

3 Gratian, successor of Valentinian I in 375.

violence at an untimely hour of the night, they were exiled to foreign lands, handed over to the sufferings of solitude until their death.[4] What follows these acts is known to everyone, even if we are silent: flight of the presbyters, flight of the deacons, and plundering of all the clergy. It is necessary either to adore the image or to be handed over to the painful flame of the lashes.[5] There are the groans of the people, continuous weeping throughout the homes and in public, since all bewail their sufferings with each other. No one is so stony-hearted as, when deprived of his father, to bear his orphanhood quietly. There is the sound of people lamenting in the city, it is in the fields, on the roads, in the solitudes. There is only one voice of all, who recount their pitiable and sad condition. Gladness and spiritual joy are done away with. Our feasts are turned into mourning;[6] our houses of prayer are closed; the altars of our spiritual service are idle. No longer are there assemblies of Christians, no longer presiding of teachers, no instructions of salvation, no festal assemblies, no nightly singing of psalms, nor that blessed joy of the souls which at the religious gatherings and at reception of Holy Communion is born in the souls of those who believe in the Lord. It is proper for us to say: 'Neither is there at this time prince, or prophet, or leader, or oblation, or incense, or place of firstfruits before the Lord, that we may find mercy.'[7]

We are writing this to you although you are aware of it, since there is no part of the world which is ignorant now of our misfortunes. Therefore, you should not suppose that we

4 Cf. Theod. 4.13, where the expulsion of Eusebius from Samosata is described. The most striking example of death following on exile is probably that of St. John Chrysostom in 407. St. Basil, of course, did not live to see this.

5 Cf. Dan. 3.10,11.

6 Cf. Amos 8.10.

7 Cf. Dan. 3.38,39.

are writing these words to give information nor to put your Graces in mind of us. We know that you would never forget us, no more, indeed, than the mother would forget the children of her womb.[8] But, since those who are weighed down by some excessive pain are wont somehow to relieve their suffering by groans, we also are doing this very thing, that is to say, we are ridding ourselves of the weight of our grief by announcing to your Charities our manifold misfortunes, in the hope that you, being roused more zealously to prayers for us, might beseech the Lord to be reconciled to us. Now, if the afflictions were only those oppressing us, we would have determined to keep silence and to rejoice in our sufferings for Christ, since 'The sufferings of the present time are not worthy to be compared with the glory to come that will be revealed in us.'[9] But now we fear lest some day the evil increasing like some flame making its way through burning wood, when it has consumed what is near, may also seize upon that which is farther away. The evil of heresy is spreading, and there is fear lest, having preyed upon our churches, it may afterwards creep even to the sound portion of your diocese. Perhaps, then, because sin abounded among us, we first were handed over to be devoured by the ravenous teeth of the enemies of God. And perhaps—what is even more likely—since the Gospel of the Kingdom, beginning in our region, went forth to all the world, for this reason the common Enemy of our souls is striving that the seeds of apostasy, having their starting point in the same region, should spread abroad to all the world. For, upon whomsoever the light of the knowledge of Christ has shone, upon them the darkness of impiety also contrives to come.

8 Cf. Isa. 49.15.
9 Cf. Rom. 8.18.

Therefore, as true disciples of the Lord, consider our afflictions yours. It is not for money, not for glory, not for any other transient thing that we are waging war; it is for our common possession, the hereditary treasure of sound faith, that we are fighting. Share our sufferings, you who love your brethren, because, though the mouths of the pious among us have been closed, every bold and blasphemous tongue of men who 'speak iniquity against God' has been loosed. The pillars and the foundation of truth are scattered, and we, who have been despised because of our insignificance, are deprived of freedom of speech. Exert yourselves in behalf of the people, and do not look to yourselves alone because you lie at anchor in calm ports, since the grace of God has given you every protection from the storm of the winds of evil. But to those of the churches also which are being overcome by the storm stretch out your hand, lest, ever being left abandoned, they suffer complete shipwreck of the faith. Lament for us because the Only-begotten is blasphemed, and there is no one who speaks against it. The Holy Spirit is rejected, and he who is able to refute is sent into exile. Polytheism has prevailed. There is a great god among them and a small one. 'Son' is believed to be not a name of nature, but a title of some dignity; the Holy Spirit, not to be complemental of the blessed Trinity, nor sharing in the divine and blessed nature, but one of the creatures added at random and by chance to the Father and the Son. 'Who will give water to my head, and a fountain of tears to my eyes?'[10] And I shall weep many days for my people who are being driven by these depraved teachings to destruction. The ears of the more simple are being seduced; they have already become accustomed to heretical impiety. The nurslings of the Church grow up with the doctrines of impiety. In fact, what

10 Jer. 9.1.

are they to do? In their heretical hands are baptisms, attendance on those departing this life, visits to the sick, consolations for those in distress, help for the oppressed, assistance of every kind, and communion of the mysteries; all these things, brought to pass through them, become for the people a bond of unanimity with them, so that, after a short time has passed, even if there should be some freedom, there is no hope now that those held fast by long-continued deceit will be recalled once more to the recognition of the truth.

For these reasons many of us ought to meet with your Dignities, and each one become the expounder of his own troubles. At present, let this very fact be evidence to you of the misery in which we live—that we are not free as regards journeys abroad. If anyone should stay away from his church even for the shortest time, he will betray his people to those who are lying in wait. But, by the grace of God we have sent one in place of the many, the most pious and beloved brother, our fellow presbyter Dorotheus. He is able by his personal observations to fill in the details which have escaped our letter, since he has followed all things with exactness and has been from the beginning a champion of the true faith. After having received him in peace, send him back speedily to us with the good tidings of the desire which you have to assist the brethren.

244. To Patrophilus, Bishop of the Church at Aegae[1]

I have read your letter, which you sent through brother Strategius, our fellow presbyter, and have read it with pleasure. In fact, why should I not so have done, since it was written by an intelligent man and from a heart which has been taught by the precept of the Lord to direct its love to all men? And I understood more or less the cause of the silence in the past. You were like a person perplexed and greatly amazed, because the notorious Basil, who from boyhood rendered such services to a certain one, who did various things on different occasions and undertook war against numberless others to show favor to that one, now had become an entirely different person and had taken upon himself warfare instead of charity, and whatever other things you have written. And you made sufficiently evident the disturbance of your soul in the unexpected change of affairs. Even though you upbraided us somewhat, I did not take it ill. For I am not so averse to admonition as to be annoyed at the charitable rebukes of the brethren. I am, in fact, so far from being vexed at what you have written that I almost laughed at it, since, although the ties which, as I think, formerly confirmed our friendship with each other were so many and so great, you yourself, because of trifling rumors which came to you, wrote that you experienced such great consternation. You, too, then, have had the experience of the many who, neglecting to examine the nature of the facts, are intent on the men concerning whom there is

---

1 Patrophilus, a friend of St. Basil and Eustathius of Sebaste, had written expressing his surprise at the break between the two after such a long friendship. Aegae is a city in Cilicia, modern Ayas; cf. Lucan 3.227. There were also towns of the same name in Achaia, Macedonia, Euboea, and Aeolia. Cf., also, Letter 250. This letter was written in the summer of 376; cf. Loofs, *op. cit.* 17f.

discussion and become, not inquirers into the truth, but judges of the distinction of persons, forgetting the admonition that 'it is not good to admit a difference of persons in judgment.'[2]

But, since God does not take a person into consideration in the judgment of mankind, that defense which I have prepared for the great tribunal I shall not refuse to make known to you. From the beginning nothing on our part, either trivial or more important, has been the cause of the disagreement, but men who hate us for reasons which they themselves know (indeed, there is no need for me to say anything about them) were continually inventing slanders. We laid them bare once, and then again. But there was no end to the affair and no advantage from the continual defenses, since we dwelt far off and those spreading the false reports were able from near at hand to wound by the slanders against us a heart easy to conquer and not trained to keep one ear unprejudiced for him who was not present. Moreover, the citizens of Nicopolis were demanding some full assurance of faith, a thing of which you were not altogether ignorant, and so we decided to undertake the furnishing of the document.[3] We thought that we would successfully accomplish two things in the same act, that we would both persuade the Nicopolitans not to have a bad opinion of the man[4] and would close the mouths of those who are slandering us, since agreement in faith would exclude the slanders on both sides. In fact, the creed was composed and was presented by us, and it was signed. When it had been

2 Cf. Deut. 1.17.

3 This reference is to the document presented to Eustathius by St. Basil in 373 and signed by Eustathius and others. It is preserved as Letter 125.

4 Eustathius.

signed, not only a place was designated for a second synod, but also another date was assigned, so that our brethren throughout the diocese, also assembling, might be united with each other, and our communion for the future might be genuine and sincere.

We, therefore, met at the appointed time, and the brethren with us—some were present and others were streaming in, all bright and eager, as if hastening toward peace.[5] Moreover, a letter from us and couriers gave the information that we were at hand, for the place appointed for the reception of those assembling was ours. But, as no one of the other party was there, either coming in advance, or announcing the arrival of those whom we were expecting, the men we sent returned, telling of the great dejection and murmuring of the people there, as if we were proclaiming a new creed. Furthermore, they were said to have declared that they certainly would not permit their bishop to come to us. Then, too, a certain man came bringing a letter for us as a matter of form and with no mention of what had been agreed upon in the beginning. And brother Theophilus,[6] worthy of all reverence and honor on my part, having sent one of his followers, made certain declarations which he thought were appropriate for him to utter and were proper for us to to hear. For he did not deign to write, not so much because he suspected a refutation from the letter, as because he was anxious not to be compelled to address us as a bishop; at any rate, his words were exceedingly violent, and were the expression of an incensed heart. After this we adjourned, humiliated and disconsolate, since we did not have any answer to give to our questioners. Not long thereafter there

5 Cf. Letter 130.
6 Of Castabala.

was a journey to Cilicia,[7] then a return, and without delay a letter containing a prohibition of communion with us.[8]

The cause of the separation, he says, is that we wrote to Apollinaris, and that we hold our fellow presbyter Diodorus as a communicant. I have never considered Apollinaris an enemy; on the contrary, there are some reasons for which I even reverence the man. Certainly, I have not so linked myself with him as to assume the charges against him, considering that I myself also have certain accusations to bring since I have read some of his treatises. However, I am not conscious either of having asked him for the book about the Holy Spirit or of having received one that he sent. Yet I hear that he has become the most voluminous[9] of all writers. I have read few of his treatises, for I have no leisure to examine such things, and at the same time I am averse to the acceptance of more recent writings, since my body does not permit me to remain steadfast even in diligently and fittingly reading the God-inspired Scriptures. What, then, is this to me, if someone wrote something not pleasing to a certain man? Yet, if it is necessary for one to render an account for another, let him who is accusing me because of Apollinaris answer to us for Arius, his own teacher, and for Aetius, his own pupil. But we were neither taught anything by him nor did we become a disciple of him whose charges they turn upon us. Diodorus,[10] however, as the disciple of the blessed Silvanus, we accepted from the beginning, and even now we love and respect him because of the grace of speech which he possesses, through which many of those coming in contact with him are made better.

7 Cf. Letter 130.
8 Cf. Letter 226.
9 Cf. Letter 263.
10 This Diodorus, at the time a presbyter of Antioch, became Bishop of Tarsus some time after St. Basil's death.

Affected, as was understandable, by this letter, and amazed at the change so unexpected and so sudden, I was not even able to reply. My heart was constricted, my tongue was unnerved, my hand grew numb, and I experienced the sufferings of an ignoble soul (for the truth will be told, yet it is worthy of pardon). I was almost driven into a state of misanthropy. Every line of conduct I considered a matter of suspicion, and I believed that the virtue of charity did not exist in human nature, but that, although it was a specious word which gave some glory to those using it, this disposition did not really exist in the heart of man, if he who seemed from childhood to late old age to have practiced watchfulness over himself was so easily made unfeeling by such allegations. He took no account of our side of the question and did not regard his experience in the past as more significant than so paltry a slander, but, like some untamed colt not yet taught to carry its rider well, he reared up because of a slight suspicion and shook off and threw to the ground those in whom formerly he had gloried. What must we surmise concerning the others, with whom we do not have such pledges of friendship, and from whom there is no such proof of watchfulness of manners? Revolving these thoughts in my mind and continually turning them over in my heart, or rather, my heart being overturned by them, since they were biting and pricking me so at my recollection of them, I gave no answer to that letter. I was not silent through contempt (do not think this, brother, for we do not defend ourselves to men, but we plead our cause in Christ before God), but through perplexity and helplessness and the inability to say anything commensurate with my grief.

While we were in this state of perplexity, another letter reached us, written, as it was pretended, to a certain Dazizas, but in truth sent out for all men, as its distribution, so rapid that in a few days it was spread throughout the whole Pontus and was circulating in Galatia, gave evidence. Some say that the messengers of these good tidings, traveling even through Bithynia, reached as far as the Hellespont itself. Now, what was written against us to Dazizas you assuredly know. For they do not consider you so far from their friendship as to leave you alone without the favor of that honor. But, if the letter has not reached you, at least I shall send it to you. In it you will find the accusations brought against us: deceit and want of principle, corruption of churches, and destruction of souls, and, what in their opinion is truest of all, that we made that exposition of faith with an insidious intention, not serving the Nicopolitans, but we ourselves intending to obtain the confession deceitfully. The Lord is the judge of these matters. For, what clear proof could there be of the thoughts in a heart? Yet, on this one point I have wondered at them, that, although they had subscribed to the document we presented, they were subject to so much disagreement that they were confusing truth and falsehood for the satisfaction of those accusing them; but they do not consider this, that their written confession of the Nicene Creed is reserved in Rome, and that by their own hand they gave to the synod at Tyana the document from Rome, which contains this same Creed and is deposited with us. Moreover, they have forgotten their own speech delivered at that time in public and deploring the deceit through which they were led on to agree to the document[11] composed by the party of Eudoxius and so they devised this defense for that fault—go to Rome, and there accept the Creed of the Fathers, in order that whatever harm they had done to the churches by agreeing to the evil they might

11 Perhaps the Creed of, Ariminum.

correct by introducing something better. But they who submitted to the longest journeys for the sake of the faith and delivered these wise speeches are now slandering us, on the grounds that we are proceeding deceitfully and under the guise of charity are doing the works of schemers. Moreover, the letter now being circulated makes it evident that they have condemned the Nicene Creed. For they saw Cyzicus and returned with another creed.

Why should I mention their inconstancy in words, since from their actions I have much greater proofs of their change to the opposition? For, although they would not yield to the decision of the 500 bishops[12] which was pronounced against them, nor consent to resign from the administration of the churches when so many were in agreement on the sentence of their deposition, because, they said, those were not partakers of the Holy Spirit nor were they managing the churches by the grace of God but had seized the positions of honor through human power and with a desire of empty glory, yet they now are receiving as bishops men they consecrated.[13] Ask them for me—even though they despise all men as having neither eyes nor ears nor a heart capable of perception, at least, so much as to enable them to perceive the inconsistency of what is happening: 'What idea do they have in their mind? How can there be two bishops, one deposed by Euippius[14] and one consecrated by him?' Both are acts of the same hand. If he had not the grace given to Jeremias to destroy and to build up, to root out and to plant,[15] he would not have uprooted the one and set up the other. But, if you give him the one power, you will yield the other, also, to him. Yet their one aim is,

12 Those who met at Constantinople in 360.
13 I.e., the 500 bishops.
14 Cf. Letter 228.
15 Cf. Jer. 1.10.

as it seems, to seek their own interests everywhere, and to consider him a friend who co-operates with their desires, but to judge as an enemy him who opposes their desires,[16] and to spare no slander against him.

Really, what are their present proceedings against the Church! Terrible because of the carelessness of those who are carrying them on, and pitiful because of the insensibility of those who are suffering them. Children of Euippius and grandchildren of Euippius,[17] summoned to Sebaste from foreign lands by a trustworthy embassy, they were entrusted with the people. They took possession of the altar, they became the leaven of the Church there. By them we are persecuted as defenders of 'consubstantiality'; and Eustathius, who brought the expression 'consubstantial' in the document from Rome to Tyana, this man now is associated with them, although he was not able to be received into their much desired communion, either because they feared the multitude of those who were united against him or respected their authority. Indeed, who those were who were assembled, and how each was ordained, and from what sort of a life originally he came to this present position of dignity—may I never have so much leisure as to explain their affairs! For I have learned to pray: 'That my mouth may not speak the works of men.'[18] And you yourself, if you search, will learn these things; and even if they escape you, assuredly they will not escape the notice of the Judge.

Nevertheless, the feelings I experienced I will not refuse to mention also to your Charity: that last year when I was ill with a most violent fever and was near to the very

16 For St. Basil's view on the validity of the ordinations by heretics, cf. Canon 1, Letter 188.

17 I.e., the clergy whose spiritual descent is to be traced to Euippius. The see over which the latter presided is unknown.

18 Cf. Ps. 16.4.

gates of death, and then was called back by the loving kindness of God, I was annoyed at my return, considering the kind of evils to which I was again returning; and I questioned within myself as to what it could possibly be that was reserved in the depth of the wisdom of God, for which days of life in the flesh were granted to me. When I understood these things, I concluded that the Lord wished us to see the churches freed from the tempest which they had previously experienced in the separation from those who had been entrusted with all things because of their feigned holiness. Or, perhaps the Lord wished to strengthen my soul and to render it more serious at least for the future, so that it might not be intent on men, but might be put in order through the precepts of the Gospel, which are changed neither with the times nor with the state of human affairs, but remain always the same, continuing just as they were uttered by the truthful and blessed mouth.

Men are like clouds which with the changing of the breezes[19] are borne to one part of the air at one time and again to another. And these especially, of whom our discourse treats, appear to be the most fickle of all who have come within our experience. Even though those who live with them might speak in regard to the other affairs of life, yet, as to their inconstancy concerning the faith which was evident to me, up to this time I have not been conscious myself either of having observed it in others or of having heard of it from others. They were followers of Arius in the beginning; they transferred to Hermogenes, who was diametrically opposed to the heterodoxy of Arius, as the creed originally promulgated by that man at Nicaea[20] makes

19 Cf. Jude 12.
20 Cf. Letter 81. Hermogenes preceded Dianius as Bishop of Caesarea. While still a deacon he acted as secretary at Nicaea.

evident. Hermogenes fell asleep and again they changed to Eusebius, the party leader of the circle about Arius, as those who have had experience say. Departing from there for some cause or other, they again returned to their native land, and again kept secret their Arian tendency. Promoted to the episcopate—to omit the intervening facts—how many creeds they set forth! One in Ancyra,[21] a second in Seleucia,[22] another in Constantinople,[23] that well-known one, another in Lampsacus,[24] and after this the one in Nice of Thrace,[25] and now again one in Cyzicus.[26] Of this one I am ignorant on other points, but I have heard this much, that they made no mention of 'consubstantiality,' and now add 'likeness in substance,' and with Eunomius sanction the blasphemies against the Holy Spirit. Now, of the creeds which we have enumerated, even if all are not opposed to each other, they certainly all alike give proof of the inconstancy of their character, since they never stand by the same words. These assertions are true, though countless other points have been passed over in silence.

And, since these have now gone over to you, we beg you to write back through the same messenger (I mean our fellow presbyter Strategius) as to whether you have continued the same toward us or have been alienated as a consequence of your conference. For it was not likely that they were silent, nor that you yourself, who have written such things to us, did not use freedom in your speech to them. If, then, you would remain in communion with us, that is excellent and deserving of the most earnest prayer. But, if they have

21 In 358, when *homoioúsion* was accepted.
22 In 359.
23 In 360.
24 In 364.
25 The Creed of Nice in Thrace was the Creed of Ariminum revised.
26 In 375 or 376. This formula is referred to in Letter 251 as the latest.

drawn you over to themselves, it is distressing. How would the separation from such a brother not be so? But, even if in nothing else, at least in bearing such losses we have been harassed enough by them.

245. *To Bishop Theophilus*[1]

Although I received the letter from your Charity long ago, I was waiting to give my answer through an appropriate person, in order that the carrier of the message might supply whatever was lacking in the letter. Accordingly, when our most beloved and pious brother, Strategius, arrived, I decided that it was a real opportunity to use him as a messenger, since he both knows our mind and is able to serve our interests sincerely and at the same time religiously. Be assured, therefore, most beloved and most honored friend, that we value highly our brotherly love for you, in which, as far as regards the affection of our soul, we are not conscious of

---

1 Theophilus, a leader of the semi-Arians, was elected bishop of Eleutheropolis in Palaestina Prima and took an oath not to accept any other bishopric (Sozomen, *Hist. Eccl.* 4.24). Later, however, he consented to be transferred to Castabala by Silvanus, the metropolitan of Tarsus, who, partly for this reason, was deposed by the synod of Constantinople in 360. In 362 he joined with Silvanus, Basil of Ancyra, and other leading semi-Arians, in a communication to Jovian begging him to confirm the decrees of Seleucia, banish the Anomoeans, and convene a general council. Cf. Socrates, *Hist. Eccl.* 3.25, and Sozomen, *Hist. Eccl.* 6.4. After the Council of Lampsacus, when Valens declared himself the supporter of the thorough Arians, Theophilus, Eustathius, and Silvanus were commissioned in 365 to communicate with him. Valens, however, had already started on his Gallic campaign, so they went on to the Bishop of Rome. When they presented a confession of faith, signed by fifty-nine semi-Arians, almost identical with that of Nicaea, Pope Liberius recognized their orthodoxy, and admitted them to communion. Theophilus and his party then went to Sicily, where they repeated the same declaration of faith at a synod of bishops of the island, and then returned home. Cf. Socrates, *Hist. Eccl.* 4.2; Sozomen, *Hist. Eccl.* 6.10-12.

having failed at any time, even though there have been many and great causes of reasonable grief. But now, this is our decision, setting the pleasant against the more unpleasant, as in a scale, to add our opinion to the weight of the good. However, since the matters have been changed by those by whom this ought least to have been done, pardon us, also, not because we changed in our opinion, but because we are changed in our position. Rather, we remain in the same position, but the others are continually changing, and at present are even openly deserting to our opponents. How much value we placed on the communion of these as long as they were in the sound party, not even you yourself are ignorant. But now, if we do not follow along with them and if we avoid those who hold the same opinions as they do, we should justly meet with pardon, since we consider nothing more precious than the truth and our own salvation.

246. To the Nicopolitans[1]

When I see, on the one hand, evil prospering, and on the other, your Reverences toiling and exhausted because of the continual abuses, I am filled with sadness. But, when anew I consider the mighty hand of God and realize that He knows how to raise again the fallen, to show affection for the just, to crush the arrogant, and to put down the powerful from their seats, again, in turn, I become lighter in spirit through hope, and I am confident that because of your prayers the Lord will show us a speedy calm. Only do not grow weary of praying; whatever you teach by words, endeavor in the present critical times to exemplify clearly to all by your deeds.

1 Letters 246 and 247 were written in the summer of 376; cf. Loofs, *op. cit.* 16 n. 6.

247. To the Nicopolitans

When I read the letter from your Holinesses, how much I groaned and lamented, because I had heard these additional troubles: lashes and insults against you yourselves, plundering of homes and wasting of the city and disruption of all the country, persecution of the Church and banishment of the clergy, incursion of wolves and scattering of flocks. But, when I had ceased from my groaning and my tears, I looked to the Lord in heaven, and I understand and am convinced. And this I wish you also to know, that help will be speedy, and the abandonment will not last forever. What we have suffered we have suffered because of our sins, but the Loving One will show us His aid because of His love and compassion for the churches.

Of course, we have not ceased beseeching personally those in power and writing to those at court who regard us with affection, that the man, raging with anger, be kept in check. And I think that a censure will reach him from many, unless, perchance, the time so filled with confusion[1] may afford those engaged in state affairs no leisure for these matters.

248. To Amphilochius, Bishop of Iconium[1]

Whenever we consider our own longings, we are grieved at being so far separated from your Reverence, but, when we regard the tranquility of your life, we give thanks to the

---

1 An allusion to the general state of affairs in the Empire. The Goths at this time, being driven south by the Huns, were becoming dangerous. Cf. Amm. Marc. 31.4.

---

1 Written in 376.

Lord, who has removed your Reverence from this conflagration which has particulary consumed our diocese. The righteous Judge has given to us according to our deeds 'an angel of Satan'[2] which buffets us considerably, vehemently defends heresy, and carries on war against us to such an extent as not even to spare the blood of those who believe in God. Assuredly, it has not been unnoticed by your Charity that a certain Asclepius,[3] because he did not choose communion with Doeg, was beaten by them and died under the lashes, or rather, through the lashes he was transferred to life. And you may believe that all the rest is on a par with that—persecutions of presbyters and of teachers, and whatever else men might do who are using the authority derived from their office according to their own will. But through your prayers the Lord will grant us both release from these evils and endurance, so that we may bear the weight of our trials in a manner worthy of our hope in Him.

But do you yourself deign to write to us frequently about your affairs. If you find anyone who can be trusted to carry to you the book which we have prepared, deign to send for it, in order that, inspired with confidence by your judgment, we may send it out into the hands of others. By the grace of the Holy One may you be granted to me and to the Church of the Lord healthy and happy in the Lord and praying earnestly for me.

---

2 Cf. 2 Cor. 12.7.

3 This Asclepius cannot be identified with certainty.

249. Without an Address, for a Pious Man[1]

I congratulate this brother both because he is delivered from the disturbances here and because he is going to your Reverence. For he has chosen for himself an excellent provision for eternity, a good life passed with those who fear the Lord. We also commend him to your Honor, and through him I entreat you to pray for our wretched life so that we may be freed from these trials and may begin to serve the Lord according to the Gospel.

250. To Patrophilus, Bishop of the Church in Aegae[1]

After a long time I have received the answer to my earlier letter; still, I received it through the most beloved Strategius, and I gave thanks to the Lord because you remain the same in your love for us. And what you have now been so kind as to write on the same subject contains a proof of your good will, because you are properly disposed and you advise us to our advantage.

Yet, since I see again that my discussion will be rather long, if I am to answer each separate point written by your Intelligence, I am saying this much: in respect to the blessing of peace, if it is limited to only the name of peace, it is ridiculous for those men to select this particular person and that one, and to accord reconciliation to them alone, but to exclude countless others from participation in the blessing. Now, if union with pernicious men produces under the appearance of peace hostile acts against those accepting it, consider who these men are with whom they have joined

1 Written in 376.

1 Written in the summer of 376; cf. Loofs, *op. cit.,* p. 8 n. 2.

company—men who have hated us with an unjust hatred; really, men belonging to the party of those not in communion with us. I do not need now to mention them by name. These latter have even been summoned by the former to Sebaste and have received the church and performed the divine services at the altar and distributed to all the people their own sacramental Bread,[2] being proclaimed bishops by the clergy there[3] and being escorted through all the country as if they were holy men and were in communion. If we ought to embrace their party, it is ridiculous to begin from the tips of the toes and not to converse with the heads.[4]

If, then, we should not consider anyone at all heretical or turn away from him, for what reason, tell me, do you separate yourself and avoid the communion of certain persons? But, if some are to be shunned, according to the rule of accuracy let them tell us—they who are accurate in all things—to which party those belong whom they brought over to their side from Galatia.

If these things seem to you deserving of grief, ascribe the separation to those who are responsible for them, but, if you decide that they are indifferent matters, pardon us for not consenting to be of the leaven of those who teach otherwise than right.[6] Therefore, if it seems best, get rid of these

2 Holy Eucharist was distributed to the people by the newly proclaimed bishops, despite the fact that the latter were in heresy.

3 In the early days the people elected the bishop. According to St. Cyprian, the choice of the bishop rested with the community and the neighboring bishops. The Council of Nicaea later required that at least three bishops of the province be present at the election, while the others should confirm the choice in writing. The final confirmation of a bishop so elected was reserved to the metropolitan. The clergy in question evidently disregarded this rule.

4 I.e., if communion with those whom Eustathius advocates is to be accepted, it is ridiculous not to give the same honor to their leaders, Euzoius, Eudoxius, and other Arians.

5 Cf. Matt. 16.12.

6 Cf. Gal. 2.14.

specious arguments and refute with all frankness those who are not walking uprightly according to the truth of the Gospel.[7]

251. To the People of Evaesae[1]

Even though the number of troubles surrounding us is great and our heart is oppressed with countless care, we have never banished from our memory solicitude for your Charities, but we beg of our God that you will continue in the faith in which you stand and exult in the hope of the glory of God.[2] For, at the present time it is truly difficult to find and very rare to see a church that is unimpaired, in no way harmed by the difficulties of the times, but preserving pure and untouched the teaching of the Apostles, such a church as He who reveals those in each generation who are worthy of His vocation has now shown yours to be.

And may the Lord grant you the blessings of Jerusalem above[3] in return for your having thrown the deceitful slanders against us back onto the heads of those who are spreading false reports and not giving them entrance into your hearts. I both know and I am convinced in the Lord that your reward is great in heaven,[4] especially because of this action. You have wisely deduced this among yourselves, which is indeed according to truth, that they who are repaying me evil for good and hatred for my love[5] toward them are now

7 Gal. 2.14.

1 Written in December, 376; cf. Loofs, *op. cit.*, p. 8 n. 2. Evaesae is probably Ptolemy's Seiousa, now Yogounes.
2 Cf. Rom. 5.2.
3 Cf. Gal. 4.26.
4 Cf. Matt. 5.12.
5 Cf. Ps. 108.5.

accusing me on those points on which they themselves are found to have given written confessions.

And not only have they fallen into this inconsistency of bringing forward their own writings to you instead of an accusation [against me], but also into this, that, although they were unanimously deposed by those assembled at Constantinople,[6] they did not accept their deposition, calling them a synod of disloyal men and not consenting to acknowledge them as bishops, in order that they[7] might not ratify the vote brought against them.[8] And they assigned as the reason of their not being bishops that they were, as it was said, the leaders of a wicked heresy. This happened less than seventeen years ago. The leaders of those deposing them were Eudoxius, Euippius, Georgius, Acacius, and others who are unknown to you. These who are now ruling the churches are successors of those men, some having been ordained in their place, others promoted by those very men.

Now, then, let these who are accusing us of heterodoxy tell us how those men were heretical whose deposition they did not accept, but these, who were appointed by them and who preserve the same sentiments as their fathers, are orthodox. In fact, if Euippius was orthodox, how is it possible that Eustathius, whom he deposed, is not a layman? And, if he is a heretic, how is it possible that he who was ordained by his hand is now in communion with Eustathius? But these are mere games, childishly pursued against the churches of God for the advantage of those undertaking to slander men and again to commend them.

Eustathius, in passing through Paphlagonia, overturned the

6 In January, 360. Cf. Sozomen, *Hist. Eccl.* 4.24.
7 Those gathered at Constantinople.
8 The deposed.

altars of Basilides[9] of Paphlagonia and offered the sacrifice on his own tables; now he is a suppliant of Basilides, asking to be received by him. He excommunicated the most pious brother Elpidius because of his union with those in Amasia;[10] now he is a suppliant of the Amasenes, seeking union with them. As to his proclamations against Euippius, even you yourselves know how terrible they were. And now he extols for their orthodoxy those who hold the opinions of Euippius, if only they will co-operate in his effort to restore him. We are slandered, not because we are doing any wrong, but because he thought that this brings him credit among those in Antioch. The men whom they summoned last year from Galatia, that they might be able through them to demand the full liberty of the episcopal office, are of such a kind as even they can perceive who have associated with them for only a short time. But, may the Lord never grant me so much leisure as to be able to enumerate all their actions! Nevertheless, escorted by their most honorable bodyguards and fellow priests, they traversed their whole country, receiving the honors and the attentions accorded to bishops. They were led with much show into the city and held an assembly with full authority. The people were entrusted to them; the altar was handed over. When those, going to Nicopolis, were unable to accomplish anything of what they had promised, they who were present know how they returned and how they were looked on during their return. Thus, they always appear to be doing everything for their own advantage. But, if they say that they have repented, let them show their repentance in writing and in an anathematization of the Creed of

---

9 Bishop of Gangra; cf. Letter 226.

10 I.e., with the Arian bishop of Amasia, who was intruded into the place of Eulalius. Cf. Sozomen, *Hist. Eccl.* 7.2, on the condition of the Amasene church at this time.

Constantinople[11] and in separation from the heretics, and let them not deceive the more simple souls. Such, then, are the matters pertaining to them.

We, beloved brethren, insignificant and lowly, but by the grace of God always the same, have never been affected by the vicissitudes of affairs. The Creed we hold is not one in Seleucia, another in Constantinople, another in Zela,[12] another in Lampsacus, and still another at Rome; that circulated at present is not different from our former Creed, but is always one and the same. As we received from the Lord, so are we baptized; as we are baptized, so do we believe; as we believe, so also do we give glory, neither separating the Holy Spirit from the Father and Son nor placing Him before the Father nor saying that the Spirit is anterior to the Son, as blasphemous tongues maintain.[13] For, who is so bold that, rejecting the commandments of the Lord, he would dare to devise an order of his own for the names? But we neither say that the Spirit is a creature, since He is ranked with the Father and the Son, nor do we dare to call Him who is in authority a servant. Moreover, we urge you, being mindful of the threat of the Lord, who said: 'Every kind of sin and blasphemy shall be forgiven to men; but the blasphemy against the Spirit will not be forgiven . . . neither in this world nor in the world to come,'[14] guard yourselves from the harmful teachings against the Spirit. 'Stand fast in the faith,'[15] look around at the world, and see that this part which is diseased is small, but all the rest of the Church, which has received the Gospel from one end of the world to the other, remains

11 Not the Constantinopolitan revision of the Nicene Creed in use today; cf. the earlier portions of this letter.

12 Cf. Letter 226.

13 Cf. *De Spiritu Sancto* 12.

14 Matt. 12.31,32.

15 1 Cor. 16.13.

in this sound and unperverted doctrine. Not only do we pray not to fall from the communion of these but we also join in prayer that we may have part with you on the righteous day of our Lord Jesus Christ, when He shall come to give to each according to his deeds.

252. To the Bishops of the Diocese of Pontus[1]

The honoring of martyrs is much to be desired by all those who have hoped in the Lord, and especially by you who are seeking after virtue and who through your affection for your celebrated fellow servants[2] have manifested your good will toward our common Master, but, above all, because your life of rigid discipline possesses a certain kinship with those who have been brought to perfection through patient endurance. Therefore, since Eupsychius[3] and Damas and their company are most distinguished martyrs whose commemoration is celebrated yearly by our city and all the neighboring country, the Church, urging you through our voice, suggests that you, her own special ornament, should resume your former custom of visiting us. As, then, a great task lies before you among the people who are seeking edification from you, and since there are rewards stored up for the honoring of martyrs, receive our request and consent to the favor, granting us a great boon with little labor.

---

1 The Pontic diocese was one of the thirteen civil divisions established by Constantine. This letter was written in 376.

2 Martyrs.

3 On these martyrs cf. Letters 142 and 176. September 7 was the day of the feast at Caesarea.

253. To the Presbyters of Antioch[1]

The solicitude which you have for the churches of God, the most beloved and most pious brother Sanctissimus, our fellow presbyter, will in part relieve by relating the love and good will of all the West toward us; in part, he will also rouse and stimulate it the more, describing personally to you with great clarity how much zeal the present circumstances demand. All the others announced to us, as it were, by halves, both the opinions of the men there and the condition of their affairs; but he, being a man capable of understanding the policies of men and of accurately investigating the state of affairs, will tell you everything and will guide your goodly zeal in all things. Therefore, you have material proper for your perfect purpose, which you have always shown in your solicitude for the churches of God.

254. To Pelagius, Bishop of Laodicea in Syria[1]

May the Lord grant me, at some time or other, to come into the presence of your true Reverence, and personally to supply those accounts which we have omitted in our letter.

1 This and the three following letters were brought by Sanctissimus to various parties on his return to Rome, either on his first or second journey. Cf. Letters 120 and 221. Letters 253-257 were probably written in 376, although Loofs, *op. cit.*, p. 28ff. would place them in the spring of 375.

1 At the Council of Constantinople in 381, Pelagius, Bishop of Laodicea in Syria Prima, was named as one of those orthodox Eastern bishops communion with whom was a test of orthodoxy, and to whom the administration of the churches of the East was entrusted. Cf. Socrates, *Hist. Eccl.* 5.8; Sozomen, *Hist. Eccl.* 7.12; 7.9.

We have been late in beginning to write, and there is great need of an apology from us. Since, however, the most beloved and pious brother Sanctissimus, our fellow presbyter, is at hand, he himself will tell you the news both from us and from the West. And in this latter he will truly gladden you, but, in speaking of the disturbances that are pouring down upon us, perhaps he will add on some grief and care to those already lying upon your good heart. Nevertheless, it is not unprofitable for you who are able to beseech the Lord to be grieved. Your solicitude will reach out to our need and I know that we shall obtain help from God when we have the assistance of your prayers. If you will pray with us for deliverance from our cares and will ask for some additional strength for our body, the Lord will render us successful in the fulfillment of our desire, namely, in coming into the presence of your Modesty.

255. To Vitus, Bishop of Charrae[1]

Would that it were possible for me to write even daily to your Reverence! Ever since I have become acquainted with your Charity, I have a great longing, above all, to be with you, but, if that is not possible, at least to write and to receive letters, in order that I may be able not only to give you some information of our affairs, but also to learn about your condition. However, since not what we wish, but what the Lord gives, is granted us, we ought to receive it with thanksgiving; therefore, we have thanked the good God who

1 Vitus, Bishop of Charrae (a city of Mesopotamia, the Charan or Haran of the Scriptures, cf. Gen. 11.31), was one of the signers of Letter 92, which the oriental prelates addressed to the bishops of Italy and Gaul. He was present at Constantinople in 381. Sozomen, *Hist. Eccl.* 6.33, speaks of him as famous for his sanctity.

has provided us with an opportunity for a letter to your Reverence—the arrival of the most beloved and pious brother Sanctissimus, our fellow presbyter, who having undertaken the labor involved in a journey abroad will relate to you with accuracy everything that he has observed in the West. For this we ought both to give thanks to the Lord and to adore Him, that He may give us also the same peace, and that we may freely receive each other. Salute all the brotherhood in Christ in our name.

256. *To Our Most Beloved and Pious Brethren, Fellow Presbyters, Acacius, Aetius, Paulus, and Silvanus, and Deacons, Silvinus and Lucius, and the Rest of Our Brethren, the Monks, Basil the Bishop*[1]

When I heard of that grievous persecution rising up against you, and how immediately after Easter those who 'fasted for debates and strife,'[2] coming to your tabernacles, consigned all your labors to the fire, preparing for you a home in heaven not made by human hands,[3] but laying up as a treasure for themselves the fire[4] which they used to injure you, I bemoaned the incident, not compassionating you, brethren (may that not be!), but those who were so submerged in evils as to extend their wickedness to such a limit.

---

1 This Acacius is probably the same one who in 375 had brought an invitation to St. Basil in the name of the church at Beroea. Letter 220 is St. Basil's answer to this invitation. Although celebrated later as Bishop of Beroea, Acacius brought dishonor on his name by his evil attacks on St. John Chrysostom. The churches of Beroea and Chalcedon had for some time been suffering persecution, but in 376, immediately after Easter, the heretics confiscated and burned the dwellings of the monks. St. Basil here writes to console them in this trial.

2 Cf. Isa. 58.4.

3 Cf. 2 Cor. 5.1.

4 Cf. 2 Pet. 3.7.

I expected that you would all run immediately to your ready place of refuge, our Lowliness, and I was in hopes that the Lord would give me a respite from the continual distresses by embracing you, and that, having received on this slothful body the glorious sweat which you let fall for the sake of truth, I would have some participation in the rewards stored up for you by the Judge of truth. But, since this did not even come into your mind, and you did not expect to receive any solace from us, I was desirous at least to find frequent occasions for writing to you, in order that, like those who acclaim the contestants, I myself also might give some applause through letters to you for an encouragement in your noble conflict. Even this was not easy for us, for two reasons: one, that we did not know where you were living; the other, that there are not many people who travel from here to you.

But, the Lord now has guided to us the most beloved and pious brother Sanctissimus, our fellow presbyter, through whom we are addressing your Charity, and we entreat you, who are rejoicing and exulting because your reward is great in heaven,[5] to pray for us and, because you have confidence in speaking to the Lord, not to cease night and day crying out to Him[6] to check this storm of the churches, to give back the shepherds to the people, and to restore the Church to its own dignity. I am convinced that, if a voice is found importuning the good God, He will not for a long time delay His mercies, but 'with the tempation He will also give us now a way out that we may be able to bear it.'[7] Greet all the brethren in Christ for us.

---

5 Cf. Matt. 5.12.
6 Cf. Luke 18.7.
7 Cf. 1 Cor. 10.13.

257. To the Monks Oppressed by the Arians

What I said to myself when I heard about the trial which had been brought upon you by the enemies of God, this I have thought it well to report to you in writing, namely, that in a time which is considered to be peacful you procured for yourselves a blessing which is reserved for those who suffer persecution for the name of Christ. Not just because a gentle and mild name invests those performing wicked deeds ought we on this account to consider that the acts are not hostile. I judge that a war on the part of those of the same race is harder to bear, because it is even easy to guard against enemies who have been publicly proclaimed, but, in the case of those who mingle with us, it is necessary to be exposed to all harm. This you yourselves, too, have experienced. Our fathers also were persecuted,[1] but by idolaters, and their property was plundered and their houses were ruined and they themselves were banished by those who were openly making war on us because of the name of Christ. But the men now appearing as persecutors hate us no less than those, and for the purpose of deceiving the many put forward the name of Christ in order that the persecuted may not even have consolation from their confession of it, since the many and the simpler souls admit that we are wronged but do not account our death for the truth as martyrdom for us. For this reason I am convinced that the reward reserved by the just Judge is greater for you than for the martyrs of that time, since they not only had the approbation conceded by men but also received the reward from God, but to you, for equally virtuous acts, the honors from the people are not granted. Therefore, the likelihood is

1 Cf. Matt. 5.12.

that a manifold recompense for your sufferings for the sake of piety is reserved for you in the future life.

For this reason we urge you not to be faint-hearted in your afflictions, but to renew yourselves in your love for God and daily to increase your zeal, being conscious that in you ought to be preserved the remnants of true religion which, when the Lord comes, He will find upon earth.[2] And, if bishops have been driven from their churches, let this not cause you to waver, or, if traitors have sprung up among the clergy themselves, let not this weaken your confidence in God.[3] The names are not the things which save us, but our motives and our sincere love for Him who created us. Consider that even in the plot against our Lord the chief priests and the scribes and the elders contrived the treachery[4] and few of the people were found really accepting the teaching; moreover, that it is not the multitude that is saved, but the elect of God.[5] Therefore, never let the crowd of people dismay you, since they are borne hither and thither like the water of the sea by the winds. For, if even one is saved, as Lot in Sodom,[6] he ought to persevere in his right judgment with hope in Christ unchanged, because the Lord will not abandon His holy ones. Salute all the brethren in Christ for me; offer up sincere prayers for my pitiable soul.

2 Cf. 2 Cor. 4.15,16; also, Eph. 3.13.
3 Maran believes that this is an allusion to Fronto, Arian bishop of Nicopolis in Lesser Armenia, who originally belonged to the orthodox party.
4 Cf. Mark 14.1,2.
5 Cf. Matt. 22.14.
6 Cf. Gen. 19.

258. To Bishop Epiphanius[1]

It has long been expected from the prediction of the Lord, and now finally confirmed by the test of events, that, 'because iniquity has abounded, the charity of the many would grow cold.'[2] This, though it was already prevailing among us, the letter brought from your Honor seemed to refute. Truly, it is an example of charity not at all trifling, in the first place, that you remember us who are so insignificant and of no worth, and secondly, that you send to visit us brethren who are fit to be messengers of letters of peace. Indeed, no sight is rarer than this, since at present everyone is inclined to suspect everyone else. Nowhere is there compassion, nowhere is there sympathy, nowhere a brotherly tear for a suffering brother. Not persecutions for the truth, nor lamentations of churches with their whole people, nor this long succession of difficulties surrounding us are able to stir us to solicitude for each other. But we leap upon the fallen; we irritate their wounds;[3] we, who seem to share the same

1 Epiphanius was elected Bishop of Constantia in Cyprus, the ancient Salamis, in 367 and governed the church there for thirty-six years. He covered the island with monastic institutions and remained in uninterruped communication with the monks of Palestine. About 376 Epiphanius was active in the Apollinarian controversies. Toward the end of 382 he went to Rome with St. Jerome and other legates of the Constantinopolitan Synod of 382 to confer with Pope Damasus on the Apollinarian heresy. Later, in an alliance with St. Jerome, he took up the Origen controversy. These controversies in which Epiphanius engaged illustrate his character. Honest, credulous, a zealot for orthodoxy, he was often found promoting divisions where a moderate course would have enabled him to maintain the peace of the Church. Although he was not present at the Council of Constantinople in 381, which ensured the triumph of the Nicene Creed in the East, his own Creed, found in his work, the *Ancoratus*, agrees almost word for word with the Constantinopolitan Creed. This letter was written in 377.

2 Cf. Matt. 24.12.

3 Perhaps a reference to the impetuous and too often injudicious zeal displayed by Epiphanius.

opinion, intensify the insults from the heretics; those who are in agreement in the most vital matters are, on some one point at least, utterly at variance with one another. How, then, shall we not admire under such circumstances him who has shown a pure and guileless love toward his neighbor, and who through so great a sea and land that separate[4] us in body bestows all possible care on our souls?

I have admired this in you, that you regarded with pain even the dissension of the brethren in Elaeon[5] and wished that they would reach some agreement with each other. And the fact that not only what had been fabricated by some and was producing disorders[6] in the brotherhood did not escape your notice, but that you even took upon yourself solicitude for these things, this also I have approved. One thing, however, I have not considered to be worthy of your Intelligence, that you have entrusted the correction of such great matters to us, a man who is neither led by the grace of God because he is living with sin, nor possesses any power in speaking because he has gladly separated from vanities and has not yet acquired the proper skill in the doctrines of truth. Accordingly, we have already written[7] to our beloved brethren, those in Elaeon, to our brother Palladius,[8] and to Innocent the Italian,[9] in answer to the letters which they sent to us, that we are not able to add anything at all to the Nicene Creed, not the slightest thing, except the glorification of the

4 St. Basil in Cappadocia and Epiphanius in Cyprus.

5 I.e., the Mount of Olives.

6 A reference to the heresy of Apollinaris.

7 This letter is lost.

8 A Palladius, a presbyter of Caesarea, wrote to Athanasius about 371, urging him to rebuke some of the monks there who were opposing St. Basil and causing a disturbance. This may be the Palladius here referred to.

9 One of the monks in the monastery of the Mount of Olives who had been previously in the service of the Roman government in Constantinople and whose biography was written by Palladius.

Holy Spirit, because our Fathers made mention of this part cursorily, since at that time no inquiry had yet been stirred up regarding it. But the doctrines[10] which are being interwoven in that Creed concerning the Incarnation of the Lord we have neither inquired into nor accepted, on the ground that they are too profound for our comprehension.[11] We are aware that, when we shall once disturb the simplicity of the Creed we shall find no limit to our words, since the arguments will always lead us on farther, and we shall confuse the souls of the simpler folks by the introduction of strange material.[12]

As for the church in Antioch,[13] I mean the one agreeing in the same doctrine, may the Lord at some time permit us to see it united. It, especially, runs the risk of lying open to the plots of the enemy, who bears a grudge against it because the name of 'Christians'[14] was first applied to the people there. Not only is heresy divided against orthodoxy, but even right doctrine against itself.[15] Still, since he who first spoke openly for the truth and fought that glorious combat in the time of Constantius, the most revered Meletius, is the bishop, and my church held him as a communicant, having loved him exceedingly because of his strong and unyielding stand, we hold him even up to now as a communicant by the grace of

---

10 Of Apollinaris.

11 The Benedictine editors remark: '*Cum nonnulli formulae Nicenae aliquid de Incarnatione adderent ad comprimendos Apollinaristas, id Basilius nec examinaverat,*' etc.

12 Yet St. Basil here admits an addition which he holds justified, in the case of the glorification of the Holy Spirit. He would have probably agreed also with the necessity of the additions made in 451.

13 On the affairs at Antioch, cf. Letter 66 n. 7.

14 Cf. Acts 11.26.

15 In 377 Meletius was in exile, and Paulinus the Bishop of the Eustathians was opposing Vitalius, who had been consecrated by Apollinaris. St. Jerome, Letter 16, discusses the confusion resulting from these three nominally orthodox claimants.

God, and we shall certainly continue to hold him so, if God wills. Even the most blessed Father, Athanasius, when coming from Alexandria, desired by all means to establish union with him, but through the malice of counselors their union was postponed until another time.[16] Would that it had not been! But of those who came afterwards we have not yet approved the communion of any, not because we judged them unworthy, but because we are not able to condemn Meletius in any way. Although we have heard many things from the brethren, nevertheless we have not accepted them, because the accused were not confronted with their accusers according to what is written: 'Does our law judge a man unless it first give him a hearing, and know what he does?'[17] Therefore, we are not yet able to write to them, most honored brother, nor ought we to be forced to it. It would be proper to your peaceful purpose not to join the one and tear apart the other, but to bring together the separated parts into the original unity. And so, first, pray; then, as far as you are able, urge that, casting ambition out of their souls both in order to restore strength to the Church and to destroy the insolence of the enemies, they should be reconciled with each other. Now, this has exceedingly encouraged my soul—the addition made by your Integrity to the other clear and accurate theological statements, that it

16 After his fourth exile, St. Athanasius, having assembled a council, framed a synodical letter in which the Nicene Creed was embodied. On September 5, 363, St. Athanasius went to Antioch with the letter. He was disposed at first to recognize Meletius, but the latter, keenly annoyed by the consecration of Paulinus, held aloof from all proposals of accommodation or put off Athanasius with vague promises. As a consequence, Athanasius, who ever since he had worshiped with the Eustathians in 346 had given them his warm sympathy, now recognized their bishop, Paulinus, as the true head of the Antiochene church on his appending to his signature on the synodical letter a full and orthodox declaration.

17 John 7.51.

is necessary to confess the three Persons. Therefore, let also the brethren at Antioch learn this from you; surely, they have learned it already. For you evidently would not have accepted communion with them unless you had been reassured particularly on this point.

The nation of the Magusaeans[18] (which you deigned to mention to us in another letter) is scattered among us in great numbers throughout nearly the whole country, having been introduced among us formerly as colonists from Babylon. They follow their own peculiar customs and do not mix with other men; it is entirely impossible to reason with them, in so far as they have been taken captive by the Devil according to his will. There are no books among them, nor teachers of doctrines; they are brought up in an unreasoning manner, the son receiving the impiety from the father. Besides these things, which are seen by all, they reject animal sacrifice as defilement, slaughtering animals according to their need through the hands of others; they are mad after illegal marriages; they consider fire as a god, and other such things.[19] As to their descent from Abraham, none of the Magi up to now has told us that myth, but they declare that the founder of their race is a certain Zarnuas. Therefore, I am able to write nothing more about them to your Honor.

259. To the Monks, Palladius and Innocent[1]

The measure of my love for you, you ought to surmise from the extent of your love for us. In truth, I have always desired to be the author of peace and, since I am failing in

18 From Magusa in Arabia. Cf. Pliny, *Nat. Hist.* 6.32.
19 Cf. Eusebius, *Praep. Evan.* 6.275, and Epiphanius, *In Exp. Cathol. Fid.*

1 Written in 377. Cf. Letter 258 nn. 8-9.

my purpose, I am grieved. Why should I not be? Yet, I cannot be angry at anyone because of this, being aware that long ago the blessing of peace was taken away from us. But, if the cause of the disagreement lies in others, may the Lord grant that those bringing about the dissension may cease to do so. Of course, I do not ask for continual visits from you; therefore, do not for this reason make apologies to me. I know that men who have chosen a life of hard work and always provide the necessities for themselves through their own hands are unable to sojourn a long time away from their own homes. But, wherever you may be, remember us. And pray for us in order that we at least may have peace with ourselves and with God, and that no disturbance may dwell in our thoughts.

260. To Bishop Optimus[1]

I would be happy to see your noble children in any event, not only because of the stability of their character, which is beyond their age, but also because of their near relationship to your Reverence, which makes it possible to expect something great of them; but, when I saw that they were coming to me with a letter from you, I felt a twofold love for them. When I read the letter and perceived in it both the anxious care of your Affection for the churches and also your solicitude in reading the holy Scriptures, I gave thanks to

---

1 Optimus, Bishop of Antioch in Pisidia, one of the most distinguished orthodox prelates of his time, firmly defended the Catholic faith under Valens. He was present at the Council of Constantinople in 381. During his time Antioch was appointed one of the centers of Catholic communion for the Eastern Church by the Council of Constantinople and Emperor Theodosius. He signed the will of St. Gregory of Nazianzus as a witness and also shared in the bounty of Olympias for the poor of her diocese. This letter was probably written in 377.

the Lord, and I prayed for blessings on those who brought such a letter to us, and even before them on him who wrote to us.

For you inquired into that much-talked-of passage which is being circulated to and fro among all—what its interpretation is: 'Whoever kills Cain shall be punished sevenfold.'[2] By this, to begin with, you yourself have given proof that you keep carefully the bidding which Paul[3] had given to Timothy, for it is evident that you are attentive to reading. Then, too, although we are old and already numb through age and weakness of the body and through the great number of afflictions which, stirred up around us at present, have weighed down our life, nevertheless you have roused us and, fervent in spirit, are bringing us, chilled like the hibernating animals, back to a moderate wakefulness and living activity.

Now, the statement can be interpreted offhand in a simple manner and can admit of an elaborate explanation. The simpler meaning and the one that might easily occur to everyone is this: that it is necessary for Cain to pay the sevenfold penalty for his sins. Indeed, it is not the duty of a just judge to determine the requitals on a basis of equal for equal, but he who has been the originator of the evil must pay the debt with additional compensation, if he himself is to become better by the punishment and is to make others more prudent through his example. Therefore, since it has been prescribed that Cain should fulfill sevenfold the penalty of his sins, he

---

2 Gen. 4.15. This passage has always caused difficulty to translators since the Hebrew version itself admits of two distinct translations and the Greek translators in the Septuagint multiplied the difficulties by using ambiguous terms to render what they did not understand. For a complete discussion of the entire question, see Vigouroux, *Dictionnaire de la Bible* (Paris 1899), art. 'Cain,' Vol. 2, col. 39; J. Skinner, *A Critical and Exegetical Commentary on Genesis* (New York 1910) 110.

3 Cf. 1 Tim. 4.13.

who kills him shall discharge, it is said, the decision pronounced against him by the divine judgment. This is the meaning of this passage which occurs to us at first reading.

But, since the mind of the more industrious is by nature prone to investigate the deeper meaning, it inquires how justice is fulfilled in the expression 'sevenfold,' and what are the sins which are being punished. Does it mean that there are seven sins, or one sin and seven chastisements for the one? Now, Scripture always prescribes seven as the number of forgiveness of sins. 'How often,' it says, 'shall my brother sin against me, and I forgive him?' (Peter is the one speaking to the Lord.) 'Up to seven times?' Then comes the answer of the Lord: 'I do not say to thee seven times, but seventy times seven.'[4] The Lord did not, in fact, change to another number, but, multiplying the seven, so fixed the limit of forgiveness. Moreover, after seven years the Hebrew was freed from slavery.[5] Seven weeks of years in ancient times produced the celebrated jubilee, in which the earth kept the sabbath, debts were canceled, slaves were set free, and as it were, a new life was established again, the old one in a certain way attaining its fulfillment in the number seven.[6] These things are figures of this present age[7] which revolves through the seven days and passes us by; an age in which the penalties for the lesser sins are paid according to the loving care of the good Lord, so that we may not be handed over for punishment in the age without end. Therefore, the term 'sevenfold' is used because of its relation to this world, on the ground that the lovers of the world ought to be punished especially in those things for which they chose to act wickedly.

4 Matt. 18.21,22.
5 Cf. Deut. 15.12.
6 Cf. Lev. 25.10.
7 I.e., this world or era in contrast to the world to come.

And as for the sins which are being punished, you will find seven, whether you would mean the sins committed by Cain or the punishments brought against him by the Judge, and thus you will not lose the sense. Now, among the daring deeds of Cain, the first sin was envy at the preference of Abel; the second, deceit, with which he addressed his brother when he said: 'Let us go out into the field';[8] third, murder, an additional evil; fourth, that it is also fratricide, a still greater evil; fifth, that Cain is also the first murderer, leaving a wicked example to all mankind; the sixth, wrong-doing, that he caused sorrow to his parents; seventh, that he spoke falsely to God, for, when he was asked 'Where is your brother Abel?' he said: 'I do not know.'[9] Therefore, seven retributions were made by killing Cain. When the Lord said: 'Cursed be the ground which has opened to receive your brother's blood,' and 'Groaning and trembling shall you be upon the earth,' Cain said: 'You are driving me today from the soil, and from your face I shall be hidden. And I shall be groaning and trembling on the earth, and whoever finds me will kill me.' To this the Lord said: 'Not so. Whoever kills Cain shall be punished sevenfold.'[10] For, since Cain believed that he was an easy prey to everyone because he did not have safety on earth (for the earth was accursed on his account), and because he was bereft of the help of God, who was angered at him in consequence of the murder, as if no help was left to him either from the earth or from heaven, he said: 'It will come to pass that whoever finds me will kill me.' Scripture refutes his error, saying: 'Not so,' that is, you will not be destroyed. Death is a gain for those who are being punished, since it brings

8 Gen. 4.8.
9 Gen. 4.9.
10 Cf. Gen. 44.11-15 (Septuagint).

deliverance from their pains. But your life will be prolonged in order that the chastisements may be measured to you according to the desert of your sins. And, since the *'ekdikoúmenon'* is understood in a twofold manner, namely, the wrong done, for which there is retribution, and the form of the chastisement by which retribution is made, let us see if seven forms of torment were imposed upon the iniquitous man.

The foregoing explanation, then, enumerated the seven sins of Cain. And now we examine whether the penalties imposed on him were seven, and we say as follows. After the inquiry of the Lord, 'Where is your brother Abel?' the loving Lord, not wishing to learn, but providing an occasion of repentance for him, led him on, as the words themselves manifest. Indeed, when Cain denied the knowledge, He quickly refuted, saying: 'The voice of your brother's blood cries to me.'[11] Therefore, the question, 'Where is your brother Abel?' was giving him an opportunity for perceiving his sin; it was not assisting the knowledge of God. If, in fact, he had not experienced the visitation of God, he would have an excuse on the ground that he had been abandoned and had received no opportunity for repentance. But, now, the Physician presented Himself to him, in order that the sick man might flee to Him for refuge. He, however, not only conceals his wound, but produces another, adding to the murder a lie, 'I do not know. Am I my brother's keeper?' From there on enumerate the punishments. 'Cursed be the ground because of you.'[12] One chastisement. 'You will till the soil.' This is the second. Some ineffable duress was yoked with him, forcing him to the work of the earth, so that not even if he wished was he able to rest, but that he continued always to suffer

11 Cf. Gen. 4.9,10.

12 This expression is more like that addressed to Adam. Cf. Gen. 3.17.

hardship from his hostile earth, which he had made accursed for himself, having stained it with his brother's blood. Therefore, 'You will till the soil'—a fearful chastisement, to live with those who hate, to have as companion an enemy, an insatiable foe. 'You will till the soil,' that is, tightly bound to the labors of agriculture, you will never slacken, being released neither night nor day from your labors but enduring an ineffable duress harsher than any relentless master pricking you on to work. 'And it shall not give its strength.' And even if the unceasing application to the work did furnish some fruit, the labor itself was an intolerable trial for one who was always overworked and weary. But, since the labor was never-ending and the hard work connected with the earth was fruitless (for it did not give its strength), this is the third chastisement, the fruitlessness of the labors. Groaning and trembling shall you be upon the earth.'[13] Two other chastisements have been added to the three—a continual groaning and a trembling of the body, because his limbs did not have the steadiness of strength. Indeed, since he had used the strength of his body badly, its vigor was destroyed, so that he trembled and shook, and he could neither easily carry bread nor lift up drink to his mouth, for after the unholy deed his wicked hand was not permitted henceforth to serve even the proper and necessary needs of the body. There is another chastisement which Cain himself revealed when he said: 'You are driving me now from the soil, and from your face I shall be hidden.' What does the expression, 'You are driving me from the soil,' mean? It means: You are excluding me from its benefits. He was not transferred to another place, but was deprived of its blessings. 'And from your face I shall be hidden.' Separation from God is the

13 Gen. 4.12 (Septuagint).

severest chastisement for those of right-judging mind. 'And it will come to pass,' he says, 'that whoever finds me will kill me.' He infers this in consequence of what has gone before. If I have been driven from the soil, if I shall be hidden from Your face, it remains for me to be destroyed by everyone. What, then, does the Lord say? 'Not so.' But He placed a mark upon him. This is the seventh chastisement, that the punishment is not hidden, but proclamation is made to all by a mark in plain evidence that this man is the author of unholy deeds. To one who reasons rightly shame is the severest of chastisements; this we have learned concerning the judgment, that 'some will rise unto life everlasting, and others unto everlasting shame and reproach.'[14]

A question of the same kind follows this in regard to the statement of Lamech to his wives, 'For I have killed a man for wounding me, a youth for bruising me. If Cain shall be avenged sevenfold, Lamech seventy times sevenfold.'[15] Some think that Cain was destroyed by Lamech on the grounds that he lived until that time to pay the longer penalty. But that is not true. For Lamech seems to have perpetrated two murders from what he tells us. 'I have killed a man and a youth; the man for wounding and the youth for bruising. Now, a wound is one thing and a bruise another; and a man is one thing and a youth another. "For Cain shall be avenged sevenfold, but Lamech seventy times sevenfold." It is right for me to undergo four hundred and ninety chastisements, if truly God's judgment against Cain is just, that he should undergo seven punishments. In fact, as he did not learn to murder from another, so he did not see the murderer undergoing the penalty. But I, having before my eyes the man groaning and trembling and also the greatness of the

14 Cf. Dan. 12.2 (Septuagint).
15 Cf. Gen. 4.23,24.

anger of God, was not brought to my senses by the example. Therefore I deserve to pay four hundred and ninety penalties.'

But some have urged this opinion, not falling short of the doctrine of the Church: that from Cain until the flood seven ages passed by and the chastisement was inflicted upon all the earth, because there was a great deluge of sin. However, the sin of Lamech does not need a flood for its cure, but Him 'who takes away the sin of the world.'[16] Count, therefore, the generations from Adam until the coming of Christ, and you will find, according to the genealogy of Luke,[17] that the Lord was born in the seventy-seventh generation.

These matters, then, have been investigated according to our power, although many points that could have been examined were passed by in order that we might not draw out our explanation beyond the length of a letter; moreover, even scanty seeds suffice for your Intelligence. 'Give an occasion,' it is said, 'to a wise man, and wisdom shall be added to him,'[18] and 'A wise man accepting a word will praise it and will apply it to himself.'[19]

The words of Simeon to Mary possess no subtlety nor depth. For 'Simeon blessed them, and said to Mary his mother, "Behold, this child is destined for the fall and for the rise of many in Israel, and for a sign that shall be contradicted. And thy own soul a sword shall pierce, that the thoughts of many hearts may be revealed." '[20] Here I marvel at this—how it can be that, passing by the preceding words as clear, you have inquired into this one: 'and thy own soul a sword shall pierce.' Yet, there does not seem to me less difficulty in how the same one is destined 'for the fall and for the rise,'

16 Cf. John 1.29.
17 Cf. Luke 3.23-38.
18 Prov. 9.9.
19 Cf. Eccli. 21.18.
20 Luke 2.34,35.

and what 'the sign that shall be contradicted' is than in the third, how 'the sword shall pierce the soul of Mary.'

I think, therefore, that the Lord is 'for the fall and for the rise,' not because some fall and others rise, but because our lower nature falls and our better nature rises. The manifestation of the Lord is destructive of the carnal passions, but stimulative of the spiritual qualities. As when Paul says: 'When I am weak, then I am strong,'[21] the same man is both weak and strong, but he is weak in the flesh and he is strong in the spirit. So, also, the Lord does not provide occasions to some of falling and to others of rising. Those who fall, fall down from the state in which they once were. Yet, it is evident that the faithless man never stands, but is always trailing on the ground with the serpent which he follows. He does not have any place, therefore, whence he may fall, because he has been previously cast down by his infidelity. So, then, the first benefit is for him who stands in sin to fall and die, then to live in justice and rise again, since faith in Christ bestows both upon us. Let the lower nature fall, in order that the better may seize the opportunity for its resurrection. If fornication does not fall, chastity does not rise; if the irrational is not crushed, the rational in us will not blossom. In this sense, then, He is 'for the fall and for the rise of many.'

And 'for a sign that shall be contradicted.' We know that in the Scripture the cross is called in a special sense a sign. It says: 'Moses placed the serpent upon a sign,'[22] that is, upon a cross. Or else the sign is an indication of something strange and obscure, seen by the simpler and understood by the ready of mind. Since, therefore, men do not cease disputing about the Incarnation of the Lord, some declaring that He

21 Cf. 2 Cor. 12.10.
22 Cf. Num. 21.8.

assumed a body, others that His sojourn was incorporeal; some that He had a body subject to suffering, others that He fulfilled His life in the flesh by a certain appearance; again, some that He had an earthly body, and others a heavenly one; some, also, that He had an existence from all eternity, and others that He had His beginning from Mary; for this reason He is 'For a sign that shall be contradicted.'[23]

And Scripture calls by the name of sword the word which has the power of trying and of discerning thoughts, and which 'extends even to the division of soul and spirit, of joints also and of marrow, and is a discerner of thoughts.'[24] Since, therefore, every soul at the time of the Passion was subjected to a sort of test, as it were, according to the words of the Lord, who said: 'You will all be scandalized because of me,'[25] Simeon prophesies also concerning Mary, that standing beside the cross,[26] and looking at what was happening, and hearing His words, even after the testimony of Gabriel,[27] after the secret knowledge of her divine conception,[28] after the great showing of miracles, 'Even you will feel,' he says, 'a certain perplexity about your soul.'[29] For the Lord must taste of death for the sake of all, and, being made a propitiation for the world, He must justify all men in His blood.[30] Therefore, some doubt will touch even you yourself who have been taught from above concerning the Lord. That is the sword. 'That the thoughts of many hearts may be revealed'

23 I.e., arousing contradictory explanations.
24 Cf. Heb. 4.12.
25 Matt. 26.31.
26 Cf. John 19.25-27.
27 Cf. Luke 1.32,33.
28 Cf. Luke 1.35.
29 The Benedictine editors strongly resent this slur on the faith of our blessed Mother. They attribute its source to Origen's Homily 27 on St. Luke, and refer to Petavius, *De Incar.* 14.1, where a list of later commentators who followed Origen is to be found.
30 Cf. John 11.50.

means that, after the scandal which happened at the cross of Christ to both the disciples and to Mary herself, some swift healing will follow from the Lord, confirming their hearts in their faith in Him. Thus we see that even Peter, after having stumbled, clung more firmly to his faith in Christ. What was human, therefore, was proved unsound in order that the power of the Lord might be manifested.

261. To the Citizens of Sozopolis[1]

I read the letter, most honorable brethren, which you wrote concerning your troubles. And we rejoiced in the Lord that you associated us with you in your solicitude for the care of things needful for you and demanding attention. But we felt much sorrow on hearing that, in addition to the disorder brought upon the churches by the Arians, and the confusion which they have produced concerning the doctrines of faith, still another novelty has appeared among you, throwing the brotherhood into great grief, as you have written to us, namely, that men are introducing innovations and dogmas unfamiliar to the ears of the faithful as if they were, as they pretend, from the teaching of the Scriptures. You have written, in fact, that there are some among you who are doing away with the Incarnation of our Lord Jesus Christ, as much as they are able, and rejecting the grace of the great mystery kept secret from eternity but manifested in His own time,[2] when the Lord, after having gone through all things pertaining to the care of the human race, in addition to all else bestowed upon us His own sojourn among

---

1 Sozopolis or Suzupolis was a town in southern Pisidia. This letter was written in 377.

2 Cf. 1 Tim. 3.16.

us.[3] For He aided His own creature, first through the patriarchs, whose lives have been set forth as examples and rules for those desiring to follow in the footsteps of the saints and through a zeal like theirs to arrive at the perfection of good deeds. Then, He gave a law for his assistance, delivering it by angels through Moses;[4] then, Prophets, who proclaimed beforehand the salvation that was to be,[5] judges, kings, and just men, who performed their mighty works with hidden hand. After all these, in the last days, He Himself was manifested in the flesh, 'born of a woman, born under the Law, that he might redeem those who were under the Law, that we might receive the adoption of sons.'[6]

If, therefore, the sojourn of the Lord in the flesh did not take place, the Redeemer did not pay to death the price for us, and He did not by His own power destroy the dominion of death. For, if that which is subject to death were one thing, and that which was assumed by the Lord were another, then death would not have ceased performing its own works, nor would the sufferings of the God-bearing flesh have become our gain; He would not have destroyed sin in the flesh;[7] we who had died in Adam would not have been made to live in Christ;[8] that which had fallen asunder would not have been restored; that which was shattered would not have been repaired; that which had been estranged through the deceit of the serpent would not have been again made God's own. For, all these things are done away with by those who say that the Lord made His sojourn with a heavenly body.[9] And what was the need of the blessed Virgin,

3 Cf. Gal. 4.4.
4 Cf. Gal. 3.19.
5 Cf. Acts 3.18.
6 Cf. Gal. 4.4,5.
7 Cf. Rom. 8.3,4.
8 Cf. 1 Cor. 15.22.
9 The doctrine of the Apollinarians.

if the God-bearing flesh was not to be assumed from the substance of Adam? But who is so bold as now to revive once more through sophistic words and the testimony, as they pretend, of the Scriptures the teaching of Valentinus[10] which was silenced long ago? This impiety of the 'appearance,'[11] in fact, is not something new, but it was begun long ago by the weak-minded Valentinus, who, taking a few detached phrases of the Apostle, constructed the impious fiction for himself, saying that He had taken on 'the nature of a slave,'[12] and not the slave himself, and that the Lord had been made 'in the form,' but that humanity itself had not been assumed by Him. These men, whom we ought to deplore bitterly since they are bringing new disturbances upon you, seem to be uttering words akin to those.

Now, as to their saying that human feelings pass over to the Godhead Itself, that is characteristic of those who never preserve any consistency in thoughts and are unaware that some feelings are of the flesh and others of flesh endowed with a soul, and still others of a soul using a body. Now, it is a property of flesh to be cut and lessened and destroyed, and, again, of flesh endowed with a soul to suffer weariness and pain and hunger and thirst and to be overcome by sleep; and the properties of a soul using a body are griefs and anxieties and cares and all such things. Some of these are natural and necessary to the living creatures, but some are

10 Valentinus, an Alexandrian, taught in Rome from the year 130 until he was excommunicated in the year 140. He died in Cyprus in 161. He pretended to be a follower of a certain Theudas, the disciple of St. Paul. His system was most elaborate and ingenious, and his sect was the most widely spread of the Gnostic heresies.

11 Docetism, the common doctrine of many Gnostic sects, signified that Christ had no real human body, but had merely assumed an ethereal or phantom body. However, Valentinus and his followers taught that Christ had assumed a body. Each school had a different teaching on this point, but all denied the real Incarnation.

12 Cf. Phil. 2.5-8.

due to a depraved will, brought on by a life that is dissolute and not trained to virtue. Therefore, it is evident that the Lord took on the natural feelings for a confirmation of the true Incarnation and not of one according to appearance, but rejected as unworthy of the undefiled Godhead the feelings arising from vice which soil the purity of our souls. For this reason it is said that He was 'made in the likeness of sinful flesh,'[13] not, indeed, in the likeness of flesh, as these men think, but in the likeness of sinful flesh. Accordingly, He took our flesh with its natural feelings, but He 'did no sin.'[14] Yet, even as death in the flesh, which was handed down to us through Adam, was swallowed up by the Godhead, so also sin was utterly destroyed by the justice which is in Jesus Christ, so that in the resurrection we resume our flesh, which is neither liable to death nor subject to sin.[15]

These are, brothers, the mysteries of the Church; these are the traditions of the Fathers. We earnestly beg every man who fears the Lord and is awaiting the judgment of God not to be led astray by various teachings. If anyone teaches otherwise than right and does not have recourse to the sound words of faith, but, rejecting the sayings of the Spirit, makes his own teaching of greater authority than the evidence from the Gospels, guard against such a one.

May the Lord grant that at some time we may meet together, so that whatever has now escaped our explanation we may supply by a personal interview. Out of many things we have written few to you, since we do not wish to go beyond the limits of a letter, and since at the same time we are convinced that for those who fear the Lord even a brief reminder is sufficient.

---

13 Cf. Rom. 8.3.
14 1 Pet. 2.22.
15 Cf. Rom. 5.12,17.

262. *To the Monk Urbicius*[1]

You did well in writing to us, for you have shown the fruit of charity in no slight measure. In fact, do it frequently. Yet, do not think that you need to apologize when you write to us. We know ourselves and we are aware that by nature every man has equal honor with all the rest, and pre-eminence among us is not due to race, or abundance of money, or the condition of the body, but depends upon the superiority of our fear of God. Therefore, what prevents you, who fear the Lord more, from being greater than we in this very respect? Write to us frequently, then, and let us know how the brethren about you are, and which of the members of your church are sound, in order that we may know to whom we should write and on whom we should rely. Since I hear that there are some who are falsifying by distorted opinions the right doctrine concerning the Incarnation of the Lord, I urge them through your Charity to refrain from that absurd notion which some are reported to us to be holding, namely, that God Himself was turned into flesh and did not assume the substance of Adam through the holy Mary, but He Himself in His own divinity was transformed into the material nature.

This absurdity is very easy to refute. But, since the blasphemy is immediately clear, I think that to one who fears the Lord the reminder alone is sufficient. For, if He was 'turned,' He was also changed. But, far be it from us either to say or to think this, since God has said: 'I am and I change not.'[2] Then, how did the benefit of the Incarnation

1 Urbicius is evidently the same person to whom St. Basil wrote Letter 123 in 373. Nothing more is known of him. However, from the last sentence of this letter it may be inferred that he was the superior of a monastery or an ecclesiastic of some rank. The heresy here referred to is the Apollinarian. This letter was written in 377.

2 Mal. 3.6.

pass over to us, unless our body, united with the divinity, became more powerful than the dominion of death? For, if He was turned, He gave substance to His own body which subsisted after the divine nature was made material.[3] But, how was the boundless Godhead circumscribed in the space of a little body, if, indeed, the whole nature of the Only-begotten was 'turned'? I do not think, however, that anyone who is endowed with intelligence and possesses the fear of God is afflicted with this disease. But, since the report has come to me that some of your Charity's followers have this infirmity of mind, I thought that our letter should not be made a mere greeting, but should contain some such thing as would also be able to edify the souls of those who fear the Lord. Therefore, we urge that these matters meet with ecclesiastical correction and that you refrain from communion with the heretics, knowing that indifference in these affairs destroys our freedom in Christ.

263. To the Westerners[1]

May the Lord our God, in whom we have put our trust, bestow upon each of you the grace to obtain the hope placed before you in a measure commensurate with the joy with

3 The Benedictine editors belive that the '*ou*' in this sentence—'*ou gàr trapeìs, oikeîon hypestésato sôma, hóper, pachuntheisēs autôi tês theikês physeōs, hypéstē*'—should be either '*ei*' or '*ho*.' I have accepted their decision, since the sense of the following sentence seems to demand it.

1 The first visit of Dorotheus and Sanctissimus to the West in search of aid for the East had proved unsuccessful and the outcome of the second seemed little better, although it is known that Apollinaris was condemned at the Synod of Rome in the presence of Peter of Alexandria. The Benedictine editors place the date of this second embassy in the spring of 377; Loofs, in the summer of 377.

which you yourselves have filled our hearts not only through the letter which you sent us by our most beloved fellow presbyters,[2] but also through the sympathy which you, putting on a heart of mercy,[3] expressed for us in our distresses, as the aforementioned have announced. Even if our wounds remain the same, nevertheless it brings us some relief to have physicians at hand who are able, if they can find the opportunity, to effect a speedy healing of our painful hurts. Therefore, we again[4] address you through our beloved brethren and we urge you, if the Lord gives you an occasion for coming to us, not to hesitate to visit us. The visitation of the sick is a duty deriving from the greatest commandment.[5] But, if the good God and wise Administrator of our lives reserves this grace for another time, still write to us whatever you should write for the comfort of the afflicted and the restoration of the crushed.[6] Many, already, have been the tribulations of the Church and great is our affliction from them. Moreover, we have no expectation of aid from elsewhere unless the Lord shall send out His healing through you who serve Him sincerely.

Now, the bold and shameless heresy of the Arians, which has been openly broken off from the body of the Church, remains in its own error and harms us little because their impiety is evident to all. Those who have clothed themselves in sheep's skin[7] and are affecting a gentle and mild appearance, but from within are unsparingly tearing to pieces the flocks of Christ and, because they originated from among us, are easily inflicting harm on the simpler folks, these are the ones that are dangerous and hard to guard against. These are the

2 Dorotheus and Sanctissimus.
3 Cf. Col. 3.12.
4 The Easterners had sent the same two to the West in 374.
5 Cf. Eccli. 7.39.
6 Cf. 2 Cor. 1.3,4.
7 Cf. Matt. 7.15.

men we ask your Integrity to make known publicly to all the churches in the East, in order that they may walk uprightly and be with us in all sincerity, or, if they stand fast in their perversion, that they may keep their harm to themselves alone, not being able through an unguarded communion to share their own disease with their neighbors. It is necessary to mention them by name in order that you yourselves also may become acquainted with those who are causing the disorders among us. Do make this clear to our churches, too. Our statements are viewed with suspicion by many, as if, perhaps, because of some personal rivalry we have adopted a captiousness toward them. But you, as the distance that you happen to live from them is greater, are considered so much the more trustworthy by the people, in addition to the fact that the grace of God works with you for the care of the oppressed. Moreover, if more of you will teach concurrently the same things, it is evident that the great number of those who are teaching will make the acceptance of the doctrine by all an indisputable fact.

Now, one of those who is causing us great grief is Eustathius[8] of Sebaste in Lesser Armenia. He was formerly a disciple of Arius and, when Arius flourished at Alexandria, composing his wicked blasphemies against the Only-begotten, he followed him and was numbered among the most steadfast of his disciples. When he returned to his own country, he gave to the most blessed Bishop Hermogenes of Caesarea, who was condemning him for heterodoxy, a confession of sound faith. Thus he received ordination from him, but, after the death of that bishop, he hurried to Eusebius of Constantinople who, himself, yielded to no one in defending the

8 Eustathius apparently attempted by suppressing the Nicene Creed to secure the favor of the Arian party, and he even used his former recognition by Liberius as a means of giving his words and actions the authority of one in close communion with Rome.

impious doctrine of Arius. Then, after he had been driven out from there for some cause or other, returning he made his defense again to the people of his native land, concealing his impious views and offering some orthodox pronouncements. When, as it chanced, he had obtained a bishopric, he immediately appears to have written an anathema of consubstantiation in the synod they[9] held at Ancyra.[10] And what he, in conjunction with those who were of like doctrine with him, did on going from there into Seleucia everybody knows.[11] In Constantinople he again agreed with the propositions of the heretics. And so, after having been expelled from his bishopric because of his previous deposition in Melitine,[12] he devised as a means for his restoration the journey to you. And what the propositions were that were made to him by the most blessed Bishop Liberius,[13] and what the agreements were which he himself made, we do not know, except that he brought a letter restoring him, and, having shown it at the synod at Tyana, he was restored to his place. This man is now destroying that Creed on the basis of which he was received, and is joined with those who are anathematizing consubstantiation, and he holds the first place in the heresy of the Pneumatomachi.[14] Now, since

9 The Arians.

10 In 358, when *'homoioúsion'* was accepted, and twelve anathemas were formulated against all who rejected it.

11 At the Council of Seleucia, Eustathius held a prominent place and was sent at the head of the ten episcopal deputies to Constantinople to lay their report before Constantine. Cf. Soz., *Hist. Eccl.* 4.22,23.

12 Before 359. Melitine in Armenia Minor. Cf. Letter 266 n. 7.

13 Ordained Bishop of Rome, May 22, 352, as successor to Julius I.

14 Eustathius was unwilling to call the Holy Spirit either God or a creature, but Macedonius, Marathonius, and others taught that the Holy Spirit must be a creature, a minister and servant of God. The new sect was known as the Macedonians, Marathonians, or Pneumatomachi ('Combaters against the Spirit'). Cf. Soc., *Hist. Eccl.* 2.45; Soz., *Hist. Eccl.* 4.27.

his power to harm the churches has been given to him from the West, and since he uses the freedom which you bestowed upon him for the ruin of the many, it is needful that the correction also come from there, and that letters be sent to the churches saying what the conditions are on which he was received, and how now, having changed, he nullifies the favor given to him by the Fathers at that time.

After him comes Apollinaris, who is also troubling the churches not a little. With ability to write and with a tongue that is able for any subject, he has filled the whole world with his writings, taking no heed of the charge of him who said: 'Guard against making many books';[15] and in their great quantity, surely, there are many errors. How, in fact, is it possible 'in the multitude of words to avoid sin'?[16] In point of fact, he has discussions of theology based not on Scriptural proofs but on human argumentation. He also has books concerning the resurrection, composed like a legend, or rather, like a Jewish story, in which he says that we shall again turn back to the form of worship according to the Law, and that we shall again be circumcised, and observe the sabbath,[17] and refrain from meats, and offer burnt sacrifices to God, and adore in Jerusalem at the Temple, and from Christians become wholly Jews. What could be more ridiculous than these statements, or, rather, more foreign to the teaching of the Gospel? Then, also, his explanations concerning the Incarnation produced such confusion among the brethren that few now of those who have read them preserve their former standards of true religion, and many, being intent on innovations, have been diverted into inquiries and contentious investigations of these unprofitable words.

15 Eccli. 12.12 (Septuagint).
16 Cf. Prov. 10.19.
17 I.e., Saturday.

Of a truth, as regards Paulinus, if he has anything reprehensible about his ordination, you yourselves could say; but he causes us distress because he has been devoted to the teachings of Marcellus[18] and has admitted his followers without investigation into his own communion. You know, most honorable brethren, that the teaching of Marcellus contains a rejection of all our hope, since it neither admits the Son in His own Person but as brought forth and having again returned to Him whence He came forth, nor concedes that the Paraclete subsists in His own Person, so that one would not err in denouncing the heresy as absolutely foreign to Christianity and calling it a corrupted Judaism. We beg you to undertake the care of these matters. And this would be done if you should consent to write to all the churches in the East, that, if those who are falsifying these things would correct themselves, they are in communion, but, if they should wish contentiously to maintain the innovations, you are separated from them. We ourselves, indeed, do not fail to realize that we ought to have held a council with your Wisdoms and to handle these matters in a general deliberation. But, since the time does not permit it, and a postponement is hurtful because the harm coming from them is being firmly established, we have of necessity sent the brethren, so that, by personally explaining whatever escapes the instructions of the letter, they may stir up your Reverences to furnish the requested assistance to the churches of God.

---

18 Bishop of Ancyra in Galatia and a contemporary of St. Basil. Although at first an earnest defender of the Catholic faith against the Arians, later, in refuting the heterodox writings of Asterius, he was accused of promulgating doctrines combining the errors of Sabellius and Paul of Samosata. Thus he seems to have taught that the Son had no real personality, but was merely the external manifestation of the Father, and was called the Son of God, viewed as man only.

264. To Barses, Bishop of Edessa, during His Exile[1]

To Barses, the bishop truly most beloved of God and deserving of all reverence and honor, Basil sends greetings in the Lord. Since the most noble brethren, Domninus[2] and his disciples, were setting out in the direction of your Lordship, we gladly seized the opportunity of writing, and through them we are greeting you. We pray the holy God that you may be preserved in this life until such a time as we may be considered worthy to see you and to enjoy the gifts of grace that are in you. Only pray, I urge, that the Lord may not hand us over finally to the enemies of the cross of Christ,[3] but may keep His churches intact until the time of peace. This peace the just Judge Himself knows when He will give.[4] For He will give it and will not abandon us utterly. But, just as for the Israelites He assigned a space of seventy years[5] as the sentence of captivity for their sins, so, perhaps, the Almighty, after having handed us over for some definite time, will finally call us back and re-establish us in the peace which we had from the beginning, unless, perhaps, apostasy is somewhere near and the present happenings are a prelude of the entrance of the Antichrist.[6] If this ever be so, pray

1 The two letters numbered 264 and 267 and addressed to Bishop Barses should be assigned to the last years of the reign of Valens, perhaps to 377, according to the Benedictine editors (Chap. 37), since in both St. Basil expresses the hope of approaching peace, as the persecution had reached its height. This first letter Barses did not receive; at any rate, he did not receive it before he wrote again to St. Basil to complain of the latter's silence. Accordingly, St. Basil wrote again, this time entrusting his letter to certain Cappadocians then on their way to Egypt.

2 The identity of this Domninus is not clear. The name is a common one at this period.

3 Cf. Phil. 3.18.

4 Cf. 2 Tim. 4.8.

5 Cf. Jer. 25.12.

6 Cf. 1 John 2.18; also, 2 John 7.

that the good God may turn aside the afflictions or may keep us without stumbling in the midst of our tribulations. We salute through you the whole synod which has been deemed worthy of being with your Reverence. All our brethren greet your Reverence. By the grace of the Holy One, may you be preserved for the Church of God healthy and happy in the Lord and praying for me.

265. To Eulogius, Alexander, and Harpocration, Bishops of Egypt in Exile[1]

Stupendous in every respect do we find the providence of the good God toward His churches, so that even events which seem gloomy and which turn out absolutely contrary to our will, even these are dispensed for the benefit of the many in the inscrutable wisdom of God and the unsearchable judgments of His justice.[2] For, behold, the Lord, having compelled your Charities to go out from the land of Egypt, led you into the midst of Palestine and settled you there in imitation of Israel of old, whom He led in captivity into the land of the Assyrians, and by the sojourn of His saints extinguished

1 Shortly after writing to the Westerners, St. Basil wrote to the exiled confessors of Egypt in Palestine, many of whom had written a joint letter to Apollinaris. These confessors had been stirred and their suspicions had been roused about Paulinus of Antioch when Apollinaris, already in open heresy, had written to him about the testimony of the confessors and their letters. Later, when some of the works of Apollinaris reached them, they did not remain silent about the injury done to the Church, but wrote their thoughts on Apollinaris to the monks of Nitra. When St. Basil learned of their zeal in refuting heresies, he sent the deacon Elpidius with this and the following letter in order to foster communion with them. Cf. *Vita S. Basilii* 37.3-7. Nothing more is known of this Eulogius and Alexander. Harpocration was Bishop of Bubastus (Basta) in Egypt, one of the bishops consecrated by Melchius. Cf. Athan., *Apol. contra Arianos.* This letter was written in 377.

2 Cf. Rom. 11.33.

idolatry in that place.[3] And thus now by inference we find that the Lord, while putting before you a struggle for the sake of religion, has opened for you through your exile a stadium of blessed contests, and through your noble conduct has bestowed on those who come in contact with you clear examples for salvation. Since, then, by the grace of God we have become acquainted with your orthodoxy in faith and with your concern for the brethren, and have learned that you provide the things which pertain to the common benefit and which are necessary for salvation neither perfunctorily nor negligently, but that you choose to accomplish whatever is for the edification of the churches, we have concluded that it is right to be in communion with your good party and to join ourselves with your Reverences by letter. Therefore, we have sent our most beloved son and fellow deacon, Elpidius,[4] who is carrying our letter and at the same time is able personally to report to you whatever is beyond the explanation in our letter.

But, what especially strengthens us in our desire for union with you is the account of your Reverences' zeal for orthodoxy —the fact that neither by a vast number of treatises nor by subtlety of sophisms was your firmness of heart overcome, but that you recognized those who were making innovations contrary to the teachings of the Apostles and did not consent to cover over in silence the harm wrought by them. Truly, we have found great grief among all those who are clinging to the peace of the Lord because of the manifold innovations of Apollinaris of Laodicea,[5] who has grieved us so much the

3 Cf. 4 Kings 17, and Isa. 10.11.

4 This Elpidius is mentioned in Letter 138. Nothing further is known about him.

5 On Apollinaris, cf. Letter 263. He was highly esteemed both by St. Athanasius and St. Basil for his classical culture, piety, and loyalty to the Nicene Creed during the Arian controversy, until he brought out a Christological heresy which is called after him and which in some respects prepared the way for Monophysitism.

more in that he seemed to belong to our party in the beginning. In fact, any suffering from an evident enemy, even if the pain is excessive, can somehow be borne by the one afflicted, as it is written: 'For if my enemy had reviled me, I would verily have borne with it.'[6] But, to experience some hurt from one who is of like spirit and an intimate friend, this is most certainly hard to bear and holds no consolation. For, him whom we had expected to have as a fellow defender of the truth, him, I say, we have now found hindering in many places those who are being saved, by perverting their minds and drawing them away from the right doctrine. In fact, what that is bold and hotheaded in deeds has he not done? What that is novel and hazardous in words has he not conceived? Was not the whole Church divided against itself, and especially after he had sent out men to the churches governed by the orthodox in order to cause schisms and to vindicate some singular illegal congregation?[7] Is not the great mystery of godliness[8] mocked when bishops go around without people and clergy, bearing an empty name and accomplishing nothing for the advancement of the Gospel[9] of peace and salvation? Are not his words about God full of impious teaching, since through his writings the earlier impiety of the weak-minded Sabellius has now been renewed?[10] For, if what the Sebastenes are circulating has not

6 Cf. Ps. 54.13-15.

7 Apollinaris and Vitalis organized a third church at Berytus, of which a certain Timothy became bishop, in addition to their own two churches at Antioch and Laodicea. Other bishops were consecrated and sent to a distance.

8 Cf. 1 Tim. 3.16.

9 Cf. Phil. 1.12.

10 Duchesne, *The Early History of the Church* 2, 469, says: 'It appears, however, that upon the question of the Trinity there was nothing serious with which to reproach him [Apollinaris]. With regard to the Incarnation, he taught as follows: Christ had received from humanity a body inspired by a soul, but the human mind had been replaced in Him by the Divine element.' The Sabellians imagined God as a

been fabricated by enemies, but is truly his writings, he has left no farther limits for his impiety, since he says that the Father and the Son and the Spirit are the same, and also commits some other dark sacrileges which we did not consent even to admit to our ears, praying to have no part with those who were uttering such words. Has not the doctrine of the Incarnation been confused by that man? Has not the saving dispensation of our Lord been called into question by the many because of his foul and obscure questions concerning the Incarnation? To bring all these things together and set them in order for a refutation requires much time and many words. And who has so obliterated and obscured the passage containing the promises, as he did by his invention of myths? In truth, he dared to explain so basely and so contemptuously the blessed hope which is laid up for those who conduct their lives according to the Gospel of Christ,[11] that it was changed into old wives' tales and Judaizing doctrines.[12] He proclaims anew the restoration of the Temple, the observance of worship according to the Law; again a figurative high priest after the true High Priest, and a sacrifice for sins after the Lamb of God who takes away the sin of the world;[13] also partial baptisms after the one Baptism,[14] and ashes of

---

monad who extends Himself in a Trinity—Father, Son, and Holy Spirit—according to the needs of the creature. When once this need has ceased, the Divinity again draws itself in. There was disagreement upon the subject of the divine Sonship. Some made it consist in the humanity of Christ; others, in the blend of Word and humanity; others, again, said that the Word assumed the character of Son at the Incarnation, which was transitory and ceased before the sending of the Holy Spirit.

11 Cf. Col. 1.5-6.

12 Apollinaris explained the Scriptures in their natural sense. In this way he found himself led to deduce from the Apocalypse the promise of the Reign of a Thousand Years and of an earthly restoration of the Temple and of the Law. Cf. 1 Tim. 4.7.

13 Cf. John 1.29.

14 Cf. Eph. 4.5.

a heifer sprinkling the Church which through faith in Christ does not have spot or wrinkle or any other such thing,[15] and purification from leprosy after the impassibility of the resurrection; and an offering of jealousy,[16] when they neither marry nor are given in marriage,[17] the showbread after the Bread from heaven;[18] lighted lamps after the true Light;[19] and, on the whole, if now the law of the commandments has been abolished in our teachings, clearly then the teachings of Christ will be nullified in the precepts of the Law.

Because of these facts shame and humiliation have covered our faces and a profound grief has filled our hearts. We urge you, therefore, as skilled physicians who have learned how to instruct your opponents in gentleness, to try to lead him back to the good discipline of the Church and to persuade him to despise the wordiness of his writings,[20] for he has confirmed the passage in Proverbs: 'In the multitude of words there shall not want sin';[21] and to propound to him solidly the teachings of the orthodox faith in order that his amendment may be evident to all, and that his repentance may be known to the brethren.

It is also wise to remind your Reverence of Marcellus[22]

---

15 Cf. Eph. 5.27.
16 Cf. Num. 5.15.
17 Cf. Matt. 22.30.
18 Cf. John 6.32.
19 Cf. John 1.9.
20 Apollinaris was a most prolific writer. He assisted his father in reconstructing the Scriptures on the classical models. He wrote in defense of Christianity against Julian and Porphyry, and of orthodoxy against the Manichaeans, Arians, Eunomius, and other heretics. He also produced Biblical commentaries and other works, of which only fragments remain. His exegesis was famous.
21 Cf. Prov. 10.19.
22 The Benedictine editors remark: 'It seems strange and at first sight almost incredible that Marcellus had left the Church on account of his impious errors. St. Athanasius had suspected his teachings, but finally believed him cleansed from his errors. His disciples presented

and his disciples, in order that you may be neither inconsiderate nor careless in prescribing for them. But, since he departed from the Church because of his impious doctrines, those following him must be admitted to communion only after having anathematized that heresy, so that, joined to us through you, they may be received by all the brethren. For, even now, no moderate grief has taken possession of many, who have heard that you received those men when they came to your Honors and that you shared with them ecclesiastical communion. Yet, you should have known that, by the grace of God, you are not alone in the East, but that you have many of your own party who vindicate the orthodoxy of the Fathers who in Nicaea set forth the true doctrine of the faith. Moreover, all those in the West are really in agreement with you and with us. We received from them and we possess their document of faith, and we follow its sound teaching. Now, all who are associated in the same communion with you ought to have full assurance, in order that the present conditions may be more securely established by the consent of the majority, and that peace may not be torn asunder by the departure of some because of the accept-

---

letters from Athanasius to the confessors of Egypt. Epiphanius declared that various judgments were passed on him. Paulinus received his disciples without discrimination. Basil (Letter 69) complained that he had been received into communion by the Church of Rome. Basil's testimony is further strengthened by the fact that during the last years of his life he removed Marcellus from his communion. Moreover, if Athanasius had always been in communion with him, there would have been no need of his disciples requesting the confessors of Egypt to receive them into communion. Furthermore, Peter, the successor of Athanasius, would not have complained as he did in his reply to Basil (cf. Letter 216, Basil) of the violation of the canons if Marcellus and his followers had always been in communion. Therefore, it can be concluded that Marcellus fell into error toward the end of his life, that he was cut off from communion with Athanasius. Deserted by the entire East, the communion which he had been granted at one time by the Church of Rome could have been of little profit.'

ance of others. So, then, you should have deliberated seriously and with moderation concerning matters which belong to all the churches in the world. For, not he who has made his deliberation hastily is deserving of praise, but he who has regulated every detail firmly and unchangeably, so that the decision when examined in subsequent time seems even more excellent. This man is acceptable both to God and man, as one who orders his words with judgment.[23]

These points, in so far as our communication by letter permitted us, we have addressed to your Reverences. May the Lord also grant us at some time to meet together in order that, having arranged all things with you for the good order of the churches of God, we may receive with you the reward prepared by the just Judge for His faithful and wise stewards. But now, in the meantime, be so kind as to write to us the conditions on which you received the disciples of Marcellus, realizing this, that, even though you are made altogether safe as regards your own interests, you ought not to leave such a matter to yourselves alone, but those in communion both in the West and in the East must be of the same opinion on their restoration.

266. To Peter, Bishop of Alexandria[1]

Rightly and in a manner becoming to a spiritual brother who has learned true love from the Lord have you upbraided

23 Cf. Ps. 111.5.

1 Peter, at the recommendation of St. Athanasius, succeeded him in May, 373. This recommendation had been sought in order to insure the peaceful succession of an orthodox bishop. St. Gregory of Nazianzus describes Peter, who had been a companion of his labors (cf. Theod. 4.20, as honored for his wisdom and his gray hairs (cf. Orat. 25.12) . This letter was written at the end of 377 or the beginning of 378. Cf. Loofs, *op. cit.* 48; also, Letters 133 and 265.

me, because we do not inform you of all particulars, whether great or small, of affairs here. Certainly, it is proper both for you to be interested in our concerns and for us to report our affairs to your Charity. But, be assured, our most honorable and most beloved brother, that our continuous afflictions and this great turmoil, which at present is agitating the churches, causes us to be surprised at nothing that is taking place. As those in the forges whose ears are assailed by the din become accustomed to the noises, so we, because of the frequency of the unwonted messages have become accustomed at length to keep our heart undisturbed and undaunted as regards the unexpected. Now, the long-standing fabrications of the Arians against the Church, even though many and great and proclaimed throughout all the world, are, nevertheless, endurable to us because they came from open enemies and men hostile to the word of truth. It is when these do not make their customary attacks that we marvel, not when they dare some great and rash act against true religion. But what is being done by those of like doctrine and of like mind with us grieves and disturbs us.[2] Even these doings, however, because they are so many and fall so continuously upon our ears, do not seem incredible. Therefore, we were neither disturbed at the recent disorderly happenings nor did we weary your ears with them, on the one hand, knowing that rumor of itself carries the news of things done, and on the other, waiting for others to be the messengers of painful tidings. And, again, we did not judge that it was reasonable for you to be vexed at such things, as if angered because you were overlooked. However, to the perpetrators themselves of these deeds we wrote what was proper, urging them, since the brethren there were suffering some disagreement, not to withdraw from charity, but to await a correction by those

2 Cf. Ps. 54.13-15.

who were able to remedy the error in due ecclesiastical form. Since you, rightly and becomingly aroused, did this, we praised you and we thanked the Lord that there was a remnant of the good order of earlier times preserved in you and that the Church had not lost its strength in our persecution. For, the canons were not also persecuted with us. Although I have been frequently importuned by the Galatians, I have never been able to answer them, because I was awaiting your decisions.[3] And now, if the Lord grants it and they are willing to bear with us, we hope to lead the people back to the Church, in order that we ourselves may not be reproached for having agreed with the followers of Marcellus, but that they may become members of the body of the Church of Christ.[4] Thus the evil censure, poured out upon them because of the heresy, may be wiped out by our taking them back, and we may not be put to shame as though we had submitted to them.

The brother Dorotheus has grieved us because, as you yourself wrote, he did not discuss all the matters fittingly and calmly with your Modesty.[5] Really, I attribute this to the difficulty of the times. For we seem to prosper in nothing because of our sins, if, indeed, the most zealous of our

3 Cf. Letter 265 n. 1.

4 Cf. Eph. 5.29,30.

5 Dorotheus, in defending the cause of Meletius before Pope Damasus and Peter, Bishop of Alexandria, by whom Meletius and Eusebius were charged with heresy, vented his wrath on Peter. Cf. *Vita S. Basilii* 37.2. In 360 the choice for the see of Antioch had fallen upon Meletius, who belonged to Melitine in Armenia Minor. A council held in the city in 358 had deposed Eustathius, Bishop of Sebaste, and Meletius had agreed to replace Eustathius, but the people of Sebaste refused to accept him. He thereupon retired to Berea in Syria. Some claimed that Meletius signed the Acacian formula—the then official formula of the imperial government. However, in his discourse at his accession to the see of Antioch he allowed it to be seen that he was no Acacian, but a Nicene. At the end of the month he was exiled. Later recalled, he was driven out a second time in 365 (?), and a third time in 370.

brethren are found to be unrefined and ill adapted for their duties, since they do not accomplish all their tasks according to our will. On his return, Dorotheus related to us the conversation which he had had with your Honor before the most revered Bishop Damasus, and he distressed us when he said that our brethren and fellow ministers dearly beloved of God, Meletius and Eusebius, had been included among the Ariomaniacs.[6] Even if nothing else recommends their orthodoxy, at least the hostility on the part of the Arians offers no slight proof of their rectitude to those who can draw reasonable conclusions. Moreover, fellowship in afflictions borne for the sake of Christ ought to draw your Reverence to them in charity. And be persuaded of this, most truly honored friend, that there is not one word of orthodox faith which was not preached with all freedom by these men. I speak with God as witness and ourselves as hearers. We would not have accepted union with them at the time, if we had found them wavering concerning the faith. But, if it seems best, let us leave the past alone and let us give to the future a peaceful beginning. We all need one another, in the communion of the members, and especially now, when the churches of the East are looking to us and will take your agreement in opinion as a means of support and firmness; but, if they perceive that you labor under any suspicion toward each other, they will relax and will let their hands fall, so as not to raise them against the enemies of the faith.

6 The Benedictine note shows that this charge was outrageous, and points out with what delicacy St. Basil approaches it without directly charging Peter, from whom it must have come, with the slander involved.

267. To Barses, Bishop of Edessa, in Exile[1]

Because of the affection which I have for your Reverence, I longed to be present myself and personally to embrace your true Charity, and to magnify the Lord[2] who has gained great glory in you and has made your honorable old age illustrious among all those in the world who fear Him.[3] But, since an oppressive weakness of body weighs me down and an unspeakably great concern for the churches[4] lies upon me and I am not my own master in regard to traveling wherever I wish and meeting with those for whom I long, I am relieving by this letter the yearning which I have for the enjoyment of your noble qualities, and I beseech your unsurpassed Reverence to pray for me and for the Church, that the Lord may give us the grace to pass through the distressful days or times of our sojourning[5] without offense. And may He allow us to see the peace of His churches and to hear concerning the rest of your fellow ministers and fellow athletes that for which we are praying, and concerning you yourself, that which the laity under you ask of the Lord of justice[6] day and night.

But realize that, though we did not write frequently, not even as often as was due, nevertheless we did write to your Reverence. And, perhaps, the brethren entrusted with the carrying of the letters were not able to preserve our greetings. But now, since we have found our own brethren journeying to your Honor, we have gladly placed the letter in their hands, and we have sent certain messages which we beg that

1 Cf. Letter 264 n. 1.
2 Cf. Luke 1.46-53, the Magnificat.
3 Cf. Matt. 5.16.
4 Cf. 2 Cor. 11.28.
5 Cf. 1 Peter 1.17.
6 Cf. Ps. 4.2.

you deign to receive from our Lowliness without contempt and to bless us in imitation of the patriarch Isaac.[7] And, if we have overlooked anything that is proper, both because we are occupied and because we have our mind submerged in a multitude of cares, do not lay that to our account and do not be grieved, but act according to your own perfection in all things, in order that we, also, like all the rest, may enjoy your virtue. May you be granted to me and to the Church of God healthy and happy in the Lord and praying earnestly for me.

268. To Eusebius in Exile[1]

The Lord has shown even in our times that He does not abandon His holy ones,[2] for with His great and mighty hand[3] He has protected the life of your Holiness. In fact, we regard this as very like to the incident of the holy man remaining without hurt in the belly of the whale[4] and like that of the men who feared the Lord remaining unscathed in the raging fire,[5] seeing that He even kept your Reverence unharmed when, as I hear, the war had spread around you on all sides.[6] And may Almighty God indeed preserve for us in the future,

7 Cf. Gen. 27.27.

1 Tillemont places this letter at the end of 377 or the beginning of 378; the Benedictine editors, on the evidence of Ammianus 31.6, assign it to the summer of 377; so does Loofs. It was at that time that many, unable to bear the heavy burdens of taxation, joined with the invading Goths. Valens, upon hearing of this, sent troops to Antioch and vicinity. This seems to be the army of which St. Basil speaks. Cf. *Vita S. Basilii,* 38.

2 Cf. Josue 1.5.

3 Cf. 2 Esdras 1.10.

4 Cf. Jonas 2.1-11.

5 Cf. Dan. 3.20-50.

6 The uprisings of the Gothic settlers in Thrace. Cf. Soc., *Hist. Eccl.* 4.24-25.

if we are still living, the much-desired sight, or at any rate, for the others who are waiting for your return as for their own salvation.[7] I am convinced that the loving God will give heed to the tears of the churches and the lamentations which all are pouring forth for you, and will preserve you in this life until He grants the favor to those who day and night are asking it from Him.

Of what has happened to you up to the time of the visit of the beloved brother, our fellow deacon, Libanius,[8] we have been sufficiently informed by him as he passed through, but we want to learn what has taken place since that time. For we hear that meanwhile still greater and harsher sufferings have been inflicted in those regions.[9] May we learn even more quickly, if it is possible, but if not, at least through the most pious brother and fellow presbyter Paul[10] when he comes, that these things are as we pray, namely, that your life is preserved unharmed and unmolested. Because we have heard that all the roads are filled with robbers and deserters,[11] we have been afraid to place anything in the hands of the brother, lest we become responsible for his death. But, if the Lord grants a moderate calm (since we are hearing of the arrival of the army), we shall endeavor to send one of our brethren to visit you and to report all the details of your affairs to us.

7 The Arians, Eunomius and Lucius, were successively placed in charge of his see after the departure of Eusebius. The people of Samosata steadfastly refused allegiance to both.

8 Nothing more is known of this Libanius. He is not the Libanius of Letter 92, nor the Libanius, the professor of rhetoric, of Letter 335.

9 It appears that Eusebius suffered more from the suspicions aroused at Rome as to his orthodoxy than from the barbarian ravages of the Goths.

10 Nothing further is known of this Paul.

11 Eusebius was an exile in Thrace where the Goths were now closing round Valens.

269. A Letter of Condolence to the Wife of the Commander Arintheus[1]

It was in accordance with and due to your position that we ourselves should be at hand and share with you what is happening. Thus we might have allayed our own grief and have reasonably discharged our duty of consolation to your Dignity. But, since my body no longer endures the more tedious journeys, we have had recourse to a conversation by letter in order that we may not seem to be altogether uninterested in regard to the occurrence.

Who, indeed, did not bewail that man? And who is so stony-hearted as not to pour forth burning tears for him? Truly, it has filled me exceedingly with sorrow when I think of the personal regard of the man for me and his general protection of the churches of God. Nevertheless, I considered that, being a man and having performed the tasks belonging to this life, he was taken in the proper time to Himself by God, who directs our concerns. And we urge your Wisdom, pondering these facts, to be calm in what has come to pass, and, as much as posible, to bear the misfortune with moderation. Certainly, time is able both to soothe your heart and to give entrance to reason; nevertheless, your excessive love for your husband and your kindness toward all I view with fear, lest you may at some time give yourself up entirely to your feelings, since through the simplicity of your

1 In 355, when the Goths were invading northern Italy, Arintheus with two other officials turned the impending defeat into a victory for Emperor Constantius by attacking the enemy without waiting for orders from the emperor. In 363, Arintheus was commander of the left wing of the cavalry in Julian's expedition against the Persians. In 372 he was consul and in 378 he was present when the general Trajan rebuked Valens for the persecution of the Catholics. Cf. also Letter 179, addressed to Arintheus himself; also Theodoret, *Hist. Eccl.* 4.30. This letter was written in 378.

character you have received deeply the blow of your grief. Now, the teaching of the Scriptures is useful always, but especially on such occasions. Remember, then, the declaration of our Creator, according to which all of us who are of dust again return to dust, and no one is so mighty as to become superior to dissolution.[2]

In truth, that excellent man was noble and great, and the strength of his body matched the virtue of his soul, and, in fact, I must say, he was not surpassed in either; but he was a man and he died, just as did Adam, or Abel, or Noe, or Abraham, or Moses, or whomever you might mention of those who have shared the same nature.[3] Let us not, therefore, be grieved because we have been deprived of him; rather, let us give thanks to Him who joined us with him that we lived with him at all. To be deprived of a husband is the lot which you share in common with other women, but in consideration of such a marriage I do not think that there is another woman who is able to have equal glory. In truth, the Creator fashioned that man as a unique example of human nature, so that all eyes were fastened upon him and every tongue related his achievements. Moreover, painters and sculptors fell short of his true worth, while historians relating his brave deeds in the wars seem to fall into the incredible fiction of the mythical. Wherefore, many refused to trust the report which brought that sad message and, in short, to admit that Arintheus was dead. Nevertheless, he has suffered what will happen to the heavens and to the sun and to the earth.[4]

He departed from this life, having made a brilliant end, not bent down by old age, not surrendering any of his

2 Cf. Gen. 3.19.
3 Cf. Rom. 5.14.
4 Cf. Ps. 101.26,27.

renown; great in the present life, and great in the future; suffering no loss of his present splendor in view of the hoped-for glory, because every stain of his soul in the very departure from life was wiped away in the bath of regeneration.[5] That you yourself have been protector and co-worker with him in these achievements holds the greatest comfort. Transfer your mind, too, from present affairs to solicitude for the future, so as to be deemed worthy through your good works to receive a place of rest equal to his. Spare your aged mother, spare your young daughter, to whom you alone have been left for consolation. Be an example of courage for the rest of womankind; and moderate your suffering in such a way as neither to cast it out of your heart nor to be swallowed up by your grief. In all things look forward to the great reward of patient endurance which was promised to us by our Lord Jesus Christ in recompense for the deeds of this life.[6]

270. Without an Address, concerning an Abduction[1]

I am grieved exceedingly because I find that you are neither indignant at the forbidden deeds nor able to understand that this abduction which has taken place is a lawless and tyrannical act against the very life and existence of man, and an insult to free men. For I know that, if all of you had such an opinion, nothing would prevent this evil practice from having been banished long ago from our country. Take upon yourself, therefore, at the present time, the zeal of a Christian,

5 Arintheus was baptized just before his death in accordance with a common custom of the day. Cf. Titus 3.5,6.

6 Cf. Matt. 25.34.

1 *Harpagé* probably means here the forceful removal of a woman to a place where she may be induced or forced to marry. This letter was written after 374.

and be roused in a manner worthy of the wrong-doing. Moreover, take away the girl by force, wherever you may find her, and restore her to her parents. Exclude the man himself from prayers and excommunicate him. Those, also, who were his accomplices, exclude with their whole families from the prayers for the space of three years according to the canon[2] we have already published. And the village which received the girl who was carried off and kept her, or fought for her possession, this, also, cut off with all its people from the prayers, in order that all, considering the ravisher a common enemy, like a serpent or any wild animal, may learn to drive him away in the same manner, and to succor those who are wronged.

271. A Letter of Recommendation to Eusebius[1] His Companion, in Behalf of the Presbyter Cyriacus[2]

What is the need to mention how disheartened I was at missing you when I stopped at the city immediately after, even on the very heels of your departure, to say it especially to a man who does not require words, but knows by experience, through having suffered the same disappointment? How much I would have appreciated seeing the all-excellent

2 The canon referred to is probably No. 30 of Letter 199 in which the same sentences are decreed. Some would understand here a letter sent broadcast to promulgate the excommunication of the guilty party.

1 This Eusebius was a college friend and roommate of St. Basil at Athens. Nothing more is known of him than is contained in this letter, which was written some time after 374.

2 The Benedictine editors do not identify this Cyriacus with the one mentioned in Letter 188. It does not seem improbable, however, that they are the same person.

Eusebius and embracing him, returning again in memory to our youth, and recalling those days in which we had but one home, one hearth, and the same teacher, recreation, interests, luxuries, want, and all things shared in common! How highly, think you, I would have valued it to renew in memory all those things by a conversation with you, and, having stripped off this heavy old age, to seem to have been changed again from an old man into a young one. Though the enjoyment of those pleasures escaped me, I have not been deprived of speaking with your Eloquence by means of a letter and of consoling myself in every possible manner through a meeting with our most revered fellow presbyter, Cyriacus, whom I am ashamed to recommend to you and to make your friend through my efforts, lest, perhaps, I may seem to be doing something heedless by introducing to you that which is your own and special possession. Yet, since I must also be a witness of the truth[3] and freely bestow upon those who are joined with me spiritually the greatest favors in my possession, although I think that the integrity of this man in his priestly life is evident even to you, I also corroborate it, knowing of no abuse directed against him by those who lay their hands on all and who do not fear the Lord. Even if something had been done by them, the man was not, therefore, unworthy. But the enemies of the Lord confirm the ecclesiastical orders of those against whom they fight rather than deprive them of any of the grace bestowed upon them by the Spirit. Only, as I said, nothing has been invented against this man. Therefore, so deign to regard him as a presbyter free from calumny and united with us and deserving of all reverence, and benefit yourself while doing us a favor.

---

3 Cf. John 18.37.

272. To the Master Sophronius[1]

Actiacus,[2] the deacon, announced to me that some men had caused you to be vexed at us, slanderously saying that we are not favorably disposed toward your Dignity. I am not surprised if there are some flatterers who attend so great a man. Somehow, these servile attendants are accustomed to attach themselves to important positions. These men, because of their lack of personal good, by which they might be known, secure approval of themselves through the evils of others. And, as the rust, when it is on the grain itself, is destructive of the grain, so flattery, insinuating itself into friendship, is the ruin of friendship.[3] Therefore, I am not surprised, as I said, if some men, like drones humming around the hives, hum thus around your brilliant and admirable hearth.

But this seems to me astonishing and altogether beyond reason, that you, a man especially conspicuous for the dignity of your character, should consent to open both ears for them and to accept the slander against me, who, although I have loved many from my early youth until this present old age, know that I have preferred no one to your Perfection as a friend. In fact, even if reason had not persuaded me to love you because you are so excellent a man, our intimacy from boyhood would suffice to attach me to your soul. And you know how much power for friendship habit possesses. If, however, I show nothing deserving of this affection, pardon my weakness. You yourself will not demand some deed from me as a proof of my good will, but an affection which

1 For this Sophronius, cf. Letters 32, 76, 96, 180, and 192. The *Magister officiorum* (Master of the Offices) was the supreme magistrate of the palace, inspected the discipline of the civil and military schools, and received appeals from all parts of the empire. This letter was written in the later years of St. Basil's life.

2 Nothing more is known of him.

3 Cf. Plato, *Republic* 609A.

assuredly joins with you in prayer for blessings. Indeed, may your concerns never sink into such a state as to need the services of those as insignificant as I am.

How, then, was I likely to say or do anything against you in the matter concerning Memnonius.[4] This is what the deacon has reported to me. And how would I consider the wealth of Hymetius[5] preferable to your friendship, when the man so freely squanders his substance. Certainly, none of these reports is true; I have neither said nor done anything against you. But this, probably, gave the occasion to those who are telling the lies, namely, my remark to some of those who were causing disturbances: 'If the man has publicly given orders to carry his decision into action, whether you make a disturbance or not, nonetheless, what is being undertaken will assuredly be accomplished, whether you talk or keep quiet. But, if he changes his mind, do not drag in the revered name of our friend, and, indeed, do not under any pretext of zeal for your patron try to gain for yourselves some profit from those circumstances through which you hold out fear and threats.' To the man himself who wrote the will, neither of myself nor through another did I utter any word, either trifling or important, concerning this affair.[6]

---

4 Nothing further is known of him.

5 Otherwise unknown.

6 The matter at issue is not too clear from the context. It seems that a certain person in authority ('the man'), for whom St. Basil has little respect, has given orders about an unknown matter, which are so objectionable to certain persons with whom St. Basil is in touch that they raise a storm of protest. They pretend to desire to serve the interests of their 'patron,' who evidently is Sophronius, to whom this letter is addressed. But St. Basil, in trying to restrain them, intimates that their real object is to advance their own interests by threatening the author of the objectionable commands, and urges them not to drag in his 'friend's' name, i.e., apparently that of Sophronius. The resentment of Sophronius against St. Basil was due to a misleading report of these words to Sophronius. In some connection Sophronius has also supposed that St. Basil influenced some person, perhaps Hymetius, regarding a will, and this will may have been involved in the incident which St. Basil here explains.

Really, you ought not to distrust these words, unless you think that I am absolutely to be despaired of and that I regard lightly the great sin of lying. But you yourself, by all means, free us from suspicion in this matter, and for the future, consider my affection for you above all slander, imitating Alexander,[7] who, at the very time that he happened to take up his medicine to drink it, received a letter charging that his physician was plotting against him and was so far from trusting the slander that, as he read the letter, he drank the medicine. I do not hesitate to regard myself as no more dishonorable than any of those who are renowned for their friendship, since I have never been found sinning against friendship, and, besides, since I have received from my God the precept of love, in which I am your debtor not only in so far as concerns human nature in general but also because I recognize that you personally are a benefactor to me and to my country.

273. Without Address, in Behalf of Hera[1]

Being fully persuaded that your Honor loves us in such a way as to consider our concerns your own, I am recommending to your marvelous Excellency our most revered brother Hera, whom we call our brother not from mere habit but from an affection that is most genuine and can go no further in friendship. I also urge you to look upon him with a friendly spirit, and, according to your power, to extend to him your patronage in whatever matters he may ask it of your Lordship, so that I may be able to reckon this good deed among the many blessings which I have obtained from you.

7 Cf. Plutarch, *Alexander* 19.3.
8 Cf. John 13.34.

1 Letters 273-275 were written toward the end of St. Basil's life.

274. To the Master Himerius[1]

That my friendship and intimacy with the most revered brother Hera began with earliest childhood and by the grace of God has endured even until old age, you yourself know better than anyone else. The Lord bestowed on us the love of your Excellency almost from the very time from which He also granted us an acquaintance with each other. Since, then, he needs your patronage, I urge you and I entreat that, favoring us with your early affection and devoting yourself to this present urgent necessity, you make his affairs your own in such a way that he will need the patronage of no other, but will return to us with everything accomplished according to his prayers. And so, with the many blessings which we have enjoyed from you, we may be able to include this one also, which we claim as our own, not finding any more important for ourself nor bearing more on our concerns.

275. Without an Address, concerning Hera

You anticipated our appeals in your affection for our most revered brother Hera and you have proved yourself better toward him than we had prayed, not only by the extraordinary honors which you have shown to him but also by your protection on every occasion. Nevertheless, we also, since we are not able to bear in silence his present state of affairs, urge your unsurpassed Honor for our sake to add to your zeal for the man and to send him back to his country victorious over the abuses of his enemies. At the present time, certainly, he is not beyond the darts of envy, since

1 The Himerius of this letter seems to be a Christian and not the contemporary Sophist of that name.

many are attempting to disturb the tranquility of his life. Against these we shall find one invulnerable means of safety, namely, if you yourself would be willing to hold a protecting hand over the man.[1]

276. To the Elder Harmatius[1]

Not only does the common law of all men make the elders common fathers, but also the law peculiar to us Christians places us old men in the position of parents to such men. Therefore, do not think that I am overbusy or meddling beyond necessity, if I serve as intercessor with you for your son. We consider it right for you to demand his obedience in other respects, for he is responsible to you as regards his body both by the law of nature and by this civil law under which we are governed. As to his soul, however, since he has derived it from a diviner origin, it is proper to consider that it is subject to another, and that it owes debts to God which hold precedence over all debts. Since, therefore, he preferred the God of us Christians, the true God, to the many gods among you which are served by material symbols, do not be angry with him. Rather, admire the nobility of his soul, that he placed as more precious than the fear and compliance due to his father, the fact that he was made a friend of God through a knowledge of the truth and a life of virtue. Now, nature itself, as well as the gentleness and kindness of your disposition toward everyone, will entreat

1 Cf. Solon, fr. 2, Bergk, 1.5.

1 Nothing more is known of the two Harmatii. This letter was written toward the end of St. Basil's life.

you not to permit to yourself even in the slightest degree any anger toward him. Assuredly, you will not esteem lightly our intercession or, rather, that of your city, undertaken by us. Its citizens, in their love for you and in their prayers for all blessings upon you, even think that they have welcomed you as a Christian. So very glad has the report which has suddenly come into the city made them.

277. To the Scholar Maximus[1]

The excellent Theotecnus[2] brought back to me news of the affairs of your Dignity, and, clearly delineating in his speech the character of your soul, inspired me with a longing to meet with you. He kindled in me such an affection for you that, if I had not been weighed down by old age and restrained by my usual infirmity and fettered by the innumerable cares of the Church, nothing could have kept me from visiting you. In truth, it is no small profit for a man from a great house and an illustrious race, entering upon the evangelical life, to bridle his youth by meditation, to subject the passions of the flesh to reason, to embrace the humility proper to a Christian who ponders, as is his duty concerning himself, both whence he came and where he is going.[3] The consideration of our nature checks the swelling of the spirit, banishes all false pretense and arrogance, and, on the whole, makes one a disciple of the Lord, who said: 'Learn from me,

1 Nothing further is known of this Maximus, although he is sometimes confused with the philosopher Maximus. This letter was written toward the end of St. Basil's life.

2 This Theotecnus is probably not the deacon nor the layman of the same name, both of whom were friends of St. Gregory of Nazianzus.

3 Cf. John 8.14.

for I am meek and humble of heart.'[4] Truly, most beloved of sons, the only thing much to be desired and worthy of praise is the everlasting good. And this is the honor which comes from God.

These human things are fainter than a shadow and more deceptive than dreams. Youth drops away more swiftly than the spring flowers, and the beauty of the body is withered by disease or age.[5] Wealth is untrustworthy and glory is fickle. The pursuit of the arts comes to an end with the span of this life. And even eloquence, a thing much desired by all, possesses charm only as far as the ear. The practice of virtue, however, is a precious possession to him who has it and a very pleasing sight to those who encounter it. Cultivating this, you will make yourself worthy of the blessings reserved by the Lord in His promises. Now, to say in what manner you might arrive at the acquisition of these blessings and how you might preserve those obtained, would take longer than is consistent with the purpose of my letter. In truth, it occurred to me to address these words to you because of these which I heard from our brother Theotecnus, whom I pray always to speak the truth, especially in his words concerning you, in order that the Lord may be glorified more in you who, drawn from an alien root, are abounding in the precious fruits of piety.

4 Matt. 11.29.
5 Cf. Job. 14.1,2.

278. To Valerian[1]

Even when I was in Orphanene[2] I was desirous of seeing your Nobility. In fact, I hoped that you, since you were living in Corsagaena,[3] would not hesitate to cross over to us, if we were holding the synod in Attagaena. But, when I missed that synod, I was eager to see you in the hill country. For, there again, Evesus,[4] as it was near at hand, held out the hope of a meeting. As I missed both, I determined to write, in order that you might deign to come to me, at the same time doing what is right—a young man making the trip to the old one—and likewise, receiving through our conference some advice from us, because your troubles with some of the residents in Caesarea need our mediation for their correction. If, then, it is convenient, do not hesitate to come to us.

279. To the Prefect Modestus[1]

Even though there are many who carry letters from us to your Honor, nevertheless, because of the extraordinary esteem which you have for us, I think that the great number of letters affords your Excellency no annoyance. For that reason I have readily given the present letter to this brother, knowing that he will obtain all that he desires and that we shall be

1 Nothing further is known of this Valerian. This letter was written during the episcopate.
2 A district of Asia Minor.
3 In the Pontus.
4 Cf. Letter 251. Evesus is about fifty miles north of Caesarea.

1 On Modestus, cf. Letter 104. Letters 279-281 were written during the episcopate.

counted by you among your benefactors, since we are procuring for your good will opportunities for beneficence.

Now, the affair for which he asks your protection he himself will tell you, if you will condescend to look upon him with a kindly eye and will give him courage to speak out in the presence of your great and august Highness. We, through this letter, are presenting our view that whatever is done for him we consider as a personal gain, especially because he, setting out from Tyana,[2] came to us for this purpose, on the ground that he will have some great advantage if he can offer our letter in lieu of the suppliant's olive branch. In order, then, that he himself may not be disappointed in his hopes and that we may enjoy our accustomed honor and that your zeal for the good may be fulfilled also on the present occasion, we beg that he be received kindly and be numbered among your closest friends.

280. To the Prefect Modestus

Even if it is a daring act to address by letter supplications to so great a man, the honor which in the past we received from you takes the fear out of our heart, and we make bold to write to you in behalf of men related to us by kinship and worthy of honor because of the uprightness of their character. Futher, he who is presenting this letter of ours stands in the position of son to me. Since, then, he needs only your good will to procure that which he seeks, deign to receive my letter, which the aforementioned is presenting to you in lieu of the olive branch, and grant him an opportunity to describe his situation and to converse with those who are able to

2 A town of Cappadocia in the Taurus Mountains.

assist him, so that by your command he may speedily obtain what he is striving for, and that it may be granted to me to pride myself on the fact that there has been given to me by the grace of God such a patron as considers my relatives his own suppliants and clients.

281. To the Prefect Modestus

I have kept in mind the great honor you bestowed on me, that among other things you gave me also the encouragement to write to your Excellency. Accordingly, I have made use of the privilege and I am enjoying your most kind favor, both delighting myself by conversing with so great a man and also affording your Lordship an opportunity to honor us by your answers. Since I supplicated your Clemency in behalf of our companion Helladius,[1] our leading citizen, that he, having been relieved of the responsibility of the assessment, might be permitted to labor in the affairs of our country, and since I was deemed worthy of a gracious consent, I am making again the same intercession and I earnestly entreat you that a command be sent to the governor of the province to relieve him of the annoyance.

282. To a Bishop[1]

When you are not invited, you complain, and when you are invited, you do not heed. From the second observation,

1 Nothing further is known of him; he is, however, usually distinguished from the Helladius of Letters 107 and 109.

1 Letters 282-289 were written during the episcopate.

it is evident that you made use of the former excuse without reason. You would not have come, in all probability, even if you have been invited then. Give ear, therefore, to those who are inviting you now, and do not again be inconsiderate, since you know that one ground of complaint added to another confirms it, and the second makes the accusation of the former more credible. I urge you always to be patient with us, but, if you will not be patient with us, it is not right to neglect the martyrs, whose commemoration you are called to share.[2] Grant, then, the favor primarily to both of us,[3] but if this does not seem good to you, at least grant it to the more honorable.[4]

283. To a Widow

We hope to find a suitable day for the synod after those which we are about to assign for the hill country.[1] But no other opportunity for a meeting, apart from the celebration of the synod, appears to us, unless the Lord makes some adjustment beyond our expectations. You ought to surmise this from your own affairs. For, if around your Nobility, who have the responsibility of one home, there lies such a throng of cares, with how many occupations do you think we are engaged each day?

2 Cf. Letter 252 n. 1.
3 The martyrs, as well as the writer.
4 The martyrs.

1 St. Basil uses the term 'synod' in many different significations: a council of bishops; assemblies of the faithful as the celebration of the festivals of martyrs; and, as here, the meeting of country presbyters held on St. Basil's visits to their regions.

I think that your dream shows more perfectly that it is necessary to pay some attention to spiritual contemplation and to train the mental sight by which God is wont to be seen. And having consolation from the divine Scriptures, you will need neither us nor anyone else to understand what is proper, since you will have in sufficient measure from the Holy Spirit counsel and guidance to what is expedient.

284. To an Assessor,[1] in Behalf of Monks

I think that some rule has been in force with your Honor in behalf of the monks, so that we need not at all request a special favor in their case, but it suffices for them if they can enjoy the kindness that is common to all. Believing, nevertheless, that it is incumbent upon me to take thought, as far as possible, for such men, I am writing to ask your mature Intelligence to free from taxation those who long ago renounced this life, mortifying their bodies, so that they are able to furnish nothing useful to the state either by means of money or of bodily service. For, if they are in truth living according to their profession, they have neither money nor bodies, having been dispossessed of the one through alms for the needy and having worn out the other in fasts and prayers. But I know that you, more than anyone else, will hold in reverence men who have lived thus and will want to secure them as assistants to yourself, since they are able through their life according to the Gospel to importune the Lord.

---

1 An assessor was a special official under the empire whose duty was to evaluate property for taxation in a province or a portion of a province. According to the burdensome tax system of Diocletian, still operative, monks, being laymen and not clergy, were not eligible to the immunities granted to the clergy.

285. Without an Address, for the Protection of the Church

He who cares for our church and has in his hands the charge of its possessions, he himself is the one presenting this letter to you, our beloved son.[1] Be so kind as to grant him freedom of speech concerning the matters which he is referring to your Modesty, and to take heed of what he is asserting, so that at least from now on our church may be enabled to recover itself and to be freed from this many-headed hydra.[2] For the possessions of the poor are such that we are always seeking someone to take them, because the church spends more than any profit it has from its possessions.[3]

286. To a Prison Official

Some men in this synod were caught committing evil deeds and, in contravention of the command of the Lord,[1] stealing the cheap garments of poor people, whom they ought rather to clothe than to strip. Now, since men who have charge of ecclesiastical discipline arrested them, I, believing that the acceptance of the responsibility for such men was of importance to you who are engaged in state affairs, wrote informing you that it was proper for crimes committed in the churches to meet with the appropriate correction from us,

1 St. Basil deliberately refrains from putting the bearer's name into writing.
2 Taxation.
3 On entering the monastery, men could give their property either to the monastery or to relatives, if they did not wish to sell it and give the proceeds to the poor. In the first case, the monastery was responsible for all taxes; in the second, the relatives.

1 Cf. Exod. 20.15.
2 Cf. Matt. 25.34,40.

and for the judges not to be concerned about such matters. Therefore, I enjoined that the stolen property, which the document in your possession as well as the indictment made before all those who were present clearly lists, should be taken in charge, and some reserved for the applicants who shall yet come and some distributed to those who are now present. As to the men, they shall be corrected in accordance with the teaching and admonition of the Lord.[3] And I think that in the name of God I will make them better for the future. For, what the lashes of the courts do not effect, this we know the terrible judgments of the Lord often successfully accomplish. But, if it seems best to you to refer this matter also to the Count, we feel such confidence in the justice and in the uprightness of the man, that we permit you to do what you wish.

287. Without an Address, against Retaliators

The case of this man seems to be very hard to handle. We do not know how to treat a character so versatile and, as it is possible to infer from our observations, so desperate. In fact, if he is summoned to judgment, he does not comply, and if he does present himself, he uses such a superfluity of words and oaths as to make us glad to get rid of him quickly. I have often seen him even twist the charges around against the accusers. In short, there is no nature among all creatures living upon this earth so subtle and so susceptible to evil as that of this man, as can be recognized from a little experience with him. But, why do you ask me? Why do you not persuade yourselves to endure the injuries from him as some God-sent visitation of wrath? Yet, that you may

3 Cf. Eph. 6.4.

not be defiled by contact with sinful actions, let him with his whole family be excluded from prayers and from all other communion with the clergy. Perchance, having been made an example of,[1] he will be put to shame.

288. *Without an Address, against Retaliators*

Those whom the usual penalties do not recall to their senses, and even exclusion from prayers does not lead to repentance, must be subjected to the canons given by the Lord. For it has been written: 'If thy brother sin, go and show him his fault, between thee and him. But if he do not listen to thee, take with thee another. And if not even thus, appeal to the Church, but if he refuse to hear even the Church, let him henceforth be to thee as the heathen and the publican.'[1] Now, this truly has been done in the case of this man. Once he was accused; in the presence of one or two he was convicted; a third time, in the presence of the Church. Since, therefore, we have solemnly protested to him and he has not acquiesced, let him for the future be excommunicated. And let it be announced to all the village that he is not to be admitted to any participation in the ordinary relations of life, so that, by our refusal to associate with him, he may become wholly the food for the Devil.[2]

---

1 By excommunication.

---

1 Cf. Matt. 18.15-17.

2 Cf. 1 Tim. 1.20.

289. Without an Address, concerning an Afflicted Woman

I, judging it to be an equal fault either to permit the sinners to go unpunished or to overstep the measure in chastisement, have imposed on this man the penalty incumbent upon me to pass, excluding him from ecclesiastical communion. Moreover, I have advised those who were wronged not to avenge themselves, but to entrust the retribution to the Lord.[1] Therefore, if there would have been any assistance from my admonitions, I would have been heeded then, since I made use of speech more impressive by far than the urgency with which a letter could entreat.

But, when I heard statements that carried much weight, not only was I silent then, but even now I do not think that it is proper for me to talk about these same things. 'For I,' she said, 'had forgone a husband and the bearing of children and the world that I might obtain this one thing, namely to be considered worthy of approval from God and of a better name among men.[2] When a man trained from childhood in the corruption of homes fell upon our home once with his accustomed boldness, forcing his way in, and became known to us only by a bare acquaintance, and I in my ignorance of his character and because of a certain inexperienced modesty was ashamed to drive him out openly, he proceeded to such a point of impiety and insult as to fill the whole city with slanders against me and to denounce me by public proclamation which was affixed to the entrances of the church. Even though he had met with some annoyance from the laws[3] because of these things, he came again and renewed

1 Cf. Rom. 12.19.

2 Cf. 1 Cor. 7.34.

3 According to the Benedictine editors, this statement shows that the author of the calumny had been condemned to exile by the civil authorities.

his slanders. Again the market place, the gymnasiums, the theatres, and the homes of those who received him because of the similarity of their lives were full of his revilings against me. And, in consequence of his most shameful charges, not even for the better qualities in which I was conspicuous was I permitted to be known, because I had become notorious among all for my shameless reputation.'

'In regard to these things,' she says, 'some are delighted with the slanders, because men naturally rejoice in revilings; others say that they are grieved, but they do not show sympathy; others are persuaded that the abusive charges are true; still others are doubtful, giving heed to the great number of his oaths. There is no one who shares my sufferings. Truly I have experienced loneliness, and I bewail myself, having no brother, no friend, no relative, no servant, no freed man, absolutely no one among men who sympathizes with me. And, as it seems, I find my lone self more pitiable than the whole city in which there is so little hatred of evil. Men do not realize that this abusive violence committed against one another travels in a circle and that they themselves will one day be seized.'

After she had related to me these and still far more impressive things with untold tears, she went away, not, however, leaving me free from blame, because, when I should be sympathizing with her in a fatherly way, I am indifferent to so much evil and philosophize on the sufferings of others. 'For you do not order me to disdain the loss of money, nor to endure bodily sufferings, but that I be ruined in reputation itself, the damage to which becomes a common loss to the clergy.'[4]

Choose what you wish me now to say to her in answer to these words, O admirable Sir, since I have this decision in

4 As a nun, she reckons herself with the clergy.

my own mind, not to hand over to the authorites the evil-doers and, nevertheless, not to rescue those who have been handed over. To them the Apostle long ago said that in their evil deed they should fear authority: 'For not without reason,' he says, 'does it carry the sword.'[5] As, then, to hand over is inhuman, so also to rescue is the act of one fostering abusive treatment. Pehaps there might be some delay of the investigation until our own arrival; then we shall show that our help profits nothing because there are none who obey.

290. To Nectarius[1]

May many blessings be bestowed on those who are moving your Honor to a steady correspondence with us by letter. Do not think that we speak such words through custom, but that from a true affection we esteem your utterances most highly. For, what could be dearer to me than Nectarius, who from childhood was known to us for his most noble qualities and who now has risen to such high distinction by the exercise of every virtue? Therefore, he who brings your letters to me is the most loved of all friends.

Certainly, in regard to the election of those who shall be in charge of the districts, if I ever do anything for the sake of bestowing favors on men, or giving in to supplications, or yielding to fear, may I not make the selections. I will not then be an administrator, but a huckster, exchanging the gift of God for human friendship. But, if the votes cast are

5 Cf. Rom. 13.4.

1 Nectarius is probably the Nectarius of Letters 5 and 6, a layman of noble birth and high official position. Nectarius had written to urge the claims of a friend of his in the coming election of the chorepiscopi, a grade of priests between the bishops and the presbyters, i.e., suffragan bishops.

cast by men who are able to testify only from the outward appearance to whatever they testify, but the selections of the more suitable men are entrusted by our Lowliness to Him who knows the secrets of hearts, perhaps it would be better for everyone, after having set down his evidence, to refrain from all zeal and contention as if his testimony was given in behalf of his personal interests, and to pray to God that what is best may not escape our observation. Thus, we shall no longer ascribe to a man the outcome in each case, but we shall feel grateful to God for what happens. Furthermore, if these things are done through man, they are not done at all, but there is an imitation and it falls altogether short of the truth.

Beware lest, seeing that there is no slight danger to him who strives in every way to gain his own end, we may at some time draw to ourselves the party of those who are wrong. For, many sins might be committed even by those who would never have been expected to commit them, because of the proneness of human nature to sin. Again, in our private life when frequently we have given excellent advice to friends, even if we seem unconvincing to those taking counsel, we do not become angry; in matters, then, which involve not man's advice but God's decision, shall we become indignant at not being preferred to God's judgment? If, therefore, this decision is given by men, what need is there to seek it from us and not for each man to take it from himself? But, if by God, it is proper to pray and not to be vexed, and in our prayer not to demand our own will, but to entrust it to God who dispenses what is best. May the holy God divert every painful trial from your home, and may He measure out to you yourself and to all your relatives a life in all prosperity free from sickness and harm.

291. To the Suffragan Bishop Timotheus[1]

Now, I am aware that to write everything I think is neither consistent with the length of a letter nor otherwise proper to that sort of a greeting, yet to pass it by in silence is almost impossible to me, since my heart is inflamed with a just indignation against you. Therefore, I shall take the middle path, writing some things and disregarding others. For, I wish to reprove you, if it is meet and right, with a friendly frankness of speech.

If you are that Timotheus whom we have known from boyhood so earnest as regards an upright and ascetic life as to be accused of excess in it, do you now, shrinking in every way from the consideration of what must be done that we may be associated with God, pay attention to what seems best to so-and-so concerning you? And do you keep your life dependent on the opinion of others? And ponder as to how you may not be useless to your friends nor ridiculous to your enemies? And fear disgrace before the many as something terrible? And do you not understand that, while you delay concerning these things, you are, unawares, neglecting your own higher life? In fact, the holy Scriptures are full of utterances which have taught us that it is not possible to have possession at the same time of both the goods of the world and the life according to God. Even nature itself is full of such examples. For, in the operation of the mind it is absolutely impossible to think two thoughts at the same time, and in sense perceptions it is not possible to receive and distinguish at the same moment two sounds falling together upon the ears, and this, although two paths of hearing are

---

1 For the term suffragan bishop, cf. Letter 53 n. 1. The recipient of this letter, written during the episcopate, is probably to be identified with the Timotheus of Letter 24.

open to us. The eyes, too, if both are not fixed on some one of the visible objects, cannot perform their duty accurately. And these are examples from nature. But to relate to you those from the Scriptures is no less ridiculous than 'to bring the owl,' as it is said, 'to Athens.'[2]

Why, then, do we attempt to mix things that will not mix—civil turmoils with the exercise of piety—and not rather, withdrawing from turmoils and from having troubles ourselves and causing them for others, become masters of ourselves and confirm by our actions the aim of the religious life which we formerly proposed to ourselves, and show to those who wish to abuse us that it is not in their power to grieve us whenever they wish? This will be whenever we show ourselves immune from every attack. So far, then, for such matters. Would that we might some day meet and take counsel more exactly concerning the interests of our souls, that we may not be preoccupied with solicitude about vain matters when inevitable death comes upon us.

I was delighted with the articles sent by your Charity, which were really very pleasing according to their nature, but the added circumstance of your being the sender made the pleasure manifold. Gladly accept our gifts from Pontus, the beeswax and the restoratives, when we send them; at present we do not have them at hand.

---

2 I.e., do something superfluous, like our 'bring coals to Newcastle.'

292. To Palladius[1]

The holy God fulfilled half of our desire when He arranged the meeting with our most modest sister, your wife. And He is able to grant the rest, also, so that we, seeing your Nobility, may return perfect thanks to God. We are possessed of a great desire, especially now, since we have heard that you have been invested with a great honor, the immortal garment,[2] which, enveloping our humanity, has utterly destroyed death in the flesh and absorbed that which was mortal in the garment of immortality.

The Lord has made you very close to Himself through His grace, alienating you from all sin, opening the kingdom of heaven, and showing you the paths which lead to happiness there. We, therefore, urge you, a man who excels the rest of mankind so far in prudence, to receive the grace wisely, and to become a faithful guardian of the treasure, vigilantly keeping the custody of the royal deposit. Thus, having preserved the seal unsullied, you may stand beside the Lord, shining with the brightness of the saints, having put no stain or wrinkle in the garment of immortality, but retaining sacredness in all your members, as having put on Christ.[3] Therefore, let all your members be holy that they may be worthy to be covered by that holy and radiant robe.

1 Letters 292-366 belong to the third class of letters as arranged by the Benedictine editors. This class comprises those whose date has not been established, as well as doubtful or clearly spurious letters. This Palladius may be the same man who wrote to St. Athanasius about 371 telling of the opposition of some of the monks of Caesarea to St. Basil, and begging that he counsel them. In that case, this letter must be placed before 371, since at this time Palladius had just received baptism. However, the name Palladius was very common.

2 Christianity.

3 Gal. 3.27.

293. *To Julian*[1]

How has your health been during these intervening days? Have you regained completely the use of your hand? And how about the other concerns of life? Are they progressing according to your desire, as we pray and as is due to your principle of action? In fact, for those whose opinion is prone to change, it is not at all unnatural for their life also to be disorderly; but as for those whose mind is fixed, always constant and the same, it is consistent for them to conduct their life in harmony with their principle of action. For, truly, it is not granted to a pilot to bring about a calm whenever he wishes, but for us it is even very easy to make life smooth for ourselves if we silence the tumults aroused within us by our passions and fix our mind above attacks from without. Neither losses, nor illnesses, nor the other hardships of life will touch the virtuous man as long as he has his mind engaged with God and fixed on the future, lightly and easily passing beyond the storm stirred up from the earth. Those who are excessively occupied by the cares of life, like very fleshy birds which have wings to no purpose, crawl along somewhere below with fatted beasts.

We have been permitted to see that you are such under your troubles as swimmers who race each other in the sea. But, since even from the claw it is possible to know the whole lion,[2] we believe that from our brief experience we know you sufficiently. Therefore, we also value highly the fact that you hold our affairs in some regard and do not dismiss

1 Julian is probably the one mentioned in Letter 21. If Leontius of Letter 21, and also of Letters 20 and 35, is to be identified with 'the good Julian' (cf. Letter 21 n. 1), this letter must have been written about 365, in the same correspondence.

2 The origin of this proverb is found in Lucian, *Hermatimus* 34. cf. Letter 9 n. 2.

them from your mind, and that we are continuously with you in memory. And a proof of remembrance is your writing. Indeed, the more frequently you write the greater is our joy.

294. To Festus and Magnus

Surely, forethought for their own children is proper to fathers, care for plants or seeds to farmers, and solicitude for their pupils to teachers, especially when because of their natural ability they begin to show in themselves hopes for improvement. The farmer rejoices in his labors when his ears of corn mature and his plants grow, and the pupils delight their teachers and children their fathers, the first when they advance in virtue, the latter when they advance in growth. But we have a solicitude in your case so much the greater and a hope so much the stronger in proportion as piety is nobler than every art, than all living things and fruits likewise. This piety, rooted and nourished by us in your souls while still tender and pure, we pray to see also making progress to perfect maturity and to fruits in due season, since your love of learning is helped by our prayers. Indeed, you well know that both our good will toward you and the assistance of God are placed in your wills; if they are directed toward what is proper, God will be at hand as a helper when summoned, or even when unsummoned, and every man who loves God will offer himself freely for teaching. For, the willingness of those who are able to teach something useful is unconquerable when the souls of the learners are free from all resistance.

Therefore, not even is the separation in the body a hindrance, since our Creator through the superabundance of His wisdom and kindness has not circumscribed the intellect by the body nor the power of speech by the tongue, but has given something more, even in the element of time, to those who are able to give assistance, so that they can transmit their teaching not only to those situated at a distance, but also to those who will be born in much later generations. And experience confirms this statement for us, since those who existed many years ago teach the young, the doctrine being preserved in their writings; and we, although separated so far in body, are always together in mind and we discourse together easily, because teaching is hindered neither by land nor by sea if you have any solicitude for your own souls.

295. To Monks[1]

I believe that, by the grace of God, you need no other exhortation after the words which we addressed personally to you, encouraging all of you to accept the common life in imitation of the apostolic manner of living. You received this as good instruction and gave thanks for it to the Lord. Since, then, that spoken by us was not mere words but instructions which should pass into action for the advantage of you who accepted them, for the consolation of us who suggested the idea, and for the glory and praise of Christ, whose name is invoked upon us, for this reason I have sent our most beloved brother, that he may become acquainted with your zeal, may rouse your sluggishness, and make clear to us what is your opposition.

For, I desire greatly both to see you united and to hear

1 Very probably the monks of the monastery founded by St. Basil in the Pontus in 358, with whom, even after his elevation to the archbishopric of Caesarea, he remained in close touch. The letter was written about 370.

concerning you that you do not like the life without witnesses, but, rather, that you all are pleased to be not only guardians of each other's exact discipline, but also witnesses of the works accomplished. Thus, each one will receive both the perfect reward for himself and that for the advancement of his brother. This reward it is proper for you to provide for each other by word and example from your constant intercourse and exhortation. Especially, we urge you to remember the faith of the Fathers,[2] and not to be shaken by those who are attempting to confuse you in your solitude, knowing that strictness of life in itself, if not illuminated by faith in God, is of no advantage, nor will a right profession of faith, if bereft of good works, be able to commend us to the Lord; but it is necessary for both to be present, so that the man of God may be perfect and our life may not be incomplete because of any deficiency. For, the faith which saves us, as the Apostle says, is 'the faith which works through charity.'

296. To a Widow[1]

Considering your disposition toward us and knowing the zeal which you have for the work of the Lord, we recently behaved boldly toward you as toward our daughter, and used your mules for a longer time, working them sparingly as if they were our own, but, nevertheless, prolonging the time of their service. It was necessary, therefore, to write these things to your Dignity, so that you might know that what has been done is a proof of our affection.

2 I.e., the Nicene Creed.

1 Since St. Basil borrowed the widow's mules, this letter was probably written before his episcopate, while he was still a monk tilling the soil at Pontus, i.e., about 370.

At the same time we remind your Modesty by letter to remember the Lord and always to keep before your eyes your departure from this world and to order your own life with a view to the defense before the Judge who cannot be deceived, so that you may have confidence because of your good deeds before Him who will reveal the secrets of our hearts in the day of His visitation.

We greet your most noble daughter through you; I urge her to spend her life in meditation on the sayings of the Lord, in order that her soul may be nourished by the good doctrine and that her mind may develop and become greater than does her body by nature.

297. To a Widow[1]

Judging that it is absolutely incumbent on me both because of my advanced age and because of the sincerity of my spiritual affection not only to visit your incomparable Nobility when you are bodily present, but also when you are absent not to fall short but to satisfy with letters for what is wanting, since I have found this suitable carrier for the letter to your Dignity, I am addressing you through her. Chiefly do I urge you on to the work of the Lord, in order that the good God, letting you spend with honor the days of your sojourning in all piety and seriousness, may make you worthy of His future blessings.

1 One manuscript gives the title 'To the Widow Julitta.' Since St. Basil here speaks of his old age, although he was only about forty-nine or fifty years old when he died, this letter must have been written toward the end of his life; consequently, about 378.

Then, I also entrust to you our aforesaid daughter, so that as my daughter and as your own sister you may receive her and be personally concerned about the matters which she will communicate to your gracious and pure soul, and that you may assist her, first of all, as receiving the reward from the Lord, and then, as giving consolation to us who have filled up the measure of our love for you in the heart of Christ.[2]

298. Without an Address, in Behalf of a Pious Man

Because you deign to use us as adviser in all things and sharer of your thoughts, you do what is proper for your own perfection. May God requite you for your love for us and your diligence in regard to your life. I am surprised that the deception of this man has taken hold upon you, and that you have believed that there is some strange power in water, and this, when no testimony has confirmed the report. Certainly, there is no one there who received for his body either more or less of that for which he had hoped—his own benefit—unless some consolation fell to a certain one accidentally, such as naturally comes upon those sleeping or engaged in some other activities of life. But he who destroys charity[1] is persuading the simpler souls to attribute accidental happenings to the nature of water. That our statement is true it is possible for you to learn from experience itself.

2 Cf. Phil. 1.8.

1 The Devil.

299. To an Assessor[1]

You wrote to me, although I was already aware of it, that you are dissatisfied with the administering of public affairs. And, in fact, it is an old saying that those who lay claim to any virtue do not gladly thrust themselves into offices. Really, that which is peculiar to doctors I see is also peculiar to rulers. They see terrible sights and have disgusting experiences, and they reap the distress belonging to the misfortunes of others, at least they do who are truly rulers. Yet, for men who are engaged in commerce, looking toward wealth and agitated about this present glory, it is considered the greatest blessing to get control of some power by which they will be able to treat their friends well, to ward off their enemies, and to obtain for themselves what they desire. But you are not such a one. Impossible! You, who even voluntarily withdrew from civil power although it was so great, and, when it was possible for you to rule over the city as over one home, you chose a life simple and quiet, considering that not having trouble nor causing it for others was worth more than the value others put upon being disagreeable.

But, since the Lord did not wish the country of Ibora[2] to be in the power of knavish men, nor the taking of the census to be like a slave market, but He wished each one to be registered as is right, accept the office, otherwise troublesome, but still capable of securing for you approval from God. Do not bow down to power; do not despise poverty; but for those who are governed provide an exactness in your reckonings more exact than any scale. Thus your zeal for justice

1 From its tone it may be surmised that this letter was written during the episcopate. For the duties of an assessor, cf. Letter 284 n. 1.

2 A diocese and a Roman military district in the Pontus. St. Basil's birthplace, Annesi, and his monastic retreat were situated in this district.

will become evident to those who have put their faith in you, and they will admire you beyond all others. Or, even if it does escape their notice, it will not escape the notice of our God, who sets before us great prizes for our good works.

300. A Letter of Condolence to the Father of a Scholar[1] *Who Had Died*

Since the Lord has placed us in the second rank of fathers to Christians, having entrusted to us the formation through piety of the children of those who believe in Him, we have considered that the fate of your blessed son is also our personal grief, and we have lamented the untimeliness of his departure. Sympathizing especially with you, we have taken into account how great would be the weight of the sorrow to him who is father by nature, since, even to us who have been made akin according to precept, there has been such grief of heart. Now, in his regard there was no need either to regret or to lament; they are to be pitied who failed in the realization of their hopes in him. Truly, they are deserving of many tears and sighs who sent their son in the very flower of his age for the study of literature, only to receive him back in this long and dreadful silence. This naturally stirred us as men and we shed uncontrolled tears and gave forth from the midst of our heart unbecoming sighs, when the calamity suddenly, like some cloud, enveloped our reason. When, however, we gained control of ourselves and looked clearly with the eye of our soul at the nature of human things, we

1 As it is evident that St. Basil was teacher of this boy, this letter was probably written after 360, when St. Basil was ordained deacon, but before 365, when as priest in Caesarea he was in the midst of the problems of the Church and had no time for teaching.

begged pardon of the Lord because our mind had acted precipitately in regard to this occurence, and we admonished ourselves to bear this moderately, since it had been allotted to the life of man by God's decision of old.

A boy has departed, at the very age that is most worth living, one conspicuous in the groups of his comrades, dear to his teachers, able from a mere meeting to win the most passionate to good will, quick in his lessons, gentle in disposition, sedate beyond his age; even if anyone should say more than this, he would speak less than the truth. Nevertheless, he was man, born of man. What, therefore, is it proper for the father of such a one to consider? What else, certainly, than to remember that his own father died? What wonder is it, then, that, having been born of a mortal, he should be the father of a mortal? That it was before his time, and before he was satiated with life, and before he had reached the measure of his age, and before he was conspicuous among men, and before he had left behind him successors for his race—these things are not an increase of suffering, as I am convinced, but a consolation for what has happened. The dispensations of God ought to be received with thanks, that he did not leave children orphans upon earth, that he did not leave a wife alone as a widow given over to long affliction, intending to live in wedlock with another man and to neglect the children of her former marriage. And as to the fact that the life of your son was not prolonged in this world, who is so senseless as not to consider this to be the greatest of blessings? In truth, continuance here for a longer time is an occasion of more evils. He did no evil; he did not plot treachery against his neighbor; he was not compelled to mingle in the associations of wicked men; he was not involved in the evils of the marketplace; he did not submit to the compulsion of sins, nor to lying, nor to arrogance, nor to avarice, nor to voluptuousness, nor to the passions of the flesh, vices which are wont to spring up in dissolute souls; he departed, his soul unstained by any blemish, but he withdrew pure to a better lot. Earth did not conceal your loved one; heaven received him. God, who dispenses our lots, who ordains for each the limits of time, who brought us into this life, He Himself has removed him. We have a lesson for the time of extreme misfortune, that celebrated utterance of the great Job: 'The Lord gave, and the Lord hath taken away: as it hath pleased the Lord so is it done: blessed be the name of the Lord forever.'[2]

301. A Letter of Condolence to Maximus[1]

How we were affected on hearing of your misfortune no word of ours would suffice clearly to describe, for at one moment we were taking account of the loss which the community of the pious suffered—the principal lady of those of her own rank having perished—at the next we were considering into how much sadness the joyousness of your Dignity had been changed, beholding in thought a home which was deemed happy by all fallen to its knees,[2] and a companionship which was firmly cemented by the most perfect harmony dissolved more quickly than a dream. How would it be possible, even if we were hard as adamant, that our soul would not be bent down? On our part, even from our first meeting a certain friendship has existed for your

---

2 Cf. Job. 1.21.

---

1 In most Mss. and in all editions prior to the Benedictine this letter is entitled 'Without an Address.' Codices Harl. and Clarom. have 'To Maximus.' This Maximus is otherwise unknown.

2 A common expression for a fallen soldier, from Solon down.

Grace, and we have been won over to such an extent by your virtue as to have your praises on our tongue at every hour. Then, when we became acquainted with that blessed soul, also, truly we were persuaded that the saying of the Proverbs was confirmed in you, that 'Woman is joined to man by God.'[3] You were so united in your way of life, each showing in himself as in a mirror the character of the other. Even though one might say many things he would not attain to even a fraction of her worth.

But, what should we feel in regard to a law of God which has long prevailed—that he who has come into existence must at the proper time again withdraw, and that each soul, when it has performed the necessary duties in life, must then be freed from the fetters of the body?

We are neither the first, admirable Sir, nor the only ones who have suffered, but whatever our parents and grandparents and all those of our race before them experienced, of these experiences we also have made trial. And the present life is full of such examples. But for you, who surpass the others so much in virtue, even in the midst of your sufferings it is proper to preserve the nobility of your soul without dejection, not as being unable to put up with the loss, but feeling grateful to the Giver for the gift in the beginning. Now, to die is the common lot of those who share the same nature, but to have lived with a good wife has been granted to the few who have been pronounced happy in their life; whereas the very fact of grieving at the separation is no insignificant gift of God, if the matter is considered reasonably, for we have known many who welcome the dissolution of an incompatible marriage as the putting aside of a burden.

Gaze upon this sky and the sun, and look around upon the whole creation, considering that these things which are so

---

3 Prov. 19.14 (Septuagint).

many and so great will not be seen a little later; and from all these things deduce this, that, being a part of the creation that will perish, we have undergone what belongs to us from our common nature. Yet, marriage itself is a consolation for death. For, since it was impossible to remain alive forever, the Creator devised a permanence of life by the succession of the race. But, if we are grieved because she has departed sooner than we, let us not envy her who was not filled for a long time with the troubles of life but, like the beauty of flowers, left us still longing for her. Before all things let the doctrine of the resurrection rejoice your soul, seeing that you are a Christian and are conducting your life in the hope of future blessings.

It is becoming, then, for us to think of her in this way—as having passed by a certain way which we shall have to travel; and, if she went before us, this is not deserving of lamentations. In fact, a little later, perchance, our lot will be more pitiable, if, having lived for a longer time, we become responsible for more penalties. But, after our reason has thrown off the burden of our sorrow, let it substitute a solicitude about how we should be well pleasing to the Lord for the future.

302. A Letter of Condolence to the Wife of Briso[1]

Why should we even mention how much we lamented at the tidings of the death of the most excellent of men, Briso? Surely, there is no one with such a stony heart, who, after he had gained some experience of that man and had then heard that he was suddenly snatched away from among men,

1 Otherwise unknown. The year 370, i.e., after St. Basil had become Archbishop of Caesarea, is the probable date.

has not considered the loss of the man the common loss of mankind. But, immediately upon our grief there succeeded a solicitude for you, when we considered how your soul is likely to have been affected by the calamity, if what has happened is so grave and hard for those to bear who are far removed from kinship. Your soul is naturally so kind and inclined to pity because of the gentleness of your disposition, and so subject to suffering as to be sensible of a sort of severing in two parts, as it were, in the separation from your husband. If, in truth, according to the word of the Lord, 'they are no longer two, but one flesh,'[2] such a parting is clearly no less painful than if the half of our body was torn away.

But there are such sorrows and even greater than these. What, however, is the consolation for what has come to pass? First of all, there is the law of God, which has prevailed from the beginning, that it is absolutely necessary for him who has come into existence to depart from life at the proper time. If, then, things human have been constituted thus from Adam until our times, let us not be grieved at the common laws of nature, but let us accept God's dispensation for us. He ordered that noble and unconquerable soul to depart from the world, not when his body was spent by disease or withered by time, but to break off his life in the flower of his age and in the splendor of his successes in war. Therefore, we ought not to be unable to endure the separation from so good a man; let us give thanks to the Lord that we have been deemed worthy of living with such a one, of whose loss nearly the whole Roman province has become sensible, whom even the king called to and the soldiers mourned and men in the highest rank bewailed as a true son.

2 Matt. 19.6.

Since, therefore, he has left for you the memory of his personal excellence, believe that you have a sufficient consolation for your affliction. Then, also, I wish you to know this, that he who does not fall down under his afflictions, but bears the burden of his grief because of his hope in God, has a great recompense from God for his patient endurance. For, in accordance with the precept of the Apostles, we are not permitted to grieve as the heathens do over those who have fallen asleep. And let your children be like living images, softening the absence of him for whom you long. And so, let the occupation of rearing your children draw your soul away from its griefs, and, being solicitous about how you may spend your remaining time in a manner well pleasing to the Lord, you will devise a noble occupation for your thoughts. The preparation of our defense in the presence of our Lord Jesus Christ and our eagerness of being found numbered among those who love Him are sufficient to overshadow our grief, so that we are not swallowed up by it. May the Lord grant to your heart the consolation of the blessing which comes from His Spirit, in order that, when we hear of your condition, we may cease from worry and that you may be a good example of a virtuous life to all your companions of like age.

303. To the Prefect of the Emperor's Private Estate[1]

The people of this district persuaded your Honor by false accusations, I think, to impose on these men a tax of mares.[2] Now, since that which is being done is unjust and for this

1 This letter is placed some time during St. Basil's episcopate.
2 Cappadocia was famous for its horses, consequently, references to taxes of horses are not uncommon. Cf. St. Gregory of Nazianzus, Letter 184.

reason ought to be displeasing to your Honor, and since it is distressing to us because of the friendship which we have for those who have been wronged, we have hastened to urge your Excellency not to allow those who are attempting to do wrong to continue their abusive treatment.

304. To Aburgius[1]

This is the man in whose behalf I previously have had some communications with you through the deacon. Now, since he has come with a letter from us, may he depart with what he wishes from you.

305. Without an Address, for Some Virtuous Man[1]

This man is already well known to you, as the accounts themselves of the man prove. On every occasion his tongue makes mention of you; in reminiscences of the orthodox, in hospitality toward ascetics, and in every virtue the man holds you first. Even if any one of the masters is mentioned he does not suffer others to be placed before you, and, if they speak of champions of piety and those capable of refuting the plausible arguments of heresy, he would not wish to enumerate another before you, ascribing to you in everything a virtue unconquerable and incomparable. And it is no great labor for him to persuade, when he says these things. For he tells his tale in the ears of men who are acquainted

1 Aburgius was an influential lay compatriot of St. Basil, upon whom the latter frequently called for aid. Cf. Letters 33, 75, 147, 175, and 196. This letter probably belongs to the time of St. Basil's episcopate.

1 Written after 370.

with mightier deeds than those which one might be thought to be reporting with exaggeration.

Now, since he is returning to you, he asked for a letter, not that he might make himself a friend of yours through us, but that he might show me a kindness by providing me with an opportunity of greeting my friends; may the Lord reward him for his good intention. But do you, to the best of your ability, bestow on him your favor by prayers and by your good will toward all. Acquaint us also with the condition of the churches.

306. To the Commander at Sebaste[1]

I am sensible that your Honor receives our letters with pleasure and I know the reason. Indeed, being a lover of good and inclined to beneficence, since on each occasion we furnish some suitable material for you to engage the nobility of your good will, you run for our letters, as holding opportunities for good deeds. Now, then, another opportunity has come which can receive the impress of your kindness and which at the same time provides a herald for your virtues.

Certain men, who set out from Alexandria in compliance with a necessary duty and one owed by the common consent of all mankind to the departed, are asking for your patronage, that you will command by public ordinance that they be permitted to remove the body of their relative, who ended his life during the sojourn of the army in Sebaste; that, moreover, all possible assistance be provided for them by the state conveyance, so that they may find some consolation through your Nobility for their long wandering. And that

1 Probably written after St. Basil's elevation to the archbishopric of Caesarea in 370.

these deeds will travel even as far as the mighty Alexandria and will supply men there with admiration for your Honor, is evident to your Intelligence, even if I should not say it. We shall count this favor also with the many which we have already received.

307. Without an Address[1]

Contentious natures frequently reject even good ideas and judge as noble and useful not that which seems so to all others, even if it is advantageous, but that which is pleasing to them alone, even if it is hurtful. And the cause is folly and perversity of disposition, not heeding the advice of others, but trusting to their own opinions only and to whatever considerations enter their mind. Those things in which they take pleasure enter the mind, and they take pleasure in what they want. Now, he who thinks that what he desires is advantageous is not a safe judge of the right; he is like the blind who are led by the blind.[2] Hence, also, he easily incurs losses, and he has only experience as teacher of what is useful.

He who is closely joined with this man here is now facing this misfortune. Although he should have entrusted the judgment to common friends, or, rather, although he has been judged frequently by many who have a care for justice and truth, he has now had recourse to the magistrates and to the decision of the courts, and prefers, after having suffered great losses, to make slight gains. And these decisions given by the magistrates do not bring even a victory without loss.

1 The subject of this letter may be the same as that of Letter 320. It is apparently an attempt to keep litigation involving ecclesiastics out of the civil courts.

2 Cf. Matt. 15.14.

Come to the assistance, my dear friend, preferably of both of these who are contending (for that is a pious duty), preventing their approach to the magistrate, and acting for them in the place of that judge. But, if one refuses compliance and quarrels with the decision, co-operate with the one who is wronged and bestow the weight of your influence on him who is seeking to obtain justice.

308. Without an Address, for Patronage[1]

Even when your Honor was present with the brethren, I spoke in behalf of the people from the district of Caprales,[2] and I introduced them to your Clemency, urging you that, keeping before your eyes the recompense from the Lord, you should succor them as being poor and afflicted in every way. And now again I renew the same petition by letter, praying to the holy God that both the distinction which you possess and the splendor of your life may be preserved and may reach to even greater limits, so that through your greater power you may be able to perform more valuable services for us. For I believe that you are convinced that our one prayer is the salvation of all your house.

1 From the fact that St. Basil used the title *hēmerótēs,* which he has otherwise applied only to laymen, and also that the people for whom patronage is sought are evidently subject to both of them, it is quite probable that this letter, written after 370, is addressed to the Governor of Caesarea.

2 Probably to be identified with the country about Carbala or Caprales (modern Gelvere), the suburb of Nazianzus, wherein St. Gregory's estate was situated.

309. Without an Address, for a Needy Person[1]

I severely condemned this brother for being solicitous about the registration of his house for taxation, since he certainly has beforehand the necessary exemption because of his poverty. For, from a wealthy life, the Lord dispensing thus for the profit of his soul, he has now been reduced to extreme poverty, so that he scarcely has enough food for each day and does not rule over even one slave out of the many which he formerly had in his service. There remains to him only his body, and that weak and aged, as you yourself see, and three children, an additional care for a poor man.

That he did not need our intercession at all, having sufficient poverty to importune you because of the kindness of your disposition, I clearly understood. But, since those who petition are hard to please, I was afraid lest at some time something of what is owed to him might be omitted and so I have written, knowing that for him the day on which he will first see your Dignity will be the beginning of a happy life for the future and will give some change for the better in his affairs.

310. Without an Address, in Behalf of Relatives

I myself was most desirous to meet your Eloquence for many reasons; first, indeed, to enjoy after a long interval of time the noble qualities which you possess, and then, to appeal to you in behalf of the men of Ariarathia, to whom after being long afflicted, the Lord has granted a worthy consolation, bestowing upon them the care of your Rectitude.

1 Probably written after St. Basil's elevation to the episcopate.

There is also a certain other possession of my relatives which is exceedingly burdensome and which is almost the chief cause of the poverty at Ariarathia. This situation I also urge your Excellency to remedy as far as is in your power, so that it may become endurable for the future to those who possess it.

311. To an Official

Men who do not pay attention to our assurances, but in their own interests seek something personal and exceptional, force us to write many letters to your Honor. For, long ago we protested to them that you would be so impartial and fair a guardian of justice for us that no one would seek for anything more as regards kindness unless, perhaps, he is excessively greedy. Nevertheless, to satisfy this man we have given him a letter, recommending him to you and urging you to look favorably upon him and, because his house has in the course of time been hard pressed by public services, to consider it deserving of all possible alleviation.

312. To an Assessor

You know both the profits and the losses which come to men from the registration for taxes. Therefore pardon this man who is taking great pains not to suffer any harm, and be willing to co-operate with all your strength to obtain justice for him.

313. To an Assessor[1]

It is not possible from afar to see the dispensations of God, but through littleness of soul we men pay attention to what is near at hand and frequently, although we are being led to a good end, we become angry, while the Lord, who manages all things in His wisdom, suffers our stupidity. You remember, I presume, how angry we became at the time against the office imposed upon us, how many friends we invited in order through their assistance to oppose the abuse. Thus, indeed, we called the affair.

But, now, you see what the present situation is like. God has offered you an opportunity of bringing to light your nobility of character and of leaving to all your posterity occasions for a good remembrance. In fact, of whatever sort these assessments are, memories of them of the same sort are naturally preserved by those who come after. Yet, it would not have been possible for the Galatians, even though they prayed for it, to meet with a kindlier character, I am firmly convinced. However, not only the Galatians am I able to deem happy because of your patronage, but myself also. For I, too, have a house in Galatia, and, by the help of God, certainly the most splendid of homes. Now, if I should obtain some assistance for it from you (and I shall obtain it as long as friendship possesses its proper strength) I will be very grateful to God.

If, then, your Honor has any esteem for my friendship, allow me to urge you for our sake to furnish some suitable aid to the house of the most admirable magistrate, Sulpicius,[2] so as to deduct some of the present assessment, an amount especially notable and worthy of your Lordship and, I will

1 Written after 370.
2 Otherwise unknown.

add, of the intercession of us who love you. But, if not that, at least as much as the times allow and the nature of the affair permits. At any rate, deduct something and do not leave it in the same condition, so that, in return for the numberless benefits which we have received from the good magistrate, we may repay this one favor through your Dignity.

314. Without an Address, in Behalf of a Servant[1]

Really, how could I overlook a suitable opportunity for a letter and not address your Honor, when this man was setting out in your direction? He, indeed, is sufficient of himself both to describe our affairs and to discharge the duty of a letter; but he wished also to become the bearer of a letter because he is very fond of us and is devoted to us with his whole soul. He desires also by all means to carry back your words and to be of service to you.

We therefore have given him the letter, through which, in the first place, we pray for all good things for you, both those which this life holds and those which are reserved and make sure the blessing in the promises, and next, we beg of the holy God to arrange for us a second meeting with you while we are still upon earth. That you will make manifold your love for the aforementioned brother for our sake, I do not doubt. Therefore, let me urge you to give him an actual trial.

1 Written some time after the beginning of his episcopacy.

315. Without an Address, in Behalf of a Relative[1]

Since I was quite persuaded that I would fail to obtain nothing for which I might justly appeal to your Honor, I willingly consented to give a letter to this most orderly guardian of orphans who lives in a home more troublesome than a many-headed hydra.[2] In addition to all this, it happens that we are related to each other by blood. Therefore, we urge your Nobility, while both honoring us and defending the honor owed to the grandfather of the orphans, to provide some assistance so that the ownership for the future may be made bearable for us.

316. Without an Address, in Behalf of an Oppressed Man[1]

I was quite convinced that those approaching your Clemency needed no letters at all because you do more from nobility of character than all that anyone by his entreaties might influence you to do for a good end. Nevertheless, because I was extremely concerned about this son, I was induced to write to your pure and guileless soul, recommending the man to you and urging that you should provide him with your assistance to the best of your power, in whatever way it might be possible, for the tasks lying before him. That he will need no other patron, if you will deign to use for his protection all the power which the Lord has given to you, I am keenly aware.

---

1 Probably written during the episcopate.

2 I.e., as the Hydra which Hercules destroyed grew two heads for every one cut off, so the troubles occasioned her by her property never ceased, continually succeeding one another.

---

1 Probably written after 370.

317. Without an Address, in Behalf of a Needy Person[1]

The infrequency of replies received here occasions on our part few letters to your Honor. For we consider our not receiving answers each time to letters which we write evidence that our letter brings annoyance to your Honor. But, again, the consideration of the mass of business about you gives us a different opinion, and we pardon for forgetting us him who has so much on his hands. For, even if there were all leisure and quiet, it would not be easy to be mindful of us because of the lowliness of our life.

May the Holy One lead you, then, to even greater distinction, and may He preserve you by His grace in your present splendor. We answer with letters at every opportunity, and not the least at the present one through this man, whom we entrust to you and ask that he will receive some notice for his service of carrying our letter.

318. Without an Address, in Behalf of a Countryman[1]

The very claim of our country recommends to you those who have arrived from our native land, although by the kindness of your manner you bring under your own care all who need any help whatsoever. Accordingly, receive him, the son of this man, who is placing this letter in the hands of your Modesty, not only as a fellow countryman but also

1 The reference to 'the lowliness of our life' seems to indicate that this letter was written before 370, probably while St. Basil was still a monk.

1 This and Letter 319 were probably written after 370.

as one who needs help, and as one who has been recommended to you by us; and for all these reasons let one favor be granted to him—the obtaining of all possible aid from you for the tasks lying before him. It is evident that there are rewards for good deeds not from us insignificant men, but from the Lord, who requites our good intentions.

319. Similarly, in Behalf of a Stranger

Immediately after your departure this son who is presenting this letter to you approached us with the need (as a man living in a foreign land) of all the consolation owed by Christians to strangers. Now, he himself will tell you his business more clearly, and you on your part will provide assistance to the best of your ability and as is necessary for the present tasks. If the governor is at hand, you yourself will, of course, lead the stranger to him, since you will furnish him with what he desires through those who are administering the government. For, it concerns me not a little that he return with all things accomplished according to his intention.

320. Without an Address, with a Friendly Greeting[1]

Only after a considerable time has it been granted to us to address your Honor, because he who carries our replies delayed long in our district and fell in with men and affairs rather hard to manage. In fact, for a whole year he alienated himself from the country which bore him. After having

1 The letter was probably written in 372, if we may assume that the late bishop was St. Basil's predecessor.

been led on by deceits and compromises of men to think that, if he would overcome the evil-doing about him, he would become master of the whole affair, he at length became sensible of his total loss, his sense of awareness having been stolen away by gradual deceit.

Since he is returning, freed not only from the troubles of the climate but also from the rascality of men, we greet you through him, urging you to remember us in your prayers (for we need much assistance from prayers). At the same time we inform you that those left responsible by the blessed bishops for the payment of the debt (for the debt was mentioned in his will, as well as from where and by whom it should properly be paid), neglecting the friendly reminders, are awaiting compulsory measures by the courts. Therefore, our companion has returned unsuccessful and has asked that these facts be attested by us, so that he may not be charged with idleness or laziness by your Honor. So far, then, for such a matter. As to what the situation of the churches is, whether it is conceded that they are remaining in the same state, or whether affairs have fallen into a worse condition, or what hope of a change for the better there is, deign to inform us through one of the true brethren.

321. To Thecla[1]

During the past year there was a heavy frost in our country and it injured the eyelids of the grapevines which were already being loosened for travail, and they, remaining barren, caused our bowls to be parched and unmoistened. Now,

1 This letter is found in the Mss. of St. Gregory of Nazianzus' letters and is generally conceded to be his. It reflects rather his gaiety than St. Basil's simplicity and gravity of style. This letter, with several others, is believed to have been added to St. Basil's collection about 389 or 390.

why in the world have we been induced to describe so tragically the unfruitfulness of our plants? In order that you yourself might become for us, according to Solomon,[2] both a blooming vine and a fruitful branch, not putting forth a cluster of grapes, but pressing out the dew of the grapes for the thirsty. And who are the thirsty? Those who are enclosing the precincts of the church.[3] Since I am unable to refresh them with a drink from the mountains, I have come to your right hand which is rich in grapes, so that you may order your fountains to flow to us like a river from your city on the river. Now, if you do this quickly, you will care for the dry mouths of many and you will, as much as is possible, gladden me, the Atticizing beggar, first of all.

322. Without an Address, on Celebrating Easter with a Friend

I was delighted at receiving your Honor's letter, as was likely, and I gave thanks to the Lord and was ready to answer if anyone had made timely mention of copies.[1] The matter about which you had given us directions was settled in the process of time, but it was not safe to answer anything before the final adjustment. This is the cause of our silence; it was certainly not indifference or ignorance of what is proper. In fact, even if we had been really indifferent, we would, at any rate, have desired to throw a shadow over

2 The passage is rather a reflection of Solomon's Canticle of Canticles, but there is no direct quotation.

3 A four-walled enclosure built some distance from the church. Cf. *Vita Constantini* 4.59; also, *Cod. Theod.* 9.45.

1 The 'anyone' was probably the addressee, who had neglected to remind St. Basil. The 'copies' evidently had to do with the business or legal matter with which St. Basil had been charged.

our faults in the presence of your Honor. But now it is not possible for us to forget you, not even for the briefest moment (or, rather, one might sooner fail to know himself). Whether we write or not, we bear you around firmly fixed in our heart, and we endure with such difficulty the long waning of the winter as to pray that, if it is not possible for you yourself, because of your occupations of which I have heard, to leave your country people, an occasion may arise for us to come suddenly to your district and to enjoy the true constancy of your character and the decorum of your life. At all events, you will strive to pass the saving day of Easter with us, together with your modest wife, whom we also greet through you and urge to co-operate with us in making you visit us.

323. To Philagrius Arcenus[1]

Thanks be to the holy God! I certainly would not say that I am grateful to those who wronged you because they have become for me the occasion of a letter. But the Lord, who shows us kindness on every side, knows how to fill us with consolations frequently even through sorrows. And for this reason He made the thoughtlessness of those who deserted you an occasion of joy for us.

But may you write to us on every pretext, just such things as you write, from a judgment so good and from a tongue so pure. Even if we do not affirm that we take to ourselves delight in the words, nevertheless in some way we are naturally charmed by it, and you who are graceful in speech

1 This Philagrius is probably the intimate friend and fellow student of Caesarius, brother of St. Gregory of Nazianzus. This letter was probably written during the episcopate.

hold us, as others hold the bees with their melodies. At any rate, send many letters, and those as long as possible, for brevity is not the mark of excellence of a letter, no more, certainly, than it is of a man.

And write to us how conditions are at home, and what is the state of your physical health, and whether the situation of the churches is peaceful, for you are concerned about these things and you do well. Of course, if there is any opportunity to labor together for the peace and unity of the dissidents, do not refuse it.

The good Cyriacus[2] formerly set to work with zeal and at that time he gave the letter to us; for the rest of the affair he had us as co-worker as far as was possible to us. In fact, we wrote to the suffragan bishop of the places. As to whether he carries out any of the commands, the affair itself will acquaint us.

324. To Pasinicus, a Doctor[1]

An evidence that you are not just casually disposed toward us is the fact that you saluted us immediately, at the very doors, so to say, of the entrance. Now, even to receive a friendly letter is in itself worthy of our zeal, but, if what is written brings about the needed result in most important matters, it is certainly of much more worth.

Therefore, understand well that Patricius, a man excellent in all respects, bears such charms of persuasiveness on his lips that, even if he would get hold of any Sauromatian or Scythian, let alone anything you have written, he would easily

2 St. Basil, intentionally obscure, is evidently referring to some secret negotiations.

1 Otherwise unknown; and the date cannot be ascertained.

win him over in whatever matter he would wish. Of a truth, those words of good cheer are not from his heart. This practice, in fact, has been pursued for a long time; that men, as far as their words go, are simple and ignorant, as they pretend, and ready to entrust their affairs to any judge, but, when it comes to their actions, may you certainly not happen to be there.

But let me tell you these things in order that you may know that the man is not in any way easily led, and that you may still be persuaded on your part not to pay attention to the speciousness of his words, but to await the proofs from his actions.

325. To Magninianus[1]

The letter from your Dignity was sufficient to bring us every joy. And now, too, the most modest of women, Icelium, our common daughter, who presented the letter, has increased our joy more than twofold, not only because she is the living image of your Excellency, but also because she has shown in herself every care for virtue. Therefore, although at first we received her gladly because of you, later reversing the order, we pronounced you happy because of her, since rewards from the Lord God await you for such rearing of your children. But, may we at some time see you yourself also and enjoy your noble qualities, without illness or any other difficulty hindering our meeting.

---

1 If this Magninianus is the person to whom Letter 175 was addressed, since in this he is not addressed as *kómēs* and must consequently have no longer held that office, the date of this letter must be some time after that of Letter 175, which was written in 374. However, as St. Basil uses the title *sémnótēs* in speaking of him, he must have been a layman of distinction.

326. Without an Address, for the Sake of Admonition[1]

The holy God has given us a most convenient occasion for the matter at hand, having made known to us this brother, the man whom we have used as carrier of this written communication of ours on his return to your Honor, and we pray to God that, advancing to a higher degree of distinction and glory, you will do honor both to us and to your whole fatherland by your own personal virtue.

We urge you during all your life to be mindful of God who created and honored you, in order that in addition to the splendor of this life you may still be deemed worthy of the heavenly glory also, for the sake of which we, who are directing our life toward the blessed hope, must do all things.

327. Without an Address, for Encouragement[1]

Because you honored us while we were present and deign to remember us when we are absent (for the report has come to us), may you receive a reward from the good Lord, and on the great day of the righteous judgment of our God may we see you glorious because of your good deeds, in order that, just as you were considered deserving of renown here, so also you may enjoy a place of dignity beside the heavenly King.

Therefore, we urge chiefly that you exhibit sufficient zeal for the Church of God, and then that you increase your good will toward us, considering us worthy of every remem-

1 Date cannot be established.

1 Nothing definite can be determined concerning the date or addressee.

brance and protection, and that you honor us with letters, so that, having a proof that we do not weary you by writing, we may be encouraged to write more frequently to your Lordship.

328. To Hyperechius[1]

I both salute your Honor and I pray for blessings for you, but I also inform you, since you are evidently desirous to know all about us, that I am faring not at all better than usual. In fact, I refrain from more foreboding words that I may not grieve one who is praying for the greatest blessings for us.

329. To Phalerius

I was very agreeably delighted with the fish from the river, having begrudged their escape which they had made by stealing under the shelter produced by the cold.[1] However, your letter is more prized by us than the fish. Therefore, send letters[2] rather than gifts. But, if you have an inclination to be silent, at least do not leave off praying for us.

330. Without an Address

That I love you you may learn from what I write. That

1 Otherwise unknown.

1 I.e., under the ice.
2 St. Basil is here making a play upon the words *epístelle* and *apóstelle,* which cannot be reproduced in English.

you hate me I know because you keep silent. Write me, at least in the future, with pen and ink and a short piece of paper, loving us who love you.

331. Without an Address

It is foolish to write twice about the same things. Either the matter does not have a nature capable of correction and those coming to us trouble us in vain, or those receiving the letters disregard us and we are foolish, writing to men who despise us. Now, since you have already received a letter about this same matter and we have been forced to write a second time, either correct yourself, if you have the strength, or make known to us the reason why our orders were not carried out long ago.

332. Another without an Address

One indication of life is speech. How, then, could you be considered to be upon earth, since you never speak? But put aside your silence, writing to us and making it evident that you are living.

333. To a Scribe

Words have a winged nature. For this reason they have need of symbols, that the writer may attain their speed when they are on the wing. Therefore, my son, make your characters perfect and punctuate the passages consistently. For, by a slight irregularity a great speech has failed, and by the carefulness of the writer that which is said is kept correct.

334. To a Calligrapher

Write straight and keep your lines straight; neither let your hand swing upward nor move downhill. Do not force your pen to go slantwise like the crab in Aesop's fable,[1] but go forward in a straight line as if moving along a carpenter's rule, which preserves absolute evenness and does away with all irregularity. The slant is offensive, but the straight line pleasing to those who observe it, since it prevents the eyes of the readers from traveling up and down like a pump handle. Some such thing happened to me when I was reading your letter. For, as the lines lie in the position of a ladder, whenever there was need to pass from one line to the other, it was necessary to raise my eyes to the beginning of the next line. When at that end the natural sequence did not appear anywhere, I had again to retrace and search for the correct order, going back and 'following along the furrow,' just as they say Theseus[2] followed Ariadne's thread. Write, therefore, in a straight line and do not confuse our mind by the crookedness and slant of your writing.

1 Cf. Aesop 187 (Halm).
2 Cf. *Od.* 11.321; Plutarch, *Theseus*; Catullus 64.

335. To Libanius[1]

I am ashamed that I bring the Cappadocians to you one by one and do not persuade all the youth to seek after eloquence and learning and to use you as teacher in their training. But, since it is not possible to meet at one time with all who are choosing the proper pursuits for themselves, we send to you those whom we have persuaded on each occasion, showing as great a favor to them as that which they who lead to the fountains show to the thirsty.

He who is now coming will a little later, after he has associated with you, be valued for his own sake. At present, however, he is known because of his father, who has a distinguished name among us for his uprightness of life and political power. He is also joined to me in the closest friendship. In exchange for this friendship I am bestowing this favor on his son, making him known to you—an act deserving of most earnest prayer on the part of those who know how to judge the excellence of a man.

1 Libanius was the greatest of the pagan rhetoricians of the fourth century. St. Basil was, for some time, a pupil of his, and Libanius is said to have had a great admiration for the young Christian because of his extraordinary intelligence and virtue. Twenty-five letters, numbers 335-359 in the Benedictine edition of St. Basil's letters, are ascribed to St. Basil and Libanius. The authenticity of this correspondence, however, has been the subject of much dispute. In summing up the evidence available to the present time it may be concluded that Letters 335-343 and Letters 345 and 358 are authentic because of their position in the manuscript tradition and because of the historical information contained in them; that Letters 344 and 346 are authentic because of their position next to Letter 345 in the Aa family and because of the relation of Letter 344 to Letter 343; that Letters 347-356 are spurious in spite of the mention of the speech of Libanius in several of them, since they are ignored in the best manuscripts of both St. Basil and Libanius, and since their contents and style are so unworthy of the two men; and that Letters 357 and 359 are spurious or, at least, very doubtful, since they are lacking in all the Basilian manuscripts and show no reason for being considered authentic.

336. Libanius to Basil[1]

After some time a young Cappadocian has come to us. This is one gain—he is a Cappadocian. And, moreover, this Cappadocian is of a first family. That is the second gain. But he is also the bearer of a letter from the admirable Basil to us. Than this, who could mention a greater gain? For I, who you think have forgotten you, even revered you long ago when you were young, seeing you competing with the old men in self-control, and that, too, in that city[2] teeming with pleasures, and also seeing you already possessed of a great measure of eloquence. But, since you thought that you ought to visit Athens also and you persuaded Celsus[3] to go, I congratulated Celsus because he was dear to your heart. Then, when you returned and dwelt in your fatherland, I said to myself: Well, what is Basil doing now, and to what manner of life has he turned? Is he engaged in the courts, vying with the orators of old? Or is he perfecting as orators the sons of fortunate fathers? But, when some came announcing that you were traversing a better road by far than these, and were examining how you might rather be a friend to God than amass gold, I pronounced both you and the Cappadocians blessed, you for desiring to be such a man, and them for being able to boast of such a citizen.

That the well-known Firmus[4] has cóntinued to be master everywhere I well know; it is from there that he possesses the power of eloquence. But, although he has enjoyed much praise, surely never yet as much as I have now heard in

1 Clearly an answer to the preceding.
2 Constantinople.
3 A Cilician, the son of Hesychius and a disciple of Libanius. According to Libanius (Letter 634), Celsus pronounced a panegyric on the emperor on his entrance into Cilicia.
4 Probably the father of the young student mentioned here.

your letters. In fact, that you are the one who says that no one could excel him in honor—how great a tribute to him must we deem it!

You seem to me to have sent these men before you saw Firminus.[5] Otherwise, the letter would not have failed to mention him. And now, what is Firminus doing, or what is he planning? Is he still longing for marriage? Or has he stopped that long ago, and is the Senate pressing him, and is it absolutely necessary for him to remain? Or what are the hopes that he will again share our lectures? Let him give us some answer, and may it be something good, but, if it even causes some grief, it will free us at least from looking toward the gates.[6] Now, if Firminus happened to be at present in Athens, what would your senators do? Would they send the Salaminia[7] for him? You see that it is only by your fellow citizens that I am abused. Nevertheless, I shall not cease loving and praising Cappadocians. I pray that they become kinder toward me, yet, if they remain in the same dispositions, I shall endure it. Firminus was with us for four months and he was not idle a single day. How much information he picked up you yourself will know and, perhaps, you will not be dissatisfied. Now, as regards his being able to come here again, whom must we invite as an ally? In fact, if the senators really think aright, and this would be proper for learned men, they will honor me in the second case, since they have pained me in the first.

5 Not otherwise known.

6 I.e., looking for the return of Firminus to Athens to resume his study of rhetoric under himself.

7 The Salaminia was one of the two sacred vessels of the Athenian government, the other being the Paralos. The Salaminia was sent to summon Alcibiades from the Sicilian expedition, an incident to which Aristophanes, *Birds* 147, refers: 'By no means do we want a place by the sea, where the Salaminia will bob up bringing a summoner from that town (Athens)!' Thus the vessel and its use for bringing men back to Athens pass into a proverb. Cf. Apostolius 15.31.

337. To Libanius[1]

Behold, still another Cappadocian has come to you, even my own son,[2] for this position which we now hold gives all men in adoption to us. Therefore, according to this he would be a brother of him who came previously and deserving of the same zeal both on my part as father and on yours as teacher, if, indeed, it is at all possible for those who come from us to receive anything more. And I say this, not because your Eloquence would not bestow any further favors on your friends of earlier days, but because your bounteous assistance is offered to all.

It would be sufficient for the youth, before he is proved by time, to be placed among your friends. May you send him back to us, worthy of our prayers and of your own reputation, which you have acquired for eloquence. Moreover, he is bringing in a comrade with equal zeal for letters, a youth both of a noble family himself and related to us. We trust that he will receive nothing less than the others, even if he falls very short of them in wealth.

338. Libanius to Basil

I know that you will frequently write this: 'Behold, still another Cappadocian has come for you.' You will send, I think, many, since you are always and everywhere using complimentary expressions about me, and by this very act stirring up both the fathers and the sons.

1 This letter also was written during the residence of Libanius in Athens.

2 This use of 'son' for a young man to whom one is attached is common from Homer down. Cf. *Iliad* 9.945; Herodotus 6.57; Plato, *Legg.* 923C. As St. Basil intimates above, all the young men in a priest's spiritual charge are 'sons by adoption.'

At any rate, what happened in regard to your beautiful letter it would not be beautiful to pass over in silence. There were seated beside me not a few others who hold government positions, and also Alypius,[1] a man excellent in every respect, a cousin of the famous Hierocles. Now, when those bringing the letter gave it to me, after going through the whole in silence, I said, laughing and at the same time rejoicing: 'We have been conquered.' 'And by what victory have you been conquered?' they asked, 'And how is it that you are not pained at having been conquered?' 'In beauty of letters,' I said, 'I have been proved inferior; and Basil has conquered. But the man is my friend and for this reason I rejoice.' When I said this, they wished themselves to see the victory from the letter. Alypius read it while those present listened. The vote was given that I was not at all deceived. And the reader went out with your letter to show it, I suppose, to others, also, and he scarcely returned it at all. Write, therefore, letters of the same kind and conquer. For this is victory for me.

You rightly infer this, that our services are not measured by money,[2] but it suffices for him who is not able to give to be willing to receive. In fact, if I notice that any poor person is a lover of eloquence, he is preferred to the rich. And, though we have not had experience of such teachers, nothing will prevent us from being better than they in this way. Therefore, let no poor person hesitate to come hither, if he possesses that one gift alone, the knowledge of how to work.

1 Alypius, cousin of Hierocles of Antioch (Amm. 23.1-2; Lib., *Ep.* 327), was a brother of Caesarius (Jul., *Ep.* 29), a nephew of Hierocles (Lib., *Ep.* 1583), after whom he named his son (Lib., *Ep.* 327; Amm. 29.1,44). As vicar in Britain under Julian (Lib., *Ep.* 327), he became a friend of the emperor (Jul., *Ep.* 29) and was commissioned by him to rebuild the temple of Jerusalem (Amm. 23.1-3). In 371, he and his son were banished (Amm. 29.1,44) on a charge of attempted poisoning.

2 The Sophists charged a fee for the instruction (Aristotle, *Eth.* N. 9.1,7) and this was the practice of the rhetors of the fourth century. Libanius, the most famous teacher of his time, charged a high fee. Cf. Letter 348.

339. To Libanius[1]

What can a man who is a Sophist not say, and such a Sophist, one for whom it is admitted that it is the distinguishing property of his art to make great things insignificant whenever he wishes, and to give to insignificant matters greatness?[2] Truly, something of such a sort you have shown in our case, too. For, that letter, a slovenly one, as you who possess such elegance of expression might say, although it was not at all more to be endured than this one now in your hand, you extolled so highly in your words that you were, as you pretended, vanquished by it and yielded to us the first prize for writing. You are doing something that is similar to the games of fathers, when they permit their sons to pride themselves on their victories over them, not suffering any loss themselves but nourishing the ambition of their sons.

And truly, it is impossible to say how much sweetness the words in your game with us possessed, just as if some Polydamas[3] or Milo[4] would decline a contest in the pancration[5] or in boxing with me.[6] Though I examined much, I found no sign of weakness. Consequently, those seeking pre-eminence in words admire you more for your ability in this, since you are so able to come down to our level in play, than if you had led the barbarian when he sailed over Athos.[7] But we, admirable Sir, are engaged with Moses and

1 Clearly an answer to the preceding.
2 Cf. Plato, *Phaedr.* 367A-B.
3 The famous athlete of Scotussa.
4 The athlete of Crotona.
5 The pancration included both boxing and wrestling.
6 A reference to his anything but athletic body.
7 Xerxes' feat of digging a canal through the promontory behind Mt. Athos was a source of never-ending wonder to the Greeks. Cf. Herodotus, 7.22-23. Later Greeks regarded the whole story as a fable. Traces of the canal, however, are said to be still visible.

Elias and such blessed men who hold their conversations with us in barbarous tongue and we speak out their utterances, true in meaning, but unpolished in phrase, as these words themselves manifest. Although we did learn something from you, we have forgotten it in the course of time.

But, do you yourself write to us, taking other subjects for your letters, which will both show you forth and will not put us to the test. I have already introduced to you the son of Anysius as my own son. If he is my son, he is the child of his father, a poor son from a poor father. What is said is well known to a wise man and a Sophist.

340. Libanius to Basil[1]

If you had considered for a very long time how you might best confirm what we wrote about your letters, you would not have seemed to me to do this better than by writing such things as you have now written. You call me a Sophist, and you say that it is characteristic of such a one to be able to make insignificant things great, and, again, great things insignificant. What is more, you say that my letter pretended to show forth yours as beautiful, although it was not beautiful; and that it was not at all better than the present one you have sent; and that you have absolutely no power of eloquence, since the books which you at present have at hand do not produce this and the eloquence which you formerly had has faded away. In attempting to persuade us of this, you have produced this letter, of which you speak abusively, so beautiful, too, that those who were with us could not keep from leaping up when it was read. I was surprised, therefore, how in trying thus to tear down the first letter by saying that the

1 An answer to the preceding.

former is like to this you embellished the former by means of this one.

He who wished this should have made the latter inferior for a slander to the former. But, it was not, I think, your intention to compromise the truth. Yet, it would have been compromised if you had purposely written more roughly and had not made use of your abilities. Again, it would be fitting for the same man not to censure what it is right to praise, lest the action should throw you back among the Sophists, trying to make things base. Therefore, cling to the books whose style you say is inferior, but the thought superior, and no one hinders you. But, of that which has always been ours and formerly was yours, the roots remain and will remain as long you shall exist, and no length of time would ever cut them out even if you would not water them in the least.

341. Libanius to Basil

You have not yet given up your grievance against me, so that in the midst of my writing I tremble. But, if you have given it up, why do you not write, excellent Sir? And, if you still retain it, a thing foreign to every learned soul and yours, how is it, when you proclaim to others that we must not continue in our wrath until sunset,[1] that you yourself have continued in it for many suns? Or, perchance, did you wish to punish me, by depriving me of your honey-sweet utterances? At all events do not do so, noble Sir, but be gentle and grant me the favor of enjoying your all-golden tongue.

1 Cf. Eph. 4.25,26.

342. To Libanius[1]

Those who are attracted to the rose, as is likely for lovers of beauty, arc not annoyed even with the thorns themselves from which the blossom grows forth. And I have heard from someone, perchance in jest or even in earnest, some such thing about them—that, just like stings of love to lovers, nature has grown those delicate thorns upon the flower, stimulating those who pluck them to a greater longing by the pleasantly stinging pricks.

What is my purpose in introducing the rose into my letter? It is not at all necessary for you to be told if you recall your own letter which possessed the bloom of the rose, spreading out for us by the sweetness of your speech the whole spring, but which was prickly with certain censures and charges against us. However, even the thorn of your words is sweet to me, inflaming me to a greater desire for your friendship.

343. Libanius to Basil[1]

If these are the words of an unpolished tongue, what would you be if you should whet it? In your mouth lie fountains of eloquence mighter than the onrush of flowing waters. But as for us, if we should not be watered daily, there remains only silence.

1 Although the style here is quite unlike that of St. Basil's genuine letters, the superficial thought and decorative language are in keeping with the spirit of the period.

1 This letter is probably an answer to Letter 344.

344. To Libanius

That I should not write frequently to your learned self, both fear and ignorance persuade me, but that you should most determinedly keep silence, how will that be free from blame? And, if anyone would consider the fact that, living even in the midst of letters, you hesitate to write, he will find you guilty of forgetfulness of us. To whom the art of speaking is easy, for him the art of writing is not difficult. He who possesses these arts and, nevertheless, is silent quite clearly does this either through contempt or forgetfulness. I shall answer your silence with a salutation. Farewell, then, most honored Sir, and write, if you should be willing; do not write, if that also is agreeable to you.

345. Libanius to Basil

I believe that there is more need of an apology from me because I did not begin to write to you long ago than there is of an excuse because I have begun to do so at present. I am the one who ran after you whenever you appeared, and offered my ears with the greatest pleasure to the flow of your tongue, rejoicing when you spoke, departing with difficulty, and saying to my companions: 'This man is so much more excellent than the daughters of Achelous[1] in that he charms in the same way as they, but does not harm as they do. And not to harm is certainly a little thing, but it is evident that his strains are a gain to him who hears them.' Now, that I, who am thus disposed in my thoughts, believing that I am

1 The water nymphs were said to be the daughters of Achelous and one of the Muses. By their charm they lured their victims to destruction.

even loved, and seeming to possess eloquence, would not dare to write would be a mark of extreme laziness and would be the action of a man punishing himself. It is evident that you will answer my brief and trivial letter with a great and beautiful one, and you will be on your guard, I presume, lest you wrong me a second time. But, I think that many will cry out against that word and will crowd around shouting against the facts: 'Has Basil done any wrong, even a slight one? Then so have also Aeacus and Minos and his brother.'[2]

I grant that you have been victorious otherwise, for who is there who has seen you and does not envy you? But, you have sinned in one respect against us; if I remind you of it, persuade those indignant men not to shout out. No one who has gone to you asking a favor which it was easy to grant has gone away without obtaining it. Yet, I am one of those who have asked a favor and have not obtained it. What, then, did I ask? Frequently, when I was with you in the camp,[3] I desired with the aid of your wisdom to enter into the depth of Homer's inspiration. 'And, if the whole is not possible,' I used to say, 'nevertheless, introduce us to the part about the casting of the lots.' And I was desirous of the part in which, after the Greeks had fared ill, Agamemnon conciliated with gifts him whom he had insulted.[4] When I

2 I.e., Rhadamanthus, judge in the lower world and the embodiment of justice. In Servius, *ad Aen.* 6.566, Rhadamanthus, Minos, and Aeacus are said to be sons of Zeus and Europa.

3 The place referred to is obscure. The *stratēgion* in Athens was the office of the general; in Constantinople, it was used for the camp. However, it is certain that St. Basil was never in a camp with Libanius. Consequently, the use of this term is an argument against the authenticity of this letter.

4 Libanius teasingly pretends that St. Basil has wronged him by not granting him the favor of an exposition of Homer. The two passages are selected because of their analogy to the case of St. Basil 'victorious' over Libanius in epistolary style. The passages are evidently *Iliad.* 7.92ff. and *Iliad* 19.183ff.

said this, you laughed, not being able to deny that you could if you wished, but being unwilling to bestow the favor. Now, to you and to those who are indignant because I said that you did wrong, do I not seem to have been wronged?

346. Libanius to Basil

If we have added anything in the way of eloquence to the young men whom you have sent, you yourself shall judge. But, I hope that this, even if it is little, will win the reputation of something great[1] because of your friendship for us. As to what you praise in preference to eloquence, that is, self-control and the refusal to surrender our souls to ignoble pleasures, they took care of this perfectly, and I kept them, as was right, mindful of him who had sent them. Welcome, then, what is your own, and praise those who by their character have adorned both you and me. But, to urge you to go to their assistance would be the same as to urge a father to go to the assistance of his sons.

347. Libanius to Basil

Every bishop is a very grasping sort of person. And, as for you, as much as you outstrip the others in eloquence, to that extent do you cause me fear lest in some way you may refuse my request. Yet, I need crossbeams. Another Sophist might have said poles or stakes, not because he wanted them, but because he takes pride in his pretty words instead of serving his need. But for my part, if you should not provide them, I shall pass the winter under the open sky.

1 Cf. Letter 340.

348. To Libanius

If making profit[1] is said to be the same as grasping, and the phrase which your sophistic art selected for us from the innermost shrines of Plato has this meaning, consider, admirable Sir, who is the more grasping, we, who are so staked[2] in by your epistolary power, or the race of sophists, whose art consists in taking toll for words. Who of the bishops has placed a toll on his sermons? Who has made his disciples payers of fees? It is you who set out your eloquence for sale, like confectioners do their honey cakes. Do you see how you have provoked the old man to leap up?

But, I have ordered that there be furnished for you, who are pluming yourself upon your declamations, crossbeams equal in number to the soldiers who fought at Thermopylae,[3] all of them large, and according to Homer, 'long-shadowing,'[4] which the holy Alphaeus[5] has promised to deliver.

349. Libanius to Basil

Will you not cease, Basil, filling these sacred precincts of the Muses with Cappadocians, and that, too, when they are redolent of the frost[1] and snow and other good things there? They have almost made me a Cappadocian, always chanting

1 Plato does not use the word *gripizein,* but often disparages money making, e.g. Plato, *Pol.* 9.581A-583B.
2 A play on the word *chárax* ('stake') in the previous letter.
3 Herod. 7.202 gives the number of the Spartans there as 300.
4 Cf. *Iliad* 3.346,355, and elsewhere.
5 Otherwise unknown.

1 The meaning of this word (*gritē*) is uncertain. Maas thinks that it is a kind of garlic; others consider it akin to *krióte,* and translate it 'frost'; still others make it equivalent to *grúte,* 'frippery.'

to me their 'I make obeisance to you.'[2] Yet it must be endured, since Basil commands it. Understand, therefore, that, although I understand accurately the manners of your country, I shall clothe the men with the nobility and good taste of my Calliope, so that they may seem to you to be tame doves instead of wild pigeons.

350. To Libanius

Your annoyance is ended. Let this, indeed, be the prelude of my letter. As for you, mock and ridicule our customs, either in jest or in earnest. Yet, why did you make mention of snow or frost, when it was possible for you to exult over us with your gibes? For my part, Libanius, that I may stir you to loud laughter, I have written my letter while covered over with a blanket of snow. When you receive it and touch it with your hands, you will perceive how icy-cold it is in itself and how it characterizes the sender who is kept inside and is unable to put his head out of the house. For the houses we possess are tombs until the spring arrives and restores to life the corpses which we were, again bestowing upon us, as upon plants, the gift of existence.

2 The Persian and western Asiatic form of greeting a superior was to prostrate the body, and this was the custom insisted upon in the court of Byzantium. The ordinary polite formula of the Greeks was *chaíre* or *aspázomai*.

3 Cf. Plato, *Theaet.* 199B.

1 An answer to the preceding.

351. To Libanius

Many of those about you who happened to meet us have marveled at your excellence in the art of speaking. They said that there had been a certain exceedingly brilliant demonstration. It was, they remarked, a most extraordinary contest, to the extent that all assembled and no one else in the city, except Libanius alone, appeared contending for the prize, and people of every age were listening. No one was willing to be absent from the contests, not he who possessed dignity of position, nor he who was famous in the military registers, nor he who was devoted to the manual arts. Even the women were already hastening to be present at the contests. And what was the contest? And what was the speech which had brought together an assembly of all the people? Well, they reported to me that the speech described the character of a querulous man.[1] That which was so admired do not hesitate to send to me, that I also may be a praiser of your eloquence. For, since I praise Libanius even without his works, what shall I become now, when I have found material for my praises?

352. Libanius to Basil[1]

Behold, I have sent the speech, although I am dripping with sweat. Indeed, how is it likely that I would not be, when I am sending my speech to that man who is able by his skill in oratory to show that the wisdom of Plato and the cleverness of Demosthenes are vaunted in vain, while my

1 The writer is imitating the speech of a peevish and irritable husband to a garrulous wife.

1 In answer to the preceding.

skill is like a gnat compared to an elephant? Therefore, I shiver and shake, thinking of the day on which you will review my words; and I have almost lost my wits.

353. To Libanius[1]

I have read your speech, O wisest of men, and I have admired it exceedingly. O Muses, O Eloquence, O Athens, what gifts you bestow on your lovers! What fruits they bear away who associate with you for some brief time! Oh, for your strong-flowing fount![2] What learned men has it shown those to be who have drawn inspiration from it! In fact, I seemed to see in the speech the man himself engaged in conversation with his garrulous little wife.[3] Libanius on earth has written a living speech, he who alone has given a soul to his words.

354. Libanius to Basil[1]

I know now that I am what I am called; since Basil has praised me, I have the victory over all. And it is probable that I, having received your vote, may walk with a swaggering gait, like some braggart who despises all men. Now, since you have prepared with much labor a speech against drunkenness, we wish to read it. I am not trying to say anything clever,[3] but your speech, when seen, will teach me the art of speaking.

1 In answer to the preceding.
2 The fount is Athens, from whose schools of philosophy and eloquence men like Libanius drew their training and inspiration.
3 Cf. Letter 351 n. 1.

1 This letter was written, as it seems, in answer to Letter 353.
2 St. Basil, *Homilia* 14.
3 The writer hastens to correct the idea that he may be making a witticism as if he needed a cure.

355. Libanius to Basil[1]

Do you live in Athens, Basil, and have you forgotten yourself? For, the sons of the Caesareans could not have listened to such things. In fact, my tongue was not accustomed to them. But, struck dizzy by the novelty of the words, just as when one is traveling through beetling cliffs, it said to me its father: 'Father, you have not taught those things.' This man is a Homer; nay, a Plato; nay, an Aristotle; nay, a Sousarion,[2] who knows all things. And these words, indeed, my tongue spoke. Would that it might be possible, Basil, for you to give such praise to us.

356. To Libanius

Receiving what you write is a delight, but being required to reply to what you have written involves a struggle. Now, what could I say in answer to so Attic a tongue, except that I am the disciple of fishermen? I confess it and I love it.

357. Libanius to Basil

What is the matter with Basil that he was annoyed at a letter, the symbol of philosophy? We were taught by you to jest. Nevertheless, our play is dignified and, as it were, becom-

1 This letter would seem to have been written after the writer had read St. Basil's oration 'Against Drunkenness,' which was referred to in the preceding letter.

2 Sousarion is considered the originator of Attic comedy. He was a native of Tripodiscus, a village of Megaris, and is said to have introduced Megarian comedy into Attica between 580 and 564 B.C.

ing to gray hairs. But, by our friendship itself and by our common pastimes, deliver me from this sadness which your letter has produced in me[1] . . . in no way different.

358. Libanius to Basil

Oh, for those times in which we were all things to each other! Now we are relentlessly separated. You, for your part, have one another,[1] but I have no one like you to replace you. And I hear that Alcimus[2] in his old age is undertaking the pursuits of youth and is hastening to Rome, putting upon you the labor of remaining with the lads. But you, always a gentle person, will bear not even this with annoyance, since you were not vexed with us at having to write first.

359. To Libanius

Although you have enclosed in your mind all the art of the ancients, you are so silent as to permit us to gain nothing whatsoever by your letters. Now, if the art of the teacher[1] were safe, having made Icarian wings, I would have come to you. Nevertheless, since it is not possible to trust wax to the sun, instead of using Icarian wings I am writing you words which prove our friendship. Moreover, it is the nature

1 A lacuna occurs here in all the Mss.

1 I.e., his comrades among the clergy.
2 A rhetorician of Nicomedia, who spent some time with Libanius at Antioch.

1 I.e., Libanius. His art, as brilliant as the sun, makes it unsafe for anyone to fly to him on waxen wings.

of words to reveal the love in the soul. And for this reason are my words. You may carry them wherever you wish; and although you possess such great power, you are silent. Give in exchange to us, however, the founts of eloquence which flow from your mouth.

360. From His Letter to Julian the Apostate[1]

According to the undefiled faith of the Christians, transmitted to us by God, I confess and agree that I believe in one God the Father Almighty, God the Father, God the Son, God the Holy Spirit; one God, the Three I adore and glorify. And I confess also the Incarnation of the Son, and holy Mary, Mother of God, who bore Him in the flesh. I accept the holy Apostles also, the Prophets, and the martyrs, and I call upon these for their prayers of supplication to God, in order that through them, or rather, through their mediation, the loving God may be propitious to me, and there may be made and be offered for me atonement for my sins. For this reason, also, I honor and kiss the features of their likenesses, especially since they have been handed down from the holy Apostles and have not been forbidden, but have been represented in all our churches.

1 This letter is clearly spurious. It is lacking in all the Mss. and it does not have the vocabulary or the style of St. Basil's authentic letters. It has in general been attributed to the Greek Iconoclasts.

361. To Apollinaris[1]

To my most revered master Apollinaris, I, Basil send greetings. We wrote to you at an earlier date concerning some obscure passages in the Scripture, and we rejoiced both in your answers and in your promises. But now, a greater care concerning more important matters has come upon us, for which we are unable to call upon any other associate and leader of the present day as capable as you, whom God has given to us, exact both in knowledge and in speech, and likewise accessible.

Since, then, those who are throwing all things into confusion and filling the whole world with arguments and inquiries have repudiated the word 'substance' (*ousía*) on the grounds that it does not exist in the divine Scriptures, deign to inform us how the Fathers employed it, and whether you have found it used anywhere in the Scriptures. For they loathe the 'daily bread' (*epioúsion*) and the 'acceptable people' (*perioúsion*) and any other such expression as having

1 Letters 361-364 have been the subject of much controversy. Apollinaris, Bishop of Laodicea, was condemned as a heretic by the Synod of Alexandria in 362, also by the Synod of Rome under Pope Damasus and by the Council of Constantinople. Although St. Basil wrote to Apollinaris when they were laymen, it was not on matters of faith, as he testifies in his own letters. It is known that Eustathius changed the text of a letter written by St. Basil to Apollinaris and circulated it in order to convict St. Basil of being in communion with Apollinaris. That letter, however, does not seem to be in this group of letters, which were probably forged for the same purpose. Another point of importance is that these letters are entirely lacking in all but two of the Mss. of St. Basil's Letters, and both of these are Mss. of the lowest reliability. Unfamiliar usages in the language of both Letters 361 and 363, but more especially St. Basil's own statements in his authentic letters, confirm the Ms. testimony that these letters were clever forgeries by some of his enemies. For a fuller discussion of the authenticity of these letters, cf. Sister Agnes Clare Way, 'On the Authenticity of the Letters Attributed to Saint Basil in the So-called Basil-Apollinaris Correspondence,' *American Journal of Philosophy* 52 (1931) 57-65.

nothing in common with it (*ousía*). Then, of course, concerning 'consubstantial' itself (because of which I believe they are trumping up all these things, violently slandering 'substance' in order to leave no place for 'consubstantial'), be pleased to expound to us more fully what meaning it has, and how it might be used with a sound sense in things in which there is discerned neither a common overlying class, nor any pre-existent underlying material, nor a division from a first into a second. How, then, we should say that the Son is consubstantial with the Father without falling into any one of the meanings mentioned, please describe more fully to us. In fact, we have interpreted that, whatever by way of hypothesis the substance of the Father is understood to be, this the substance of the Son absolutely must be understood to be. Therefore, if anyone should say that the substance of the Father is light intellectual, eternal, and unbegotten, he will say that the substance of the Only-begotten also is light intellectual, eternal, and unbegotten. But, for such a meaning it seems to me the expression 'alike without difference' fits better than the word 'consubstantial.' For light which does not differ from light either more or less, I think can rightly be said not to be the same (because each exists in its own limit of substance), but to be alike in substance, exactly and without difference. Now, whether we should discuss these ideas or receive other better ones instead, as a wise physician (for we have revealed to you what is in our heart) cure our illness, support our weakness, and strengthen us in every way.

I salute the brethren with your Reverence, and I beg them to pray with you for us, that we may be saved. Our companion, Gregory, choosing a life with his parents, is with them. May you be preserved to us for a very long time in health, aiding us both by your prayers and by your knowledge.

362. Apollinaris to Basil[1]

You believe piously and inquire learnedly; therefore, for the sake of charity, good will is due on our part even though satisfaction should not follow upon our words because of our deficiency and the extraordinary character of the task.

Substance is said to be one not only in number, as you say, and as to what is in one sphere, but also properly of two men and any other whomsoever that are united by race. Therefore, in this way at least, both two and more are the same in substance, according as we men are all Adam, being one, and David is the son of David, as he is the same as the former; just as you say rightly that the Son is identical in substance with the Father. Not otherwise would the Son be God, since the Father is confessed to be the one and only God; just as, certainly, there is one Adam, the founder of mankind, and one David, the author of the kingly race.

In this way, too, it undoubtedly will be removed from our supposition that there is one overlying race or one underlying material in the case of Father and Son, when we admit the genarchic principle of the first beginning and the races coming from the founders of the race with reference to the only-begotten offspring of the one beginning, for within due limits do things of such a kind reach a similarity. Just as of Adam, as one formed by God, and of us, as born of man, there is not one overlying race, but he himself is the beginning of men, neither is there a material common to him and to us, but he himself is the starting point of all men. And certainly not of David and of the race which came from David is there any previous perception as to how far it is David, since the individuality of David begins from David, and the starting point of all who are derived from him is himself.

1 This same subject matter is fully treated in Letter 8.

But, since all these things fail in so far as there are other universal qualities of all men in relation to each other, as those of brothers, yet in the case of the Father and the Son there is no such thing, but the Father is entirely the beginning and the Son is from the beginning.

Therefore, there is not a division of the first into the second, as in the case of bodies, but a generation. For, the individuality of the Father is not, as it were, divided into the Son, but that of the Son has come forth from that of the Father, the same in difference and different in sameness, just as it is said that the Father is in the Son and the Son in the Father. In fact, neither will difference preserve absolutely the truth of sonship nor again will identity preserve indivisibleness of the Person, but each is interwoven and simple, the same differently and the different in the same manner, to express in a forced way words which do not attain clarity. For, the Lord had confirmed our opinion that the Father is greater in equality, but the Son possesses equality in His subordination; wherefore He taught us to apprehend the Son in a homogeneous but inferior light, not changing the substance, but considering the same as excelling and in subordination. They who have admitted substance in no identity bring in likeness from the outside and impose it upon the Son, but this certainly passes over to men also who are made like God.

Now, they who know that likeness is proper to creatures join the Son to the Father in identity, but in an inferior identity, lest He be the Father Himself or a part of the Father. And these things are ably demonstrated by the expression, 'another is the Son'; thus He is God, not as the former, but from Him, not the archetype, but an image. He is consubstantial, transcendentally in all respects and singuarly, not as that which is homogeneous, not as that which is divided, but as from one class and nature of the Godhead, one only Offspring by undivided and incorporeal procession, through which that which generates, remaining in its generative individuality, has proceeded to the begotten individuality.

363. To Apollinaris

To my master, my most revered brother, Apollinaris, I, Basil, send greetings. We missed the opportunities by which it was possible to address your Reverence, although we would gladly have written in reply to those letters. We rejoiced that you silently took pleasure in the former ones. In truth, you alone seemed to us to be learned (but the shadows of the interpreters dart about), as you led your explanation toward so sound a sense. And now, actually, the desire for the knowledge of the divine Scriptures fastens more tightly upon my soul. However, I hesitate to propound to you any of the difficulties, lest I seem to make use beyond measure of your frankness. Again, I do not have the strength to keep silence, being in an agony of mind and still desiring to make progress. Therefore, it has seemed best to me to inquire of you whether you will permit us, O admirable Sir, to submit any of our difficulties, or whether we must keep silence. Whatever you shall answer, that we shall observe for the future. May we possess you always in good health and cheerful and praying for us.

364. Apollinaris to Basil

To my master, my most beloved brother, Basil, I, Apollinaris, send greetings in the Lord. Where was I myself, Master, and where were the most beloved voice and the customary letter? Why do you not give aid by your presence, or in your absence give encouragement, since so great a war against true religion has broken out and we, as if in the midst of the battle, are crying out to our companions because of the violence of the enemy? But we do not know how we should seek you, since we do not even find out where you happen to be staying. However, I did seek you in Cappadocia, since those who had met you in Pontus reported that you had promised to return rather soon. But, I did not find you where I had hoped. Now, having heard that you are still tarrying in the same place, I immediately handed this letter to my informant. When you receive it, do not refrain from answering, as this man also is traveling with you.

Realize that in the meantime we have had a visit from the bishops of Egypt, and there were handed over documents in harmony with our former writings and also with the divine Scriptures themselves, and with that which was written in agreement with the divine Scriptures at Nicaea. But a repetition of the same points with an explanation was necessary because of the unsound interpretation of the texts, a misinterpretation which those introduced who long ago spoke openly in contradiction, but now have gotten around the contradiction by pretence of an explanation. In this there was a malicious repeal of 'consubstantial,' as if it was bound not to be understood by reason of even one Greek denial; but there was as a substitute for 'consubstantial' 'likeness according to substance,' which was invented, confusedly named, and maliciously intended, since likeness is of things that are in substance, that is, of substantial things, so that, in fact, a 'substance made like' might be considered a substance just as a statue of a king would be in relation to a king.

To these statements a reply was written by men who know how and who wish to live piously, that 'consubstantial' does not mean 'like to God,' but 'God,' as it were, a true offspring and of the same substance as He who has begotten it. There was also brought in the statement about the Spirit, as placed by the Fathers in the same creed with God and the Son, that He is in the same Godhead.

Now, as to the leadership of this act of religion, who was so likely to have a part as the most zealous[1] among us, along with my master Gregory, who likewise does not write from anywhere and gives absolutely no information? May you be in good health, most beloved Master.

365. To the Great Emperor Theodosius[1]

A calamity has occurred in our country, not from any bodily vicissitudes, but from the influx of waters. Whence this came I shall explain. There was a great downfall of snow in our marshy region. Before it had yet frozen a warm breeze followed and rain from the south fell upon it. Now, as the melting was sudden, immense streams transcending

1 Intended to refer to St. Basil himself.

1 It seems evident that this letter must be spurious from the following facts: its style is unlike St. Basil's, it contradicts St. Basil's statement elsewhere about the forty martyrs, and is contained in only five Mss. of St. Basil's letters. Tillemont believes that it is not unworthy of St. Basil as a young rhetorician and would place its date as of the year 356. Since Theodosius became emperor only in 378, shortly before St. Basil's death, in such case it could only have been written to some other official and not to the emperor.

tongue and eye were put in motion and joined an ever-flowing river, the Halys, and that when it was a torrent. This is the neighboring river which falls to our share. It pours out of the country of the Armenians, emptying into the most sacred lake of the Sebastenes, onto which the so-called noble forty soldiers of Christ were fastened when a terrible north wind was blowing. From there on (accept my words as the truth, your Excellency), this river, encircling us like some warlike host of formidable men, alarms us not a little. For, as it is never crossed on foot at any time or in any manner, it does not permit our indispensable and profitable districts to carry seasonable merchandise across. I mean the districts of the Galatians, the Paphlagonians, and the Hellenopontians, through whom and from whom we secure the necessities of life, especially an abundance of bread, when the ground round about is frozen and fettered by the surrounding climate and the overpowering wrath of lightning, thunder, hail, and river. And not a little does the arrogance, too, of Mount Argeos,[2] our hereditary cause of suffering, threaten us.

Since, therefore, your Excellency, you have been entreated, be pleased to show a patriotic zeal for your tributary land, in order that thus, by the liberal gift of a bridge, making it possible for the river to be crossed, you may show it as if it were a new Red Sea affording passage. For the Lord, having had compassion on the life of the Jews, which was full of groaning, was well pleased for them to walk with unwet feet in the Red Sea as on dry land, having given them Moses as guide. Now, the character of our river is violent; it has become death for men. And, when it has formed an inland sea and is pressing upon all the grass-producing land, and

2 The loftiest mountain of Asia Minor, nearly in the center of Cappadocia; an offset of the Anti-Taurus. At its foot stood the celebrated city of Mazaca or Caesarea.

the land is covered with mud, necessarily the steer for plowing is hungry, as well as all the animals of the land round about. Truly, if it had been man wronging man, we would not have ceased making use of the courts. But, in the case of the immense river which does not obey, what measure should one take? Therefore, it is necessary, your Excellency, to pray to you, who are able in one moment of time to remove the danger to the travelers.

366. To Urbicius, a Monk, concerning Continence[1]

You do well in setting forth strict standards for us, in order that we may know not only continence but also its fruits. Now, its fruit is a participation in God. For, incorruption is a sharing in God, just as corruption is a participation in the world. In fact, continence is a denial of the body and an assent to God. It withdraws from everything mortal, having, as it were, the Spirit of God as a body. Possessing neither jealousy nor envy, it causes us to be joined with God. For, he who loves a body passionately envies another, but he who has not taken into his heart the disease of corruption is strengthened thereafter for all labor, albeit dying in the body, yet living in incorruption. And, when I examine closely, God seems to me to be continence, because He desires nothing, but has everything in Himself; and He

1 Since the publication of Garnier and Maran's edition of St. Basil's letters, several others, Letters 366-368, have been found and attributed to St. Basil. Letter 366 was included by Mai and also by Migne in their editions of the letters. Letters 367 and 368, lately discovered by Mercati, are contained in Deferrari's edition of St. Basil's Letters. Letter 366 seems to be spurious because of its poor Ms. tradition. It is found in only three Mss. and they are of the late date. According to Bessières, it is contained in none of the ancient Mss. and is not in Marcianus 61, as Mai asserts.

reaches after nothing, nor does He have any lust of the eyes nor of the ears, but, being in want of naught, He is wholly satisfied. Concupiscence is a disease of the soul; continence is soundness.

Yet, not only with one meaning, as referring to sexual pleasures, must we look at continence, but also in regard to all other things which the soul, not being satisfied with necessities, evilly desires. Envy comes because of gold, and numberless other wrong-doings because of other desires. To refrain from becoming intoxicated, as well as from bursting by overeating, is continence. Moreover, prevailing over the body is continence, and also mastering our evil thoughts as often as some fancy, which is neither good nor true, has disturbed the soul, and has delivered the heart over to consider many things without fruit. In every way continence sets man free, being at the same time a remedy and a power; it does not teach temperance, but provides it.

Continence is a grace of God. Jesus appeared to be continence when He was made light on land and sea. For, the earth did not support Him, nor the sea, but, just as He walked on the sea, so He did not weigh down the earth. Indeed, if from corruption is death and from absence of corruption immortality, Jesus wrought divinity, not mortality. He ate and He drank in a peculiar way, not giving up the food again;[2] so great a power was continence in Him that His nourishment was not corrupted in Him, since He did not have corruption.

If we possess continence to some little degree we are higher than all others. For, we have heard that even the angels became incontinent, having been cast down from heaven because of concupiscence. They, in fact, were conquered; they did not go down. What was the disease itself doing

2 I.e., not passing the residue through the bowels and kidneys.

there, unless there was some such eye there as to detect it? For this reason I said: If we have continence in a slight degree and do not passionately desire the world but the higher life, we shall be found there where we raise our mind; for this, it seems, is the eye which can see the invisible things. Truly is it said: 'The mind sees, and the mind hears.'[3] Although these words seem few to you, I have written much, because each single word is a thought. I know that in reading you will perceive it.

367. To Basil[1]

He who in your opinion is a mimic, but in ours a pious man, asked me for a letter to you that he might be heard with joy.

368. Basil to Gregory

He who in our opinion is a mimic, but in yours a pious man, came to us on a desired and joyous day and departed in a manner truly befitting a god.

3 Cf. Epicharmos as quoted by Plutarch, *'De sollertia animalium,' Moralia* 961A.

1 Mai, in (*'Über einen neuen Brief,'* in *Bibliotheca Nova Patrum* 3 (1845), considers this and the following letter genuine because they are found in all the important Mss. of St. Gregory's correspondence as well as in a Ms. of St. Basil; also, because any motive for their being forged is lacking.

INDEX

INDEX

abduction, *2*: 107, 259
Abel, *1*: 119; *2*: 225, 226, 258
Abraham, *1*: 110; *2*: 161, 172, 221, 258
Abraham, Bishop of Batnae, *1*: 203, 273
Abraham, Bishop of Urimi, *1*: 203
Aburgius, *1*: 79, 181, 295, 340; *2*: 41, 298
Acacians, *1*: 135; *2*: 252
Acacius, Bishop of Beroea, *2*: 103, 121, 123, 213
Acacius, Bishop of Caesarea, *1*: 64; *2*: 207
Achab, *2*: 94
Achaea, *2*: 77
Achelous, *1*: 48; *2*: 327
Actius, *1*: 41
Adam, *2*: 7, 10, 164, 226, 229, 233-236, 258, 296, 339
adultery, *2*: 5, 20, 49, 51, 56, 58, 61, 62, 109-111, 114, 157
Aecus, *2*: 328
Aegae, *2*: 190
aeons, *2*: 8
Aeschylus, *1*: 179
Aesop, *2*: 26, 317
Aetius, heretic, *1*: 24; *2*: 133, 193
Aetius, presbyter, *2*: 213
Africans, *2*: 6, 7, 77, 82
Alcibiades, *2*: 320
Alcimus, rhetorician, *2*: 335
Alcinous, *1*: 177
Alcmaeon, *1*: 48
Alexander, Bishop of Corydalia, *2*: 118
Alexander, Bishop of Egypt, *2*: 244
Alexander the Great, *1*: 43, 64, 211; *2*: 264
Alexandria, *1*: 4, 208, 284; *2*: 5, 6, 128, 220, 299, 300
almshouse, *1*: 292, 301, 339
Alphaeus, *2*: 330
Alypius, *2*: 322

Amasea, *1*: 292; *2*: 143, 208
Ambrose, St., *1*: 161, 201, 282, 305, *2*: 42
Amphilochius, Bishop of Iconium, *1*: 298, 300, 319, 323, 338; *2*: xiii, xiv, 4, 34, 37, 47, 51, 62, 64, 105, 117, 153-156, 202
Amphipolis, *1*: 47
Ancyra, *1*: 64, 73, 75, 224; *2*: 143, 173, 174, 199, 240
Andronicus, *1*: 236
Annesi, *1*: 13; *2*: 87
Anomoeans, *1*: 41, 266; *2*: 90, 97, 133, 165, 200
Anthimus, Bishop of Tyana, *1*: 148, 203, 250-253; *2*: 92
Antichrist, *2*: 243
Antioch, *1*: 130, 147, 161, 162, 168, 197, 249, 250, 266, 273, 282, 286, 308; *2*: 47, 48, 100, 142, 144, 208, 211, 219, 220, 221, 246, 252, 255
Antiochus, *1*: 294, 311, 329; *2*: 176, 177
Antipater, Governor of Cappadocia, *1*: 280; *2*: 3, 4
Apocrypha, *2*: 60
Apollinarians, *2*: 4, 233
Apollinaris, Bishop of Laodicea, *1*: 266, 267, 272, 273; *2*: xv, xvi, 131, 134, 136, 146, 193, 218, 219, 237, 241, 244-248, 279, 337-343
Apostolius, *2*: 320
Apotactitae, *2*: 60
Arcadius, Bishop, *1*: 131
Arcadius, imperial administrator, *1*: 48
Arendzen, J.P., *2*: 10
Argeos, Mount, *2*: 344
Arians, *1*: 22, 80, 155, 160, 161, 164, 166, 228, 256, 265, 266, 271, 276, 289, 304; *2*: 4, 48, 77, 100, 139, 142, 143, 159, 200, 205, 215, 232, 238, 242, 248, 251, 253, 256
Ariarathia, *2*: 302, 303
Arintheus, *1*: 224, 304, 341; *2*: 256, 258, 259
Ariomaniacs, *2*: 253
Aristenus, *2*: 16, 54, 56, 58, 59, 62, 107, 111, 112, 115
Aristophanes, *1*: 10; *2*: 320
Aristotle, *1*: 23, 41, 96, 190, 276; *2*: 17, 128, 322, 334
Arius, *1*: 167, 169, 200, 202, 204, 256, 259, 269, 270; *2*: 129, 133. 144, 146, 183, 193, 198, 199, 239, 240
Armenia, *1*: 219, 222, 223, 252, 255, 263; *2*: 150, 177
Armenia, Lesser, *1*: 171, 251, 266; *2*: 41, 239
Armenians, *1*: 252; *2*: 77, 150, 344
asceticism, *1*: 104-111, 187, 245
Ascholius, Bishop of Thessalonica, *1*: 305-307, 323, 324, 326
Asclepius, *2*: 203
Astydamas, *1*: 97
Atarbius, Bishop of Neo-Caesarea, *1*: 158, 261, 338, *2*: 70, 81, 90

Athanasius, St., Bishop of Alexandria, *1*: 96, 154, 159, 160, 162, 164, 166, 185, 188, 197, 198, 201, 271, 274, 282, 306; *2*: 6, 21, 43, 77, 100, 218, 220, 244, 245, 248, 250, 283
Athanasius, Bishop of Ancyra, *1*: 62, 64, 73
Athanasius, Father of Athanasius, Bishop of Ancyra, *1*: 62
Athens, *1*: 3, 179; *2*: 260, 282, 319
Athos, Mount, *2*: 323
Augustine, St., *1*: 335

Baal, *1*: 311
Balaam, *2*: 30, 94
Balsamon, *2*: 13, 16, 22, 23, 49, 56, 58, 60, 62, 106, 107, 109, 112, 114-116
baptism, *1*: 35, 36; *2*: xv, 5-12, 23, 50, 60, 61, 145, 170, 189, 247, 283
Baronius, *2*: 9, 142
Barses, Bishop of Edessa, *2*: 243, 254
Basil, St., works cited: *Adversus Eunomium, 1*: 49, 53, 66; *Book of Ascetic Discipline, 1*: 61; *De Spiritu Sancto, 1*: 66, 338; *2*: 84, 155; *Hexaemeron, 1*: 115; *Homilia, 2*: 333
Basilides, Bishop of Gangra, *2*: 143, 208
Beroea, *2*: 121, 122, 213, 252
Bessieres, J., *1*: 21, 49, 96, 102, 111, 115, 142; *2*: 345
Bianor, presbyter, *2*: 47
bishops, Western, *1*: 160, 197, 249, 268; *2*: 100
Bosporius, Bishop of Colonia, *1*: 133, 135, 290
Briso, *2*: 295
Bythos, *2*: 8

Caesarea, *1*: 3, 61, 99, 147, 151, 170, 173, 176, 187, 209, 214, 250, 255, 262, 282, 288, 295, 298, 300, 307, 325, 333; *2*: 10, 65, 132, 174, 218, 269, 283, 299
Caesaria, *1*: 208
Caesarius, *1*: 66, 77, 78; *2*: 311, 322
Cain, *2*: 223-229
calligraphists, *1*: 275
Callisthenes, *1*: 173, 174
calumny, *2*: 126
Candidianus, *1*: 12
Canonesses, *1*: 135, 335
canons, *1*: 205, 290; *2*: xiii, xvii, 4-24, 47-62, 105-117, 140, 252, 260, 276
Cappadocia, *1*: xv, 12, 80, 130, 154, 155, 169, 176, 179, 181-183, 193, 218, 238, 242, 278, 307, 324, 327; *2*: 42, 43, 65, 70, 92, 124, 145, 218, 243, 270, 297, 318, 319-321, 330, 342
Cappadocia Secunda, *1*: 133, 217, 250; *2*: 154
Cappadocia Tertia, *2*: 143

Carbala, or Caprales, *1*: 22, *2*: 301
Carmel, Mount, *1*: 109
Cathari, *2*: 5, 9, 10
Catholic Church, *1*: 257, 258, 288; *2*: 7
Catullus, *2*: 317
Celsus, *2*: 319
Cephallenians, *1*: 295
Chalcedon, *2*: 132, 213
charms, *2*: 19
Chilo, *1*: 102
Christ, *1*: 6, 17, 26-28, 31-33, 36, 58, 61, 62, 71, 73, 105, 106, 110, 111, 115, 118-120, 122, 125, 127, 131, 139, 141, 151, 159, 168, 169, 173, 187, 200, 207, 234, 241, 248, 253, 266, 284-287, 294, 298, 305, 309, 312, 316, 320, 325, 327-329, 338, 343, 344; *2*: 6-8, 10, 20, 38, 43, 44, 48, 50, 60, 66, 69, 79, 82, 86, 90, 91, 98, 113, 119, 122, 123, 125, 128, 130, 135, 141, 142, 147, 148, 165, 166, 169, 170, 179-183, 187, 194, 213-216, 229, 230, 232-235, 237, 238, 243, 247, 248, 252, 253, 283, 286, 289; as High Priest, *2*: 247; as Lord, *1*: 52, 60, 111, 115, 131, 259; *2*: 150, 151, 165, 184, 210, 232, 259; as Master, *1*: 33, 70, 71, 147, 194, 225, 231, 235, 345; *2*: 50, 98, 210; as Redeemer, *2*: 233; as Saviour, *1*: 30, 31, 36, 110, 116, 118, 124, 285; *2*: 7, 32, 98; as Son, *1*: 23-41, 66, 87-96, 124-126, 137-139, 200, 230, 253, 257-260, 266, 267, 288, 312-314, 334; *2*: 28-33, 61, 90-94, 101-103, 144-147, 160, 165-168, 171, 188, 209, 336-340; as Word, *1*: 23, 26, 28-31, 38, 127, 167, 257, 265
Christian, *1*: 17, 54-60, 77, 131, 149, 171, 211, 225, 231, 241, 276, 284, 302, 304, 324, 325, 342; *2*: 26, 37, 45, 104, 139, 180, 184-186, 219, 241, 259, 265-267, 291, 295, 308, 336
Cicero, *1*: 156, 190
Cilicia, *1*: 18, 80, 130, 164, 269, 270; *2*: 60, 193
Cleanthes, *1*: 14
Cleobulus, *1*: 40
Colonia, *1*: 263; *2*: 41, 147, 150, 152
Communion, *1*: 198, 208-209; *2*: 13, 15, 108-111, 114; Holy, *2*: xiv, 15, 52, 60, 108, 114-116, 186; Blessed Sacrament, *2*: xiii, 108-110, 112; Holy Viaticum, *2*: 15, 113
communion, *1*: 199, 200, 219, 221, 222, 230, 240, 250, 252, 268, 269, 274, 290; *2*: 5, 12, 13, 15-17, 23, 49, 53, 57, 58, 70, 78, 79, 108, 111, 115, 116, 134, 136, 142, 143, 146, 174, 181, 189, 192, 193, 197, 201, 205, 210, 221, 237, 239, 242, 245, 249, 250, 253, 276, 277
congregations, illegal, *2*: 6-8

Constantine the Great, *1*: 143; *2*: 5, 240
Constantinople, *1*: 3, 14, 135, 183, 242, 289; *2*: 104, 142, 196, 209, 212, 218, 240
Constantius, *1*: 99, 271, 289; *2*: 43, 210, 219, 257
consubstantiality, *2*: 101, 103, 197, 199
consubstantiation, *2*: 240
contemplation, *1*: 30, 31, 38, 40, 43
Cornelius, St., Pope, *1*: 142; *2*: 5
Council of Ancyra, *1*: 256; *2*: 108; Canons of, *2*: 13, 19, 48, 51, 55, 109, 110, 115, 116, 139
Council of Ariminum, *1*: 166
Council of Chalcedon, *1*: 84
Council of Constantinople, *1*: 158, 273, 305; *2*: 4, 36, 37, 217, 222, 337; Canons of, *2*: 6, 11, 12
Council of Elvira, *1*: 144; Canons of, *2*: 109, 111, 114
Council of Laodicea, Canons of, *2*: 5, 6, 11, 15, 61
Council of Milan, *2*: 43
Council of Nicaea, *1*: 187, 256; *2*: 145; Canon of, *1*: 144
Council of Nice, Canons of, *2*: 5, 11, 23, 49, 61, 113
Council of Rimini, *1*: 166
Council of Rome, *1*: 201
Council in Trullo, Canons of, *2*: 6, 11, 12, 56, 60
Creed, *1*: 257, 263, 268; *2*: 219, 240; of Antioch, *2*: 132; of Ariminum, *1*: 42, 133, 135; *2*: 132, 195, 199; of Constantinople, *1*: 134; *2*: 132, 199, 208; of Nicaea, *1*: 240, 256, 258, 289, 312; Nicene, *1*: 255-260, 264, 266, 269, 289; *2*: 144, 145, 195, 196, 209, 217, 218, 220, 239, 245, 287
Croesus, *1*: 238
Cyprian, St., *1*: 101, 143, 209; *2*: 8-10, 12, 205
Cyprus, *2*: 217, 218, 234
Cyriacus, *1*: 241; *2*: 21, 22, 260, 261, 312
Cyril, Bishop of Armenia, *1*: 222, 250
Cyrus the Great, *1*: 238
Cyzicus, *2*: 196, 199

Damas, *1*: 339; *2*: 210
Damasus, Pope, *1*: 132, 168, 197, 200, 282; *2*: 100, 177, 252, 253, 337
David, *1*: 8, 10, 25, 37, 103, 319, 327; *2*: 168, 169, 339
deaconesses, *1*: 229; *2*: 59, 60
Deferrari, Roy J., *1*: xvii; *2*: 345
Demosthenes, *1*: 12; *2*: 332
Demosthenes, Vicar of Pontus, *2*: 139, 140, 143, 154, 173
Demophilus, *1*: 130
Devil, *1*: 15, 22, 24, 28, 36, 85, 95, 98, 107, 108, 117, 119, 131, 141, 146, 202, 223, 263, 284,

290, 299, 319; *2*: 16, 17, 83, 117, 152, 179, 203, 221, 276, 289
devils, *1*: 25, 38
Dianius, Bishop of Caesarea, *1*: 21, 129, 133, 134, 187, 228; *2*: 198
Diatimus, *2*: 118
Didymus the Blind, *1*: 66
Diocletian, *1*: 169; *2*: 45, 273
Diodorus, *1*: xiv, 221, 276, 314; *2*: 193
Diogenes, *1*: 14, 43, 180
Dionysius of Alexandria, *1*: 41, 42, 169; *2*: 6, 9
Dionysius of Corinth, *1*: 169
Dionysius of Milan, *2*: 42-44
Dionysius of Rome, *1*: 42, 170
disciples, *1*: 30, 32, 34, 37, 41, 104, 105, 153, 171, 204, 287, 301; *2*: 3, 6, 32, 38, 66, 85, 90, 161, 176, 180, 188, 243, 249, 250, 334
Doara, *2*: 154, 177
Docetism, *2*: 234
Domitian, *1*: 237
Dorotheus, deacon, *1*: 162, 163, 165, 189, 194, 197, 310
Dorotheus, presbyter, *2*: 103, 177, 189, 237, 238, 252, 253
Doxology, *1*: 139, 202, 313; *2*: 91
Duchesne, P., *2*: 246

Ecdicius, *2*: 143, 173, 176
Echinades, *1*: 48
Egypt, *1*: 4, 161, 169, 208, 246, 281, 284, 316; *2*: xv, 8, 33, 77, 82, 84, 128, 169, 244, 249, 342
Elias, *1*: 109; *2*: 324
Elias, Governor of Cappadocia, *1*: 191, 209, 218
Eliseus, *1*: 103; *2*: 24
Elpidius, *1*: 156, 157, 183, 184; *2*: 154, 208
Elpidius, deacon, *1*: 281; *2*: 244, 245
Elpidius, bishop, *2*: 79, 80
Emmelia, *1*: 18, 74; *2*: 130
Encratites, *2*: 10-12, 60, 170
Epiphanius, St., *1*: 161; *2*: 121, 217, 218, 221, 249
Esdras, *1*: 109
Ethiopian, *1*: 270, 271
Eudoxius, *2*: 142, 143, 195, 205, 207
Euippius, *1*: 164, 265; *2*: 176, 196, 197, 207, 208
Eulancius, *2*: 86
Eulogius, *2*: 244
Eumathius, *1*: 342
Eunomius, *1*: 49, 132, 199, 248, 256
Eupaterius, *1*: 312
Euphronius, Bishop of Colonia, *2*: 41, 147, 148, 150-152
Eupraxius, *1*: 327
Eupsichius, martyr, *1*: 224, 291, 338, 339; *2*: 64, 210
Euripides, *1*: 156, 318
Eusebius, Archbishop of Caesarea, *1*: 128, 129
Eusebius, Bishop of Samosata, *1*: 68, 74, 75, 79, 130, 202,

212, 216, 223, 247, 249, 253, 255, 262, 263, 273, 278, 279, 281, 289, 293-295, 311, 321, 327, 329, 340, 342, 343; *2*: 45, 172, 175, 181, 186, 252, 253, 255, 256
Eusebius, Bishop of Vercelli, *1*: 282; *2*: 43
Eusebius, historian, *1*: 169
Eusebius, reader, *2*: 46
Eusebius, school companion of St. Basil, *2*: 260, 261
Eustathians, *2*: 147, 219, 220
Eustathius, Bishop of Himmeria, *1*: 344
Eustathius, Bishop of Sebaste, *1*: 161, 164, 184, 203, 212, 217, 219, 220, 247, 251, 253, 255, 260, 263-265, 269, 270, 283, 303; *2*: 65, 79, 87, 97, 104, 125, 126, 129, 130, 139, 143, 144, 174, 190, 191, 197, 200, 205, 207, 239, 240, 252, 337
Eustathius, bishop, *2*: 144
Eustathius, deacon, *1*: 129, 279
Eustathius, philosopher, *1*: 3
Eustathius, physician, *1*: 302; *2*: 25
Eutyches, martyr, *1*: 324, 325
Euzoius, *2*: 134, 144, 205
Evaesae, *2*: 206
Evagrius, *1*: 282, 283, 308
Evesus, *2*: 269
excommunication, *2*: 107, 260, 276

Fabius of Antioch, *1*: 142
faith, *1*: 21-40, 255-260, 261, *2*: 75-78, 161, 162, 165, 180, 181, 188, 189, 191, 195, 198, 209, 235, 248, 249, 253, 287
famine, *1*: 75
Fathers, *1*: 61, 69, 72, 135, 136, 142-145, 199, 200, 202, 206, 207, 242, 256, 265, 288, 289, 312, 325, 327, 334; *2*: 8, 10, 11, 23, 43, 48, 56, 69, 71, 77, 101, 109, 114, 115, 147, 185, 195, 219, 235, 241, 249, 287, 337, 343
Festus, *2*: 285
Fialon, E., *1*: xiii, xv, xvii
Firmilian, *2*: 8, 10, 12
Firminus, *1*: 244, 245; *2*: 320
Firmus, *2*: 319
fornication, *2*: 5, 13, 15, 16, 19, 20, 51-53, 56, 58-60, 62, 109, 111, 114, 230
Fronto, *1*: 260; *2*: 147, 174, 175, 177, 216

Galatia, *2*: 140, 163, 173, 174, 195, 205, 208, 242, 252, 304, 344
Gaul, *1*: 197, 273; *2*: 8, 184, 212
Gelasius, *2*: 138
Genethlius, *2*: 135
Gentiles, *2*: 30, 68, 116, 147, 170
George, Bishop of Laodicea, *1*: 135
Getasa, *1*: 219, 221, 253
Glycerius, *1*: xv, 330-333
Gnosticism, *2*: 8, 10

God, Creator, *1*: 7, 31, 40, 335; *2*: 156, 162, 166, 258, 285; Divinity, *1*: 24, 31, 32, 42, 338; *2*: 27, 247; Father, *1*: 18, 22-42, 66, 86, 87-96, 110, 128, 137-139, 200, 230, 257-260, 266, 267, 288, 312, 313, 334; *2*: 28-33, 61, 90-94, 101-103, 144-147, 160, 165-168, 171, 188, 209, 336-340; Godhead, *1*: 256; *2*: 27-29, 32, 33, 91, 103, 171, 234, 235, 237, 341; Good Shepherd, *1*: 114, 127; Holy One, *1*: 45, 193, 232, 306; *2*: 36, 38, 64, 65, 71, 106, 155, 203, 244, 307; Judge, *1*: 16, 133, 136, 243, 284, 285, 287, 324, 336; *2*: 197, 203, 214, 215, 225, 243, 250, 288; Lord, *1*: 16, 19, 20, 25, 26, 33, 39, 44, 45, 50, 56, 57, 60-62, 72, 81, 92, 95, 102, 103, 105, 109, 117, 120, 122-124, 127, 130, 132, 134-136, 138, 139, 142, 145, 146, 152, 155, 158, 160, 162, 186, 189, 194, 197, 199-207, 215, 220, 222, 225, 227, 229-231, 240, 241, 248, 256, 259, 260, 263, 266, 271, 274, 278, 283, 284, 286, 291, 294, 300-302, 305-311, 319-325, 327, 330, 334, 335, 339, 340, 343-345; *2*: 15, 19, 22, 24, 28, 35, 36, 38-44, 48, 49, 54, 59, 61-74, 78-85, 94, 97-99, 106, 113, 114, 116, 117, 119, 121-124, 127, 130, 141, 143-147, 149, 151, 154, 155, 161, 162, 164, 165, 169, 175, 176, 178-182, 185-188, 190, 195, 198, 201-204, 206, 208, 209, 212-214, 216, 217, 219, 222-226, 228, 230-238, 243-245, 247, 250, 252, 254-256, 261, 265, 267, 268, 272-276, 283, 286-290, 292, 295-299, 301, 302, 304, 306, 308, 310, 311, 313, 340; Mighty One, *2*: 66; Most High, *1*: 320; Only-begotten, *1*: 27, 42, 87, 88, 93-96, 139, 167, 259, 288; *2*: 90, 160, 165, 166, 188, 237, 239, 338

Goths, *1*: 324; *2*: 202, 255-257

Gratian, Emperor, *2*: 185

Greeks, *1*: 117, 118; *2*: 137

Gregory of Nazianzus, St., *1*: 5, 14, 20-22, 46, 52, 66, 76-79, 128, 161, 170, 171, 209, 216, 217, 242, 246; *2*: 41, 106, 131, 174, 222, 250, 253, 262, 267, 273, 297, 301, 304, 309, 311, 327, 329, 330, 333, 338, 339, 347

Gregory of Nazianzus, the Elder, *1*: 202, 298

Gregory of Nyssa, St., *1*: 46, 49, 64, 84, 108, 148, 161, 203, 217, 224; *2*: 25, 92, 104, 139, 154, 174

Gregory Thaumaturgus, St., *1*: 70, 72; *2*: xiv, xv, 71, 76, 84, 86, 89, 92

Gregory, Bishop, uncle of St. Basil, *1*: 148, 150, 151, 153

Gregory VII, Pope, *1*: 250

Haceldama, *1*: 141
Hades, *1*: 126
Halys River, *2*: 344
Harmatius, *2*: 266
Harpocration, *2*: 244
hearers, *2*: xiv, 7, 15, 52, 56, 62, 108-111, 114-116
heaven, *1*: 33, 37, 38, 51, 123, 128, 258, 272, 288, 325; *2*: 85, 91, 167, 175, 180, 206, 213, 214, 225, 248
heavens, *1*: 19, 36, 112, 113; *2*: 24, 101, 158, 170, 258
Hefele, *2*: 9, 10, 12, 13, 15, 17, 19, 20, 23, 48, 51, 52, 108, 109, 111, 113-116, 145
hell, *1*: 141
Helladius, *1*: 232, 233; *2*: 271
Hellenius, *1*: 171, 216
Hera, *2*: 264, 265
Heracleidas, *1*: 298, 300, 323
Hercules, *2*: 306
heresy, *1*: 129, 166, 169, 170, 200, 202, 204, 206, 230, 251, 253, 259, 266, 268, 270, 325; *2*: xv, xvi, 6, 7, 50, 121, 124, 129, 136, 137, 178, 187, 203, 205, 207, 219, 236, 244, 249, 252, 298
heretics, *1*: 29, 36, 73, 161, 207, 267, 270; *2*: 6, 8, 9, 15, 16, 50, 97, 99, 118, 124, 133, 142, 143, 156, 173, 183, 197, 207, 209, 213, 218, 237, 240, 248
Hermogenes, *1*: 187, 288; *2*: 198, 199
Herod, *2*: 55, 169
Herodotus, *1*: 238, 318; *2*: 321, 323, 330
Hesychius, *1*: 157, 173; *2*: 319
Hierocles, *2*: 322
Hilarius, *2*: 95, 118
Himerius, *2*: 265
Hippolytus, *2*: 10
Homer, *1*: 3, 4, 46, 154, 157, 176, 177, 295; *2*: 3, 178, 317, 321, 328, 330, 334
homicide, *2*: 22
Homoiousians, *1*: 266; *2*: 133, 199
homoiousion, *2*: xvi, 240
Horace, *1*: 176
Huns, *2*: 202
Hydroparastates, *2*: 10
Hyperechius, *2*: 315
Hypsinus, *2*: 143, 173

Iamblichus, *1*: 156
Ibora, *2*: 290
Icelium, *2*: 313
Iconium, *1*: 283; *2*: 34, 47, 119
Illyrians, *1*: 197, 201; *2*: 77
Illyricum, *1*: 169, 204
Incarnation, *1*: 26, 31, 215; *2*: 90, 102, 155, 167, 219, 230, 232, 234-236, 241, 246, 247, 336
incest, *2*: 111, 114
Indians, *1*: 99
indiction, *1*: 143
Innocent, monk, *2*: 218, 221

Innocent, Pope, *1*: 132, 186
Irenaeus, *2*: 10
Iris River, *2*: 131, 143
Isaac, *1*: 278, 279; *2*: 255
Isauria, *1*: 80, 196; *2*: 34-37, 77, 104
Israel, *1*: 110, 316, 319, 320; *2*: 94, 163, 229, 244
Israelities, *1*: 320; *2*: 243
Ister, *1*: 324
Italy, *1*: 164, 197, 202, 273, 282, 2: 7, 8, 184, 212, 257
Izois, *2*: 12

Jackson, B., *1*: xvii, 56; *2*: 71, 183
Jacob, *1*: 109, 110; *2*: 170
Jechonias, *2*: 168, 169
Jerome, St., *1*: 166, 201, 256, 282; *2*: 217, 219
Jerusalem, *1*: 29, 116, 200; *2*: 168, 176, 206, 241
Jews, *1*: 117, 118; *2*: 8, 137, 146, 241, 344
John, *1*: 51, 203
John the Baptist, St., *1*: 109, 110, 119, 120, 301
John Chrysostom, St., *1*: 14, 132, 161, 186; *2*: 186, 213
Joseph, *1*: 8, 110, 124, 203
Jovian, *2*: 100, 200
Jovinus, Bishop of Perrha, *1*: 203, 247, 262
Jovinus, Count, *1*: 322
Judaism, *2*: 26, 89, 93, 242
Judas, *1*: 103, 104, 141; *2*: 180
Judea, *2*: 163, 168-170
Julian, *1*: 54: *2*: 284
Julian, Emperor, *1*: 96-101, 224; *2*: 257, 322, 336
Julitta, *1*: 231, 232; *2*: 288, 289
Julius, Bishop of Rome, *1*: 166
Justin, *1*: 82, 209
Juvenal, *2*: 3

knowledge, *2*: 161-168, 226

Laban, *1*: 22
Laconian Ceades, *1*: 179
Laconian Dispatch, *1*: 12
Laestrygones, *1*: 295
Lamech, *2*: 228, 229
Lampsacus, *2*: 132, 143, 199, 200, 209
Laodicea, *2*: 8, 246
Leontius, Bishop of Caesarea, *1*: 187, 288
Leontius, peraequator, *2*: 45
Leontius, sophist, *1*: 52, 54, 81
Libanius, bishop, *1*: 203
Libanius, deacon, *2*: 256
Libanius, rhetorician, *2*: 318-335
Liberius, Pope, *1*: 166, 269; *2*: 145, 200, 239, 240
Libya, *2*: xv, 84, 154
litanies, *2*: 84
Lollianus, Bishop of Phelus, *2*: 118
Longinus, *2*: 21, 22
Loofs, F., *1*: 216, 218, 223, 226; *2*: 45, 62, 64, 65, 70, 81, 87, 95, 99, 103, 104, 117, 141, 153, 155, 156, 159, 161, 165, 172, 175, 176, 184, 190, 201, 204,

206, 211, 249, 250, 255, 266, 273, 308, 319, 321, 322, 329
Lucan, *2*: 190
Lucian, *1*: 40; *2*: 284
Lucius, *2*: 256
Lucius, deacon, *2*: 213
Lycaonia, *2*: 34, 63
Lycia, *2*: 118

Maas, *2*: 330
Macedonians *1*: 188; *2*: 4, 77, 240
Macedonius, *1*: 289; *2*: 106, 240
Macrina, *2*: 76, 87, 130
Maenads, *1*: 177
Magi, *2*: 221
Magninianus, Count, *1*: 337; *2*: 313
Magnus, *2*: 285
Magusaeans, *1*: xv; *2*: 221
Mai, *1*: xvii; *2*: 345, 347
Mambre, *1*: 109
Manichaeans, *2*: 5, 7, 60, 240
manna, *2*: 36
Maran, P., *1*: 83, 108, 155, 198, 203, 217, 242, 247; *2*: 99, 155, 216
Marathonius, 2: 240
Marcellinus, Ammianus, *1*: 54, 304, 341; *2*: 202, 255
Marcellus, *1*: 166, 167, 256, *2*: 82, 178, 242, 248-250, 252
Marcion, *2*: 8, 10, 60, 61
marriage, *1*: 120, 121, 124, 318, 319; *2*: 7, 8, 10, 14-16, 19, 20, 48-54, 56, 59-62, 83, 107, 111, 221, 248, 258, 292, 295
Martinianus, *1*: 176
martyrs, *1*: 132, 224, 291, 308, 323, 324, 326, 327, 339; *2*: 45, 64, 65, 80, 180, 185, 210, 215, 272, 336, 343
Mary, *2*: 164, 229-232, 236, 336
Massagetae, *1*: 179
Maximilla, *2*: 6
Maximus, *2*: 293
Maximus, Governor of Cappadocia, *1*: 218, 295-297
Maximus, philosopher, *1*: 40
Maximus, scholar, *2*: 267
Melcher, R., *1*: 21
Meletius, Bishop of Antioch, *1*: 147, 161-163, 165, 197, 198, 202, 212, 217, 221, 249, 255, 262, 266, 273, 309; *2*: 7, 48, 92, 99-101, 104, 144, 219, 220, 252, 253
Meletius, officer, *2*: 63
Meletius, physician, *2*: 39
Meletius, presbyter, *2*: 79, 141
Melitine, *1*: 266; *2*: 240, 252
Mercati, *1*: xvii; *2*: 345
Mesopotamia, *2*: 7, 83, 99, 128, 169, 212
Messalians, *2*: 4
Mesteia, *2*: 21, 22
Milo, *2*: 324
Mindana, *2*: 21, 22
Minos, *2*: 328
Moabites, *2*: 94, 169
Modestus, prefect, *1*: 228, 234, 235; *2*: 269-271
Montanists, *2*: 6, 8, 9
Morel, C., *1*: 96

Moses, *1*: 8, 69, 103, 186; *2*: 23, 33, 181, 230, 233, 258, 324, 344
mourners, *2*: 15, 56
murder, *2*: xiii, 5, 12, 13, 17-19, 23, 55, 56, 107, 108, 225, 226, 228
Muses, *2*: 330
Musonius, Bishop of Neo-Caesarea, *1*: 68; *2*: 89
Myra, *2*: 118

Naaman, *2*: 24
Nabuchodonosor, *2*: 168
Nazianzus, *2*: 106, 301
Nectarius, *1*: 14, 17; *2*: 279
Neo-Caesarea, *1*: 13, 68, 74, 156, 158, 271; *2*: xv, 15, 70, 81, 84, 86-88, 105
Newman, John Henry, Cardinal, *1*: 166, 200; *2*: 70
Nice, *1*: 166, *2*: 8, 199
Nicaea, *1*: 136, 166, 206, 242, 288, 289; *2*: 198, 249, 342
Nicopolis, *1*: 216, 217, 219, 221, 255, 261, 262; *2*: 41, 148-152, 174, 175, 177, 178, 191, 195, 201, 202, 208
Nitra, *2*: 244
Noe, *2*: 258
Novatians, *2*: 5, 7, 8, 11, 61
Nyssa, *2*: 36, 174, 177

Odysseus, *1*: 3, 176, 295
Olives, Mount of, *1*: 109; *2*: 218
Olympians, *2*: 3
Olympias, *2*: 222
Olympius, *1*: 13, 45, 271, 273; *2*: 95
Optimus, *2*: 222
Origen, 1: 41, 50; *2*: 6, 231
Orphanene, *2*: 269
Osroene, *1*: 196
Otreius, *1*: 342
Ozizala, *1*: 298

Paeonius, *1*: 275
Palestine, *1*: 108, 281, *2*: 83, 217, 244
Palladia, 1: 280
Palladius, Arian bishop, *1*: 201
Palladius, presbyter, *2*: 218, 221, 283
pantheism, *2*: 8
Paphlagonia, *2*: 207, 344
Paregorius, *1*: 144; *2*: 22
Parnassus, *1*: 155; *2*: 143, 173
Pasinicus, *2*: 312
passions, *1*: 5, 7, 9, 56, 104, 122, 144, 145, 254, 294, 318, 319; *2*: 18, 48, 83, 94, 114, 230, 267, 293, 294
Patricius, *2*: 312
Patrophilus, Bishop of Aegae, *2*: 190, 204
Paul, St., *1*: 25, 26, 37, 89, 102, 122; *2*: 48, 163, 223, 230, 234
Paul, presbyter, *2*: 256
Paul of Samosata, *1*: 136; *2*: 82, 242
Paulianists, *2*: 8
Paulinus, *1*: 161, 308; *2*: 100, 105, 219, 220, 242, 244, 249
Pausanias, *1*: 179

peace, *1*: 165, 166, 168, 189, 206, 215, 220, 241, 261, 263, 264, 309, 324, 326; *2*: 66, 70, 94, 99, 103, 120, 125, 140, 150, 181, 192, 204, 217, 221, 222, 243, 246, 249, 254, 312
Pelagius, Bishop of Laodicea, *1*: 203; *2*: 211
Pentheus, *1*: 177
Pepuzeni, *2*: 6, 8, 9
Pergamius, *1*: 145
perjury, *2*: 115, 116
persecution, *2*: 5, 185, 202, 203, 213, 215, 217, 243
Persians, *1*: 98; *2*: 257
Persons, *1*: 258; *2*: 27, 86, 90, 92, 93, 102, 103, 137, 146, 159, 167, 171, 221, 242, 340
person, *1*: 21, 41, 42, 84-96, 138, 257; *2*: 102, 171
Petavius, *2*: 231
Peter, Bishop of Alexandria, *1*: 274; *2*: 237, 249, 250, 252, 253
Peter, Bishop of Sebaste, *1*: 84; *2*: 89, 105
Peter, presbyter, *2*: 70
Phalerius, *2*: 315
Pharaoh, *1*: 155; *2*: 33, 36
Phargamos, *1*: 212
Pheidias, *1*: 40
Philagrius Arcenus, *2*: 311
Philippolis, *2*: 172
Philo, *2*: 36
Philocares, *2*: 139
Phinehas, *1*: 119
Phocas, Emperor, *2*: 23
Phoenicians, *2*: xv, 84
Phrygia, *2*: 6, 60, 77
Pilate, *2*: 169
Pisidia, *1*: 319; *2*: 77, 104, 232
Plato, *1*: 12, 96, 97, 277; *2*: 262, 321, 323, 330-332, 334
Pliny, *2*: 221
Plutarch, *1*: 54, 64, 180, 264; *2*: 317, 347; pseudo-, *1*: 17
Pneumatomachi, *1*: 289; *2*: 240
Podandus, *1*: 179-181
Poemenius, Bishop of Satala, *1*: 226, 252; *2*: 147, 151
Poemenius, presbyter, *1*: 220
Polydamus, *2*: 323
polygamists, *2*: 14
polygamy, *2*: 15, 114
polytheism, *2*: 93, 188
Pompeianus, *1*: 282
Pontus, *1*: xiii, 46, 48, 184, 224; *2*: 65, 104, 105, 118, 174, 195, 210, 269, 282, 286, 287, 290, 342
pope, *1*: 250
poverty, *1*: 13, 14, 29, 60, 77, 81, 113, 196, 301, 303; *2*: 290, 302, 303
prayer, *1*: 7, 9, 11, 15, 19, 121, 123, 161, 192, 197-199, 201, 205, 210, 213-216, 219, 223, 224, 227, 286, 307-309, 312, 321, 322, 325, 327, 336, 337; *2*: xiv, xv, 36, 49, 68, 83, 84, 113, 118, 128, 149, 152, 176, 180, 183, 186, 187, 199, 201, 203, 210, 216, 260, 265, 267, 276, 280, 285, 299, 301, 309, 336, 338

Priscilla, *2*: 6, 9
professions, religious, *2*: 49, 50
prostrates, *2*: xiv, 56, 58, 108-111, 114-116
Protagoras, *1*: 277
psalmody, *2*: 83-85
Ptolemy, *2*: 206
Pythagoras, *1*: 54, 190

rainbow, *1*: 91, 92
Ramsey, W. M., *1*: xv, 176, 330
rebaptism, *2*: 6, 9, 61
Rebecca, *2*: 164
Restitutus of Carthage, *1*: 166
Resurrection, *1*: 26; *2*: 90
resurrection, *1*: 16, 36, 37, 125, 126; *2*: 8, 241, 248, 295
Rhadamanthus, *2*: 328
Rome, *1*: 99, 160, 163, 165, 166, 169, 189, 269, 283; *2*: 8, 61, 101, 104, 195, 197, 209, 211, 217, 234, 237, 239, 249, 256, 335
Routh, *2*: 19
Rufinus, *1*: 40, 115

Sabas, martyr, *1*: 307, 325, 326
Sabellius, *1*: 41, 42, 138, 257, 262, 267; *2*: 6, 26, 82, 89, 90, 93, 102, 133, 137, 146, 171, 242, 246
Sabinus, *1*: 197, 199, 201, 204
Saccophori, *2*: 60
Saul, *2*: 30
Sagadares, *1*: 98
Salaminia, *2*: 320
Salathiel, *2*: 169
Samosata, *1*: 198, 217, 229, 273, 343; *2*: 45, 119, 256
Sanctissimus, *1*: 249, 251, 267, 273; *2*: 177, 212-214, 237, 238
Sapor, *1*: 98
Saracens, *1*: 99
Sasima, *1*: 175
Satala, *1*: 218, 221, 222, 226, 227; *2*: 151
Satan, *1*: 141; *2*: 16, 17, 83, 203
Saturninus, *1*: 273; *2*: 10, 12
Schafer, J., *1*: 21, 68, 73, 74, 79, 140, 142, 144
schism, *2*: 6-10, 246
Scripture, Holy, *1*: xv, 8, 18, 22, 25, 27, 30, 31, 36, 38, 55, 86, 87, 95, 100, 106, 107, 111, 113, 119, 125, 128, 138, 166, 259, 260, 262, 286, 301, 313, 314, 317, 320, 327, 335, 338; *2*: xiv, 8, 22-24, 27, 30, 32, 33, 36, 40, 43, 48, 66, 67, 69, 79, 83, 90, 94, 102, 113, 116, 126, 127, 140, 161, 165, 166, 183, 185, 187, 193, 198, 204, 206, 209, 222, 224, 225, 230-232, 235, 241, 246-248, 256-258, 273, 281, 282, 294, 337, 341, 342; quotations from, or references to, individual Books:

Acts of the Apostles, *1*: 22, 30, 32, 34, 57, 140, 141, 265, 301, 319; *2*: 53, 91, 118, 154, 173, 180, 219, 233
Amos, *1*: 114, 317; *2*: 42, 186
Apocalypse, *2*: 136

Canticle of Canticles, *1*: 230; *2*: 310
Colossians, *1*: 60, 87, 141; *2*: 28, 238, 247
1 Corinthians, *1*: 26, 32, 34, 37, 38, 57-59, 63, 87, 106, 123, 139, 141, 158, 256, 285, 287, 318; *2*: 17, 19, 20, 53, 56, 59, 71, 73, 74, 76, 85, 98, 119, 127, 158, 163, 166, 182, 184, 209, 213, 233, 277
2 Corinthians, *1*: 15, 25, 32, 35, 36, 56, 59, 62, 122, 123; *2*: 44, 128, 138, 203, 213, 216, 230, 238, 254
Daniel, *1*: 126; *2*: 186, 228, 255
Deuteronomy, *1*: 25, 26, 119; *2*: 135, 191, 224
Ecclesiastes, *1*: 133, 154; *2*: 125, 126
Ecclesiasticus, *1*: 40, 149; *2*: 229, 238, 241
Ephesians, *1*: 38, 56, 57, 60, 62, 121, 317; *2*: 37, 94, 126, 145, 216, 247, 248, 252, 275, 325
1 Esdras, *2*: 169
2 Esdras, *2*: 255
Exodus, *1*: 38, 63; *2*: 12, 23, 33, 133, 164, 181, 274
Ezechiel, *1*: 103, 114; *2*: 132
Galatians, *1*: 158; *2*: 100, 157, 163, 205, 206, 233, 283
Genesis, *1*: 37, 109, 189, 299, 317, 318; *2*: 24, 117, 164, 169, 170, 216, 225-228, 255, 258
Hebrews, *1*: 29, 33, 37, 55, 57, 59, 110, 111, 119, 124, 241, 260, 285; *2*: 128, 160, 169, 180, 231
Isaias, *1*: 29, 34, 114, 119, 121, 127, 150; *2*: 94, 122, 127, 163, 170, 187, 213
James, *1*: 56
Jeremias, *1*: 23, 73, 110, 114, 118, 119, 122-125, 270; *2*: 19, 30, 51, 66, 126, 136, 168, 188, 196, 243
Job, *1*: 16, 25, 51, 86, 122, 203; *2*: 125, 268, 293
John, *1*: 22, 27-34, 87, 96, 118, 126, 208, 313; *2*: 15, 32, 38, 66, 67, 71, 90, 142, 160, 161, 166-168, 220, 229, 231, 243, 247, 248, 261, 264, 267
1 John, *2*: 56
Jonas, *2*: 182, 255
Josue, *2*: 255
1 Kings, *1*: 26, 319; *2*: 30, 123
2 Kings, *2*: 170
3 Kings, *2*: 94
4 Kings, *1*: 103; *2*: 24, 169
Lamentations, *1*: 15, 113
Leviticus, *1*: 69, 315-317; *2*: 224
Luke, *1*: 15, 25, 29, 35, 38, 55-60, 102, 105, 118, 124, 125, 128, 132, 138, 188, 301; *2*: 19, 74, 127, 138, 141, 154, 164, 167, 214, 229, 231, 254
2 Maccabees, *1*: 18
Malachias, *2*: 236
Mark, *1*: 31, 58, 60 125, 126; *2*: 19, 71, 127, 165, 167, 216

Matthew, *1*: 5, 18, 26, 32, 34, 37, 38, 56, 58, 60, 105, 111, 117, 119, 125, 127, 134, 136, 139, 152, 201, 215, 241, 260, 301, 317, 334; *2*: 9, 19, 38, 42, 55, 61, 74, 85, 90, 108, 127, 137, 138, 141, 146, 150, 161, 165-167, 205, 206, 209, 214-217, 224, 231, 238, 248, 254, 259, 268, 274, 276, 296, 300
Nahum, *2*: 14, 57
Numbers, *2*: 30, 94, 230, 248
Osee, *1*: 113, 122, 124
2 Paralipomenon, *2*: 169
1 Peter, *1*: 56, 57, 106, 320; *2*: 235, 254
2 Peter, *2*: 213
Philippians, *1*: 52, 55, 57, 58, 71, 74, 102, 111, 312; *2*: 34, 43, 128, 146, 234, 243, 246, 289
Proverbs, *1*: 33, 40, 60, 114, 118, 133, 201, 344; *2*: 4, 19, 51, 229, 241
Psalms, *1*: 25, 29, 35-39, 60, 74, 90, 104, 105, 109, 110, 114, 126, 127, 129, 132, 133, 300, 319, 320, 327; *2*: 23, 30, 42, 55, 85, 93, 98, 119, 126-128, 164, 182, 197, 206, 246, 248, 250, 251, 254, 258
Romans, *1*: 25, 35, 56-58, 67, 89, 122, 124, 145, 204, 240, 270, 285, 313; *2*: 19, 28, 50, 71, 136, 141, 162, 187, 206, 233, 235, 244, 258, 277, 279
1 Thessalonians, *1*: 58, 70, 106, 111, 123, 155, 226, 319
2 Thessalonians, *1*: 58, 285; *2*: 151
1 Timothy, *1*: 25, 59, 60, 114, 120; *2*: 23, 48, 53, 54, 98, 223, 232, 246, 247, 275
2 Timothy, *1*: 56, 59, 106, 120, 334; *2*: 34, 74, 145, 164, 243
Titus, *1*: 56-59; *2*: 153
Wisdom, *1*: 36, 39; *2*: 119, 136
Zacharias, *1*: 226; *2*: 94

Scylla, *1*: 295
Scythia, *1*: 169, 179, 307
Sebaste, *1*: 216, 283; *2*: 174, 197, 205, 246, 252, 299, 344
seduction, *2*: 52, 53
Seleucia, *1*: 24, 135; *2*: 199, 200, 209, 240
Semi-Arians, *1*: 166; *2*: 70, 139, 143, 145, 200
Septuagint, *1*: 60, 118, 122, 124, 125, 127, 145, 150; *2*: 4, 12, 14, 122, 170, 225, 227, 228, 294
Servius, *2*: 328
Severians, *2*: 10
Severus, *1*: 260; *2*: 10, 21, 22
Sicily, *2*: 200
Sida, *2*: 4
Silvanus, Bishop of Tarsus, *1*: 276; *2*: 131, 193, 200
Silvanus, presbyter, *2*: 213
Silvinus, deacon, *2*: 213
Simeon, *2*: 229, 231
Simonides, *1*: 179
Simplicia, *1*: 242
Sirens, *1*: 3
Skinner, J., *2*: 223

Socrates, *1*: 305, 335; *2*: 200, 211, 240, 255
solitude, *1*: 5, 6, 13, 43, 47, 106, 107, 109, 116, 181, 211, 280, 302; *2*: 88, 183, 186, 287; life of, *1*: 102-111
Solomon, *1*: 39, 40, 103, 133
Solon, *1*: 180
Sophar, the Minnaeai, *1*: 86
Sophocles, *1*: 4, 40
Sophronius, *1*: 229; *2*: 45
Sophronius, bishop, *1*: 333
Sophronius, master, *1*: 76, 182, 213, 339, 342; *2*: 38, 262, 263
Sophronius, monk, *1*: 247, 249, 264
Sophronius, prefect, *1*: 183
Soranus, Julius, *1*: 307, 326
Sousarion, *2*: 334
Sozomen, *1*: 101, 169, 209, 224, 335; *2*: 200, 207, 208, 211, 212, 240
Sozopolis, *2*: 232
Spartans, *1*: 12, 179
Spirit, Holy, *1*: 6, 8, 9, 22-40, 42, 60, 66, 87-90, 110, 113, 138-140, 145, 146, 151, 155, 158, 199, 200, 206, 230, 240, 242, 257, 260, 264, 266, 267, 274, 287-289, 307, 309, 313, 314, 321, 324, 325, 334; *2*: 9, 10, 28-33, 61, 63, 75, 76, 90-94, 101-103, 133, 145-147, 157, 158, 160, 171, 188, 193, 199, 209, 261, 336, 343, 345
standers, *2*: xiv, 56, 58, 115
Stephen, Pope, *2*: 6, 12
Strabo, *1*: 179
Strategius, presbyter, *2*: 199, 200, 204
Strymon, *1*: 47
substance, *1*: 21, 24, 25, 33, 35, 36, 39, 41, 42, 66, 84-96, 137, 138, 257, 258, 288; *2*: 27, 92, 102, 159-166, 171, 337-343
Sulpicius, *2*: 304
Sympius, Bishop of Seleucia, *2*: 36, 37
synod, *1*: 197, 212, 219, 220, 224, 255, 256, 283, 289, 291, 339; *2*: 174, 192, 207, 244, 269, 272, 274
Synod of Alexandria, *2*: 337
Synod of Carthage, *2*: 5
Synod of Constantinople, Acacian, *1*: 135
Synod of Elvira, Canons of, *2*: 13, 17
Synod at Iconium, *2*: 5
Synod of Laodicea, *1*: 142
Synod of Milan, *1*: 282
Synod of Nicaea, *1*: 144
Synod of Rome, *2*: 337
Synod at Synnada, *2*: 5
Syria, *1*: 4, 80, 247, 281, 294, 343, 345; *2*: xv, 8, 24, 60, 77, 84, 128, 131, 146, 169, 177, 211

tachygraphists, *1*: 275
Tarsus, *1*: 80; *2*: 239, 241
Tatian, *2*: 10, 118
Taurus, *1*: 235, 270
taxation, *1*: 228, 292; *2*: 273, 274, 302

taxes, *1*: 229, 235, 292; *2*: 274, 297, 303
Terentius, Count, *1*: 157, 218, 229; *2*: 99, 103, 105
Tertullian, *1*: 209
tetractys, *1*: 54
Tetrapolis, *1*: 164
Thebaid, The, *1*: 204
Thecla, St., *2*: 36, 309
Theodora, canoness, *1*: 335
Theodoret, *1*: 201, 209, 276, 282, 329, 341; *2*: 186, 250, 257
Theodorus, *1*: 254
Theodosius, Emperor, *2*: 4, 60, 222, 343
Theodosius, presbyter, *2*: 179
Theodotus, Bishop of Berrhoea, *1*: 345
Theodotus, Bishop of Nicopolis, *1*: 203, 212, 219-221, 251, 253, 255, 260, 269; 2: 126, 129, 139, 147, 151, 174, 175
Theophilus, Bishop of Hieropolis, *1*: 269
Theophilus, Bishop of Eleutheropolis, *2*: 192, 200
Theophrastus, *1*: 276
Theophrastus, deacon, *1*: 148, 212
Theotecnus, *2*: 267, 268
Therasius, *1*: 183; *2*: 44
Thermopylae, *2*: 330
Theudas, *2*: 234
Thrace, *1*: 253, 262, 343; *2*: 172, 255, 256
Thrasymachus, *1*: 277
Thucydides, *1*: 179; *2*: 128
Tiberina, *1*: 48
Tiberius, *2*: 169
Tillemont, M., *1*: xv, 14, 129, 158, 168, 188, 202, 208, 217, 218, 231, 247, 249, 289, 304, 329, 341; *2*: 9, 37, 104, 143, 182, 255, 343
Timotheus, *1*: 63; *2*: 281
Trajan, *1*: 296, 297, 304, 341
trigamists, *2*: 62
trigamy, *2*: 114
Trinity, Blessed, *1*: xvii, 38, 40, 84, 87-89, 92, 193, 200, 202, 267, 289, 314; *2*: 33, 188, 246
Tyana, *1*: 214, 250, 342; *2*: 145, 154, 197, 240, 270

Unbegotten, *1*: 93, 137, 139, 259
Urbicius, *1*: 253; *2*: 236, 345
Ursacius, *1*: 166

Valens, Emperor, *1*: 41, 155, 159, 176, 179, 185, 196, 209, 218, 228, 253, 284, 289, 293, 296, 304, 341, 345; *2*: 134, 183, 200, 222, 243, 255-257
Valentinians, *2*: 8
Valentinus, *2*: 8, 234
Valerian, *1*: 201; *2*: 269
Valerius, *2*: 36
Vasoda, *2*: 21
Venesa, *1*: 331
Vespasian, *1*: 206
Victor, *1*: 304
Vigouroux, *2*: 223
virginity, *1*: 120-124; *2*: 48-50, 83, 110

Vitalius, *2*: 100, 219
Vitus, Bishop of Carrhae, *1*: 203; *2*: 212
vows, *2*: 48, 54, 55
Vulgate, Latin, *1*: 60; *2*: 12

Watkins, O. D., *2*: 57, 112
Way, Sister Agnes Clare, *1*: xiv, 100; *2*: 337
Westerners, *2*: 182, 237, 244; *see also* bishops
widows, *2*: 48, 52, 53, 56, 59, 107
witchcraft, *2*: 110, 111
Wittig, J., *1*: 132
Wright, W. C., *1*: 96, 98

Xerxes, *2*: 323

Zarnuas, *2*: 221
Zela, *2*: 143, 209
Zeno, *1*: 14
Zoilus, *2*: 40
Zonaras, *2*: 9, 10, 16, 17, 22, 23, 49, 54, 56, 58, 62, 107, 109, 112-115

THE FATHERS OF THE CHURCH SERIES

(A series of approximately 100 volumes when completed)

VOL. 1: THE APOSTOLIC FATHERS (1947)
- LETTER OF ST. CLEMENT OF ROME TO THE CORINTHIANS (trans. by Glimm)
- THE SO-CALLED SECOND LETTER (trans. by Glimm)
- LETTERS OF ST. IGNATIUS OF ANTIOCH (trans. by Walsh)
- LETTER OF ST. POLYCARP TO THE PHILIPPIANS (trans. by Glimm)
- MARTYRDOM OF ST. POLYCARP (trans. by Glimm)
- DIDACHE (trans. by Glimm)
- LETTER OF BARNABAS (trans. by Glimm)
- SHEPHERD OF HERMAS (1st printing only; trans. by Marique)
- LETTER TO DIOGNETUS (trans. by Walsh)
- FRAGMENTS OF PAPIAS (1st printing only; trans. by Marique)

VOL. 2: ST. AUGUSTINE (1947)
- CHRISTIAN INSTRUCTION (trans. by Gavigan)
- ADMONITION AND GRACE (trans. by Murray)
- THE CHRISTIAN COMBAT (trans. by Russell)
- FAITH, HOPE, AND CHARITY (trans. by Peebles)

VOL. 3: SALVIAN, THE PRESBYTER (1947)
- GOVERNANCE OF GOD (trans. by O'Sullivan)
- LETTERS (trans. by O'Sullivan)
- FOUR BOOKS OF TIMOTHY TO THE CHURCH (trans. by O'Sullivan)

VOL. 4: ST. AUGUSTINE (1947)
- IMMORTALITY OF THE SOUL (trans. by Schopp)
- MAGNITUDE OF THE SOUL (trans. by McMahon)
- ON MUSIC (trans. by Taliaferro)

ADVANTAGE OF BELIEVING (trans. by Sr. Luanne Meagher)

ON FAITH IN THINGS UNSEEN (trans. by Deferrari and Sr. Mary Francis McDonald)

VOL. 5: ST. AUGUSTINE (1948)

THE HAPPY LIFE (trans. by Schopp)

ANSWER TO SKEPTICS (trans. by Kavanagh)

DIVINE PROVIDENCE AND THE PROBLEM OF EVIL (trans. by Russell)

SOLILOQUIES (trans. by Gilligan)

VOL. 6: ST. JUSTIN MARTYR (1948)

FIRST AND SECOND APOLOGY (trans. by Falls)

DIALOGUE WITH TRYPHO (trans. by Falls)

EXHORTATION AND DISCOURSE TO THE GREEKS (trans. by Falls)

THE MONARCHY (trans. by Falls)

VOL. 7: NICETA OF REMESIANA (1949)

WRITINGS (trans. by Walsh and Monohan)

SULPICIUS SEVERUS

WRITINGS (trans. by Peebles)

VINCENT OF LERINS

COMMONITORIES (trans. by Morris)

PROSPER OF AQUITANE

GRACE AND FREE WILL (trans. by O'Donnell)

VOL. 8: ST. AUGUSTINE (1950)

CITY OF GOD, Bks. I-VII (trans. by Walsh, Zema; introduction by Gilson)

VOL. 9: ST. BASIL (1950)

ASCETICAL WORKS (trans. by Sr. M. Monica Wagner)

VOL. 10: TERTULLIAN (1950)

APOLOGETICAL WORKS (vol. 1), (trans. by Arbesmann, Sr. Emily Joseph Daly, Quain)

MINUCIUS FELIX

OCTAVIUS (trans. by Arbesmann)

VOL. 11: ST. AUGUSTINE (1951)

COMMENTARY ON THE LORD'S SERMON ON THE MOUNT WITH SEVENTEEN RELATED SERMONS (trans. by Kavanagh)

VOL. 12: ST. AUGUSTINE (1951)
LETTERS 1-82 (vol. 1), (trans. by Sr. Wilfrid Parsons)

VOL. 13: ST. BASIL (1951)
LETTERS 1-185 (vol. 1), (trans. by Deferrari and Sr. Agnes Clare Way)

VOL. 14: ST. AUGUSTINE (1952)
CITY OF GOD, Bks. VIII-XVI (trans. by Walsh and Mtr. Grace Monahan)

VOL. 15: EARLY CHRISTIAN BIOGRAPHIES (1952)
LIFE OF ST. CYPRIAN BY PONTIUS (trans. by Deferrari and Sr. Mary Magdeleine Mueller)
LIFE OF ST. AMBROSE, BISHOP OF MILAN, BY PAULINUS (trans. by Lacy)
LIFE OF ST. AUGUSTINE BY POSSIDIUS (trans. by Deferrari and Sr. Mary Magdeleine Mueller)
LIFE OF ST. ANTHONY BY ST. ATHANASIUS (trans. by Sr. Mary Emily Keenan)
LIFE OF ST. PAUL, THE FIRST HERMIT; LIFE OF ST. HILARION; LIFE OF MALCHUS, THE CAPTIVE MONK (trans. by Sr. Marie Liguori Ewald)
LIFE OF EPIPHANIUS BY ENNODIUS (trans. by Sr. Genevieve Marie Cook)
A SERMON ON THE LIFE OF ST. HONORATUS BY ST. HILARY (trans. by Deferrari)

VOL. 16: ST. AUGUSTINE (1952)—Treatises on Various Subjects:
THE CHRISTIAN LIFE, LYING, THE WORK OF MONKS, THE USEFULNESS OF FASTING (trans. by Sr. M. Sarah Muldowney)
AGAINST LYING (trans. by Jaffee)
CONTINENCE (trans. by Sr. Mary Francis McDonald)
PATIENCE (trans. by Sr. Luanne Meagher)
THE EXCELLENCE OF WIDOWHOOD (trans. by Sr. M. Clement Eagan)
THE EIGHT QUESTIONS OF DULCITIUS (trans. by Mary DeFerrari)

VOL. 17: ST. PETER CHRYSOLOGUS (1953)
SELECTED SERMONS (trans. by Ganss)
ST. VALERIAN
HOMILIES (trans. by Ganss)

VOL. 18: ST. AUGUSTINE (1953)
LETTERS 83-130 (vol. 2), (trans. by Sr. Wilfrid Parsons)

VOL. 19: EUSEBIUS PAMPHILI (1953)
ECCLESIASTICAL HISTORY, Bks. 1-5 (trans. by Deferrari)

VOL. 20: ST. AUGUSTINE (1953)
LETTERS 131-164 (vol. 3), (trans. by Sr. Wilfrid Parsons)

VOL. 21: ST. AUGUSTINE (1953)
CONFESSIONS (trans. by Bourke)

VOL. 22: ST. GREGORY OF NAZIANZEN and ST. AMBROSE (1953)
FUNERAL ORATIONS (trans. by McCauley, Sullivan, McGuire, Deferrari)

VOL. 23: CLEMENT OF ALEXANDRIA (1954)
CHRIST, THE EDUCATOR (trans. by Wood)

VOL. 24: ST. AUGUSTINE (1954)
CITY OF GOD, Bks. XVII-XXII (trans. by Walsh and Honan)

VOL. 25: ST. HILARY OF POITIERS (1954)
THE TRINITY (trans. by McKenna)

VOL. 26: ST. AMBROSE (1954)
LETTERS 1-91 (trans. by Sr. M. Melchior Beyenka)

VOL. 27: ST. AUGUSTINE (1955)—Treatises on Marriage and Other Subjects:
THE GOOD OF MARRIAGE (trans. by Wilcox)
ADULTEROUS MARRIAGES (trans. by Huegelmeyer)
HOLY VIRGINITY (trans. by McQuade)
FAITH AND WORKS, THE CREED, IN ANSWER TO THE JEWS (trans. by Sr. Marie Liguori Ewald)
FAITH AND THE CREED (trans. by Russell)
THE CARE TO BE TAKEN FOR THE DEAD (trans. by Lacy)
THE DIVINATION OF DEMONS (trans. by Brown)

VOL. 28: ST. BASIL (1955)
LETTERS 186-368 (vol. 2), (trans. by Sr. Agnes Clare Way)

VOL. 29: EUSEBIUS PAMPHILI (1955)
ECCLESIASTICAL HISTORY, Bks. 6-10 (trans. by Deferrari)

VOL. 30: ST. AUGUSTINE (1955)
LETTERS 165-203 (vol. 4), (trans. by Sr. Wilfrid Parsons)

VOL. 31: ST. CAESARIUS OF ARLES (1956)
SERMONS 1-80 (vol. 1), (trans. by Sr. Mary Magdeleine Mueller)

VOL. 32: ST. AUGUSTINE (1956)
LETTERS 204-270 (vol. 5), (trans. by Sr. Wilfrid Parsons)

VOL. 33: ST. JOHN CHRYSOSTOM (1957)
HOMILIES 1-47 (vol. 1), (trans. by Sr. Thomas Aquinas Goggin)

VOL. 34: ST. LEO THE GREAT (1957)
LETTERS (trans. by Hunt)

VOL. 35: ST. AUGUSTINE (1957)
AGAINST JULIAN (trans. by Schumacher)

VOL. 36: ST. CYPRIAN (1958)
TREATISES (trans. by Deferrari, Sr. Angela Elizabeth Keenan, Mahoney, Sr. George Edward Conway)

VOL. 37: ST. JOHN OF DAMASCUS (1958)
FOUNT OF KNOWLEDGE, ON HERESIES, THE ORTHODOX FAITH (trans. by Chase)

VOL. 38: ST. AUGUSTINE (1959)
SERMONS ON THE LITURGICAL SEASONS (trans. by Sr. M. Sarah Muldowney)

VOL. 39: ST. GREGORY THE GREAT (1959)
DIALOGUES (trans. by Zimmerman)

VOL. 40: TERTULLIAN (1959)
DISCIPLINARY, MORAL, AND ASCETICAL WORKS (trans. by Arbesmann, Quain, Sr. Emily Joseph Daly)

VOL. 41: ST. JOHN CHRYSOSTOM (1960)
HOMILIES 48-88 (vol. 2), (trans. by Sr. Thomas Aquinas Goggin)

VOL. 42: ST. AMBROSE (1961)
HEXAMERON, PARADISE, AND CAIN AND ABEL (trans. by Savage)

VOL. 43: PRUDENTIUS (1962)
POEMS (vol. 1), (trans. by Sr. M. Clement Eagan)

VOL. 44: ST. AMBROSE (1963)
THEOLOGICAL AND DOGMATIC WORKS (trans. by Deferrari)

VOL. 45: ST. AUGUSTINE (1963)
THE TRINITY (trans. by McKenna)

VOL. 46: ST. BASIL (1963)
EXEGETIC HOMILIES (trans. by Sr. Agnes Clare Way)

VOL. 47: ST. CAESARIUS OF ARLES (1964)
SERMONS 81-186 (vol. 2), (trans. by Sr. Mary Magdeleine Mueller)

VOL. 48: ST. JEROME (1964)
HOMILIES 1-59 (vol. 1), (trans. by Sr. Marie Liguori Ewald)

VOL. 49: LACTANTIUS (1964)
THE DIVINE INSTITUTES, Bks. I-VII (trans. by Sr. Mary Francis McDonald)

VOL. 50: OROSIUS (1964)
SEVEN BOOKS AGAINST THE PAGANS (trans. by Deferrari)

VOL. 51: ST. CYPRIAN (1965)
LETTERS (trans. by Sr. Rose Bernard Donna)

VOL. 52: PRUDENTIUS (1965)
POEMS (vol. 2), (trans. by Sr. M. Clement Eagan)

VOL. 53: ST. JEROME (1965)
DOGMATIC AND POLEMICAL WORKS (trans. by John N. Hritzu)

VOL. 54: LACTANTIUS (1965)
THE MINOR WORKS (trans. by Sr. Mary Francis McDonald)

VOL. 55: EUGIPPIUS (1965)
LIFE OF ST. SEVERIN (trans. by Bieler)

VOL. 56: ST. AUGUSTINE (1966)
THE CATHOLIC AND MANICHAEAN WAYS OF LIFE (trans. by Donald A. and Idella J. Gallagher)

VOL. 57: ST. JEROME (1966)
HOMILIES 60-96 (vol. 2), (trans. by Sr. Marie Liguori Ewald)

VOL. 58: ST. GREGORY OF NYSSA (1966)
ASCETICAL WORKS (trans. by Virginia Woods Callahan)

VOL. 59: ST. AUGUSTINE (1968)
THE TEACHER, THE FREE CHOICE OF THE WILL, GRACE AND FREE WILL (trans. by Russell)

VOL. 60: ST. AUGUSTINE (1968)
THE RETRACTATIONS (trans. by Sr. Mary Inez Bogan)

VOL. 61: ST. CYRIL OF JERUSALEM, VOL. 1 (1969)
PROCATECHESIS, CATECHESES 1-12 (trans. by McCauley and Stephenson)

VOL. 62: IBERIAN FATHERS, VOL. 1 (1969)
MARTIN OF BRAGA, PASCHASIUS OF DUMIUM, LEANDER OF SEVILLE (all trans. by Barlow)